Keats's Negative Capability

New Origins and Afterlives

Romantic Reconfigurations:
Studies in Literature and Culture 1780–1850

Series Editors:
Professor Tim Fulford, De Montfort University
Professor Alan Vardy, Hunter College and the Graduate Center, CUNY

As befits a series published in the city of Roscoe and Rushden, a city that linked Britain to the transatlantic trade in cotton, in sugar, and in people, *Romantic Reconfigurations* reconfigures the literary and cultural geographies and histories of Romanticism. Topics featured include, but are by no means confined to, provincial and labouring-class writing, diasporic and colonial writing, natural history and other scientific discourse, journalism, popular culture, music and theatre, landscape and nature, cosmopolitanism and travel, poetics and form.

Keats's Negative Capability

New Origins and Afterlives

Edited by
Brian Rejack and Michael Theune

LIVERPOOL UNIVERSITY PRESS

First published 2018 by
Liverpool University Press
4 Cambridge Street
Liverpool
L69 7ZU

This paperback edition first published 2021

British Library Cataloguing-in-Publication data
A British Library CIP record is available

ISBN 978-1-78694-181-7 cased
ISBN 978-1-80085-672-1 paperback

Typeset by Carnegie Book Production, Lancaster
Printed and bound by CPI Group (UK) Ltd, Croydon CR0 4YY

Contents

Part II. 'examplified throughout': Forms of Negatively Capable Reading

Part III. 'pursued through Volumes', Volume I: Negative Capability in Twentieth- and Twenty-First-Century American Poetry

Part IV. 'pursued through Volumes', Volume II: Adaptations, Appropriations, Mutations

List of Figures

Acknowledgments

> But what, without the social thought of thee,
> Would be the wonders of the sky and sea?
>
> —'To My Brother George'

Like Keats, who ends his sonnet to his brother by acknowledging the power of the social, we too upon completing this book recognize the indispensable communal spirit and support that made its existence possible.

We are deeply fortunate to have worked with our imaginative and more than capable contributors. They took negative capability in new directions, opening new thoroughfares for thought, and we hope others will continue to explore and extend those paths for years to come. We thank, as well, Nicholas Roe and Jonathan Mulrooney for their excellent opening and closing notes to the volume. Tim Fulford and Alan Vardy supported and encouraged the project from an early stage. We thank them and all those with whom we worked at Liverpool University Press to help make the book a reality. Special thanks to Jenny Howard, Sarah Warren, and Christabel Scaife for their expert guidance as we moved through the final phases of the process. Additionally, we thank our two anonymous readers. Their insightful comments made this book a better one. And thanks, as well, to Sarah Nesbit, who, by allowing us to use her painting *Sift* as our cover image, made the book a more beautiful one.

Our respective universities, Illinois State and Illinois Wesleyan, provided research support, including a Pre-tenure Faculty Initiative Grant from ISU and an Artistic and Scholarly Development Grant from IWU. We are grateful for their institutional assistance.

This exploration of negative capability developed alongside another Keats endeavor, The Keats Letters Project, and the two undertakings informed and energized each other. As such, we thank our co-founding editors at the KLP for their brilliance, generosity, and conviviality: Anne McCarthy, Ian Newman, Kate Singer, and Emily Stanback.

We offer our heartfelt thanks to our families, friends, and colleagues for their interest and support. Mike dedicates his work on this book to his parents, Peter and Judy Theune. Brian extends special gratitude to Anne and Jeff Rejack, and to Josette Lorig (along with feline research assistants, George and Lady Georgina). He dedicates his work to Josette.

Abbreviations

CWWH	*The Complete Works of William Hazlitt*, ed. P. P. Howe, 21 vols. (London: J. M. Dent, 1930)
KC	*The Keats Circle: Letters and Papers and More Letters and Poems*, ed. Hyder Edward Rollins, 2 vols. (Cambridge, MA: Harvard University Press, 1969)
JJ	John Jeffrey's transcripts of Keats's letters, MS Keats 3.9 (Houghton Library, Harvard University)
LJK	*The Letters of John Keats 1814–1821*, ed. Hyder Edward Rollins, 2 vols. (Cambridge, MA: Harvard University Press, 1958)
PJK	*The Poems of John Keats*, ed. by Jack Stillinger. (Cambridge, MA: Belknap Press, 1978)
SE	Sigmund Freud, *The Standard Edition of the Complete Psychological Works of Sigmund Freud*, trans. James Strachey, 24 vols. (London: Hogarth Press, 1964)

Contributors

Robert Archambeau is Professor of English at Lake Forest College. He teaches and writes about poetry and poetics from the nineteenth century to the present, and has published several books of criticism and poetry, including, most recently, *Laureates and Heretics* (2010), *The Poet Resigns: Poetry in a Difficult Time* (2013), and *The Kafka Sutra* (2015).

Suzanne L. Barnett is Assistant Professor in the Department of English at Francis Marion University and the author of *Romantic Paganism: The Politics of Ecstasy in the Shelley Circle* (2018). She has also published articles in *Essays in Romanticism*, *Keats-Shelley Journal*, and *Romantic Circles Pedagogy Commons*.

Brian Bates is Lecturer in the Department of English at California Polytechnic State University. He is the author of *Wordsworth's Poetic Collections, Supplementary Writing and Parodic Reception* (2012), as well as several journal articles on romanticism. He is currently editing a collection of essays, *Keats and Popular Culture*, for *Romantic Circles Praxis Series*, and writing a monograph titled *Keats's Authorial Play: Pantomime and Popular Culture*.

Jeanne Britton is Curator in the Irvin Department of Rare Books and Special Collections at the University of South Carolina. Her book *Vicarious Narratives: A Literary History of Sympathy, 1750–1850* is forthcoming from Oxford. Her research has appeared in *European Romantic Review*, *Nineteenth-Century Contexts*, *Nineteenth-Century Literature*, and *Studies in Romanticism*.

Eric Eisner is Associate Professor in the Department of English at George Mason University. He is the author of *Nineteenth-Century Poetry and Literary Celebrity* (2009), as well as numerous articles on Romanticism. He is currently at work on a monograph on Keats and contemporary poetry.

Cassandra Falke is Professor of English Literature at the University of Tromsø. She has published several essays on romanticism, edited the collection *Intersections in Christianity and Critical Theory* (2010), and authored two monographs: *Literature by the Working Class: English Autobiography, 1820–1848* (2013) and *The Phenomenology of Love and Reading* (2016).

Thomas Gardner is Alumni Distinguished Professor in the Department of English at Virginia Tech. He is the author of a number of articles on contemporary poetry and has also published seven books, including *Regions of Unlikeness: Explaining Contemporary Poetry* (1999), *Jorie Graham: Essays on the Poetry* (2005), and *A Door Ajar: Contemporary Writers and Emily Dickinson* (2006).

Kurtis Hessel earned his doctorate from the University of Colorado with a dissertation examining the changing relationship between poetics and chemistry during the romantic period. His recent essays, 'Humphry Davy's Intergalactic Travel: Catching Sight of Another Genre', and 'The Romantic-Era Lecture: Dividing and Reuniting the Arts and Sciences', were published, respectively, in *Studies in Romanticism* (2015) and *Configurations* (2016).

Anne C. McCarthy is Assistant Professor of English at Penn State University. She is the author of *Awful Parenthesis: Suspension and the Sublime in Romantic and Victorian Poetry* (2018), as well as essays in *Studies in Romanticism*, *Victorian Poetry*, and *PMLA*. She is currently working on a second book-length manuscript about the convergence of personal and planetary catastrophe titled 'Catastrophic Intimacies: Looking for Love at the End of the World, 1780–1830'.

Carmen Faye Mathes is Assistant Professor of English at the University of Central Florida. She has published essays and reviews in journals including *European Romantic Review*, *Modern Philology*, *Romantic Circles Praxis Series*, and *Studies in Romanticism*. She is currently at work on two book-length projects, one of which explores *The Disappointment Aesthetic* in Romantic poetry, while the other investigates modernity as a condition of perpetual ethical concession.

Jonathan Mulrooney is Professor of English at the College of the Holy Cross and editor of the *Keats-Shelley Journal*. He is the author of *Romanticism and Theatrical Experience: Kean, Hazlitt, and Keats in the Age of Theatrical News* (2018), as well as many essays and chapters on Romantic-period poetry. He is at work on several articles on Keats which may or may not become a book entitled *Keats's Vanishing Figures*.

Walter L. Reed is William Rand Kenan, Jr. University Professor Emeritus of English and Comparative Literature at Emory University. He has published widely on romanticism, the novel, and Bakhtin, including several books, among which are *Meditations on the Hero: A Study of the Romantic Hero in Nineteenth-Century Fiction* (1974), *An Exemplary History of the Novel: The Quixotic versus the Picaresque* (1981), and *Romantic Literature in Light of Bakhtin* (2014).

Brian Rejack is Associate Professor of English at Illinois State University. He has published widely on Romanticism in journals including *European Romantic Review*, *Romanticism*, and *Romantic Circles*, and he is one of the co-founders of The Keats Letters Project (keatslettersproject.com). Currently he is at work on a monograph on Keats and media theory, titled *John Keats and Romantic Imaginary Media: The Secrets of Wondrous Things*.

Nicholas Roe is Bishop Wardlaw Professor of English Literature at the University of St. Andrews and Chair of the Keats Foundation. He is the author of several celebrated books on romanticism, Keats, and the Keats circle, including *John Keats and the Culture of Dissent* (1997), *Fiery Heart: The First Life of Leigh Hunt* (2005), *John Keats: A New Life* (2012), and, as editor, *Keats and History* (1995) and *John Keats and the Medical Imagination* (2018).

Emily Rohrbach is Lecturer in British Literature, 1750–1820, at the University of Manchester. She is the author of *Modernity's Mist: British Romanticism and the Poetics of Anticipation* (2015) and is co-editor (with Emily Sun) of *Reading Keats, Thinking Politics*, the 50th anniversary issue of the journal *Studies in Romanticism*.

Arsevi Seyran is a doctoral student at SUNY Stony Brook. She is the author of the chapbook *Quarter Past Terminal* (2013) and has published poetry in several other venues. Her dissertation examines Elizabeth Bishop's poetry from a Keatsian perspective.

David Sigler is Associate Professor of English at the University of Calgary. He is the author of *Sexual Enjoyment in British Romanticism: Gender and Psychoanalysis 1753–1835* (2015) and various articles on British Romanticism and psychoanalysis.

Michael Theune is Professor of English and Writing Program Director at Illinois Wesleyan University. He is the editor of *Structure & Surprise: Engaging Poetic Turns* (2007) and co-author of *We Need to Talk: A New Method for Evaluating Poetry* (2018). He is a co-founding editor of The Keats Letters Project (keatslettersproject.com).

Preface

Nicholas Roe

Negative capability came out of moonlight, somewhere on the cursed cold distance between London and Hampstead. Nothing is known about precisely where and when, but there are a few bearings that we can establish. Keats was at the Reynolds' home in Lamb's Conduit Street, Bloomsbury, on Christmas Eve of 1817: his friend John Hamilton Reynolds would shortly leave town and asked Keats to take his place and review a new pantomime at Drury Lane. On Christmas day Keats returned to Hampstead, encountering William Godwin on the way, and passed the evening at Wentworth Place with his friends Brown and Dilke. Next day, a Friday, all three of them set off for town and the first performance of 'a new splendid pantomimic Romance called HARLEQUIN'S VISION; or, The Feast of the Statue'.[1] That night a holiday audience was in tumultuous mood, pelting the actors with 'discharges of oranges' and eliciting 'a just and effective appeal' from the stage. Keats's satirical review appeared in *The Champion* on 4 January and a full account of the performance he saw survives in the *Morning Post*.[2]

Based on the story of *Don Juan*, *Harlequin's Vision* opened with 'a grand and terrific view of *Pluto*'s Council Hall'. The ghost of the Don's father, introduced by Mercury, implores Pluto's mercy for his son, whose dissolute life 'bids fair to send him to Tartarus'. When his request is rejected, Proserpine intervenes and

> dispatches *Mercury* to *Venus*; and these three deities uniting their efforts, lead *Don Juan* in a dream (which to the spectators is the reality of the Pantomime) through all the vicissitudes of guilt, audacity, and

[1] As advertised in the *Morning Chronicle*, 27 December 1817.

[2] 'On Don Giovanni, a Pantomime Acted at Drury Lane Theatre': *The Complete Works of John Keats*, ed. H. B. Forman, 5 vols. (Glasgow: Gowars & Gray, 1901), III: pp. 243–5.

> punishment, which usually marks the career of the libertine. After having been thrown into an ocean of living flame, he is again found on his sofa, awakened by *Venus*, and restored a reclaimed husband to the arms of his forgiving wife.

This performance of dream reality featured many splendid scenes—a temple of Venus descending through opening clouds, an amphitheater, a cemetery by night:

> the passage of the *Acheron* under stupendous arches of rocks, with the distant view of the burning mountain, is full of wildness and majesty; and the Pandemonium or palace and sea of fire, is a terrific representation of all that can be conceived of Hell. The last scene, the Palace of Pleasure, is also grand and magnificent, and the procession of *Gods*, with the descent of *Jupiter* and *Juno* in the clouds, form a most sublime and animated picture. Some of the tricks in this pantomime are very good: such as the metamorphosis of an old woman into a table and two chairs; the union of heads and legs that walk off without bodies, and of bodies and thighs that march off without heads and legs; and the extraction of *Young Punch* and *Joan* out of a punch-bowl.[3]

These extraordinary spectacles—beautiful, sublime, and grotesque—were contrived to challenge an audience to contemplate what 'can be conceived'. Where dream is the reality, do we wake or sleep? Or, as the *Literary Gazette* observed, 'this is a Pantomimic era … . Oh, enlightened age … . Oh! Wise world! … . But this has nothing to do with *Harlequin's Vision*;—it is all a waking dream'.[4]

They sauntered back to Hampstead under a full moon, with Mars high overhead and Sirius slightly lower in the southern sky. Influenced, perhaps, by that fiery planet, Keats and Dilke began what might have been a dispute—at least, that was what Keats told his brothers in a letter that survives for us only in a puzzling transcription by John Jeffrey (second husband of Georgiana Wylie Keats). 'I had not a dispute but a disquisition with Dilke, on various subjects', Keats reported and then, with Sirian brilliance,

> several things dovetailed in my mind, & at once it struck me ~~at once~~,[5] what quality went to form a Man of Achievement especially in

[3] 'Theatres. Drury-Lane', *Morning Post*, 27 December 1817.

[4] 'The Drama. Drury Lane', *Literary Gazette, and Journal of Belles Lettres, Arts, Politics, Etc.*, 3 January 1818, p. 11. Final ellipses in original.

[5] Struck through by John Jeffrey.

> Literature & which Shakespeare posessed so enormously—I mean Negative Capability, that is when man is capable of being in uncertainties, Mysteries, doubts, without any irritable reaching after fact & reason—[6]

Misdated, incomplete, with two deletions and two interlinings, Jeffrey's transcript tests our own capacities for negative capability. Can we be content with what Jeffrey has written when, as Hyder Rollins conjectured, he 'omitted some words (possibly even a page or two) after the first sentence' (*LJK*, I: p. 191 n.1)? Jeffrey's 'posessed' may and may not have been Keats's own mis-spelling: it occurs nowhere else in Keats's letters, although, significantly perhaps, the words 'possess' and 'possession' in his letters were often linked with matters of identity and selfhood and, once, 'a right to an inside place in my own Letter—I take possession' (Keats is reasserting authorship of his letter after Charles Brown had inserted a pun).[7] What Shakespeare 'posessed so enormously' was a capable dispossession—that is, unlike Keats's 'inside place', Shakespeare's genius is figuratively an occupant of an 'outside place', as if on a mail coach exposed to the elements and all that wretches feel.[8]

That this book ranges so richly, so variously, and so widely will be welcome to all readers, not least because it embodies the Shakespearean aspects of negative capability. There were many other backgrounds to the concept too. As a child Keats discovered how to live with doubts by dodging questions with rhymes, a formative Keatsian capability to which other things may have been 'dovetailed' on that moonlit December night. Among them were Leigh Hunt's idea of acting as a 'passive capacity', William Hazlitt's disinterested imagination, and Coleridge's 'suspension of disbelief'—such proto-conceptions of 'negative capability' were circulating at the time.[9] More personal for Keats was his experience of Guy's hospital, where he studied and was employed as a dresser, or house-surgeon, between October 1815 and March 1817. At a time when there were no effective drugs or cures, no anaesthetic, and no assurance that even simple surgical procedures would be successful, a physician's calling was an exemplary statement of negative capability. Equally, a

[6] John Jeffrey, transcript of John Keats to George and Tom Keats, 21–27 [?] December 1817, John Keats Collection, MS Keats 3.9 (Houghton Library, Harvard University), sequence 14, accessed 6 July 2018, https://iiif.lib.harvard.edu/manifests/view/drs:35522552$14i.

[7] It is worth noting that Jeffrey has 'posession' in two letters from 1844 and 1845 (*KC*, II: pp. 113, 119); he also has 'possessed' and 'possession' in two further letters from 1845 (pp. 117, 123).

[8] Keats's letter protracts a joke about coaching, from 'diligence' in the first line, through 'dog-cart', to 'inside place' (*LJK*, II: pp. 134–6).

[9] With Hunt, compare Keats's 'in my dramatic capacity I enter fully into the feeling' (*LJK*, II: p. 174).

Georgian operating theater with its bare wooden table, knives, and bone-saws was as much an arena for negative capability as the harrowing third act of *King Lear*, where the old king orders 'let them anatomize Regan; see what breeds about her heart' (Act III, Scene VI, lines 74–5). As a surgeon Keats operated in 'half knowledge'—tentatively feeling his way into what his letter terms the 'Penetralium', the innermost part, as when he extracted a pistol-ball from a wound in a woman's neck.[10] Perhaps a memory of his surgical experiences launched his poetic speculation about 'the feel of not to feel' and how that might be said 'in rhyme' (*PJK*, p. 221).

Finally, a word about the words themselves. Unlike 'darkling', 'forlorn', and 'mists', the words 'negative' and 'capability' are in themselves curiously un-Keatsian, yet when brought together they form a thoroughly Keatsian core of verbal energy.[11] Neither word appears in his poetry. In his letters—beyond the phrase itself—'negative' and 'capability' appear respectively only twice and once: 'Women like your London people in a sort of negative way' (*LJK*, I: p. 241); 'A is the soolishest, B the sulkiest, C is a negative' (II: p. 245); 'my Humility and capability of submission'. Of these only the last seems to have any relation to 'negative capability': it dates from 22 November 1817 and Keats's claim that 'Men of Genius are great as certain ethereal Chemicals operating on the Mass of neutral intellect ... they have not any individuality, any determined Character' (I: p. 184). To 'ethereal Chemicals' we might add astronomy: as Keats knew from reading John Bonnycastle, the greater the apparent brightness of a star, the more negative its scale of magnitude becomes. Sirius, brightest of bright stars, has an apparent magnitude of -1.46.[12]

The sixteen chapters in *Keats's Negative Capability: New Origins and Afterlives* summon us, first, to Keats's world of Shakespeare, playgoings, and pantomimes. We look into the creation of the term 'negative capability' and the role of Hazlitt's 'natural capacity' and then, as we read on, we discover how these connect with nineteenth-century women writers, the non-certainties of reading, and the unknowing capaciousness of 'knowledge enormous'. We encounter negative capability in physiology, in unknowable futures, and as a resource for some American poets—Elizabeth Bishop, Jorie Graham, Charles Olson, and Adrienne Rich. In the book's closing chapters Philip Pullman quarrels with negatively capable 'empathy' while psychoanalysis and Zen appropriate it; finally, negative capability is seen opening into a future

[10] See my essay 'Mr. Keats', *Essays in Criticism*, 65: 3 (July 2015), pp. 274–88.

[11] There are what we might call cognate phrases, such as 'not over capable in my upper Stories' (*LJK*, I: p. 138); more usually, 'capable' in Keats's letters is a positive quality as in 'capable of being'. Likewise, 'incapable' occurs only once in his letters, to describe Coleridge as 'incapable of remaining content with half knowledge' (p. 194).

[12] Bonnycastle has Sirius as a first magnitude star; see *An Introduction to Astronomy* (London, 1811), pp. 43, 198.

of unending discursive possibilities as a concept, a mode of thought, and a stance towards life. All of this, from a single moment of moonlit inspiration 200 years ago.

Welcome to Keats's universe of uncertainties, mysteries, and doubts—and prepare to make up your mind about nothing …

Introduction

Disquisitions: Reading Negative Capability, 1817–2017

Brian Rejack and Michael Theune

Fortunately for those of us invested in the literary career of John Keats generally, and in negative capability specifically, one day in May 1845 an accomplished Scottish engineer—who was responsible for bringing gas lighting to the streets of many Midwestern and Southeastern cities in the United States, including Louisville, Kentucky, where he then resided—sat down to read the newspaper and came across a notice like this one: 'A Life of Keats is preparing by Monckton Milner, M. P., himself a good poet'.[1] 'Milner' referred to Richard Monckton Milnes, the person who was at the time gathering materials for a biography of the poet (a project which Keats's friends had failed to make happen in the years since his death). The Scottish engineer was John Jeffrey, who two years earlier had married Georgiana Wylie Keats, the poet's sister-in-law, who had emigrated to America with her husband George in 1818 and been widowed in December 1841. Jeffrey thought that, with his access to the Keats family papers, he might try 'arranging them for publication some of these days when I have a little more leisure' (*KC*, II: p. 114). Milnes beat him to it. At least as early as January 1845, notices announcing Milnes's intentions to publish the biography of Keats began appearing in British newspapers and, soon thereafter, versions of those notices had made it into American newspapers; the longer notices even specifically mentioned that 'all the necessary papers have been placed in [Milnes's] hands by the family'.[2] Jeffrey would have immediately realized, since he himself had not been contacted by Milnes, that not *all* the

[1] *North American and Daily Advertiser* (Philadelphia), 13 May 1845 (Readex: *America's Historical Newspapers*).

[2] 'Varieties', *The Manchester Guardian*, 18 January 1845. There likely were earlier American notices, but the earliest we have encountered appears in 'Correspondence', *Littell's Living Age* (Boston), 3 May 1845.

necessary papers had made their way to Milnes's hands. As Jeffrey wrote to Milnes on 13 May 1845, he had, through his marriage to Georgiana, 'become possessed of papers & information relative to the poet Keats, without which, it is impossible in my opinion to give his complete life' (*KC*, II: p. 117). One of those papers was the letter Keats sent to his brothers George and Tom in December 1817, and which contained the term around which the essays in this volume revolve: negative capability.[3]

Devoted Keatsians and all others who have been taken by 'negative capability' also must be grateful that during the 1930s a young high school student in the American Midwest happened to come across the term. A teenaged Walter Jackson Bate first discovered the 'mysterious phrase' while reading John Dewey's *Art as Experience*, a book which his 'father had brought home from the town library'.[4] At the end of the book's second chapter, 'The Live Creature and "Etherial Things"', Dewey clarifies his use of a Keats quotation in his chapter's title, offering this significantly edited version of a passage from Keats's 10, 11 May 1817 letter to Benjamin Robert Haydon: 'the Sun, the Moon, the Earth and its contents, are material to form greater things, that is, etherial things—greater things than the Creator himself made'.[5] Dewey uses this passage to show that Keats was precisely the kind of artist Dewey was trying to encourage: one for whom there was no distance between creaturely, participatory living and even the most ethereal creations of art. Dewey reinforces this view by linking Keats's famous statements on humanity's essentially creaturely existence—that just like 'a Stoat or a field mouse', man is a 'Creature' that 'has a purpose and his eyes are bright with it' (*LJK*, II: pp. 79–80)—with negative capability. Immediately following the above quotations, Dewey cites '"Negative Capability"' (p. 33) and then closes out his citation of Keats's letters with his 22 November 1817 note to Bailey: 'Can it be that even the greatest philosopher ever arrived at his goal without putting aside numerous objections?' (p. 33; *LJK*, I: p. 185). As crucial as Bate is to negative capability's rising status in the twentieth century, if not for his early encounter with Keats via Dewey he may never have put the term at the center of Keats's system of thought, drawing such great critical attention to and initiating so many future engagements with it.[6]

Walter Jackson Bate is the Paul to Keats's negatively capable Jesus. Negative capability itself only appears as a kind of glimpse of an epiphany: it is momentous,

[3] Brian Rejack's chapter in this collection examines in detail the significance of Jeffrey's involvement with the transmission of the term.

[4] Walter Jackson Bate, 'The Endurance of Keats', in *The Persistence of Poetry: Bicentennial Essays on Keats*, ed. Robert M. Ryan and Ronald A. Sharp (Amherst, MA: University of Massachusetts Press, 1998), p. 55.

[5] John Dewey, *Art as Experience* (New York: Minton, Balch & Company, 1934), p. 20.

[6] See Eric Eisner's chapter in this collection for more on the connection between Bate and Dewey.

but also momentary: 'at once it struck me' (*LJK*, I: p. 193). It also seemed to be connected to other stories, parables, gnomic statements, and paradoxes strewn throughout Keats's epistolary speculations. Perhaps inspired by John Middleton Murry, who put forward the notion that negative capability 'is that quality which Christ pre-eminently possessed', a kind of cosmic 'Acceptance', Bate systematized the term, transubstantiating it and all of that material he connected with it into the ethereal thing so many know as *Negative Capability*.[7] After the mid-1960s any use of the term negative capability very likely is negative capability understood through the thinking of Walter Jackson Bate.

It is important to emphasize the chanciness of negative capability—that it occurred to Keats at all, that Milnes's advertisement was noticed by Jeffrey, that Bate picked up his father's library book and keyed in on Dewey's one reference to it—because negative capability now feels, if not stable, then like a ubiquitous presence within Keats scholarship and beyond. For Keats scholars, negative capability is a necessary touchstone, often one pliable enough to align with whatever theoretical perspective one employs to examine Keats's life and work. For example, in *Romanticism and Gender*, Anne Mellor argues for the alignment of negative capability with 'feminine empathy'; and in *John Keats and the Culture of Dissent*, Nicholas Roe works to uncover the liberal political ideology underlying negative capability, especially in the book's epilogue, which opens with a section called 'Negative Capability and its Backgrounds: Shakespeare, Politics, Theatre'.[8] One would be hard-pressed—indeed, pressed to the very last oozings—to find a recent book on Keats that does not reckon with negative capability in some way.

Negative capability has also escaped the gravitational pull of Keats studies and surfaced in discussions ranging from such various domains as contemporary poetics, Philip Pullman's His Dark Materials series, and Wilfred Bion's psychoanalytical theory (to cite a few of the discussions covered in this book), and (to cite a few not discussed here) the marketing strategy of Eben Pagan, the need to accept uncertainty related to the emergence of the Zika virus, and the minimalist style of punk rockers The Urinals, with their album, *Negative Capability … Check It Out!*[9] One can gather a sense of the ubiquity

[7] Quoted in Walter Jackson Bate, *Negative Capability: The Intuitive Approach in Keats* (Cambridge, MA: Harvard University Press, 1939), p. 41. Bate continued to spread the negative capability gospel in a more widely read context with his biography, *John Keats* (Cambridge, MA: The Belknap Press of Harvard University Press, 1963). See especially the book's central chapter, 'Negative Capability', pp. 233–63.

[8] Anne K. Mellor, *Romanticism and Gender* (New York: Routledge, 1993), p. 24; Nicholas Roe, *John Keats and the Culture of Dissent* (Oxford: Clarendon Press, 1997), p. 230.

[9] 'Negative Capability—Developing Empathy In Business', YouTube video, posted by 'Get Altitude', 11 November 2007, accessed 5 July 2018, https://www.youtube.com/watch?v=jFZaGK3GjvI; Sandro Galea, 'Uncertainty and the Zika Virus: Why Scientists

of negative capability in many of this collection's chapters, especially those in Parts III and IV, covering negative capability's uses in recent and contemporary American poetry and adaptations and appropriations of the concept in psychoanalysis (David Sigler), Zen (Anne McCarthy), and Pullman's trilogy (Suzanne Barnett). Walter Reed closes the collection by employing Bakhtinian dialogism to theorize and celebrate this multiplicity.

This ubiquity has seemed too much for some. In the late 1970s Woody Allen satirized the use of the term in *Manhattan* by having a character employ it, in Keats's terms, '*hoity-toityishly*' (*LJK*, II: p. 204), in a remark on the power of a seemingly unremarkable sculpture. In 1983 Shimon Sandbank states, '"Negative capability" ... has been not only praised but worked out of all proportion, certainly out of the ten lines it occupies in the famous letter to his brothers'.[10] In a notebook entry from the early 1980s American poet W. S. DiPiero notes, 'Keats's remark about Negative Capability seems to be becoming a literary cult object. The commentators are full of it these days.'[11] Approximately three decades later American poet Mary Ruefle laments that negative capability has become for her 'like a sickness unto death', and she wishes for a decade-long 'moratorium' on uses of the term, complaining, 'so overused are [the words 'negative capability'], so bandied about that they have come to mean just about anything one wants them to'.[12]

The sense that the numerous and varied uses of negative capability have gotten to be too much seems to have been part of what gave rise to Li Ou's treatment of the topic in her monograph *Keats and Negative Capability* (2009). In the book's preface, Li notes 'the only book-length study of the idea itself until today is Walter Jackson Bate's 1939 monograph published from his Harvard honours thesis'. The 'idea itself' is an important one for Li, for whom there is a core of negative capability that has not yet been accessed or fully revealed by scholarly criticism. Li observes that '[n]egative capability is such an essential idea of Keats's that any criticism of him has to deal with it at least in passing', but adds that its ubiquity also leads to a problem: 'more often than not, it is discussed as a key issue in the critics' overall projects in a bigger framework ... while the idea *per se* rarely constitutes the project itself'.

Need to Think Like Poets', *Cognoscenti* (blog), *WBUR*, 8 September 2016, accessed 5 July 2018, http://www.wbur.org/cognoscenti/2016/09/08/zika-sandro-galea; The Urinals, *Negative Capability ... Check It Out!* (Warning Label Records, 1997).

[10] Shimon Sandbank, 'Keats Altered by the Present', *Comparative Literature*, 35: 1 (1983), p. 43.

[11] W. S. DiPiero, 'Out of Notebooks', in *Memory and Enthusiasm: Essays, 1975–1985* (Princeton, NJ: Princeton University Press, 1989), p. 73.

[12] Mary Ruefle, 'On Fear: Our positive capability', *Poetry Magazine*, 200: 3 (June 2012), accessed 5 July 2018, https://www.poetryfoundation.org/poetrymagazine/articles/detail/69815.

Li acknowledges that negative capability has been closely investigated—she allows that some 'critics have examined the idea at a microscopic level, exploring its meaning, analysing its different aspects', but always as 'a means serving another end'. The alternative to this kind of work also has its limitations: 'When the idea does take up the central place in criticism, it is usually found in shorter pieces, which, due to their length, tend to take a rather limited perspective.' Li concludes: 'The broader discussions tend to be cursory, and the closer ones, narrow.'[13] In addition to identifying this problem, Li also takes issue with negative capability's proliferation. At the end of her introduction she notes that 'the term itself has taken on a life of its own' (p. 20), but one senses that she views that afterlife as one in need of control. Even as she recognizes that the popularity of the term 'demonstrates its vigorous life and currency' (p. 22), her study, by 'intend[ing] to make the idea the end itself', seems resistant to the more 'wild directions' negative capability has taken (pp. ix, 21).

While there is much to learn from and respect about Li's significant contribution to Keats studies—especially her analysis of what Keats gleaned about negative capability from his reading of *King Lear*[14]—Li's treatment of negative capability differs from ours in significant ways. Chief among them is Li's notion that there is a core idea itself to negative capability. Li states that '[t]he idea itself' is 'like a constellation of several stars', one that 'holds together many intricately interrelated components' (p. x). But constellations lack cores: they are human projections on a multitudinous array of discrete objects distributed across empty spaces. The projectors are always free to alter what shapes are made, to add new stars, remove old ones, or see the sky itself anew. Citing Keats's 19 February 1818 letter to John Hamilton Reynolds, Li states, 'Only by unravelling the key threads of this idea, can we clearly see how its "beautiful circuiting" weaves into "a tapestry empyrean"' (p. x). But what's allowed? Which exactly are the proper 'points of leaves and twigs' on which to construct our 'airy Citadel[s]' (*LJK*, I: p. 232)? Li acknowledges that with her book she intends 'not to open new frontiers, but rather, to till this fertile piece of land which has not yet been thoroughly ploughed' (p. x); of course, this is an allowable and fruitful strategy, but, even so, it implies that we already agree upon the boundaries of 'this fertile piece of land'. The Batean decree establishing the borders of negative capability is one we shouldn't necessarily accept. When the core idea comes together in Li's book, like Bate she conceives of negative capability as a primarily serious concept. In fact, to the core idea of (a largely Batean) negative capability, which Li glosses with the terms 'imaginativeness, experiential and artistic intensity, submission of the self, sympathetic identification, the dramatic quality of the poet, disinterestedness,

13 Li Ou, *Keats and Negative Capability* (London: Bloomsbury, 2009), p. ix.

14 See chapter 2, '*King Lear* and Negative Capability', pp. 62–107.

[and] a neutral intellect tolerating diversity and contradiction', she adds one final element: 'a tragic vision of human experience' (p. 8). In short, what Bate reifies, Li reinforces.

By contrast, we hope that Keats's description of the 'poetical Character' might apply as well to our book: 'it enjoys light and shade; it lives in gusto, be it foul or fair, high or low, rich or poor, mean or elevated'. We hope our collection's 'camelion' contributions, which would have shocked the early 'virtuous' critics of negative capability, will inform, intrigue, and provoke our readers (*LJK*, I: pp. 386–7). Taken as a whole, this collection proceeds without a strong devotion to a core idea of negative capability itself. The chapters reconsider the origins of negative capability—some familiar ones, some which will likely be 'new' for most readers. They apply an array of theories and methods, and in so doing they offer vibrant new readings of works by Keats. And they read forward to *and* backward from the varied afterlives that continue to alter Keats's nebulous, persistent phrase from 200 years ago. These chapters are plural disquisitions, not a singular one meant to restrict traffic on the thoroughfares of our minds. As such, they don't need to agree, and they shouldn't be expected to: new discoveries, new ways of engaging Keats's life, relationships, and work, and each new use of the term contribute to the meaning, the significance, the resonance of negative capability. Here is how we have organized our part in that larger conversation.

Part I, '"swelling into reality": New Contexts for Negative Capability', considers crucial but under-investigated aspects of what went into making negative capability. The section's first chapter, by Brian Bates, puts negative capability squarely into one of its most immediate but also most disregarded contexts: that of the Christmas pantomime from which Keats, along with his friends Dilke and Brown, is walking home when certain ideas about literary genius suddenly strike him. Bates reinterprets the negative capability passage in light of Keats's experiences with pantomimes, viewing it as an enactment of pantomimical theater. Brian Rejack revisits another of the letter's immediate contexts: its transcription by John Jeffrey. His chapter represents the first sustained effort to think deeply about what it means that the negative capability letter survives only via a notoriously unreliable transcriber. Drawing upon insights provided by both Bates and Rejack, Michael Theune argues in his chapter that it is possible that the creation of the term 'negative capability' involves an element of wordplay, overriding by over-writing the term 'natural capacity' (a term which Hazlitt borrows and repurposes from Thomas Hobbes). Part I concludes with Carmen Faye Mathes's consideration of three early readers of Keats—Mary Shelley, Letitia Elizabeth Landon, and Elizabeth Barrett Browning—who were not influenced by the phrase negative capability itself (their comments coming before the letter's first publication in 1848). Mathes situates her analysis in one of the most important scholarly contexts for considering negative capability: Keats and gender. However, through her engagement with these early women readers of Keats, Mathes complicates accounts that read negative capability as fundamentally rooted in openness and empathy. Part I thus closes with some resistance to our assumptions about what it means to encounter the term negative capability, and reminds us that much of the Keatsian legacy exists prior to or in contradiction with a conventional understanding of negative capability, and it bears consistent repeating that other narratives still need writing, rewriting, and reconsideration.

Part II, '"examplified throughout": Forms of Negatively Capable Reading', features essays which focus on negative capability from the side of reception instead of creation. As Cassandra Falke points out in her opening essay, negative capability tends to be associated less with the former than with the latter, even though Keats discusses both in the immediate context for the term. Earlier in the letter Keats tells his brothers that if they 'Examine King Lear', the notion that 'the excellence of every Art is its intensity' will appear there 'examplified throughout'. Unreliable as Jeffrey's transcript is, we'll take this word at its word, so to speak, and treat the process of reading as one of *exemplifying* and *amplifying* forms of knowledge, insight, and intuition, especially when those experiences register as 'uncertainties, Mysteries, doubts'. This Part thus begins with Falke's 'Negatively Capable Reading', in which she argues that French phenomenologist Jean-Luc Marion's related concepts of 'saturated phenomenality' and 'negative certainty' offer us ways to articulate what happens when we read. In Keats's terms, we might say, Marion's phenomenology explores the precise nature of experiencing aesthetic intensity. Falke concludes her chapter by turning to two poems that 'examplify' this form of reading, both of which are poems *about* reading: 'On First Looking into Chapman's Homer' and 'This Living Hand'.

Following Falke's theorizing of the process, Kurtis Hessel's, Jeanne Britton's, and Emily Rohrbach's essays each 'examplify' further what negatively capable reading looks like in three different contexts. Hessel's chapter situates negative capability at the inception of the growth of modern professionalism and shows how the physician–poet's multidisciplinarity is reflected and embodied in Keats's poetics. Hessel argues that negative capability 'both arose from the plurality of Keats's professional commitments and also served as a conceptual bridge among the disciplines'. Britton likewise roots her analysis in Keats's professional training in medicine, but with a focus on the concept of irritability. In her chapter, Britton connects irritability both with the Horatian trope of the *genus irritable vatum* ('the irritable race of poets') and with the term's physiological meanings. Irritability thus situates negative capability in relation to the mediation of sensation by the body and the mediation of literary history through writers, readers, and texts. Rohrbach concludes Part II by locating in Keats's resistance to irritable reaching a method of historically oriented thinking and reading. Negative capability specifically and Keats's figurations of plurality more broadly, she contends, offer means of conceptualizing the historical present. Rohrbach identifies 'Keatsian historical thinking' first in the negative capability letter, expanded upon in his 'vale of Soul-making' conceit, and put to effect in 'To Autumn'; her essay then concludes with a reading of William Hazlitt's *The Spirit of the Age*, a text which Rohrbach characterizes as an example of negatively capable historiography.

The collection's third Part shifts from the origins of negative capability to its afterlives. '"Pursued through Volumes", Volume I: Negative Capability in Twentieth- and Twenty-First-Century American Poetry' is the first of two 'volumes' that pursue various applications and adaptations of negative capability. The first two chapters, by Robert Archambeau and Eric Eisner, both focus on the place of negative capability within American poetry and poetics in the second half of the twentieth century. Both engage with the prominent place that the New Critics, Walter Jackson Bate, and Charles Olson all hold in the history of negative capability, but their chapters move in different directions from their shared beginnings. Archambeau homes in on the 'poetry wars' and argues that we can find a consensus between opposing camps precisely around their shared reliance on negative capability to articulate various poetic projects and aims. Eisner's chapter begins by revealing connections between Bate's and Olson's seemingly incompatible conceptions of negative capability and concludes by examining Adrienne Rich's poem 'In Memoriam: D.K.'. He reads Rich's poem as 'a negatively capable critique of negative capability', arguing that it offers a challenge to Bate and Olson's shared notion that negative capability is an unalloyed good, and to the 'masculinist gender politics' undergirding the male writers' assessments. We thus begin Part III with two (somewhat) overlapping readings of negative capability's place in postwar American poetry that, despite their common ground, demonstrate the expansive range of poetic purposes to which the concept has been put.

After the broader focuses of Archambeau's and Eisner's approaches, Part III continues with two in-depth examinations of the relationship between negative capability and the work of one particular American poet. Arsevi Seyran links Elizabeth Bishop to negative capability via the poet's particular interest in Charles Darwin's inductive method, which, as Bishop describes it, builds from the accretion of concrete particulars to 'a sudden relaxation' to transport 'into the unknown'. Seyran demonstrates how this pattern is replicated not only in Keats's own formulation of negative capability but also in three of Bishop's famous poems, 'The Filling Station', 'The Moose', and 'The Fish'. Thomas Gardner's chapter tracks Jorie Graham's close connection with negative capability through her career. In particular, he examines the poet's enactments of negative capability in her four most recent full-length collections, discovering that at key moments the poet calls upon the body to respond to situations marked by uncertainty and doubt, and the body does so by developing 'a new form of listening' that allows the poet to productively engage the occasioned questions.

In Part IV, '"pursued through Volumes", Volume II: Adaptations, Appropriations, Mutations', we move outside of poetry's 'realms of gold' and encounter some of the more far-ranging stops on the term's travel itinerary. If at this point you still harbor any doubts about negative capability's ubiquity, by the time you reach the end of Suzanne Barnett's chapter you'll have plenty of facts and reasons with which to replace them. Her essay focuses on Philip Pullman's His Dark Materials trilogy, but she begins with a thorough (though by no means exhaustive) catalogue of negative capability's uses and abuses across twentieth- and twenty-first-century literary criticism, fiction, poetry, and popular culture more broadly. Situating her argument in relation to that catalogue, Barnett demonstrates that Pullman's novels present a significantly different reading of the term than what has come to be the popular (and often scholarly) consensus about its meaning. Instead of a capacity for empathy or identification, Pullman's negative capability resembles something more in line with William Blake's or Percy Shelley's radical political visions of human subjectivity.

Our pursuit continues in David Sigler's chapter, in which he excavates negative capability from the archive of psychoanalysis, where, thanks largely to the work of Wilfred Bion, the term has a long history and still persists in contemporary practice and discourse. Sigler's approach—reading Bion's use of negative capability in relation to how Bion responds to Freud and Lacan—demonstrates Keats's continuing influence on psychoanalysis while also revealing aspects of negative capability not encountered in the standard Batean reading. The chapter concludes by turning to Marion Milner, a British psychoanalyst whose work in the 1930s brought negative capability into the discipline long before Bion did, and in markedly different ways; even if Bion's later efforts have overshadowed Milner's, Sigler's essay offers a first step toward redressing that imbalance. Like Sigler's retroactive reconstruction of negative capability's history in psychoanalysis, Anne McCarthy's chapter adopts an idiosyncratic and non-linear form of literary history. She shows that negative capability has frequently been ported into western accounts and appropriations of Zen Buddhism, but, rather than rejecting or viewing with skepticism such ahistorical, cross-cultural recognitions, McCarthy suggests that a method of this sort can become 'a negatively capable reading practice—one that recognizes the discontinuity of textual circulation as well as the possibility of contingent, non-binary modes of interpretation'. McCarthy finds an instance of this method in Reginald Horace Blyth's *Zen in English Literature and Oriental Classics* (1942), a work which offers another version of negatively capable reading while also suggesting the possibility of additional futures for such approaches.

In the spirit of multiplicity and possibility that pervades this collection, in the final chapter Walter Reed turns to Mikhail Bakhtin in order to articulate the ongoing vitality of negative capability as 'an unfinished, open-ended collaboration, a disquisition which is in fact a set of ongoing disputes'. Negative capability's dialogic context takes us from Keats's London in 1817, to Jorge Luis Borges's Buenos Aires in 1960, to Julio Cortázar's Paris in 1984, and many other times and places in between and beyond. Reed's treatment of negative capability in these contexts reveals significant insights about influences on Keats and Keats's influences on others, while also helping us '[prove] upon our pulses' Bakhtin's claim that 'There is neither a first nor a last word.'

And so, we feel compelled to ask, as Keats does in 'I stood tip-toe' after one hundred-plus lines of ardent pursuit, 'What next?' (*PJK*, p. 83). While we hope and trust that our readers will find ample satisfying information and insight in and among these collected essays, we hope and trust equally that this collection will provoke new investigations into negative capability and its multifarious manifestations. Several newly opened avenues of investigation merit additional inquiry, which we will leave to our readers to identify (although we can't help but note the tantalizing possibilities raised by some of the many intriguing texts discussed in these chapters, including Milner's *An Experiment in Leisure*, Cortázar's *imagen de John Keats*, and Blyth's *Zen in English Literature and Oriental Classics*). To bring about a whole new and decisive era in the field, those engaged in negative capability studies might also work to locate the original manuscript of the negative capability letter. Very little might more greatly transform the field.

That the letter might swell back into reality at some point in the future is not actually all that preposterous. Just over twenty years ago a long-lost manuscript of a different Keats letter turned up in the closet of a historic home in Virginia (after having likely spent most or all of the nineteenth century in Louisville).[15] Given that Jeffrey made a transcript, the negative capability manuscript was obviously in his possession in 1845. It is also almost certain that when John Gilmer Speed (George Keats's grandson, born to Emma Keats Speed) produced his edition of the letters in 1883 it was *not* in *his* possession. Although he claimed the genesis of his edition came from his realization, while reading over the manuscripts possessed by his mother, that 'the larger part of the letters were not included [in Milnes's 1848 biography]', Gilmer Speed seems to have overstated his case.[16] He does print the 5 January 1818 letter to George and

[15] For more on this letter, see Dearing Lewis, 'A John Keats Letter Rediscovered', *Romantic Circles* (November 1998), accessed 5 July 2018, http://www.rc.umd.edu/editions/keats/.

[16] John Gilmer Speed, ed., *The Letters and Poems of John Keats, in Three Volumes* (New York: Dodd, Mead & Company, 1883), I: p. ix.

Tom for this first time.[17] And he prints large portions of some of the journal letters (Feb–May 1819 and September 1819) to George and Georgiana which had not been printed before because of Jeffrey's omissions. But the negative capability letter was clearly based on Milnes's text for Gilmer Speed's edition (he follows almost exactly not only the text but also Milnes's spelling, punctuation, capitalization, etc.). To begin searching for negative capability, then, one need only look into the Keats family and its circle in Louisville between 1845 and 1883, and primarily concerning Gilmer Speed's mother Emma, 'whose pious care preserved the most valuable of the manuscripts', according to the dedication of his edition. Emma Speed at times gifted manuscripts written in her uncle's hand to recipients she judged worthy of the honor, including Oscar Wilde, whom she invited to her home in 1882 while he was traveling across the United States on a lecture tour.[18] With fine isolated—or 'insolated', via Jeffrey—bits of knowledge like these in hand, we have more clues to find, more leads to follow, and maybe even, at some point, a few basements and attics to search. The pursuit just might yield an ethereal thing or two.

And what if Keats's manuscript of the negative capability letter does reappear in the future? Perhaps we'll discover that Jeffrey screwed up royally. Perhaps what he read as 'Negative Capability' was actually 'negligent celerity'. Cleopatra's quip to a tardy and unfaithful Antony that 'Celerity is never more admired / Than by the negligent' (Act III, Scene VII, lines 24–5) may be on Keats's mind, since he does, after all, quote Cleopatra's 'sooth la' at the letter's end (*LJK*, I: p. 194 n.2). And the contradictory concept jibes well with Keats's 'delicious diligent Indolence' (I: p. 231), a passive but impassioned devotion to imagination, which even in lassitude may still result in a rapid recognition (like an imaginative truth felt all of a sudden—'at once it struck me'). Perhaps instead we'll see Jeffrey vindicated, this particular transcript turning out to have been startlingly accurate. Perhaps we'll find that his work falls somewhere in between that of royal screw-up and meticulous scribe, with his errors more minor, like transcribing 'I mean Negative Capability' instead of 'I mean a 'Negative Capability'. (Although even such a small adjustment could radically revise our notions of negative capability: '*a*' negative capability? So there's more than one?) Or perhaps we'll encounter some new details or contexts (excised by Jeffrey) which will retroactively prove a particular take on negative capability (whether in this volume or not) to have been especially prescient. But it might be best if we're all proved wrong. If the letter does turn up, it would be most exciting if everything we thought we knew up to this point were upended entirely, casting us all into even more 'uncertainties, Mysteries,

[17] Although Jeffrey transcribed this letter, Milnes curiously chose not to print it in his biography.

[18] Oscar Wilde, 'Keats's Sonnet on Blue', *The Hobby Horse* (July 1886), pp. 83–6.

doubts', but also offering us new entries into ardent pursuit. Then we'll need to work even harder to resist the temptation to irritably reach after fact and reason, and instead remain content with various forms of half-knowledge while we keep working to create new ones in the future.

Part One

'swelling into reality': New Contexts for Negative Capability

Chapter One

Keats's Negative Capability

On Pantomime and 'Irritable Reaching'

Brian Bates

> Brown and Dilke walked with me & back from the Christmas pantomime.
>
> — *LJK*, I: p. 193

This sentence, which directly precedes Keats's description of his negative capability epiphany, has been often overlooked by Keats scholars. Most notably, Walter Jackson Bate's touchstone 'Negative Capability' chapter in his *John Keats* biography (1963) only briefly mentions Keats's walk back from the Christmas pantomime before quoting and closely scrutinizing the 'famous sentences' from Keats's letter.[1] Li Ou's *Keats and Negative Capability* (2009)—the only twentieth-first-century monograph devoted solely to Keats's concept—does not include this Christmas pantomime sentence in her opening block quotation from Keats's letter, which presents the 'idea itself' and serves as the 'basic reference point of the ensuing discussion'.[2] Harry Beaudry—one of the few scholars who has commented on Keats's pantomime viewing—belittles that particular Christmas pantomime in *The English Theatre and John Keats* (1973) and offers a bemused explanation of why Keats would precede his negative capability remarks with a sentence about pantomime:

> it is a most incongruous circumstance that following this innocuous bit of stage fare Keats and Dilke should become involved in a serious discussion of Shakespeare's 'negative capability'. One can only reflect that

[1] Walter Jackson Bate, *John Keats* (Cambridge: Harvard University Press, 1963), p. 249.

[2] Li Ou, *Keats and Negative Capability* (London: Bloomsbury, 2009), p. 1. Li offers only one brief comment on pantomime.

> Keats's imagination worked in startling paradoxes at times and could make poetic sense out of incongruity.[3]

Far from an 'incongruous circumstance' of Keats 'at times' exercising the extremity of his 'poetic sense', I argue that pantomime's presence in a 'serious discussion of Shakespeare' reveals a fundamental aspect of Keats's negative capability that has yet to be explored. Moreover, Beaudry's disparaging remarks about pantomime implicitly uphold a general critical consensus, reified forty-five years later in Li's book, that Keats's negative capability should be regarded as a highly serious philosophical endeavor that leans toward a tragic poetic vision.[4] As a result of this longstanding perception, critical definitions of negative capability have not entertained how pantomime—the most popular form of Regency theater—influenced Keats's thinking about his poetic identity and poetics.[5] Spotlighting pantomime's significant role in Keats's concept reveals how negative capability involves playfulness, satire, bodily performance, and popular culture.

The pantomime Keats saw that December 1817 night was Drury Lane's *Harlequin's Vision; Or, The Feast of the Statue* (also billed as *Harlequin Libertine*).[6] In his book *Satire and Romanticism* (2000), Steven Jones notes that Keats's thinking about negative capability might be connected meaningfully with his experience watching that pantomime.[7] More broadly, Jones points

[3] Harry Beaudry, *The English Theatre and John Keats* (Salzburg: University of Saltzburg Press, 1973), p. 144. Beaudry's negative evaluation of pantomime as 'an innocuous bit of stage fare' reflects another prevailing critical consensus, which began in the eighteenth century, that pantomime is frivolous entertainment best suited for children.

[4] Arguably, Lionel Trilling's 'The Poet as Hero: Keats in his Letters', in *The Opposing Self: Nine Essays in Criticism*, ed. Leon Wieseltier (New York: Viking Press, 1955) articulates the most influential argument for negative capability as a high philosophical concept that involves pursuing the nature of evil and a tragic vision.

[5] For example, see the definition of 'Negative Capability' in the most recent edition of *The Princeton Encyclopedia of Poetry and Poetics*, 4th ed. (Princeton, NJ: Princeton University Press, 2012).

[6] I have used The Huntington Library's John Larpent Collection manuscript of *Harlequin's Vision; Or, The Feast of the Statue*, which is identified as *Harlequin Libertine*, MssLA, 2004. That opening pantomime night was almost certainly Boxing Day, 26 December 1817. See *LJK*, I: p. 194n. For more about the challenges of identifying reliable print texts for pantomimes, see Jeffrey N. Cox, '"Illegitimate" Pantomime in the "Legitimate" Theatre: Context as Text', *Studies in Romanticism*, 54 (Summer 2015), pp. 159–86.

[7] See Jones's chapter 'Turning What Was Once Burlesque into Romantic: Byron's Pantomimic Satire', in his *Satire and Romanticism* (New York: St. Martin's Press, 2000), pp. 169–97. Jones remarks, 'Even the coincidental juxtaposition, if that is all it is, of pantomime and negative capability prompts a re-examination of the Keatsian idea, usually glossed in relation to Shakespeare and Kean, in relation to the lower theatrical form' (p. 196).

out that in the early nineteenth century pantomime was 'in the air … in the repertoire of almost any author who cared to draw upon it' as a popular mass entertainment that appealed to a 'mixed-class' and 'extremely heterogeneous' audience (p. 173).[8] In his letters, Keats mentions attending four pantomime performances—*Harlequin's Vision* (26 December 1817), *Harlequin Gulliver* (2 January 1818), and *Harlequin Munchausen* (twice: 13 February 1819 and 1 March 1819) (*LJK*, I: pp. 193, 199; II: p. 68). Keats also reviewed *Harlequin's Vision* for *The Champion* in December 1817 and twice referred to pantomime elsewhere in his letters.[9] First, in an October 1818 letter, he playfully mentions 'pantomimical' when describing 'two distinct tempers of mind in which we judge of things'. Second, in a January 1820 letter, he cleverly characterizes a particular type of 'witty' person as 'Harlequin Epigram, Esqre' (*LJK*, I: p. 385; II: p. 245). Keats's 1818 poem 'Welcome joy, and welcome sorrow' makes one direct reference to pantomime—'visage sage at pantomime' (*PJK*, p. 231; line 10)—while his January 1818 'Apollo to the Graces' echoes a song from *Harlequin's Vision* and his April 1819 'Song of Four Fairies' follows the structure and song lyrics in a scene from *The Elements; Or, Harlequin Earth, Air, Water and Fire*.[10] In *Keats and the Dramatic Principle* (1958), Bernice Slote conjectures further that Keats saw *Harlequin and the Dandy Club; Or, 1818* as well as a few other pantomimes between 1815 and 1819. As the first (and virtually only) scholar to trace Keats's interest in pantomime, Slote concludes that 'Keats liked the pantomime and no doubt saw it often'.[11]

Beyond watching staged pantomime, Keats was privy to the pantomime reviews and pantomime rhetoric of his circle of 'Cockney' friends, including William Hazlitt and Leigh Hunt, the latter of whom wrote two January 1817 *Examiner* essays celebrating pantomime's mass popularity, 'animal spirit', and satirical power. Hunt's essays, which emphasize pantomime's satiric playfulness and self-reflexive audience appeal, shine a light on pantomime's significance for Keats. Pantomime's characteristic low-to-high and high-to-low transfigurations were pleasurably ridiculous and liberating for Keats, particularly its

[8] For more about Romantic period authorial pantomime rhetoric, see Beth Lau's 'Authorial Disguise and Intertextuality: Scott's *The Lay of the Last Minstrel*, Coleridge, and Keats', *Studies in Scottish Literature*, 40: 1 (2014), pp. 116–33.

[9] While his friend J. H. Reynolds was out of town during the last weeks of December, Keats took over his drama reviewing duties for the radical-leaning London weekly *The Champion*. For further information, see Laura Brake and Marysa Demoor, eds, *The Dictionary of Nineteenth Century Journalism in Great Britain and Ireland* (London: Academia Press and the British Library, 2009), pp. 106–7.

[10] Performed at Sadler's Wells, this 1818 pantomime restaged Thomas Dibdin's 1808 *Harlequin in his Element; or, Fire, Water, Earth & Air*.

[11] Bernice Slote, *Keats and the Dramatic Principle* (Lincoln: University of Nebraska Press, 1958), p. 63.

harlequinade, which reveled in a carnivalesque, tongue-in-cheek space of cultural translation, genre adaptation, character metamorphosis, and physical transformation. Pantomime granted its characters and, by extension, its diverse audience the freedom to flout cultural conventions, upend power structures, challenge elite aesthetics, and reimagine reality. Keats found aesthetic possibility and freedom in pantomime as well as in a Harlequin figure whose self-dramatizing, transformative power struck a chord with him as a new poet attempting to define his identity in Leigh Hunt's 'Cockney' circle of friends.

Pantomime's gestural acts, bodily actions, visual tropes, and welcoming of high and low provided Keats with fodder for staging his own sincere and ironically distanced transformations and poetic experiments. As Jonathan Mulrooney and John Kandl each have pointed out, Keats's negative capability involves his desire to model his poetic identity after Edmund Kean's illegitimate Shakespearian acting.[12] I argue further that Keats's negative capability description uses pantomime conventions to body forth a Shakespearian 'Man of Achievement'. That rhetorical move shadows Kean's low-to-high career trajectory from an acrobatic Harlequin and illegitimate actor of all trades to Shakespearian greatness on the legitimate stage.[13] Written within a few days of his negative capability letter, Keats's review of *Harlequin's Vision* demonstrates further his enthusiasm for pantomime's illegitimate stage power while showcasing his flair for mimicking the sincere and satirical reviewing styles of his mentors Hunt and Hazlitt. To demonstrate the versatility and changeable character of a Shakespearian 'Man of Achievement' who embodies negative capability, Keats drew on Hunt's celebration of pantomime's mixed aesthetic and satirical power while also echoing Hazlitt's satirical pantomime rhetoric, which Hazlitt used to ridicule deceptive public transformations—most notably Coleridge's. Seen through this pantomimic Hunt/Hazlitt context, I argue that Keats's negative capability lead-in—'at once it struck me'—enacts a Harlequinade scene of transformation that dovetails self-satire and serious epiphany, illegitimate and legitimate theater, a Shakespearian 'Man of Achievement' and Coleridge's 'irritable reaching', gestural acting and poetic truth. Keats's pantomime scene portrays negative capability as a self-reflexive capacity that welcomes mixed aesthetics, contrary states, character doubling, and imminent transformability.

[12] See Mulrooney's 'Keats in the Company of Kean', *Studies in Romanticism*, 42: 2 (Summer 2003), pp. 227–50 and Kandl's 'Plebian Gusto, Negative Capability, and the Low Company of "Mr. Kean": Keats's Dramatic Review for *The Champion*', *Nineteenth-Century Prose*, 28: 2 (Fall 2001), pp. 130–41.

[13] Several scholars have examined Kean's career in this manner and connected it to Keats's similar trajectory. See Jane Moody's *Illegitimate Theatre, 1770–1840* (Cambridge: Cambridge University Press, 2000), Mulrooney's 'Keats in the Company of Kean', and Jeffrey Kahan's *The Cult of Kean* (Aldershot: Ashgate, 2006).

'Pranks and witty squeaking': *Harlequin's Vision* & Mirrored Reviewing

For Drury Lane's 1817 Boxing Day performance of *Harlequin's Vision* Keats would have expected a one- to two-hour pantomime to follow the often-staged tragedy *Georges Barnwell*, which started at 7 p.m.[14] Early nineteenth-century British pantomime had two general plot movements, involving anywhere from one- to two-dozen scenes.[15] The first and shorter framing part (usually a few scenes), which gave the pantomime its name, drew on a fairy tale, nursery fable, Classical myth, literary classic, or Eastern story and featured two would-be lovers who were unable to marry because of a disapproving paternal authority. The second and larger part of the plot was the harlequinade. Unlike the mostly serious or sentimental initial plot line, the harlequinade was filled with comedic episodes and slap-stick humor, chase scenes and tricks, rapid-fire set and scene changes, spectacular visual effects and musical scores, stretched cause and effect relationships, loose narrative structures, and ellipses of time and space. The harlequinade typically began after a benevolent spirit or deity transformed the distraught lovers into Harlequin (with his magical wooden sword) and Columbine, thus enabling them to escape from the controlling paternal authority. Likewise, that same spirit or deity (or a countering evil one) transformed the paternal authority into Pantaloon, as well as that authority's servant or closest ally into Clown and often a suitor competing for Columbine into Lover. During the harlequinade, Pantaloon and company chased Harlequin and Columbine through a variety of geographical scenes while Harlequin protected Columbine and pursued a hero's task, usually assigned by the benevolent spirit. Inevitably, this knock-about series of chase, trick-work, and escape scenes led to the lovers' capture in a penultimate 'dark scene' during which Harlequin lost possession of his magical sword and Pantaloon appeared to triumph. At this point, the initial transformative spirit or deity reappeared to liberate Harlequin and Columbine and deliver them to a final celebratory wedding scene. Amidst this spectacle of elaborate processions, extravagant scenery, big heads, stock costumes, acrobatics, music, singing, dancing, and topical cultural references, Clown—owing largely to Joseph

[14] I disagree with Beaudry's claim that Keats would not have gone to see George Lillo's tragedy (first produced in 1731). Beaudry argues, 'Even if Keats had used Reynolds' pass, he would have had little interest in the bourgeois (or "domestic") tragedy of Lillo. It is most likely that the three companions went to see only the pantomime' (p. 132).

[15] British pantomime was derived from the Italian *commedia dell'arte* form. On the differences between eighteenth-century and late eighteenth-/early nineteenth-century pantomime, see David Mayer's *Harlequin in his Element, 1806–1836* (Cambridge, MA: Harvard University Press, 1969) and John O'Brien's *Harlequin Britain: Pantomime and Entertainment, 1690–1760* (Baltimore, MD: Johns Hopkins University Press, 2004).

Grimaldi's charismatic acting—had begun to steal the Regency show through his self-serving, double dealing, and tricks of construction, which competed with the popularity of Harlequin's sword-thumping, magical transformations of objects, people, and scenes.[16]

That December 1817 evening Keats and his friends—Charles Brown and Charles Wentworth Dilke—saw a 'well received' *Harlequin's Vision* amidst a 'very crowded' Drury Lane theater that seated a little over 3,000 people.[17] This pantomime version of Mozart's *Don Giovanni* is 'supposed to be a dream, which *Mercury* has conjured up in order to warn *Don Juan* from his evil courses' (*Theatrical Inquisitor*, pp. 50–1). The plot of *Harlequin's Vision* featured Don Juan/Giovanni (then Harlequin), his wife Donna Elvira (then Columbine), and Clown, as well as a wide cast of deities, most prominently Pluto, Proserpine, Mercury, and Venus. The *Literary Gazette* maintained that 'the inventor, Mr. Lethbridge, has departed so far from the original, as to impart considerable novelty to the production' (p. 11).[18] The action on stage that evening also differed in several respects from the conventional pantomime formula. Uncharacteristically, it had two Harlequins (Don Juan and Octavio), two Columbines (Donna Elvira and Leonora), and Punch and Judy—all of whom, according to *The Theatrical Inquisitor*, 'displayed unwearied activity throughout the evening—and entered into the spirit of the entertainment so completely, that the bustle of the scene was never suffered to subside' (p. 51). The pantomime's dream action played out Don Juan Harlequin's profligate exploits, duals with the husbands of women that he attempted to seduce, and subsequent escapes—all while his wife (and his father's ghost) pursued him. Finally, Don Juan Harlequin was caught by the Furies and nearly thrown into Pandemonium's liquid fire before being saved by Venus from his dream/past and reunited with his forgiving wife in a 'Palace of Pleasure' celebration that involved a host of reveling Roman gods. Even more than most pantomimes, *Harlequin's Vision* was a self-reflexive play of fun-house mirrors that celebrated the triumph of illegitimate theater over the London stage.[19] This pantomime dream vision replayed plot lines filtered through several adaptations of Mozart's opera *Don Giovanni*, which had dominated the London theater scene in 1817.

[16] For a more detailed plot description of a typical pantomime, see Mayer's *Harlequin* (pp. 23–30).

[17] *The Theatrical Inquisitor, and Monthly Mirror* (London, 1818), XII: p. 52.

[18] *The Literary Gazette; and Journal of Belles Lettres, Arts, Sciences, For the Year 1818* (London, 1818).

[19] *The Literary Gazette* reviewer laments that *Harlequin's Vision* represents illegitimate pantomime's rise to power. For him, this is a 'Pantomimical Era. The play houses are more crowded to see these shows than they have been at any former period of the season; and stage tricks are crowned with more success than the regular business of the Drama' (p. 11).

Keats's mistitling of his review, 'On "Don Giovanni", a Pantomime', suggests his sense that *Harlequin's Vision* was predominantly about the 1817 reception and adaptation of Mozart's opera, first performed on the London stage in April 1817. The review's opening sentence further exaggerates that notion: '*Don Giovanni* after having been wire drawn for years past at the neighbor theatres, made a pet at the Surrey, and fiddled away to hell at the Italian opera, has found its way into the Drury-Lane pantomime for the Christmas of 1817–18.'[20] In Regency slang, 'wire drawn' meant to 'lengthen out or extend any book, letter or discourse'.[21] Keats's 'wire drawn for years past' exaggerates the time scheme (April to December 1817) over which several adaptations in licensed, unlicensed, and private English theaters were produced, most notably its rapid transformation from its opera debut at the elite King's Theatre to 'a pet at the Surrey' one month later in *Don Giovanni; Or, A Spectre on Horseback* at the Royal Circus.[22] Keats's use of 'wire drawn' also recalls the wire-drawn Punch and Judy puppets that appeared in this pantomime as human actors. Closely related to Joseph Grimaldi's clown (and to the authoritarian power of Pantaloon), the humpback Punch (with his Jester's motley, stick, and violent actions) playfully subverted Harlequin's tricolored dress, magical wooden bat, and seemingly heroic behavior. With two Harlequins, two Columbines, Clown, Punch (a double of Clown/Pantaloon and ironic double of Harlequin) and Judy (an ironic double of Columbine), this pantomime obfuscated the conventional distinctions between harlequinade characters as well as the division between opening scenes and the harlequinade.

Keats's review mimics the zany mirroring and redounding energy of these characters as he alternately takes on the guise of overly dramatic spectators who are emotionally subsumed by pantomime and reviewers who obsessively critique its minutia. Keats mocks the self-indulgent emotional responses that *Don Giovanni* adaptations have garnered, namely the 'great delight' that male spectators have exhibited when Don Giovanni is thrown into Tartarus—'from

[20] *The Complete Works of John Keats*, ed. H. B. Forman, 5 vols. (Glasgow: Gowars & Gray, 1901), III: p. 243. Pantomime performances of Don Juan myths were over twenty-five years old in England. *Don Juan; Or, the Libertine Destroyed: a Grand Pantomimical Ballad* was first staged in October 1791 at Drury Lane. See David Worrall's *The Politics of Romantic Theatricality The Road to the Stage* (London: Palgrave Macmillan, 2007), pp. 135–65. Worrall contends that 1817 was a high water mark for Cockney theater largely because of Don Giovanni adaptations.

[21] Francis Grose, ed., *The Dictionary of the Vulgar Tongue* (London: 1811).

[22] Mozart's opera was first performed in London (in Italian) in April 1817 at the elite King's Theatre in the Haymarket before going through several anglicized adaptations (ballet, burlesque, and pantomime) in licensed and unlicensed theaters, most remarkably Thomas Dibdin's May hit *Don Giovanni; Or, A Spectre on Horseback* at the Royal Circus and Surrey Theatre. Notably, Hazlitt reviewed a spring 1817 adaptation and Hunt reviewed a summer 1817 adaptation.

a spirit of rivalry, jealousy, and certain other things which do haunt the heads and hearts of men'—as well as the 'retrospective compassion of the more soft and pitying [female] spectators' (p. 244). Following these characterizations, he chides critics who have acted as 'great antiquaries', tracking all the minute permutations of Don Giovanni's personal history and development, as well as those critics who would question the appropriateness of having Punch and Judy on the pantomime stage. Against the critical scrutiny of 'Commentators' who would offer up a host of 'frivolous objections' to Punch and Judy, Keats gleefully remarks that these two are of an 'illustrious house', and their 'pranks and witty squeaking are more popular than Giovanni himself'. He particularly delights in the bodily contrasts between Don Giovanni Harlequin and Punch, Don Giovanni's mistresses and Judy:

> if the Don is well made, Punch is ill made; if the Rake has a dozen mistresses, Punch has his Judy, who has the charms of a dozen in her summed up—if the former has a confident stamp, the latter has the neatest jerk of the left leg; if the former has his quizzing glass, the latter has his ladle. (p. 244)

Notably, Keats's only direct commentary on *Harlequin's Vision* focuses on its most illegitimate parts—Punch and Judy—and Keats judges those parts to be even more pleasing than the other pantomime characters. His exuberant description of Punch's vulgar appearance and 'jerky' behaviors and Judy's twelve-in-one charms lead him to lambaste 'caviling' critics who do not appreciate Punch and Judy's bodily capacities and, thus, 'stand against all common sense'.

Keats punctuates his review with two sentences that wryly reflect on the wrong-headedness of such reviewing critics. These critics miss the pleasure of pantomime—exemplified here by Punch and Judy—which, Keats suggests, a child is better fit to describe: 'As to the pantomime, be it good or bad, a child should write a critique upon it. We were pleased knowing how much better it ought to be—a child's is the eulogy—and that not merely in pantomimes' (p. 245). Such childish appreciation comes from the open experiencing of complementary contrasts (Harlequin/Punch), which can stimulate the imagination to consider 'how much better it ought to be'. For Keats, evaluating pantomime too narrowly or meticulously destroys such possibilities and disqualifies spectators from the pleasurable experience of losing themselves—in pantomime's spectacle, bustle, and mixed forms—before finding their way back to themselves.[23] Overall, Keats's review reads like a satirical exercise

[23] Also relevant is Meylinda Neuss's argument in *Distance, Theatre, and the Public Voice, 1750–1850* (New York: Palgrave Macmillan, 2012), in which she maintains that 'pantomime actually helped its audience adapt to new forms of spectatorship' (p. 15).

that plays high emotional sincerity and overly determined criticism against pantomime as a tongue-in-cheek form that holds a mirror up to audience responses.

Leigh Hunt's two January 1817 *Examiner* essays offered Keats a precedent for reviewing pantomime and considering its satirical, mirroring potential. Hunt's essays represent a 'Cockney' endorsement of pantomime that celebrates the form's dynamic energy and satirical power. His first essay proclaims, 'We must indulge ourselves a little this season on the subject of Pantomimes—a species of drama, for which, at whatever hazard of our critical reputation, we must acknowledge a great predilection.' Flying directly in the face of reviewing critics' propensity to scoff at pantomime as childish and nonsensical entertainment, Hunt attaches pantomime to his own reputation (and 'indulgence') and then contends:

> There is no such thing as modern comedy, tragedy, nor even farce, since Mr. Colman has left off writing it; but Pantomime flourishes as much as ever, and makes all parties comfortable; it enchants the little holiday folks; it draws tenfold applauding thunder from the gods; it makes giggle all those who can afford to be made giggle; and finally, it brings out the real abilities of our dramatic writers, who would be very pleasant fellows if they would not write comedy.
>
> Yes, there is something *real* in Pantomime: there is animal spirit in it.[24]

Hunt reverses the conventional hierarchy of legitimate and illegitimate theater forms.[25] From his smiling point of view, the bad 'dialogue and performance' of legitimate contemporary theater forms have rendered them illegitimate, while illegitimate pantomime has become the only contemporary form that legitimately can 'bring out the real abilities of our dramatic writers' and please a diverse audience. Hunt elaborates on that 'something *real* in pantomime'—its 'animal spirit'—in his second essay: 'The three general pleasures of a Pantomime are its bustle, its variety, and its sudden changes' (p. 388). Pantomime's pleasurable 'animal spirit' of constant movement, adaptation, and metamorphosis can transform hierarchical categories—the low into the high and the high into the low—while leaving spectators 'to their several powers, to imagine what supplement they please to the mute caricature before them' (p. 388). Through these energized arranger-to-actor-to-spectator transferences, Hunt sees

[24] Jeffrey N. Cox and Michael Gamer, eds., *The Broadview Anthology of Romantic Drama* (Orchard Park, NY: Broadview Press, 2003), p. 386.

[25] Pointing out the general 'badness' or disappointing nature of Regency tragedy and comedy was a common reviewing stance; however, placing pantomime above these legitimate forms was not.

contemporary pantomime as 'the best medium of dramatic satire' (p. 388). He focuses on its capacity to produce healthful social satire—through a variety of constantly moving bodies and scene changes—via audience self-reflection that works much like having 'looking glasses put before the patients'. His suggestion is that pantomime's carnivalesque, redounding energy might reveal to spectators more about themselves than anything else.

'At once it struck me': Pantomime Transformation in Negative Capability

Keats wrote his Hunt-inflected pantomime review within a few days of finishing his negative capability letter. This letter's pantomime scene-setting and the words 'disquisition' and 'dovetailed' lead to his epiphany—'at once it struck me'—thereby playing out his serious and satirical thinking, which mimics Hunt's and Hazlitt's (and Coleridge's) pantomime rhetoric. Keats's description of his epiphany enacts a Harlequin strike that depicts Keats and Dilke as characters caught up in the chaotic workings of a pantomime scene:[26]

> Brown & Dilke walked with me & back from the Christmas pantomime. I had not a dispute but a disquisition with Dilke, on various subjects; several things dovetailed in my mind, & at once it struck me, what quality went to form a Man of Achievement especially in Literature & which Shakespeare posessed so enormously—I mean *Negative Capability*, that is when man is capable of being in uncertainties, Mysteries, doubts, without any irritable reaching after fact & reason—Coleridge, for instance, would let go by a fine isolated verisimilitude caught from the Penetralium of mystery, from being incapable of remaining content with half knowledge. (*LJK*, I: p. 193)

Keats's phrase, 'at once it struck me', recalls the action of Harlequin's wooden sword, which could transform scenes, objects, and people. Moreover, as Leigh Hunt remarks in the second of his January 1817 pantomime essays, 'besides being a thing very pleasant in the imagination to handle, [Harlequin's sword] is excellent at satirical strokes. Lissom as a cane … . We always think, when we see it, what precious thumps we should like to give some persons' (p. 388). In the midst of celebrating Harlequin's thumping antics, Hunt imagines Harlequin's sword in his own hand and then fantasizes about using it on the 'backs' of a line of satirical targets with 'looking glasses put before them' so that they 'might know themselves when transformed into their essential shapes; after which

[26] Keats later styles Dilke as a character in a play, calling him 'a Godwin perfectibil[it]y Man' in an October 1818 letter to George and Georgiana (*LJK*, I: p. 397).

they might recover'. Notably, Hunt does not exempt himself from the sword. In the essay's final sentence, he proposes that someone also 'should set a glass before ourselves, and give us a thump equally informing' (p. 388). Keats's 'at once it struck me' couches the high sincerity of his transformative epiphany in the playful, thumping language of Hunt's harlequinade. Going beyond Hunt's hypothetical self-satirical thump, however, Keats presents himself as actually being struck by Harlequin's sword—an informing thump that punctuates his lead-in, 'several things dovetailed in my mind'.

The word 'dovetailed' adds a further theatrical, pantomime edge to that strike. In the Romantic period, 'dovetailed' is most often associated with wood-working, when a tightly fitted joint is made—a process that Samuel Johnson's 1785 *Dictionary* describes more broadly as a 'form of joining two bodies together, where that which is inserted has the form of a wedge reversed, and therefore cannot fall out'. Dovetailing involves joining together mirror opposites in a fitting space. The *OED* further identifies a usage particular to the Regency stage. In 1813 *The Theatrical Inquisitor* used 'dovetailed' when sneering at how, in Coleridge's play *Remorse*, the 'various compartments of the dialogue dove-tailed into each other', while in 1815 *The Sporting Magazine* deployed the word specifically in relation to the structure of farce: 'The difficulty of dove-tailing the component parts of the farce into each other'. These two examples of 'dovetailed' usages suggest the artificial forcing or over-forcing of parts together. Keats's 'dovetailed' smacks of a similar connotation. His '& at once it struck me' immediately follows the dovetailing of 'various compartments' and 'component parts' in his thinking, as if the serious, satirical, and farcical actions in a harlequinade scene are suddenly brought together. In this burlesque pantomime context, if Keats has received a Harlequin strike, then 'dovetailed' also might pun on the meaning of Columbine's name. As Leigh Hunt's first pantomime essay recounts, Columbine's name 'signifies the little dove; and such is she in her beauty, her ready flight, her elegance, and her amorousness' (p. 387). Flitting across the stage of Keats's mind, Columbine's energetic flight is followed immediately by a Harlequin strike.

With Harlequin and Columbine in mind, Keats's 'not a dispute, but a disquisition with Dilke, on various subjects' conjures up another aspect of the harlequinade that Hazlitt satirically deployed in his August 1817 review of Coleridge's *Biographia Literaria*. In mid-sentence, Keats qualifies his characterization of his verbal exchange with Dilke from 'dispute' (a disagreement) to 'disquisition' (an extended examination and systematic argument). Although 'disquisition' might signal the serious turn of their disagreement toward sustained argumentative reasoning, the word also suggests the ridiculous escalation of that exchange into high sincerity and 'consequitive reasoning', which Keats abruptly interrupts by writing '& at once it struck me'. The word 'disquisition' was used routinely in many early nineteenth-century writings, but Hazlitt's extensive review of Coleridge's newest 'disquisition' charged this word anew with satirical power. In that review, Hazlitt ridicules (among other things) Coleridge's letter from a 'Friend' at the end of chapter 13, which advises Coleridge not to publish his 'disquisition' on the imagination. Hazlitt quips,

> As Mr. C. has suppressed his *Disquisition* on the Imagination as unintelligible, we do not think it fair to make any remarks on the 200 pages of prefatory matter, which were printed, it seems, in the present work, before a candid friend apprised him of this little objection to the appearance of the *Disquisition* itself. (my italics)[27]

That 'candid Friend' was actually a masked Coleridge, who weighs the importance of those withdrawn pages against the difficulties that they would pose for the general reading public:

> who would have both right and reason to complain of … so abstruse a subject so abstrusely treated … . It will be well, if already you have not too much of metaphysical *disquisition* in your work, though as the larger part of the *disquisition* is historical, it will doubtless be both interesting and instructive to many. (my italics)[28]

Coleridge's withdrawn 'disquisition' is a trick that Hazlitt singles out and derides as Coleridge's ploy to frustrate and further entice public interest. For Hazlitt, Coleridge's already overly lengthy published disquisitions, let alone his withdrawn 'disquisition', exemplify his public career as a critic, poet, and lecturer, which has traded on sensational theatricality and abrupt political transformations. Lumping Coleridge's writings and politics with Robert Southey's, Hazlitt scoffs:

> Always pampering their own appetite for excitement, and wishing to astonish others, their whole aim is to produce a dramatic effect, one way or other—to shock or delight their observers; and they are as perfectly indifferent to the consequences of what they write, as if the world were merely a stage for them to play their fantastic tricks on. (p. 151)

[27] William Hazlitt, *The Collected Works of William Hazlitt in Twelve Volumes*, ed. A.R. Waller and Arnold Glover, 12 vols. (London: J. M. Dent, 1904), X: p. 157.

[28] Samuel Taylor Coleridge, *Biographia Literaria*, vol. 7 of *The Collected Works of Samuel Taylor Coleridge*, ed. James Engell and W. Jackson Bate (Princeton, NJ: Princeton University Press, 1983), p. 303. For more on Coleridge's letter from a friend, see my 'Opening Up Chapter 13 of Coleridge's *Biographia Literaria*', in *Wordsworth's Poetic Collections, Supplementary Writing and Parodic Reception* (London: Routledge/Pickering & Chatto, 2012), pp. 101–20.

Earlier in his review, Hazlitt sets the stage for ridiculing Coleridge's 'fantastic tricks' by lamenting the long-standing 'disease' of Coleridge's mind, which has led him to his poetic pursuits and sensational public acting. To typify how Coleridge's promised magical truths and deceptions are intertwined, Hazlitt uses a series of high/low metaphors that align Coleridge's continual metaphysical ascents and bathetic descents with pantomime aesthetics, characters, transformations, and stage tricks:

> Mr. Coleridge has ever since, from the combined forces of poetic levity and metaphysical bathos, been trying to fly, not in the air, but under ground—playing at hawk and buzzard between sense and non-sense—floating or sinking in fine Kantian categories, in a state of suspended animation 'twixt dreaming and awake—quitting the plain ground of 'history and particular facts' for the first butterfly theory, fancy-bred from the maggots of his brain,—going up in an air balloon filled with fetid gas from the writings of Jacob Behmen and the mystics, and coming down in a parachute made of the soiled and fashionable leaves of the Morning Post,—promising us an account of the Intellectual System of the Universe, and putting us off with a reference to a promised dissertation on the Logos, introductory to an intended commentary on the entire Gospel of St. John. (p. 138)

Of particular note, Hazlitt's tropes of a balloon and a parachute are likely references to Drury Lane's 1816 Christmas pantomime *Harlequin Horner*, which features a balloon that Harlequin creates out of his prison house in order to save himself from Clown, who, in a twist, becomes trapped in that prison house.[29] Hazlitt's pantomime conceit posits a two-faced Coleridge—part Harlequin magician and part trickster Clown who has caught himself up in his own prison/balloon creation.[30]

In the context of Hazlitt ridiculing Coleridge as a Harlequin–Clown combination whose withdrawn 'disquisition' is nothing more than deceptive stagecraft, Keats's 'disquisition with Dilke' redounds with knowing self-satire that pokes fun at their 'consequitive reasoning'. Keats catches himself in the midst of a Coleridge-like 'disquisition' and receives a thump. In this pantomime scene, Keats depicts Dilke and himself like a squabbling Clown

[29] Hazlitt's 'under ground' reference also might refer to other Regency pantomimes that toyed with the idea of underground scenes in relation to the much discussed Regency Thames Tunnel project. See Mayer's *Harlequin* (p. 218).

[30] This is not the only place where Hazlitt skewers one of the Lake poets with a pantomime comparison. As Moody points out in *Illegitimate Theatre*, in *The Morning Chronicle* on 11 January 1814 Hazlitt compares Robert Southey to a Harlequin who has been cut to pieces but emerges later seemingly unscathed (p. 226).

(Keats) and Pantaloon (Dilke) caught up in a 'disquisition' until a Harlequin strike thumps Keats (Clown), leading to a transformative epiphany. What that dovetailed strike produces for Keats is a new mode of seeing that leads him to speculate about a Shakespearian 'Man of Achievement' in contrast with the 'irritable reaching' of his character foil Coleridge. Keats, via Hazlitt, holds a satirical mirror up to himself in relation to Coleridge. In the next part of Keats's letter, this Coleridge shows himself to be an amalgam of Clown and Pantaloon, representing a dubious legitimate power structure.

Keats's negative capability caricature of Coleridge stages a satirical bodily depiction of him in action as an authoritarian 'Modern Shakespeare'. Keats contrasts Coleridge's dramatic gestures—'Coleridge, for instance, would let go by a fine isolated verisimilitude caught from the Penetralium of mystery, from being incapable of remaining content with half knowledge'—with the quality of 'a Man of Achievement especially in Literature & which Shakespeare posessed so enormously—I mean *Negative Capability*, that is when man is capable of being in uncertainties, Mysteries, doubts, without any irritable reaching after fact & reason'. Keats's word 'Penetralium' and gestural depiction of Coleridge letting go and reaching likely draw on *Blackwood's Edinburgh Magazine*'s October 1817 review of *Biographia Literaria*, in which Christopher North ridicules Coleridge's 'absurd self-elevation' and complains that Coleridge 'cannot put pen to paper without a feeling that millions of eyes are on him', which makes him appear 'as restlessly as any charlatan who ever exhibited on stage'.[31] From North's perspective, Coleridge will be known in the future as a man

> who overrated and abused his talents, who saw glimpses of that glory which he could *not grasp*, who presumptuously came forward to officiate as High Priest at mysteries *beyond* his ken, and who carried himself as if he had been familiarly admitted into the *Penetralia* of Nature, when in truth he kept perpetually *stumbling* at the Threshold. (my italics, pp. 330–1)[32]

Keats's irritably reaching Coleridge is very like North's: a laughable buffoon who postures and stumbles while attempting to 'grasp' and mimic the elite power of a 'High Priest'.

Keats's agitated Coleridge is unable to appreciate the value of partial truths—'a fine isolated verisimilitude caught from the Penetralium of

[31] J. R. de J. Jackson, ed., *Samuel Taylor Coleridge: The Critical Heritage*, 2 vols. (London: Routledge, 1995), I: p. 334.

[32] In his chapter 'Keats and Coleridge', in *Romantic Complexity: Keats, Coleridge, and Wordsworth* (Urbana: University of Illinois Press, 2006) pp. 41–61, Jack Stillinger argues that Keats was distinctly influenced by discussions with friends about Coleridge's *Biographia Literaria* in the fall of 1817, as well as by the quotation cited above from North's review.

mystery'—that he has grasped while stumbling near that 'mystery'. Instead, he lets go (by) and 'irritably' reaches 'after fact & reason' in order to catch the one unified vision of truth that he seeks. Unlike a Shakespearian 'Man of Achievement', Keats's Coleridge appears at best like Clown, but more nearly like Pantaloon, the authoritarian figure whose 'irritable reaching' after a fleeing Harlequin and Columbine always makes him look buffoonish and demonstrates his incapacity to function in the chaotic world of the harlequinade. Keats's critique delivers a glancing blow at Coleridge who, as a would-be 'Contemporary Shakespeare',[33] has forced Shakespearian tragedy into an elitist realm through his authoritarian, transcendent overreaching. By contrast, Keats's Shakespearian 'Man of Achievement' remains grounded, 'content with half knowledge', and comfortably at home in the 'midst of uncertainties, mysteries, and doubts'. Like Harlequin amidst pantomimic chaos, a Shakespearian 'Man of Achievement' revels in 'uncertainties' and his own 'doubts' while finding that mysterious 'half knowledge' is replete with transformative possibilities.

Pantomimic Capability

Nearly ten months after the negative capability letter, in his first letter addressed to his brother George and sister-in-law Georgiana in America, Keats turned directly to pantomime again. Using the word 'pantomimical' to illustrate his 'half-knowledge' of Jane Cox, a cousin of the Reynolds's siblings, Keats describes Cox as a 'Charmian' in front of whom he 'forget[s] himself entirely because [he] live[s] in her'. For Keats, Jane Cox represents a 'want of knowledge' that keeps him 'awake one Night as a tune of Mozart's might do' and that is embodied by how 'she walks across a room in such a manner that a Man is drawn towards her with a magnetic power' (*LJK*, I: p. 395). While openly acknowledging Cox's faults and social artifice, Keats is struck by her enthralling acting on a worldly stage, which prompts him to forget himself and presently 'live in her'. Not unlike Charles Dilke, the 'Godwin perfectibility Man' whom Keats mentions later in this letter, Cox appears as a theatrical character, who draws his attention and sense of identity within another.

In direct contrast to the Reynolds sisters, who deride Cox as a 'flirt', Keats offsets her readily apparent faults with praise:

> Yet she is a fine thing speaking in a worldly way: for there are two distinct tempers of mind in which we judge of things—the worldly, theatrical

[33] In *The Theatrical Inquisitor*'s 1813 review of Coleridge's play *Remorse*, cited in the *OED* definition of 'dovetail', the reviewer 'H' scoffs at the 'first production of the *Modern Shakespeare*, for such is the title by which his judicious friends have chosen to distinguish the author of a tragedy'.

> and *pantomimical*; and the unearthly, spiritual and ethereal—in the former Buonaparte, Lord Byron and this Charmian hold the first place in our Minds; in the latter John Howard, Bishop Hooker rocking his child's cradle and you my dear Sister are the conquering feelings. As a Man in the world I love the rich talk of a Charmian; as an eternal Being I love the thought of you. I should like her to ruin me, and I should like you to save me. (*LJK*, I: p. 396; my italics)

In this playful, direct address to Georgiana, Keats is of two minds—each of which is sub-divided into a series of three appositions in parallel with the other. Georgiana might be said to garner the highest praise from Keats because he connects her with the end of the series 'unearthly, spiritual, and ethereal' as a 'thought' that could 'save [him]'. That projected transcendent end as an 'eternal Being' notwithstanding, Keats shows an equal and opposite, parallel 'love' for the 'rich talk' of this 'Charmian' whom he, as a 'Man in the world', should like 'to ruin [him]'. Poised amidst these 'two distinct tempers of mind', Keats brings into parallel apposition the seeming opposites 'pantomimical' and 'ethereal', so that they ironically dovetail through Jane and Georgiana. As Keats occupies different character positions at the end of this passage, magnetic artifice and bodily desire redound pantomimically on high sincerity and transcendence. Keats plays for Georgiana both an ironic Clown and a magical Harlequin who can revel in worldly buffoonery and deliver a transformative strike that reveals how the seemingly low can become the high and vice-versa. Keats's own pantomimical capability is on full display.

This part of his 1818 letter also recalls Keats's turn near the end of his negative capability letter to consider the work of a 'great poet'. He contends that 'This'—Coleridge's 'irritable reaching', which represents a system of forced synthesis and reconciliation—'pursued through Volumes would perhaps take us no further than this, that with a great poet the sense of Beauty overcomes every other consideration, or rather obliterates all consideration' (*LJK*, I: p. 194). As Keats moves toward the close of his letter, ironic pursuit and high sincerity fold back on each other through the word 'perhaps'. Keats's 'perhaps' demonstrates what Steven Jones describes as Keats's capacity to intermingle 'ironic detachment' and 'sentimental sincerity', 'transcendental buffoonery' and 'Romantic transcendence' (p. 196). 'Perhaps' encapsulates the self-reflexive qualities of negative capability because it draws attention back from and redoubles attention to Keats's claim that, for a 'great poet', 'Beauty … obliterates all consideration'. Keats's 'perhaps' partially undoes his assertive, qualified over-statement, ironically leaving the obliteration of 'all consideration' open to further reflection and transformation—perhaps even to another Harlequin strike.

CHAPTER TWO

John ~~Keats's~~ Jeffrey's 'Negative Capability'; or, Accidentally Undermining Keats

Brian Rejack

The text of the negative capability letter comes to us from a single unreliable source: John Jeffrey, the second husband of Georgiana Wylie Keats (who had married John Keats's brother George and emigrated to America in 1818), and, for better or worse, the person to whom we owe a debt of gratitude for conveying to posterity the term negative capability. That the letter with Keats's coinage exists at all is fortuitous. After having come across a newspaper advertisement for an upcoming biography of the poet, and after corresponding across the Atlantic with its author, Richard Monckton Milnes, Jeffrey transcribed Keats's letter during the summer of 1845, along with fourteen others. Thereafter he sent his texts to Milnes, who used these copies for his *Life, Letters, and Literary Remains of John Keats* (1848). So it was that negative capability moved out of the private world of the Keats family and its Louisville, Kentucky circle, entering into public discourse for the first time.

At some point the manuscript itself quietly slipped out of existence (though perhaps not forever). Most of Milnes's Keatsiana, however, including Jeffrey's transcript of the negative capability letter, has stuck around, the bulk of it making its way to Harvard's Houghton Library in 1952. Thanks to the digitization of materials in the Harvard Keats Collection, Jeffrey's transcripts are now readily available for viewing by anyone with an internet connection and an appropriate device. Because original manuscripts for nine of the fifteen letters copied by Jeffrey still exist, we can compare Jeffrey's work against them and see precisely how badly Jeffrey performed his task. Hyder Edward Rollins, the editor of what remains the standard scholarly edition of Keats's complete correspondence, assesses Jeffrey's work as such: 'he changed words or phrases that he disliked or did not understand or could not decipher; he reversed the order of certain sentences, reformed spelling, punctuation, grammar. Worse yet, with no warning he omitted words, sentences, paragraphs, at times whole pages' (*LJK*, I: p. 20). To demonstrate just how egregious such omissions could be, Rollins prints the Jeffrey transcript of the September 1819 journal letter to George and Georgiana Keats, the original manuscript of which still survives, and which runs to thirty-four pages in Rollins's edition. The Jeffrey transcript fills approximately three. So it is no secret—and it hasn't been for the better part of a century—that Jeffrey's texts are deeply problematic. And yet, despite this recognition and the ready availability of the Jeffrey transcripts in digital form, not much has been made of his work beyond passing expressions of disappointment akin to Rollins's.

Since the MS of Keats's negative capability letter does not currently exist, we do not know what alterations or mistakes Jeffrey made. What we do know is that Jeffrey most certainly made *some* alterations and mistakes. The very term negative capability might not even be what Keats wrote. No less estimable a Keatsian than Robert Gittings remarks, 'some of Keats's most famous phrases, such as "Negative Capability", may have been invented or misread by Jeffrey'.[1] In this essay I (mostly) do not attempt conjuring up other terms that Jeffrey might have mistaken for what he wrote as 'Negative Capability' (Figure 2.1).[2] Rather, while keeping in mind that the term itself is suspect, I focus on one small aspect of Jeffrey's transcript which significantly affects how we read Keats's phrase: the dubious underlining of the two words. Reckoning with this particular textual 'accidental'[3] can help us to nurture skepticism about the term and about the stability of Keats's epistolary texts

[1] Robert Gittings, introduction to *Letters of John Keats*, ed. Robert Gittings (Oxford: Oxford University Press, 1970), p. xxii. In this collection Michael Theune speculates about the possibility that some wordplay on 'natural capacity' might have been at work for Keats, and perhaps was an aspect of the term that Jeffrey missed, ignored, or altered.

[2] John Jeffrey, transcript of John Keats to George Keats and Tom Keats, 21–27 [?] December 1817, John Keats Collection, MS Keats 3.9 (Houghton Library, Harvard University), sequence 14, accessed 7 July 2018, https://iiif.lib.harvard.edu/manifests/view/drs:35522552$14i. All quotations from Jeffrey's transcripts hereafter cited parenthetically as such: (*JJ*, seq. 14). While most print editions present underlining as italicized text, I keep Jeffrey's underlined text as such, and when quoting from Rollins's edition of Keats's letters, I present his italicized text as underlined. In cases where I diverge from Rollins's readings, I cite the MS directly.

[3] In bibliography and textual studies, 'accidentals' refer to formal features such as punctuation, spelling, or underlining, which carry less semantic weight than 'substantives', the linguistic elements conveying meaning. For an influential statement on these issues, see W. W. Greg, 'The Rationale of Copy-Text', *Studies in Bibliography*, 3 (1950/51), pp. 19–36. An analogous model for making sense of these different textual features, and one which emphasizes the semantic weight of formal features such as accidentals, is what Jerome McGann terms 'linguistic' and 'bibliographic' codes, which correspond respectively, though not always exactly, with Greg's substantives and accidentals. See McGann's *The Textual Condition* (Princeton, NJ: Princeton University Press, 1991), especially chapters two and three, pp. 48–87.

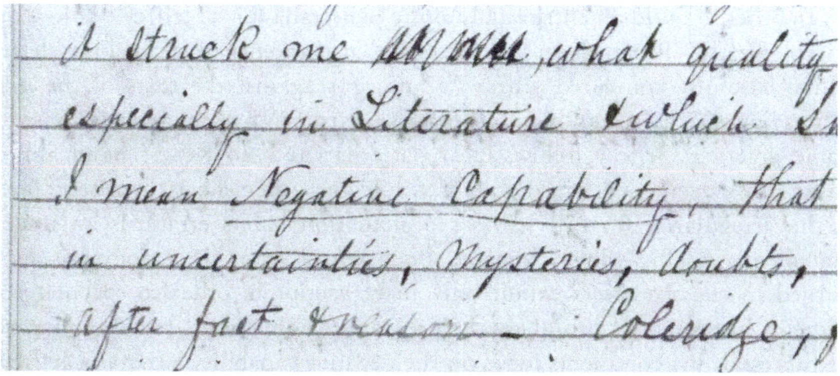
it struck me , what quality
especially in Literature & which
I mean Negative Capability, that
in uncertainties, Mysteries, doubts,
after fact & reason – : Coleridge,

Figure 2.1: Detail from John Jeffrey's transcript of Keats's 21, 27 [?] December 1817 letter to George and Tom Keats. MS Keats 3.9 (Houghton Library, Harvard University).

more broadly; furthermore, it can help us to cultivate awareness of the need to keep actively curating, revisiting, and reassessing Keats's material and textual records, always staying open to the possibility that some new planet might swim into our ken.

When just a single unreliable copy-text exists, one would think it ought to heighten our sensitivity to the inherent instability and fluidity of textuality. It seems, however, that the opposite occurs with negative capability. We all shake our heads at Jeffrey and his shoddy transcription, but then we proceed as normal and treat the letter, and the term itself especially, as if it really were a stable object immune to the transformations at work on all texts as they move through time and space. Even in those rare moments when scholars recognize how much uncertainty pervades this letter and its celebrated term, that moment of being in uncertainty is quickly abandoned in favor of the solid ground of fact and reason.[4] This essay thus tries one tack for getting us out of the habit of mistaking half-knowledge for whole. We will never arrive at any final certainty without the original manuscript itself (or even with it). But because we have a sizable amount of transcribed material from Jeffrey we can divine much about his habits. As such, my essay reaches not after fact but after mystery. While I urge us to imagine more (or less) of what the letter might have included, I recognize that the process will not lead to unchallenged certitude.

[4] In Li Ou's *Keats and Negative Capability* (London: Bloomsbury, 2009), the only contemporary monograph devoted solely to the concept (and discussed in more detail in this collection's introduction), she mentions Jeffrey only briefly before dismissing the significance of his transcriptional work by arguing that the term negative capability 'reveals a quite perceptible conceptual core' unaffected by the 'shaky ground' of its textual basis (p. 2).

In order to build an entryway into the penetralia (or, as Jeffrey has it—and maybe Keats—'Penetralium') of mystery that is the negative capability letter, I first carefully compared Jeffrey's transcripts against the texts of the nine letters for which Keats's manuscripts also exist.[5] What emerged is that, for some practices, Jeffrey follows clear patterns ('and' in Keats's hand almost invariably becomes '&' in Jeffrey's), while for others he is consistent only in his irregularity (to call Jeffrey's punctuation habits erratic is an understatement). Taking what I learned about Jeffrey from these comparisons, I turned to the six letters extant only in transcript in order to speculate on some of his potential mistakes, changes, and/or omissions. For the purposes of this essay, my comments focus on the negative capability letter and Jeffrey's underlining of the term, but there are other significant letters based solely on Jeffrey's transcripts which merit closer speculative consideration of this sort. Such work, as I show here with the negative capability letter, reveals insights about individual letters and about Keats's correspondence more broadly, and it demonstrates the value of working closely with the physical and digital materials constituting the Keatsian archive. Whether we recognize it or not, 'Negative Capability', as much as it is Keats's, has always been John Jeffrey's, too. On the list of figures who have made this '[Nothing] ... Great and dignified by an ardent pursuit', surely John Jeffrey deserves a spot, even if he felt his pursuit to be more arduous than ardent. There exists a wealth of material traces from that pursuit and others like it. Jeffrey did his part to '[stamp] the burgundy mark' on the 'bottles' of the Keatsian archive; we, too, need to engage in a continued pursuit so that we may transfer those marks to 'our Minds' (*LJK*, I: p. 243). Especially in our situation 200 years on—as the marks constituting cultural archives are being restamped (straining the metaphor a bit) onto silicon, cobalt, and the other magnetic or semiconductor materials used to create digital memory—scholars need to participate in these processes and the related task of making meaning out of the past, present, and future objects that will persist as and in the cultural record.[6]

[5] Six of these originals reside in the Harvard collection (21 February 1818 to George and Tom; 3, 5, 7, 9 July 1818 to Tom; 23, 26 July 1818 to Tom; 14–31 October 1818 to George and Georgiana; December 1818–January 1819 to George and Georgiana; and February–May 1819 to George and Georgiana), which I consulted via their digital reproductions. For the 5 January 1818 letter to George and Tom I used the facsimile from *Shelley and His Circle, 1773–1822*, ed. Donald H. Reiman, vol. 5 (Cambridge, MA: Harvard University Press, 1973). For the remaining two letters (17–27 September 1819 to George and Georgiana, MS at Princeton; 13–28 January 1820 to Georgiana, MSS (in parts) at University of Texas and Yale) I compared Jeffrey's transcripts against Rollins's edition (where he renders underlined text in italics).

[6] For an impassioned argument about the necessity of this kind of engagement, and about how to make it happen, see Jerome McGann's *A New Republic of Letters: Memory*

What, then, are some of the specific assumptions and tendencies underlying how Jeffrey bequeathed significant elements of that record to posterity? As was customary during this period, he took steps to excise or anonymize references to other people and to eliminate passages that might have been deemed too personal or too ribald for Victorian sensibilities. As was also typical for editing at the time, manuscript punctuation seems not to have mattered to Jeffrey. He was overly fond of inserting commas where Keats has no punctuation, and Keats's swift dashes often become commas or semicolons in Jeffrey. As such, the correspondence's familiar breathlessness becomes significantly more breathy when mediated through Jeffrey. In what is perhaps Jeffrey's most consistent editorial practice regarding accidentals, he converts almost every instance of 'and' in Keats's manuscripts to '&' in his transcriptions. One almost never encounters an ampersand in Keats's letters in manuscript, but in the negative capability letter, for instance, we find twenty-four, including five within the sentence introducing the term ('Brown & Dilke walked with me & back', '& at once it struck me ~~at once~~', '& which Shakespeare', 'fact & reason' (*JJ*, seq. 14)).[7] As with his liberality with commas, Jeffrey's consistent ampersands likely emerge from his personal habits and his desire for efficiency. In the many nineteenth-century editions based on Jeffrey's transcriptions, the ampersands tend to become 'ands' in print. Only well into the twentieth century—as editorial practices shift away from eclecticism and toward the standard of judiciously replicating a single copy-text—do we see Jeffrey's editorial accidentals (punctuation, capitalization, abbreviations, etc.) honored in print form. In what might come as no surprise, then, the negative capability letter looked rather different for Keats's nineteenth-century readers than it does for us. Nonetheless, such an assertion bears reiterating given the tendency not to engage with the minute particulars of this perplexing text.

The particulars covered in what follows, and which first drew me to this line of inquiry, are Jeffrey's instances of underlining, especially of 'Negative Capability'.[8] As Walter Jackson Bate remarked about his first encounter with the term, there is something 'mysterious' and seductive about the term,[9] and

and Scholarship in the Age of Digital Reproduction (Cambridge, MA: Harvard University Press, 2014).

[7] Jeffrey wrote 'at once' both before and after 'it struck me'; the second instance was struck through with right-slanting lines.

[8] To my knowledge the only substantive comment on Keats's possible underlining of the phrase comes from Susan Wolfson in 'Keats the Letter-Writer: Epistolary Poetics', *Romanticism Past and Present*, 6: 2 (1982), pp. 43–61. She cautiously posits, 'Though the letter does not exist in Keats's hand, it is tempting to think that the underscoring of the thought by which he was "struck" is his own device, an equivalent in script for the sudden force of this perception on his understanding' (p. 46).

[9] Walter Jackson Bate, 'The Endurance of Keats', in *The Persistence of Poetry: Bicentennial*

its appeal is only heightened by that act of underlining. And yet, even if we accept that Jeffrey copied the term accurately (again, not something we should easily accept), there is a significant likelihood that the underlining was not present in Keats's original manuscript. Jeffrey regularly fails to replicate Keats's underlining (or lack of underlining) with anything resembling fidelity. At times Jeffrey adds underlining for no apparent reason. For instance, Keats's 'a mind "with child" of Philanthropy' becomes 'a mind "with child" of philanthropy' (*LJK*, I: p. 321; *JJ*, seq. 21); 'This day is my Birth day—' becomes 'This my Birthday——' (*LJK*, I: p. 405; *JJ*, seq. 35); 'a little Bluebeardish' becomes 'a little blue beardish' (*LJK*, II: p. 28; *JJ*, seq. 42); and, illustrating Jeffrey's increasing inattention as he gets further along, in the penultimate letter he copied, Keats's 'I have discoverd that a little girl in the house was the Rappee—I assure you she has nearly make me sneeze' gets rendered as 'I have discovered that a little girl is the rapper, as I was the rappee I should have made her sneeze' (*LJK*, II: p. 216; *JJ*, seq. 61). At other times Jeffrey neglects to underline when Keats clearly does: Keats's 'Minx', 'a fortnight', and 'the old Cat' (*LJK*, II: pp. 13, 16, 29) all appear without underlining in Jeffrey's texts (*JJ*, seqs. 39, 40, 43); and at the start of the passage ending with his discovery of 'the Rappee' (or Jeffrey's 'rapper') Keats speaks of one joke 'play'd off at Brown' and a second 'play'd on on myself', which Jeffrey reads as 'played on myself' (*LJK*, II: p. 215; *JJ*, seq. 60). While Jeffrey does sometimes accurately follow Keats's underlining, there are far more cases of him getting it wrong than right. And even if he gets it *mostly* right, his partially wrong matters, as when Keats's 'nothing particular' becomes Jeffrey's 'nothing particular' (*LJK*, I: p. 395; *JJ*, seq. 31).

Jeffrey's underlining of 'Negative Capability' produces many possible effects; a significant one, I suggest, is the enhanced sense that the term functions as a key philosophical element in Keats's thinking which can then be transported into others'. As discussed in this volume's introduction, and as many of the essays collected demonstrate, there is no shortage of arenas into which negative capability has been thrust. Keats himself, so far as we know, did not bother to return to the term in his writing. Like many other of his famous phrases, negative capability appears just once in his correspondence. But, unlike Jeffrey's 'Negative Capability', almost all of Keats's other notable terms, concepts, and phrases do not appear underlined. The only recognizable coinage other than negative capability that involves underlining is the 'vale of Soul-making', and in that case Keats underlines to excess. More underlined words appear in that one passage than in any other comparable space in the correspondence, which likely results from Keats's vacillation between sincere philosophical speculation

Essays on Keats, ed. Robert M. Ryan and Ronald A. Sharp (Amherst: University of Massachusetts Press, 1998), p. 55.

and self-deprecating mock-seriousness (he concludes the long passage, 'There now I think what with Poetry and Theology you may thank your Stars that my pen is not very long winded' (*LJK*, II: p. 104)). Not just with notable terms, but on the whole in Keats's letters, he underlines sparingly. Out of the twenty-seven extant letters written by Keats in 1817, only eleven letters feature any underlining, accounting for a total of sixty-six underlined words. Of those eleven letters, four exist only via transcripts (three by Richard Woodhouse, one by Jeffrey), and those four transcribed letters account for forty-one of the sixty-six total underlined words. So if Keats did underline negative capability, it was uncharacteristic of him to do so. It's likely that, of the ten underlined words in the negative capability letter, some, and perhaps all, were not underlined in Keats's MS.

But even if the term 'Negative Capability' represents one of those rare instances in which Keats did underline, we should also reconsider what underlining might mean for him. First and foremost, we should view skeptically the assumption that underlining indicates Keats's intention that the term be viewed with complete seriousness or reverence. Particularly in his letters of 1817–18, the rare instances of underlining usually signal not gravity but wordplay or some other form of levity.[10] The earliest examples of underlining in Keats's correspondence occur in his 15 April 1817 letter to George and Tom. (Demonstrating how rarely Keats underlines, the thirteen extant letters preceding this one feature no underlining at all—eleven exist in MS and two others via transcripts by Woodhouse.)[11] Keats is not engaging in wordplay per se with his underlining here, but he definitely uses it to humorous effect. The first example comes amid Keats's playful catalog of objects he viewed while traveling by stagecoach from London to Southampton. One of these sights was a 'Nymph of Fountain', which, after listing, Keats clarifies: 'N.B. Stone' (i.e., no, he did not see an actual nymph). A few lines later he returns to this same method of emphasizing his playfulness when he relays that 'after having had [his] fill' of the lamplit scenes during the night, 'I popped my Head out just

[10] For other readings of Keats's playfulness in his letters, see Wolfson's 'Keats the Letter-Writer', in which she argues that 'Keats consciously exploits epistolary composition as a medium of play' (p. 44); John Barnard also treats Keats's humor and wordplay in 'Keats's Letters: "Remembrancing and enchaining"', in *The Cambridge Companion to John Keats*, ed. Susan J. Wolfson (Cambridge: Cambridge University Press, 2001), pp. 120–34; and Heidi Thomson has an extended analysis of punning in 'Keats's Letters: "A Wilful and Dramatic Exercise of Our Minds Towards Each Other"', *The Keats-Shelley Review*, 25: 2 (2011), pp. 160–74.

[11] In my accounting, I leave out Keats's 'Epistle to George Felton Mathew' (November 1815), since the earliest source for it is Keats's 1817 *Poems*, and also the joint letter from the Keats Brothers to Richard Abbey, 13 June 1816. Neither text includes any underlining, however.

as it began to Dawn—N.B. this tuesday Morn saw the Sun rise—of which I shall say nothing at present' (I: p. 128). As with the stone nymph example, here Keats's cheeky *nota bene* states the obvious: yes, the morning did indeed see the sun rise. Such underlining is anti-romantic, deflating any hope for an imaginary world of pagan wonder; it resignedly but playfully conveys acceptance that 'The world is too much with us'. There may also be a bit of Keats's 'boyish imagination' on display here.[12] That he will 'say nothing' about popping his head out or about the 'rise' at dawn suggests some youthful phallic humor, particularly as the previous underlined reference concerned a 'Nymph of Fountain'. Whatever the actual intended messages are, Keats's underlining certainly helps him approximate 'writ[ing] a wink, or a nod, or a grin' to accompany them (*LJK*, II: p. 205).

Other examples from this time period (within about a year of the negative capability letter) demonstrate further how Keats draws attention to wordplay with underlining. For instance, in the 10 May 1817 letter to Leigh Hunt he opens with an allusion to Shakespeare in which he punningly alters and underlines one word: 'The little Gentleman that sometimes lurks in a gossips bowl ought to have come in very likeness of a coasted crab and choaked me outright for not having answered your Letter ere this' (*LJK*, I: pp. 136–7). Rollins identifies the reference to Puck's self-description in *A Midsummer Night's Dream* and explains the change of 'roasted' to 'coasted' by noting that Keats was writing from Margate (on the coast of the North Sea). This example actually unites two of Keats's underlining tendencies: indicating puns and indicating references to other texts (especially Shakespeare's).

Particularly in Keats's early correspondence, lines of Shakespeare seem to crop up on nearly every page, and Keats will sometimes underline entire quotations or parts of them. In a letter sent to Benjamin Robert Haydon the day after the previous one to Hunt, Keats quotes from or alludes to *Love's Labour's Lost*, *King Lear*, *The Tempest*, and, lastly, *Antony and Cleopatra*, from which he includes several extracts while making comparisons between Antony and Napoleon (the latter of whom Haydon had recently written about in *The Examiner*). The extract Keats underlines comes from a short scene in Act Three, during which two of Antony's supporters (Enobarbus and Eros) discuss Antony's anger at his fellow triumvirs, Octavius and Lepidus, for their decision to war with Pompey: Eros reports that Antony is 'walking in the garden—thus: and spurns the rush that lies before him, cries fool, Lepidus!' Ostensibly Keats refers to this passage because it illustrates of Antony a point Haydon makes about Napoleon in his *Examiner* article, and which Keats paraphrases as such: 'his Life had been as common in particulars as other Mens' (*LJK*, I: p. 144).

[12] See Richard Marggraf Turley, *Keats's Boyish Imagination* (London: Routledge, 2004), the title of which refers to a phrase from Keats's 18–22 July 1818 letter to Benjamin Bailey.

The underlining could simply emphasize Antony's ordinariness—the anger of the great man manifests in his pacing back and forth, kicking pointlessly at the grass. I suggest, though, that Keats is also gesturing toward a pun (or two). First and most obviously, another 'rush' that Antony is futilely attempting to spurn is the oncoming rush of conflict that will be his ruin. Alternatively, a 'rush' can refer to a temporary wedding band made in a pinch from actual rushes (the *OED* cites a line from *All's Well That Ends Well* for this definition).[13] At this point in the play Antony has recently wedded, in haste, Octavius's sister Octavia and, while he furiously paces around the garden, Antony likely mentally spurns his new wife by imagining returning to Cleopatra in Alexandria (to whom he does return at the end of Act Three). In these two early examples of Keats's underlining, then, he emphasizes specific language from Shakespeare, and moreover, in one instance uses Shakespeare's words to craft a new pun, while in the other he points toward Shakespeare himself doing a bit of punning. Of course, there are other examples of Keats's underlining which function differently. But, especially in letters from 1817–18, the majority of the examples involve punning and/or Shakespeare. With those tendencies and Jeffrey's transcriptional habits in mind, then, I will now entertain five scenarios imagining what might have happened with Keats's negative capability manuscript and Jeffrey's transcription of it.

Scenario I:
Underlining was present in the MS, but JJ misreads the term

One of 'my favorite Speculation[s]' (to borrow from Keats) is that Jeffrey misread whatever Keats wrote, and the actual phrase was a Shakespearean allusion of some sort, perhaps even a punning play on Shakespeare's words, with Keats's underlining indicating as much (*LJK*, I: p. 184). Shakespeare is clearly on Keats's mind in this letter, before, during, and after the negative capability passage. The 'quality' that 'form[s] a Man of Achievement' is one that 'Shakespeare posessed so enormously', and *King Lear* makes a significant appearance earlier in the letter (*JJ*, seq. 14). Keats's thinking is likely informed by Hazlitt's writing on Shakespeare, with Coleridge on Shakespeare as another likely candidate.[14] We know from other letters to George and Tom that Keats's

[13] *Oxford English Dictionary*, 3rd ed., s.v. 'rush', accessed 5 March 2018, http://www.oed.com/view/Entry/169026?.

[14] For thorough treatments of the Hazlitt and Shakespeare connections see Li's *Keats and Negative Capability*, especially pp. 23–61. Also significant for its reading of Shakespearean influence is Nicholas Roe's epilogue to *John Keats and the Culture of Dissent* (Oxford: Clarendon Press, 1997), especially its first section, 'Negative Capability and Its Backgrounds: Shakespeare, Politics, Theatre', pp. 230–9. For the Coleridge connection, see Walter Reed's chapter in this volume, as well as Jack Stillinger, 'Keats and Coleridge', in

brothers are interlocutors receptive to reflections on or allusions to various Shakespearean fruits. So although my argument—that *the term*, if it was transcribed incorrectly, was more closely connected with Shakespeare—is by necessity full of doubt and uncertainty, the textual situation afforded us by Jeffrey's transcript makes it possible to engage in such doubt-laden speculation. If Keats did underline a part of or all of those two words, and if Jeffrey misread them as 'Negative Capability', then a punning riff on Shakespeare is a good possibility.

Scenario II:
Underlining was not present in the MS; JJ adds underlining to indicate his uncertain reading of the term

'Another favorite speculation of mine' is that Jeffrey misread what Keats wrote, but also *knew* that he misread what he wrote (*LJK*, I: p. 185). This scenario assumes what is more likely than Keats himself underlining: that Jeffrey added underlining where there was none in the MS. At times Jeffrey clearly struggled with his task. In his letter to Milnes enclosing the transcripts, he explains, 'I could scarcely comprehend the letter until I had copied it, as they were almost all miserably illegible & badly dated' (*KC*, II: p. 123). Evidence of his difficulties also exists in the transcripts themselves. Early on in the process, in the second letter he tackled, Jeffrey reaches a tricky moment and writes in brackets, 'This word illegible in the original', only to then cross out the note once he deciphers the word ('Rhyme', although Jeffrey transcribes it as 'Rhymes') (*JJ*, seq. 6; *LJK*, I: p. 197). Elsewhere Jeffrey seemingly indicates uncertainty about particular words or phrases, including one example from a letter sent to Tom during Keats's tour through Northern England and Scotland (3, 5, 7, 9 July 1818). Keats and his travel companion Charles Brown had at this point made a short detour to Ireland, whence he writes, 'The dialect on the neighbouring shores of Scotland and Ireland is much the same—yet I can perceive a great difference in the nations from the Chambermaid at this nate Inn kept by Mr Kelly' (*LJK*, I: p. 319). Keats's spelling captures the Irish pronunciation of 'neat', but it clearly befuddled Jeffrey. He transcribes it as 'nate Toone' (*JJ*, seq. 19). As such, the underlining seems to convey not that Keats himself underlined the words but rather that Jeffrey believes he's accurately copied the nonce term, or that it must be something else he cannot sort. Perhaps 'Negative Capability' was Jeffrey's best guess, and the underlining, wavy and slight as it is, gestures toward his uncertainty.

Coleridge, Keats, and the Imagination: Romanticism and Adam's Dream, ed. J. Robert Barth and John Mahoney (Columbia: University of Missouri Press, 1990).

Scenario III: Some playful spelling is excised by JJ

The 'nate Toone' example raises another issue that is more applicable in other instances, but may also have relevance for the negative capability letter. Jeffrey often indicates irregular spelling by adding underlining when Keats does not do so himself. Keats frequently plays with pronunciation by purposefully altering spelling, though not usually with an accompanying underline. As with 'nate' from his time in Ireland, 'Whuskey' and 'sax' (for whiskey and six) approximate what Keats heard from his northern neighbors in Scotland (*JJ*, seq. 18, 25). In each case Jeffrey underlines in order to emphasize that the misspellings are intentional in Keats's MSS. We know that, with 'sax', Keats did not underline it himself (*LJK*, I: p. 347). For Jeffrey's 'Whuskey' no corresponding MS in Keats's hand exists, but in the other letters from the northern tour which do Keats has either 'whiskey' or 'wiskey', sometimes with initial capitals, but never with underlining. Given that Keats tends not to underline his phonetic spellings, both 'Whuskey' and Keats's playful spelling from a later Scotch letter, 'werry romantic indeed' (*JJ*, seq. 28), seem likely instances of Jeffrey drawing extra attention to a feature that Keats himself did not. For some of Keats's idiosyncratic spellings elsewhere in the correspondence, consider that the underlined 'Milatary', 'narvus' (MS Keats 3.3, seq. 48), and 'leetle' (MS Keats 3.3, seq. 73) all come from transcripts by Woodhouse; 'ramance' (*LJK*, I: p. 253; II: p. 28), 'Saciety' (*LJK*, II: pp. 242, 244, 246), 'Sagars' (*LJK*, I: p. 150), and 'Segar' (*LJK*, II: p. 78) all exist in MS and feature no underlining. Woodhouse has 'mony' in two separate letters (MS Keats 3.3, seq. 74), while, in a third letter extant in Keats's hand, Keats has 'mony' (*LJK*, I: p. 328).

While the precise nature of the playful spelling that might have been present with negative capability remains a mystery, Keats's tendency to write *p*

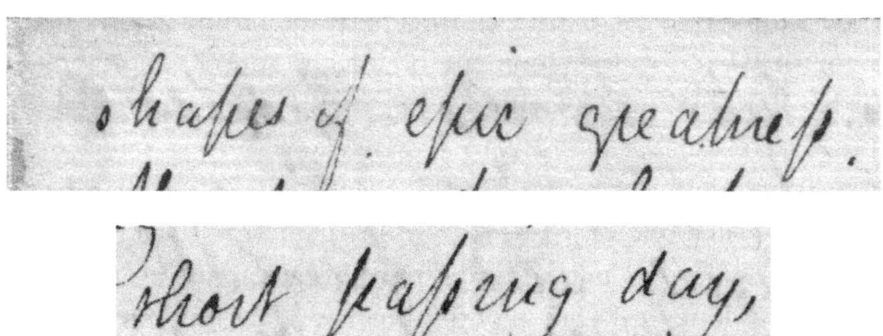

Figure 2.2: Details from John Keats's 14–31 October 1818 letter to George and Georgiana Keats. MS Keats 1.39 (Houghton Library, Harvard University).

and *ss* in a remarkably similar manner adds to the plausibility that 'capability' could have been Jeffrey's misreading of something else (Figure 2.2). While this suggestion is admittedly outlandish, the *ss* and *p* similarity could have led to Jeffrey's confusion at Keats's playing with the name of *Othello*'s Michael Cassio: 'Negative Cassio-bility', perhaps? Cassio is, after all, a character who spends significant time in uncertainties, mysteries, and doubts. In any case, it would be in keeping with Jeffrey's slapdash habits were he to identify an irregular spelling with added underlining, even while simultaneously regularizing the spelling himself.

Scenario IV:
JJ gets it mostly right, but misses some small but crucial detail

When *Keats* draws attention to irregular spelling with underlining, he does so to hint at some more involved pun (as opposed to simply indicating phonetic spelling). For instance, in a letter to his publisher John Taylor we see Keats play on the name of Henry Cary, with whom Taylor and James Hessey were in the process of negotiating a second edition of his translation of Dante: 'Remember me to Hessey saying I hope he'll Carey his point' (*LJK*, I: p. 296). Often Keats underlines just a part of a word when punning in this manner, as when he plays on 'national debt' in a letter to Benjamin Bailey, expressing his 'rational debt' to his friend (*LJK*, I: p. 288). A remarkable example of this sort occurs in another letter to Bailey from a few weeks later. Keats explains that *Blackwood's* and the *Quarterly* have begun linking his name with Hunt's in reviews of the elder poet's recent volume, *Foliage*. Keats writes, 'I have more than a Laurel from the Quarterly Reviewers for they have smothered me in 'Foliage' (MS Keats 1.30, seq. 110).[15] The joke plays on Keats's self-deprecating awareness about what it means to win the false laurel leaves of being associated in the *Quarterly* with Hunt's 'leafy luxury'. But a bilingual pun on the French *mot* (word) may also be signaled by the underlining, since the smothering is a matter of words printed in the reviews. Jeffrey himself even attempts to employ the same strategy of underlining parts of punny words when Keats neglects to: in what seems a moment of insight into Keats's habits, Jeffrey turns Keats's 'Pun-making' (playing on *pin* making) into 'pun making' (*LJK*, II: p. 214; *JJ*, seq. 60).

But, try as he might, Jeffrey fails in this regard more often than he succeeds. He does not register one of Keats's more brilliant, multilayered, and bawdy puns, where he again uses partial underlining to get across an epistolary wink and nod. In the letter to Tom mentioning the 'nate Inn' in Ireland, Keats

[15] Rollins prints the word as *smothered*, but in the MS the underline is clearly present only under the letters mot.

does a bit of 'proing and conning' about the effects of the Scottish church on national well-being (*LJK*, I: p. 156). In the negative column, he notes: 'These kirkmen … have banished puns and laughing and kissing (except in cases where the very danger and crime must make it very fine and gustful. I shall make a full stop at kissing for after that there should be a better parentthesis' (*LJK*, I: p. 319).[16] Jeffrey closes the parenthesis after 'gustful', without including Keats's deliberate full stop after 'gustful', and he has 'parenthesis' without the extra 't' or the underlining. In other words, Jeffrey fails to replicate every aspect of Keats's textual play. While Keats is by no means systematic or consistent in his orthography, examples like this one—which relies on the visual play between an open parenthesis and a period, as well as the linguistic play on gustful kissing resulting in parenting if things are not quickly brought to a full stop—demonstrate how conscious he is of the richness afforded by the epistolary medium. Again, although we remain in the realm of speculation, based on what we know about Keats's playfulness with underlining and about Jeffrey's habits of transcription, if Keats did employ some underlining with the term that Jeffrey reads as 'Negative Capability', it is less likely that Keats meant to emphasize the concept's significance and seriousness and far more likely that he was engaging in allusiveness and/or playfulness. Some small, seemingly insignificant feature, overlooked by Jeffrey, could, if it were present, drastically shift how the term and the underlining of it signify.

Scenario V: JJ mistakes some other mark for underlining

A final possibility is that Jeffrey might have been duped by the simple material contingencies of paper and ink. In at least two cases it appears that Jeffrey misread others marks as underlining. The first results from an eccentricity of Keats's handwriting: he tends to cross his *t*'s rather high on the vertical stroke. As such, a crossed *t* from one line can appear to underline a word in the line above it. If one scans a few pages of a Keats letter in manuscript, there's likely a better chance of mistaking the cross of a *t* for an underline than there is of finding a clearly intentional instance of underlining. Particularly troublesome are words with two *t*'s, as in one instance of 'identity' from the 'vale of Soul-making' letter (Figure 2.3).

Jeffrey skipped this section of the letter, so we don't know if he might have underlined 'the' in this case. But it does seem that earlier in this same text he may have misread the cross in the *t* of 'consecration' in this way.

[16] Rollins prints the last word as 'paren*t*thesis', but there is good reason to print instead the first *t* in small caps, or with the double underline (a mark used to signal in MS that small caps should be used in print). See MS Keats 1.33, seq. 120.

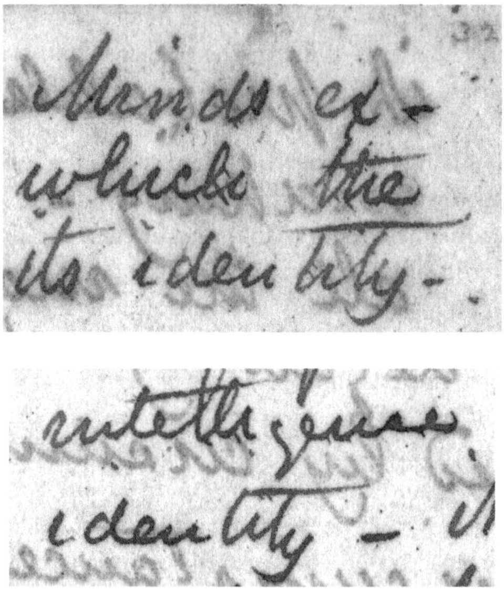

Figure 2.3: Details from John Keats's 14 February–3 May 1819 letter to George and Georgiana Keats. MS Keats 1.53 (Houghton Library, Harvard University).

While at Bedhampton with Charles Brown in early 1819 Keats attended a consecration of a chapel commissioned by and built for Lewis Way (who gave large sums of money to *The London Society for Promoting Christianity Amongst the Jews*—the newly built chapel was used for Way's conversion efforts). As Keats tells the story of attending the consecration, he relays this anecdote: '[Way] maintains a great number of poor Jews—Of course his communion plate was stolen—he spoke to the Clerk about it—The Clerk said he was very sorry adding—"I dare shay your honour its among ush"' (*LJK*, II: pp. 62–3). This passage reflects poorly on Keats, relying as it does on anti-Semitic stereotypes, including his rendering of a lateral lisp ('shay' and 'ush', for 'say' and 'us'). Jeffrey may have attempted to indicate Keats's phonetic spelling by underlining as such: 'I daresay your honour it s amongst ush' (*JJ*, seq. 46). I suggest also that Jeffrey was influenced by the cross in the *t* of 'consecration', which lines up under the first few letters of 'among' (Figure 2.4). The more forceful mark under Jeffrey's 'ush' suggests that with that word he may have caught on to Keats's phonetic spellings and added more underlining to certify the spelling. Whatever the case may have been, this example shows that the combination of Keats's handwriting and Jeffrey's disregard for accuracy in such matters could have played a part in the negative capability transcript as well. It is worth noting that 'uncertainties' or 'without', both located nearby below 'Negative Capability' in the

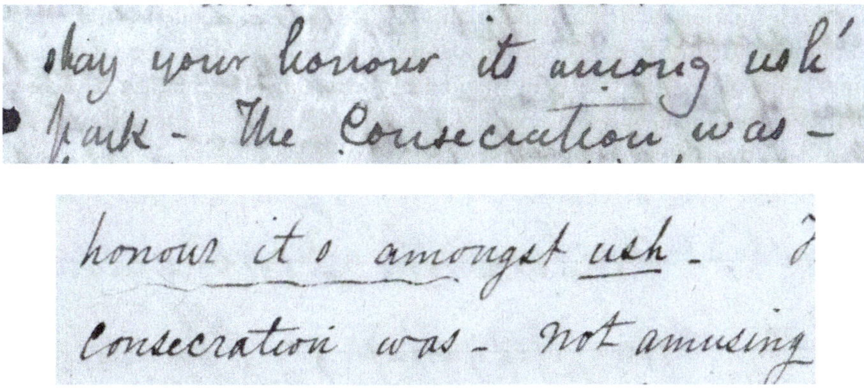

Figure 2.4: Detail from John Keats's 14 February–3 May 1819 letter to George and Georgiana Keats, and detail from John Jeffrey's transcript of the letter. MS Keats 1.53, 3.9 (Houghton Library, Harvard University).

transcript, in the original MS could have been fatefully aligned, either of the two words' double *t*'s conspiring to bless Keats's phrase with an underlining he himself withheld.

My last example shows how paper and ink, exerting a sort of agential force on the shaping of literary history, could have similarly led Jeffrey astray. With Keats's December 1818–January 1819 letter to George and Georgiana, the pages more exposed to air and light (i.e. those on the exterior of the folded sheets) have significantly faded, and, as a result, the ink from the reverse side of the page is more visible. Such a material change could have happened between 1819 and 1845, when Jeffrey made his transcripts, even if conditions worsened after that. Jeffrey has one instance of added underlining which appears to have resulted from marks on one side of the page lining up fortuitously with the words on the other side. Keats regales his brother and sister-in-law with a story of 'Uncle Redall', a well-intentioned dinner host a bit oblivious about how much wine to have at the ready for his guests ('he gave a supper and ranged his bottles of wine all up the kitchen and cellar stairs'). Ever the prankster, Keats remarks that 'it might have been a good joke to pour on the sly bottle after bottle into a washing tub and roar for more' (*LJK*, II: p. 13). Jeffrey underlines 'on the sly' (*JJ*, seq. 39), which upon first glance seems yet another instance of Jeffrey, without reason, haphazardly underlining when Keats does not (Figure 2.5). Closer examination of Keats's MS, however, shows that three distinct marks appear underneath 'on', 'the', and 'sly'—they are a dash, an extended stroke of the M in $M^{\underline{rs}}$, and the underscore of '$\underline{rs}$', bleeding through from the page's reverse side and lining up clearly enough that Jeffrey could understandably have taken them for Keats's own underlining. The sheer contingency of such an occurrence ought to give us pause when we treat with certitude matters of textual materiality as complicated, tenuous, and serendipitous as that of Keats's correspondence. While Keats, Hazlitt, Shakespeare, and Hunt played their roles in shaping negative capability, it may have been Jeffrey's encounter with the vagaries of how cotton paper reacts with ink, air, and light that helped bring us 'Negative Capability'.

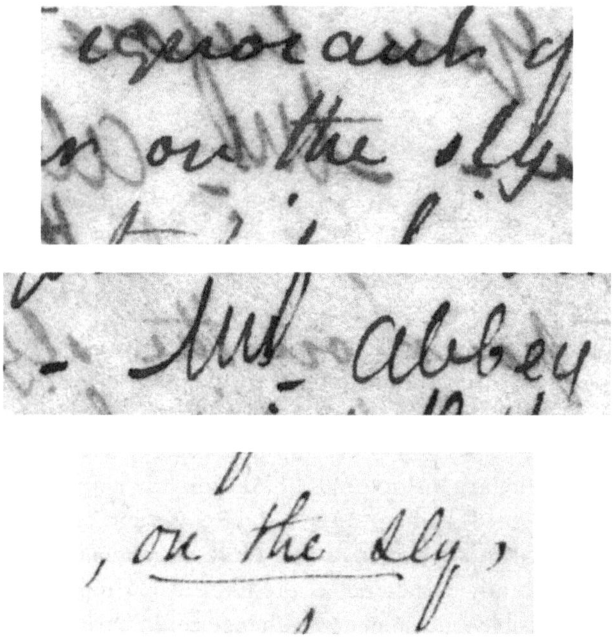

Figure 2.5: Detail from John Keats's December 1818–January 1819 letter to George and Georgiana Keats (and reverse side of page), and detail John Jeffrey's transcript of the letter. MS Keats 1.45, 3.9 (Houghton Library, Harvard University).

Chapter Three

Keats's 'Negative Capability' and Hazlitt's 'Natural Capacity'

Michael Theune

We are still getting to know mercurial Keats. Keats's friends knew this Keats very well, but he was largely lost in the course of his Victorian reception. Keats states, 'there are two distinct tempers of mind in which we judge of things—the worldly, theatrical and pantomimical; and the unearthly, spiritual and etherial' (*LJK*, I: p. 395). Employing Keats's binary we can see that Keats was kept etherial by serious, etherial minds. The twentieth century's increased critical attention to Keats has certainly made us more alert to Keats's worldliness and theatricality. With the application of a much wider variety of theoretical perspectives to a broader array of increasingly accessible materials—including, especially, the numerous important biographies and Rollins's edition of the letters—we can see more clearly what one of the great biographers calls Keats's 'ready humor', which 'could be earthy ... was certainly direct ... [and] had an element of farce', and we can hear more clearly his 'unconscious mimicry'.[1] We are more greatly attuned to and prepared to receive Keats's hoodwinkings and embarrassments, his epistolary dynamics and the productions of his often boyish imagination.[2] In fact, we should *expect* such playfulness, whether unconscious or conscious. As Christopher Ricks notes, 'Keats's mind, so alertly prefigurative, was especially liable to puns and portmanteaux, often of course quite premeditatedly; his letters

[1] Walter Jackson Bate, *John Keats* (Cambridge, MA: The Belknap Press of Harvard University Press, 1964), p. 116.

[2] Jack Stillinger, 'The Hoodwinking of Madeline: Scepticism in the "Eve of St. Agnes"', *Studies in Philology*, 58: 3 (July 1961), pp. 533–5; Christopher Ricks, *Keats and Embarrassment* (Oxford: Oxford University Press, 1974); Timothy Webb, '"Cutting Figures": Rhetorical Strategies in Keats's Letters', in *Keats: Bicentenary Readings*, ed. Michael O'Neill (Edinburgh: Edinburgh University Press, 1997), pp. 144–69; Richard Marggraf Turley, *Keats's Boyish Imagination* (New York: Routledge, 2004).

are full of conscious effects of which Lewis Carroll or James Joyce would have been proud.'[3]

But this Keats, who comes to us trailing ethereal clouds of unearthly spirituality, is still only coming into focus[4]—sometimes, even as he's right before our eyes. Ensconced in Rome approximately a month after his quarantine in Naples, Keats makes the terrible confession to Charles Brown that he feels as though he is 'leading a posthumous existence' (*LJK*, II: p. 359). This certainly is a moment of grave self-awareness, a terrifying (and heroic) acknowledgment of the state of things. But it is also a pun. Keats, exiled to Italy, away from his beloved Fanny Brawne, is leading a life like that of Posthumus, the character from Shakespeare's *Cymbeline*, who is exiled to Italy and so separated from his beloved Imogen. This connection should not be surprising. When he was younger Keats was brought to tears by Imogen's imagining of Posthumus's departure.[5] Additionally, in the very same letter—though he is desperate, and though the letter, which ends with Keats's 'awkward bow', is directed deathward—Keats notes: 'even at my worst, even in Quarantine, [I] summoned up more puns, in a sort of desperation, in one week than in a year of my life' (*LJK*, II: p. 360). Even told in the same letter by Keats that, for good or ill, he is in a pun-making mode, this detail is overlooked.[6]

It shouldn't be. Such overlooking matters. In the case of Keats's 'posthumous existence' it leads, at one level, to an incomplete reading of the term, which can lead to circumscribed notions of what Keats's self-understanding was at that time. What does it mean that Keats, consciously or unconsciously, turns himself into a literary character, a creation of the great creator, Shakespeare? How might Keats's pun contribute to his idea of living, like Shakespeare, a

[3] Christopher Ricks, 'Keats's sources, Keats's allusions', in *The Cambridge Companion to Keats*, ed. Susan J. Wolfson (Cambridge: Cambridge University Press, 2001), p. 69.

[4] In his essay 'Multiple Readers, Multiple Texts, Multiple Keats', in *The Persistence of Poetry: Bicentennial Essays on Keats*, ed. Robert M. Ryan and Ronald A. Sharp (Amherst: University of Massachusetts Press, 1998), Jack Stillinger recounts the following anecdote concerning Keats and humor: when '[s]omebody in the NASSR [North American Society for the Study of Romanticism] … user group recently raised the question of whether Keats had a sense of humor … responses poured in to such an extent that one got the idea that there were hardly any letters and poems in which Keats was not in some way being funny' (p. 24). For the purposes of this essay, what's important to note is that, even as recently as two decades ago, the question had to be asked in the first place.

[5] Charles and Mary Cowden Clarke, *Recollections of Writers* (London, 1878; facsimile rpt. Sussex: Centaur Press, 1969), p. 126. Quoted in Ricks, 'Keats's sources', pp. 161–2.

[6] I briefly discuss this punning allusion in the review 'Contradictory Keats: on Stanley Plumly's *Posthumous Keats: A Personal Biography*', *Pleiades*, 29: 1 (2009), pp. 122–8. To my knowledge, no one else has made this connection in print. Though in his essay 'Keats's sources' Christopher Ricks refers to Charles and Mary Cowden Clarke's reflections on Keats's reading and use of *Cymbeline* (pp. 161–2), he does not make the connection between Shakespeare's Posthumus and Keats's 'posthumous existence'.

life that is 'a continual allegory … a life like the scriptures, figurative', and so a life of 'worth' (*LJK*, II: p. 67)? Must we not read Keats's admission that he 'always made an awkward bow' (*LJK*, II, p. 360) as even more performative and theatrical than previously thought? Critics have not yet begun to inquire fully into such questions because Keats's pun so far has remained unrecognized.

I will not pursue these questions here because I believe that overlooking Keats's playfulness at key moments can have even more significant, and more troubling, effects which I will examine at the conclusion of this essay. For now, I turn to make the related case of another term from Keats which critics largely continue to see as 'unearthly, spiritual and etherial', but which can and should be read in a way more 'worldly, theatrical and pantomimical': negative capability.

Save for some suggestive lines about Leigh Hunt's 'passive capacity' in Nicholas Roe's biography of Keats, no one has suggested a viable source term for negative capability.[7] Keats's term thus is generally thought to be an original production, or an epiphanic emanation, of Keats's genius. However, I want to question this idea, and suggest a plausible source for negative capability: 'natural capacity', a term, originally used by Thomas Hobbes, that appears, repurposed, in the work of William Hazlitt. In my essay I first present the case for this connection, and then I argue how this connection can and should serve as an important corrective to some problematic uses of negative capability. Negative capability has spent enough time in its quarantine of tragic seriousness—we should work to summon up the wordplay that Keats himself may have implied in formulating it.

Natural capacity is a key part of what critic John Kinnaird says Hazlitt conceived of as 'one "modern system" of materialism', a 'tradition of thought' that descended 'from Hobbes through Locke, Berkeley … Hume' and others; and it is this system against which Hazlitt pits his own philosophical system.[8] Hazlitt entered this debate at the outset of his career with his first published work, *An Essay on the Principles of Human Action* (1805). In the chapter 'Negative Capability' in his biography of Keats, Walter Jackson Bate notes:

> Hazlitt's aim in this short book … was to refute the contention of Thomas Hobbes and his eighteenth century followers that self-love, in one way or another, is the main-spring of all human action, and to prove instead, as the subtitle states, 'the Natural Disinterestedness of the

[7] Nicholas Roe, *John Keats: A New Life* (New Haven, CT: Yale University Press, 2012), p. 185.

[8] John Kinnaird, *William Hazlitt: Critic of Power* (New York: Columbia University Press, 1978), p. 61, quoting *The Complete Works of William Hazlitt*, ed. P. P. Howe, 21 vols. (London: J. M. Dent, 1930), XX: p. 81. Abbreviated hereafter as *CWWH*.

> Human Mind'. … His hope was to show that imaginative sympathy was not a mere escape hatch from the prison of egocentricity, but something thoroughgoing, something indigenous and inseparable from all activities of the mind. Sympathetic identification takes place constantly—even if only with ourselves and our own desired future. Hazlitt's psychology, in effect, is a more dynamic version of Locke's. Instead of the image of the mind as a *tabula rasa* on which experience writes, we have an image of it as something more actively adhesive and projective. (pp. 256–7)

Though natural capacity is not mentioned in the *Essay on Human Action*, on three later occasions—in the essays 'On the Writings of Hobbes', 'Madame de Staël's Account of German Philosophy and Literature', and 'Mr. Locke, a Great Plagiarist'—Hazlitt offers a ten-point summary of modern materialist philosophy, announcing that, in only slightly varied language, he will offer a summary of the 'general' or 'leading' 'principles of this philosophy' 'as they are to be found in Hobbes' or 'as they are expressly laid down by Hobbes'; and in each of these, natural capacity is brought up in the final, tenth point (*CWWH*, II: pp. 144–5; XX: pp. 15–16; XX: pp. 74–6). That is, Hazlitt is offering the core features of the system of thought against which he argues, and natural capacity consistently can be found as the culminating, final point. Two of these instances—'On the Writings of Hobbes' and 'Madame de Staël's Account'—use the same wording: '10. That there is no difference in the natural capacities of men, the mind being originally passive to all impressions alike, and becoming whatever it is from circumstances' (*CWWH*, II: p. 145; XX: p. 16).

Hazlitt's two most significant uses of natural capacity, however, occur in a single essay: 'Mr. Locke A Great Plagiarist'. (Hazlitt believed Locke stole all his ideas from Hobbes.) In the second part of this essay, 'The Same Subject Continued', Hazlitt once again offers his standard ten-point rehearsal of the modern system of philosophy; however, in this instance, he formulates his tenth point a bit differently, stating, '10. That there is no such thing as genius, or a difference in the natural capacities or dispositions of men, the mind being originally alike passive to all impressions, and becoming whatever it is from circumstances, &c. &c' (*CWWH*, XX: pp. 75–6). Here, of course, the key detail is that natural capacity is defined as the aspect of mind that suggests there is no such thing *as genius*. This aspect of mind very likely would have attracted Keats's attention, as he was, during the formulation of negative capability, so interested in determining the special nature of Shakespeare's genius. Natural capacity thus is an aspect of mind Keats, following Hazlitt, will want to critique and, potentially, try to replace—perhaps also by engaging in some crafty wordplay.

Even more significantly, though, as a part of another effort to show very clearly Locke's borrowing from Hobbes, Hazlitt enumerates the topics (such as 'Sensation', 'Mind and Matter', 'Association', etc.) shared among Hobbes and Locke and other modern materialist philosophers, and then cites similar quotations intended to reveal the dependence of the whole system on Hobbes. The section titled 'Of Natural Capacity' begins with the following quotation from Hobbes:

> 'By natural capacity, I mean not that which a man hath from his birth; for that is nothing else but sense, wherein men differ so little from one another, or from brute beasts, as it is not to be reckoned. But I mean that wit which is gotten by use only and experience, without method, culture, or instruction. This natural wit consisteth principally in two things—celerity of imagining, and steady direction. On the contrary, a slow imagination maketh that defect which is commonly called dullness. And this difference of quickness is caused by the difference of men's passions'.—*Leviathan*, p. 31. (*CWWH*, XX: p. 81)[9]

Numerous points are of interest here. First, this sole offering of a definition of natural capacity, in fact, is incorrect. Here, Hazlitt misquotes Hobbes. In this part of *Leviathan*, Hobbes is differentiating between intellectual *virtues*. Hobbes states, 'These *Vertues* are of two sorts; *Naturall* and *Acquired*. By Naturall, I mean not, that which a man hath from his Birth.'[10] Additionally, with natural capacity, Hazlitt seems to be fashioning a new term, or rather giving a term a new meaning. Hobbes, in fact, does use the term natural capacity a handful of times in *Leviathan*, but he never uses it to identify an aspect of mind; rather, he always uses it to differentiate when certain agents, such as representatives, are acting in their political capacity— that is, on behalf of another's authority—and when they are acting out of their own natural capacity, on their own authority. Hobbes notes: 'every man, or assembly that hath Soveraignty, representeth two Persons, or (as the more common phrase is) has two Capacities, one Naturall, and another Politique'.[11]

Is this simply misremembered by Hazlitt? While the seemingly small, insubstantial changes in wording and the fact that Hazlitt does not build off of the term (or use it outside of his summary lists of the modern school of

[9] Although Hazlitt announced that this would be the tenth point, it is published and labeled as the ninth. Points nine and ten seem to have been switched. In Hazlitt's brief overview of the modern system of philosophy, number nine was to discuss how 'the mind acts from necessity, and consequently is not a moral or accountable agent'. However, this is the tenth point in Hazlitt's longer list of quotations, labeled '10. Of Liberty and Necessity'. Additionally, it is worth noting that Hobbes's 'not' in Hazlitt's quotation is excluded in *CWWH*.

[10] Thomas Hobbes, *Leviathan* (Oxford: Clarendon Press, 1909), p. 52.

[11] Hobbes, *Leviathan*, p. 184.

philosophy's traits) make it seem as though it may be, some details point to the fact that natural capacity was a deliberate construction. Hazlitt uses the term 'natural capacity' in three different essays—if it was misremembered, it was repeatedly misremembered. Additionally, the fact that Hazlitt cleans up the longish quotation from Hobbes, including 'capacity' and excluding 'amongst Vertues'—a very convenient forgetting—from what 'it is not to be reckoned', makes this seem more like a deliberate construction.

'Natural capacity' also supplies a term for the modern materialist philosophy that is new, and that stands out. Among the other topics covered, such as 'Sensation', 'Mind and Matter', 'Association', 'the Understanding', 'Abstraction', 'Reasoning', 'Motives of Action', and 'Liberty and Necessity', 'Natural Capacity' is the only that would strike anyone as somewhat original and inventive. Finally, Hazlitt's term employs a word that is of great importance to him: 'natural'. Hazlitt begins his career with a defense of *natural* disinterestedness. Uttara Natarajan points repeatedly to this word's importance for Hazlitt, noting that 'the term "natural" for Hazlitt describes less an independent and external quality inhering in nature, than the inwardly produced property or feeling with which it is invested by the mind, whence the equivalence of the natural and the imaginative'.[12] With his borrowing and retooling of the term 'natural capacity', Hazlitt gets what he needs: a convenient term that links his thinking directly to that of Hobbes's, which he aims to argue against, in order to indicate what is at the heart of what is at stake in the debate: the nature of the natural. 'Natural capacity' is a term that Hazlitt can use to identify the modern system's picture of the basic workings of mind, which he, and others, will resist.

Keats, I argue, is one of those others; we should understand 'negative capability' to be an overriding of natural capacity by means of over-writing. It is very likely that Keats read the essay on Locke. He certainly could have, at least. The Locke essay was published in the *Examiner* on 31 March 1816, and Keats was an avid reader of the *Examiner* since his school days at Enfield.[13] While not a clear pun, like Posthumus/posthumous, the term 'negative capability' sounds like 'natural capacity'. I trust this is clear. However, not only does Keats echo (by overwriting) 'natural capacity' with his 'negative capability', he even seems to echo Hazlitt's version of Hobbes's natural capacity. Hazlitt states

[12] Uttara Natarajan, *Hazlitt and the Reach of Sense: Criticism, Morals, and the Metaphysics of Power* (Oxford: Clarendon Press, 1998), p. 61.

[13] Keats likely was paying particularly close attention to the *Examiner* at the time, as it would have been right around the time he sent his sonnet, 'To Solitude', to the *Examiner* for publication. In *John Keats: A New Life*, Nicholas Roe notes that in the 28 April issue there is a note saying 'J.K. and other Communications, next week'; the poem appeared in the 5 May issue (p. 82). Keats may have sent in his poem just a week or two after reading Hazlitt's essay.

(that Hobbes states), 'By natural capacity, I mean not that which a man hath from his birth ... but I mean that', and Keats seems to echo Hazlitt: 'I mean *Negative Capability*, that is when man is capable of being in uncertainties.' Not only are the phrases 'natural capacity' and 'negative capability' sonically similar but so are the clarifications: 'I mean ... that'.

Keats very likely is in a linguistically mercurial mood. He always, naturally, is. Benjamin Haydon reports a story told to him about Keats: 'when he could just speak, instead of answering questions put to him he would always make a rhyme to the last word people said, and then laugh'.[14] Keats is primed to chime. The likelihood of this increases once we more fully acknowledge the immediate context of Keats's discovery of negative capability: his return, with Dilke and Brown, from a Christmas pantomime—and, more broadly, his reading and thinking about pantomime. As Brian Bates argues in his chapter in this collection, through his viewing of and reading and thinking about pantomime—which until now has been an essentially disregarded, and therefore under-theorized, context for negative capability—Keats was well-aware of pantomime's 'satiric playfulness' and took pleasure in the 'ridiculous and liberating' aspects of the genre, including its 'metamorphos[e]s' and 'transformation[s]'. Bates reads the negative capability passage as an enactment of subversive pantomimical practices, making the case that we should understand the epiphany that delivers to Keats negative capability as pantomimical transformation: 'Keats's "at once it struck me" couches the high sincerity of his transformative epiphany in the playful, thumping language of ... harlequinade.' Thus recontextualized and re-encountered, 'Keats's pantomime scene portrays negative capability as a self-reflexive capacity that welcomes mixed aesthetics, contrary states, character doubling, and imminent transformability.' I only add that we also can view Keats as harlequin, touching his bat to modern materialist natural capacity and transforming it into the articulation of genius: negative capability.

Hazlitt, of course, certainly was someone Keats wanted to and often did mimic. Keats refers to his reading of Hazlitt's work—much of which appeared in the *Examiner*—in numerous letters, revealing his close attention to Hazlitt's thought and style.[15] Additionally, Hazlitt certainly was on Keats's mind around the time he wrote the negative capability letter. Hazlitt is a tutelary spirit of

[14] Richard Monckton Milnes, *Life, Letters, and Literary Remains of John Keats*, 2 vols. (London: Edward Moxon, 1848). This story is retold, without the laughter, in Bate, *Keats*, p. 8.

[15] In *Keats and Negative Capability* (London: Bloomsbury, 2009), Li Ou provides a helpful overview of Keats's 'admiration for Hazlitt', including his avid reading of and commentary on Hazlitt's work, his attentiveness to Hazlitt's prose style, his imitation of that prose style, and his adoption of Hazlittian vocabulary (pp. 26–7). Brian Bates's close reading of Hazlitt's satirically inflected August 1817 review of Coleridge's *Biographia Literaria* in this collection will expand this list.

the letter.[16] Not even a month after sending the negative capability letter, Keats will include 'Hazlitt's depth of Taste' among the 'three things to rejoice at in this Age' (*LJK*, I: p. 203). As Natarajan notes, 'It has been indisputably established … not only that Keats admired Hazlitt, but also that many of the best-known passages on poetic identity in Keats's letters are derived from his reading of Hazlitt' (pp. 108–9).

In regard to the content of natural capacity, at one level Keats, of course, will want to oppose any concept that calls into doubt the possibility of genius. Negative capability largely is an insight into, or perhaps even more a naming of, Shakespeare's particular kind of genius: 'what quality went to form a Man of Achievement especially in Literature & which Shakespeare posessed so enormously—' (*LJK*, I: p. 193). The connection between genius and achievement is made explicit in a later letter in which Keats introduces his ideas about the nature of the 'poetical Character'—certainly a part of the constellation of ideas that shape what is thought to be the content, the significance, of negative capability—by noting that he will 'in a clerklike manner … make some observations on two principle points, which seem to point like indices into the midst of the whole pro and con, about genius, and views and atchievements and ambition and cœtera' (*LJK*, I: p. 386). Keats states elsewhere, 'I am very near Agreeing with Hazlit that Shakspeare is enough for us' (*LJK*, I: p. 143). Negative capability is Keats's own reformulation of this idea, a reformulation that could involve the reformulation of the term from Hazlitt that stands against the possibility of genius: natural capacity.

Owing to the cursory and largely suggestive nature of the deployments of both Hazlitt's natural capacity and Keats's negative capability, it is not clear *precisely* what Keats might have gleaned from natural capacity, but if we wish to read a little more deeply into Keats's formulation, natural capacity identifies the mind's general functions, specifically naming those virtuous—that is, for Hobbes, commendable—mental functions just above the intake of the senses, namely 'celerity of imagining' and 'steadiness of direction'. However, these certainly are two of the traits of mind that negative capability is described in contradistinction to. Rather than quickness of imagining, negative capability suggests it is superior to dwell, to be 'capable of being in'. Rather than steadiness of direction, negative capability recommends foregoing 'any irritable

[16] Keats reports to his brothers that his review of Edmund Kean in Burges's *Riches* appears 'in todays champion' (*LJK*, I: p. 191), and in that review Keats draws on Hazlitt's essay 'On Gusto' to praise the 'gusto' of Kean's voice. Additionally, as Rollins observes in one of his notes to the letter, in his assessment of Benjamin West's *Death on the Pale Horse* 'Keats is following Hazlitt's criticism in the *Edinburgh Magazine*, December, 1817' (*LJK*, I: p. 192 n.9). For more on the connections between Hazlitt and the negative capability letter, see the relevant sections of Li's 'Genealogy of Negative Capability' in *Keats and Negative Capability* (pp. 23–51).

reaching' (*LJK*, I: p. 193). These ideas will ripen with Keats, and turn into an increasing emphasis on receptivity and 'delicious diligent Indolence' (*LJK*, I: p. 231). Slowness is not and will not be the 'defect ... dullness', but rather a key characteristic of genius. Additionally, 'steadiness of direction' is the kind of thing that will come to seem to Keats like problematic 'consequitive reasoning' (*LJK*, I: p. 185) and 'palpable design' (*LJK*, I: pp. 223–4). Later, Keats will write in favor of letting 'the mind be a thoroughfare for all thoughts', contrasting this to what seems like Dilke's overly directional thinking: 'Dilke will never come at truth as long as he lives; because he is always trying at it' (*LJK*, II: p. 213). A mere natural capacity will not be enough. The mind is capable, but its greatest workings result from slowing up, going deeper, subtracting.

But, of course, with negative capability Keats is not systematically theorizing. Rather, he is having an epiphany, an epiphany critical of another idea and involving overriding by over-writing. With the discovery/invention of negative capability we are witnessing in a flash the kind of thinking that goes into turning the unsatisfactory idea of '"a vale of tears"' into a '"vale of Soul-making"' (*LJK*, II: pp. 101–2). In the negative capability letter we are given an account of the action Keats describes in a letter from January 1820 to Georgiana Keats in which he writes, 'T wang dillo dee ...This you must know is the Amen to nonsense. I know many places where Amen should be scratched out, rubb'd over with a pou[n]ce made of Momus's little finger bones, and in its place "T wang dillo dee", written' (II: p. 246). While it is easiest to read negative capability as a serious over-writing similar to that of the vale of tears/Soul-making, we should not discount the more clearly absurd, comedic (Momus is a god of comedy) transformation Keats describes with 'T wang dillo dee', especially given Bates's linking of negative capability and pantomime. There is a chance, too, that negative capability is a similar result of a transformative linguistic imagination. As Brian Rejack's work on the significance of John Jeffrey's underlining of negative capability informs us, there is greater likelihood that that underlining (to whatever extent it is significant at all) indicates that we are in the presence of wordplay as Keats understands it.[17]

About his own efforts to show that a passage from Book One of Francis Bacon's *The Advancement of Learning* was a source for the definition of negative capability, Roy Park states: 'In all this there is much that must remain purely conjectural.'[18] There certainly remains something that is speculative about finding the source for negative capability in natural capacity. But it should not seem that strange. In many ways, my reading contributes some small additional information to the longstanding conception of negative capability

[17] See Brian Rejack's chapter in this collection.

[18] Roy Park, *Hazlitt and the Spirit of the Age: Abstraction and Critical Theory* (Oxford: Clarendon Press, 1971), p. 34.

established by Walter Jackson Bate. In fact, given the substance of natural capacity and the term itself, it supports and corroborates the idea that, no matter the unreliability of Jeffrey's transcriptions, 'negative capability' could plausibly have been Keats's term.[19] My reading of negative capability as an over-riding/-writing of natural capacity also merely extends a bit the already clearly acknowledged debt that the *substance* of negative capability owes to Hazlitt into the *articulation* of the concept itself. Additionally, it only slightly extends Nicholas Roe's closer investigations into 'the immediate backgrounds to Keats's intellectual and imaginative life in December 1817'; as Roe notes, 'the *Examiner*'s articles about self-love, disinterest, and irritability in politics and the theater surely featured in numerous irrecoverable conversations, arguments, and jokes in which Keats participated'.[20] I broaden the range of Keats's *Examiner* reading in order to try to recover another act of playfulness right at the site of negative capability.

Regardless of *what* play is at work, recognizing that there *is* play in negative capability is significant in itself. In a recent study of negative capability's wide-ranging dispersal, I examined a number of uses of negative capability, focusing especially on its (very often non-scholarly) uses in contemporary American poetry, finding that 'some clear, and clearly troubling, trends in fact emerge'.[21] Among those trends, I discovered that 'Negative Capability is almost always thought to be a serious term, one used to endorse only serious poetry—*Negative* Capability is rarely, if ever, applied to comedic poetry'. Additionally, 'when used as shorthand to encapsulate the totality of Keats's thought and work, the result is that it seems as though Keats's thought and work are *only* serious'.

I want to be clear: this tendency is largely due to the term itself. The term 'negative capability' is mysterious and therefore seductive. In part naming the projective and adhesive nature of mind, the term itself has played a significant role in the projection and adhesion of negative capability, its broad dissemination, and its staying power. It allows for it to be connected to Middleton Murry's Christ-like acceptance and the *via negativa*.[22] In her chapter on the

[19] In his Introduction to *Letters of John Keats*, ed. Robert Gittings (Oxford: Oxford University Press, 1970), Gittings speculates that negative capability 'may have been invented or misread by Jeffrey' (p. xii).

[20] Nicholas Roe, *John Keats and the Culture of Dissent* (Oxford: Clarendon Press, 1997), p. 239.

[21] '~~Negative Capability~~ T wang dillo dee', in *Jacket*, 40 (2010), accessed 7 July 2018, http://jacketmagazine.com/40/theune-keats.shtml. Much of the rest of this essay follows closely the argument at the end of that one.

[22] John Middleton Murry, *Keats and Shakespeare* (Oxford: Oxford University Press, 1925), p. 48. Quoted in Walter Jackson Bate, Negative *Capability: The Intuitive Approach in Keats* (Cambridge, MA: Harvard University Press, 1939), p. 41. Bate sees an 'element of truth' in Middleton Murry's formulation, but also warns against its overreaching idealism, which 'we must guard against' (p. 41).

'Modernist Heritage of Negative Capability' Li states, 'The receptive openness to the mysterious, ineffable vision of the divine links negative capability with *via negativa*' (p. 179). She does this even though she knows it's not quite correct. In the note to this claim Li states, 'The two notions are connected, but *via negativa* obviously also differs from negative capability in its denial of the ordinary facts of experience in order to achieve a vision of God' (p. 194). To me this seems close to sounding like what Li pejoratively describes as one of the 'wild directions the term may take' (p. 21). But it is endorsed by the terms of the term 'negative' and by the fact that that word is taken to be solely serious.

That this is a wild direction is confirmed by the deadly swerve taken in Stanley Plumly's *Posthumous Keats: A Personal Biography*. Plumly is enchanted by the idea of negative capability—he refers to it often his book *Argument and Song: Sources & Silences in Poetry*, especially in his essays 'Seasons of Mists' and 'Reading Autumn', essays on Keats and Keats's 'To Autumn'.[23] In *Posthumous Keats*, Plumly refers to negative capability numerous times and again argues that '"To Autumn" ... becomes the resonant model of Keats's own negative capability' (p. 168). In fact, Plumly—who links Keats's walking with negative capability, as walking allowed Keats 'to separate himself from his troubles long enough to write as if they didn't exist' (p. 77)—clearly intends his biography to be negatively capable: in his preface Plumly notes that he, instead of treating Keats's life in a linear fashion, wanted to write 'with "disinterestedness," wanted 'to walk around in Keats's life and art, not simply through them'.[24]

The problem, though, with Plumly's biography is its selection of topics to walk around in: Plumly selects topics which mostly reinforce the picture of a Batean, negatively capable Keats, and excludes many details that would argue against this picture, including Keats's growing interest in concentrating his writing on political journalism, comedy, and satire. Though he refers to Charles Cowden Clarke's remembrance of Keats's strong reaction to reading *Cymbeline*, Plumly does not at all make this pun explicit, let alone investigate it (p. 122). With such exclusions, and enabled by the book's negatively capable approach, Plumly traps himself in a contradiction: though he spends much of his book arguing that Keats did not die from psychological torment—caused by bad reviews of his early work—Plumly ends up arguing that Keats in fact did die of psychological causes: from having written the perfect—that is, perfectly negatively capable—'To Autumn'. About Keats's decline and death, Plumly states:

[23] Stanley Plumly, *Argument & Song: Sources & Silences in Poetry* (New York: Other Press, 2003). In these two chapters, references to negative capability occur on pp. 65, 77, 81, and 88.

[24] Stanley Plumly, *Posthumous Keats: A Personal Biography* (New York: W. W. Norton & Company, 2008), p. 17.

> No wonder the doctors were confused as to what was ailing Keats: in a way it was neither this nor that but everything, manna as well as matter. And it starts with his most perfect poem, as if an open circle had been drawn to close. That is to say, the recognition of what is true and fated for years arrives like a vision, and that vision is 'To Autumn', whose emotional and spiritual realities represent both a full cup and exhaustion, their sequence and consequence. It is as if Keats's only choice after 'To Autumn' is to die. (p. 305)

Even though generally very positively reviewed by Keats scholars,[25] Plumly's *Posthumous Keats* surely contains one of the wildest directions any use of negative capability has ever taken. What such magical thinking reveals is the degree to which Plumly—a fine poet, a generally sharp critic, and a devoted Keatsian—is so blinded by negative capability that he is willing to sacrifice Keats to it. Far from being an isolated incident, virtually every use of negative capability—which so venerates the use of the term over the facts that surround it, and thus tends to court such recklessness—can be conceived of as aiding and abetting this outcome. Much less a destiny for Keats, Plumly's book in fact reveals the destiny of negative capability, and not even so much the substance—however convoluted—of negative capability but rather mostly the term itself: all other things being the same, it is hard to imagine Keats being so sacrificed to, say, 'Shakespearean capability', or an allusion, a bit of wordplay, a jest. Indeed, I suspect that Plumly's suggestion is just the sort of thing that Keats would be eager to 'smoke', to suss out, to critique, to ridicule.[26]

American poet Mary Ruefle has (playfully) called for a decade-long 'moratorium' on the words 'negative capability', arguing, 'so overused are they, so bandied about that they have come to mean just about anything one wants them to, especially a bebop version of *Be Here Now*, or a diffusive religious awe

[25] Appreciative reviews include Christopher Ricks, 'Keats's Afterlife', *The New York Review of Books* (11 June 2009), pp. 59–61; and Susan J. Wolfson's 'Stanley Plumly, Posthumous Keats', a review in *Romantic Circles* (11 December 2009), accessed 6 July 2018, https://www.rc.umd.edu/reviews-blog/stanley-plumly-posthumous-keats.

[26] Registering Keats's growing attention to power dynamics, James Chandler suggests that negative capability gets subsumed by Keats's awareness of and interest in the ability to—to use a word Keats employed often—'smoke' (that is, to see through and critique through withering satire) intellectual and creative work. Hearing negative capability as a critical take on natural capacity, along with a greater appreciation of Keats's involvement with the satirical power of pantomime, helps us see that the seeds of smokeability already are planted in late 1817 in negative capability. See James Chandler, *England in 1819: The Politics of Literary Culture and the Case of Romantic Historicism* (Chicago, IL: The University of Chicago Press, 1998), pp. 395–402.

in which the poet wanders'.[27] As no such moratorium is possible, nor, especially given Bates's and Rejack's inquiries into the term, advisable, my call is for something different: that we start to hear negative capability in a new way. At the conclusion of 'Ode to a Nightingale', the speaker hears the word—including its rhyming syllables—'forlorn', which strikes him suddenly and awakens him from his reverie: 'Forlorn! the very word is like a bell / To toll me back from thee to my sole self!' I hope hearing the resonance of natural capacity in negative capability has a similar effect, encouraging those hearing negative capability to be transported not to dreamy reveries about what might be connected to the term but rather specifically back to the particularity of the term, reminded of its local, limited usage and range of reference. Such would be a wake-up call, a proper chastening. To the extent that Plumly's maneuvers surprise us, we have reason to curb the appeal of Batean, solely serious negative capability. While limiting us, somewhat paradoxically this will broaden our idea of the Keats who is so often summed up by negative capability, freeing him up to be as he was: serious and playful; inventor and imitator; shade and light; mortal (and deeply aware of it) and lively; 'etherial' and 'pantomimical'. We must—to repurpose the famous phrase of F. Scott Fitzgerald's 'The Crack-Up', that 'the test of a first-rate intelligence is the ability to hold two opposing ideas in the mind at the same time yet still retain the ability to function', a phrase often linked to solely serious negative capability[28]—hold these two opposing Keatses in our minds yet still be able to appreciate and thoughtfully engage his life and work. I hope that, even if in a small way, hearing negative capability as a playful derivation of natural capacity will help us do so.

[27] Mary Ruefle, 'On Fear: Our positive capability', *Poetry Magazine* (1 June 2012), accessed 5 July 2018, https://www.poetryfoundation.org/poetrymagazine/articles/detail/69815.

[28] F. Scott Fitzgerald, *The Crack-Up* (New York: Penguin, 1965), p. 39. Stanley Plumly makes this connection in *Posthumous*, p. 361, as does Dan Simmons in 'Skinwalkers and Shapeshifters: the Writer's Curse of Negative Capability', *Journal of the Fantastic in the Arts*, 8: 4 (1997), p. 412.

Chapter Four

'that strong excepted soul'

Nineteenth-Century Women Read Keats

Carmen Faye Mathes

Introduction

This chapter explores early nineteenth-century women readers of Keats, whose reflections on the poet's life and achievements characterize the gap between his 1821 death and the publication and wider circulation of his letters. The women, Elizabeth Barrett Browning, Letitia Elizabeth Landon, and, to a lesser extent, Mary Shelley, provide an archive of critical perspectives on Keats's legacy and early reception that both challenges and reinforces the by-now-canonical accounts of his male contemporaries—Percy Shelley's *Adonais*, Leigh Hunt's 'Cockney School' of poetry, and Lord Byron's derogatory praise—as well as later views. Like their counterparts, the women tend to be laudatory but condescending. Rather than identify with the poet on the grounds of shared social inferiority, as has been suggested,[1] they generally treat him with respectful pity. Indeed, at a time when being female and taken seriously as a thinker could have meant expressly not equating beauty with authority (as Mary Wollstonecraft warned, 'it is the fate of the fairest flowers to be admired and pulled to pieces by the careless hand that plucked them'),[2] these writers, who appreciate and were influenced by Keats, are also wont to distance themselves from his perceived effeminacy and weakness. This tension, between approbation on the one hand and detachment on the other, typifies

[1] Beth Lau, 'Jane Austen and John Keats: Negative Capability, Romance and Reality', *Keats-Shelley Journal*, 55 (2006), p. 109; Margaret Homans, 'Keats Reading Women, Women Reading Keats', *Studies in Romanticism*, 29: 3 (1990), pp. 341–2.

[2] Mary Wollstonecraft, *Wollstonecraft: A Vindication of the Rights of Men and a Vindication of the Rights of Woman*, ed. Sylvana Tomaselli (Cambridge: Cambridge University Press, 1995), p. 240.

the admiring resistance of Keats's reception by the women authors: an attitude with which they judge poems and a poet as-yet-uncharacterized by explicit knowledge of '*Negative Capability*' (*LJK*, I: p. 193).

Exploring this attitude in letters, poems, and diary entries, I ask if Keats's reception by nineteenth-century women pre-figures more recent alliances (both implied and forged) between negative capability and uniquely 'female' ways of knowing. The question is not a simple one. As Susan Wolfson puts it, Keats's poetry is 'as complex and elusive in its gender as it is compelling in its genius', unsettling gender binaries whilst 'provok[ing] [the] terminology—*masculine, feminine, effeminate, patriarchal, feminist*'.[3] For Wolfson, as for Anne Mellor, Marjorie Levinson, Margaret Homans, and James Najarian, Keats's poetry resists stable categorization by enacting shifts in gender that tie pleasure to uncertainty.[4] The poet 'embodies an aspect of the feminine within masculinity itself' and, as Najarian argues, for nineteenth-century male readers this ambiguity courts a variety of queer identifications (p. 20). Yet, in the case of the female readers above, the list of Keatsian poetic provocations would require slightly different terms—*youth, authenticity, sensitivity, weakness, strength.* What the women's historical accounts centralize are observations about Keats's personal vulnerability that, while certainly not reinforcing an unambiguous machismo, aren't necessarily feminizing either. Critical reflections often give way to expressions of pity best exemplified by the addition of the adjective 'poor' to the poet's name.

So, while Keats was certainly doing something 'complex and elusive' with gender that was legible to his female readers, its centrality is often displaced, in their accounts, by the fact that he died doing it. Keats's death—and specifically Keats's foreknowledge about his own death—is the catastrophic intuition that wrests posthumous Keats from the narrative of his submission to literary-critical censure. In what follows, I examine the ways in which Keats's tragic insight shades his legacy long before negative capability became an available referent (with the 1848 publication of Richard Monckton Milnes's biography). Although an oft-cited twenty-first-century conversation about negative capability and women's 'weak ego boundaries' reflects stereotypes about female impressionability,[5] the nineteenth-century women's accounts confirm Keats's

[3] Susan Wolfson, *Borderlines: The Shiftings of Gender in British Romanticism* (Stanford, CA: Stanford University Press, 2006), p. 284.

[4] See Wolfson, *Borderlines*; Anne Mellor, *Romanticism and Gender* (New York: Routledge, 1993); Marjorie Levinson, *Keats's Life of Allegory* (Oxford: Blackwell, 1988); Homans, 'Keats Reading Women'; and James Najarian, *Victorian Keats: Manliness, Sexuality, and Desire* (New York: Palgrave McMillan, 2002).

[5] For discussions of Adrienne Rich and Barbara Charlesworth Gelpi on Keats, see Wolfson (*Borderlines*, pp. 282–3), Mellor (*Romanticism*, p. 174), and Homans ('Keats Reading Women', p. 343–5); for the original text see Rich, 'Three Conversations', in

intuitive powers as a form of agency, ego-boundedness, and strength. Negative capability has been central to readings of Keats and gender, yet we have almost thirty years (1821–48) of his reception by women as yet unexamined through its interpretive lens. What this chapter offers, then, is a significant departure from how Keats has been characterized in relation to gender in contemporary criticism, one that reads backwards negative capability's supposed openness and empathy onto an archive of women authors both critical of and captivated by the posthumous character of the poet's life and achievements.[6]

It is worth saying at the outset that Keats's views on women and historical women's views on Keats are firmly enmeshed in the misogyny and sexism of the time. Negative capability may let the poet 'take part in [the] existence [of the sparrow] and pick about the gravel', but it also describes the mindset of a 'Man of Achievement especially in Literature', best exemplified by William Shakespeare (*LJK*, I: pp. 186, 193). Homans, in her exceptional reading of Keats's fraught attitude towards women, argues that while negative capability names the potential to 'enter into' another's being, 'there is at least one "body" that his identityless, negatively capable self prefers not to enter into or to be entered by: it prefers to keep women distinct as objects of vision' (p. 345). In the letters, Keats reveals myriad sexist attitudes and assumptions, including the admission that his attachment to the abstract idea of Beauty 'stifles' the possibility of life with a real woman or domestic partner (*LJK*, I: p. 403). Notably, he also takes umbrage with the Bluestockings, a well-known group of intellectuals led by Elizabeth Montagu (*LJK*, I: p. 163; II: p. 19). Then there is the claim, from Keats's friend Richard Woodhouse to the publisher John Taylor, that Keats 'does not want ladies to read his poetry: that he writes for men' (*LJK*, II: p. 163). In Homans's account, all this explicit resistance also surfaces in telling ways in the poet's appropriation of women's voices in his letters and poems. Homans's conclusion, that Keats's ventriloquizing is a 'defense' against the 'female figure [who] promises a dissolution of the poet's identity that is at once pleasurable and profoundly threatening', finds in the very openness that negative capability affords the grounds for a psychic schism rent by the impossibility of entering safely, or 'taking part in', a woman's existence (p. 355).

Against his own bias, then, and prior to negative capability becoming a known quantity, nineteenth-century women read and wrote about Keats.

Adrienne Rich's Poetry, ed. Barbara Charlesworth Gelpi and Albert Gelpi (New York: Norton, 1975), p. 115.

[6] Keats's worries over his poems' critical reception (his concerns over the 'smokeability' of *Isabella; or, the Pot of Basil*, for example) also hinge on questions about which types of poetry 'might do very well after one's death' and which might not (*LJK*, II: p. 174). For a discussion of posthumousness in Keats's poetics see Stanley Plumly, *Posthumous Keats: A Personal Biography* (New York: Norton, 2009), and Andrew Bennett, *Keats, Narrative and Audience: The Posthumous Life of Writing* (Cambridge: Cambridge University Press, 1994).

Taking the measure of the 'Cockney School' poet, playwright, and theater reviewer, their opinions reflect the quality of his poetry, the negative reviews, his public self-presentation in the preface to *Endymion* (1818) and elsewhere, and gossip and anecdotes gleaned from those who knew him. Tones range from celebratory to disparaging. Some, such as Landon, might be called fans, while others, such as Mary Shelley, are more restrained. Each feels touched in some way by Keats, and compelled to immortalize him. There is, in other words, no shortage of women's voices on Keats, whether he would have wished it or not—although it almost goes without saying that these voices are mostly absent from our established narratives of his legacy and early reception.

Overlooking the opinions of Keats's female contemporaries, scholars run the risk of shoring up Keats's sexism even in our attempts to consider him justly. Turning up the volume on Byron and the male members of the Pisan Circle, which should include Mary Shelley in addition to Percy Bysshe Shelley, scholarship might seem to privilege male voices for reasons of celebrity. This is a mistake not least because, as Jerome McGann and Daniel Riess remind us, Landon was a literary icon on par with Byron[7]—a fact that does not stop her 'Lines on Seeing a Portrait of Keats' (1824) from receiving considerably less attention than Canto XI of *Don Juan* (1823). So, while Keats may or may not have said he does not write for ladies, it is imperative that we recognize that he could not stop an incisive Mary Shelley from noting, in a letter to Leigh Hunt, that an admittedly 'beautiful stanza' from 'Ode on a Nightingale' suffers a factual oversight: 'It was the sky lark', she writes, and 'not the nightingale that Ruth heard "amid the alien corn"—the sky lark soars and sings above the shearers perpetually.'[8] Such a blatant 'reaching after fact & reason' offers a new perspective on negatively capable Keats, revealing as it does Shelley's ornithological interest in truth as beauty. In fact, a quibble over a nightingale seems a fitting point of departure towards a more complete understanding of the legacies of both Keats and his negative capability.

Irritable Facts: Feeling Bad about Keats

That it was not the nightingale, but the skylark, is not a readerly observation but an editorial one, directed posthumously at Keats by way of Leigh Hunt. By 1844, Mary Shelley, widowed for more than two decades, had become a literary authority within the circle of writers who survived Percy Bysshe Shelley, Lord

[7] Jerome McGann and Daniel Riess, Introduction to *Letitia Elizabeth Landon: Selected Writings*, ed. Jerome McGann and Daniel Riess (Peterborough: Broadview Press, 1997), p. 11.

[8] *The Letters of Mary Wollstonecraft Shelley*, ed. Betty T. Bennett, 3 vols. (Baltimore, MD: Johns Hopkins University Press, 1988), III: p. 161.

Byron, and John Keats, and for whom she offered editorial advice and opinions, as well as connections with important publishers such as Henry Colburn and John Murray. In a letter responding to Hunt's new collection, *Imagination and Fancy; or Selections from the English Poets* (1844), Shelley both lauds its prefatory essay and lodges her complaint against 'Ode on a Nightingale', one of the many works by Keats that Hunt includes, introduces, and annotates. Two aspects of Shelley's complaint are interesting for the ways in which they characterize the poet's legacy. First, her fact-checking obliquely repudiates the very thing that Hunt celebrates, in the collection, as Keats's tendency to transform the mundane into the magical: 'Keats was born a poet of the most poetical kind ... [who] never beheld an oak-tree without seeing a Dryad' (p. 283). Second, her self-reflexive framing of the complaint suggests that she knows she should be sensitive to Hunt's desire to fix a legacy of Keatsian genius:

> Will you think me hypercritical about a most beautiful stanza of Keats—it was the sky lark and not the nightingale that Ruth heard 'amid the alien corn'—the sky lark soars and sings above the shearers perpetually—The nightingale sings at night—in shady places—& never so late in the season—May is her Month—
>
> Excuse all this. (*Letters of Mary Shelley*, III: p. 161)

Already long exposed to Byron's sarcasm and Percy Shelley's lament, Shelley reacts to Hunt's recovery project by positioning herself as editor and critic, and thus participating in a form of commentary that Hunt explicitly denigrates. Keats, claims Hunt, 'knew the youthful faults of his poetry as well as any man, [but] [t]he critic is ... almost always an inferior to a man of genius, and possesses [the genius's] sensibility neither to beauty nor to pain' (p. 286). For this reason, Shelley's desire to hold Keats to an earthly standard of factual accuracy challenges what Hunt wants for Keats's legacy, and her excessive self-consciousness about it ('Will you think me', 'Excuse all this') helps illustrate what had become, by the mid-nineteenth century, something of a standard in Keats commentary: apprehensiveness about critical disapproval endangering the poet's legacy, whilst critically disapproving nevertheless.

Indeed, little more than a decade earlier, it had seemed to a twenty-five-year-old Elizabeth Barrett (later Browning) that disappointing poems might bury the legacy along with the poet. In a diary entry of 18 August 1831 Barrett recalls: 'I finished Keats's *Lamia, Isabella, Evening of St. Agnes & Hyperion*, before breakfast ... . The first three disappointed me. The extracts I had seen of them, were undeniably the finest things in them. ... Poor poor Keats.'[9] In

[9] Elizabeth Barrett Browning, *The Barretts at Hope End; the Early Diary of Elizabeth Barrett Browning*, ed. Elizabeth Berridge (London: John Murray, 1974), p. 141.

her condescending mix of compassion and dismay, Barrett makes clear that her lack of enjoyment stems from the poems' failure to live up to the high quality of the excerpts she has already read. The syntax of her final phrase, which echoes the poet's own well known and youthfully flawed phraseology, seems both to make light of and genuinely mourn the collection's lost potential. Where Keats's 'happy, happy', becomes Barrett's 'Poor poor', the echo of a flat repetition calls to mind the additional disappointment that, while in 1831 there is definitely no future for the poet, there may not be a future for his poems either.

Barrett's mimicry (unconscious or even, compellingly, not) highlights a peculiar formal impulse when it comes to mourning Keats: that of the qualified repetition or echo. 'Poor poor' interrupts pity with helplessness. It turns legacy to tautology, and recalls Percy Shelley's own solicitous gloss, from *Adonais*, of Keats's double happiness. Of those poets who have ever striven for greatness, writes Shelley, 'happier they their happiness who knew' that their perseverance will lead 'through toil and hate, to Fame's serene abode' (lines 39, 45). While *Adonais* threads the language of Keats's self-described 'inexperience [and] immaturity' (*PJK*, p. 102) into an elegiac poem that both admires and censures, in Barrett's account what purports to be exclamatory actually resembles, as Jacques Rancière describes it, criticism's tendency to reconfigure the traps of the literature it seeks to interpret.[10] Barrett's repetition plays up Keats's inelegance while reading his legacy through his personal struggles. Like Mary Shelley, she feels bad about feeling bad about Keats. Like Percy Shelley, she parrots even as she reveals how the poems incorporate, on the one hand, the living poet's sense of limited futurity and, on the other hand, an optimistic attachment to his poems' future influence. As she closes the entry, she feels her 'spirits are very very cloudy!'[11]

Together, Mary Shelley and Barrett's accounts begin to reveal the admiring resistance that colors Keats's legacy in shades at once consolatory and critical. Keats's absent future weighs heavily on both, diluting censure with self-consciousness and centralizing his legacy's vulnerability to criticism. For Barrett in the 1840s, this vulnerability seems to have prompted something like protectiveness: a desire to canonize Keats that, while rising above 1831's disappointments, nevertheless preserves the condescending attitude. In an August 1844 letter to John Kenyon she entreats,

> And also agree with me in reverencing that wonderful genius Keats, who rising as a grand exception from among the vulgar herd of juvenile

[10] Jacques Rancière, *Dissensus: On Politics and Aesthetics*, ed. and trans. Steven Corcoran (New York: Continuum, 2010), p. 164.

[11] Barrett Browning, *Early Diary*, p. 141.

> versifiers, was an individual man from the beginning, & spoke with his own voice, though surrounded by the yet unfamiliar murmur of antique echoes. Leigh Hunt calls him 'the young poet' very rightly.[12]

Even as she excepts Keats from 'the vulgar herd', Barrett still tallies him among them, if 'young poet' and 'juvenile versifier' can properly be counted as synonymous. The reference to Hunt's *Imagination and Fancy* (the same collection to which Shelley responds above) casts Barrett as willing participant in a legacy-building project likewise invested in a young poet aware of, but not destroyed by, his limits. Indeed, Hunt's collection, with its sympathetic repackaging of Keats's self-doubt from the 1818 preface to *Endymion*, seems the work of a kindred spirit. His animated defense of Keats's immature genius Barrett here matches with her claim that, while Keats may not have been an experienced poet, he was certainly an exceptional one. Requesting agreement from Kenyon, Barrett aims to further both her and Hunt's cause: recognition that Keats can be the author of uneven poems, and still not be forgotten.

For Barrett, canonizing Keats means including him in her personal stable of 'true true poets', or what she elsewhere calls her 'Poets Record', and calling upon others to do the same.[13] It also means turning her attention to his early death, the tragic foreknowledge of which transforms Keats's potentially feminine-coded passivity into masculine activeness and agency. In a 26 October 1841 letter to her friend Mary Russell Mitford, for instance, Barrett worries that Keats's self-effacing public persona has lessened his influence. Characterizing his ineffectiveness at self-promotion as a lack of authoritative 'thunder', Barrett challenges his alleged hypersensitivity by transforming it into intuitive power:

> Much of the verse of the day [is] rather poetic than poetry, rather tuneful that music … . Keats—yes—Keats—*he* WAS a poet. But Jove is recognized by his thunder. A true true poet, from his first words to his last, when he said he 'felt the daisies growing over him'. Poor Keats! Do you know, did I ever tell you, that Mr Horne was at school with [Keats] & that they were intimate friends? 'The divine Keats'—he says of him—and will not hear the common tale, which I for one thought deteriorative to the dead poet's memory, that he suffered himself to be slain outright & ingloriously by the Quarterly reviewer's tomahawk. No,

[12] Elizabeth Barrett Browning to John Kenyon, August 1844, Browning Letters, Baylor University Libraries Digital Collections, accessed 7 July 2018, http://digitalcollections.baylor.edu/cdm/ref/collection/ab-letters/id/30124.

[13] Barrett Browning, *Early Diary*, p. 141.

> said Mr Horne to me once—'He was already bending over his grave in sweet & solemn contemplation, when the satyrs *hoofed* him into it'.[14]

Certainly Mitford, Barrett, and her friend, the poet Richard Hengist Horne, all knew of the charge that Keats was, in Byron's words, 'killed off by one critique'.[15] The accusation, popularized in *Don Juan* and based on Percy Shelley's claim, in a 17 April 1821 letter to Byron, that Keats had 'died lately in Rome from the consequences of breaking a blood-vessel, in paroxysms of despair at the contemptuous attack on his book in the *Quarterly Review*', was well known.[16] As Susan Wolfson tells it, in the contest over Keats's legacy, 'excesses of defense courted parody. While Keats's friends were bonding in sympathy, another circuit was forming, bonded by ridicule.'[17]

Yet, on Barrett's account, intuition rescues Keats from the deadly pitfalls associated with his sensitivity to censure. Almost twenty years after Byron's insult, Horne's story takes power from the bullying 'satyrs' by emphasizing not that Keats was dying anyway but that he *knew* he was. Horne implies that a poet who is conscious of his impending mortality might unattach from life while still living, might 'contemplate' 'sweet[ly] & solemn[ly]' his grave. By including Horne's story, Barrett honors Keats's legacy while retroactively granting him the opportunity to make choices, to be an agent in the life he has left to live. Her addition of Joseph Severn's account of Keats having 'felt the daisies' furthers this suggestion, giving Keats foresight about his demise in order to reclaim the narrative of his critical erasure.

That Keats's poems endure in spite of his lack of masculine-coded egotism Barrett implies in her invocation of Jove, whose thunder, like William Wordsworth's ego, draws attention to itself by dint of strength and volume. By comparison, Keats's modesty is a form of weakness. Yet, assuming that the difference between partial and fully realized artistic expression lies in essence rather than completeness, Barrett attributes to Keats's life and works a power that persists in spite of the limited time he had to develop his craft. Keats was 'an individual man from the beginning', she claims, who 'spoke with his own voice';[18] he wrote 'poems of endurant construction' because he was a 'true

[14] Elizabeth Barrett Browning to Mary Russell Mitford, 26 October 1841, Browning Letters, Baylor University Libraries Digital Collections, accessed 7 July 2018, http://digitalcollections.baylor.edu/cdm/ref/collection/ab-letters/id/25836.

[15] Lord Byron, *Don Juan*, ed. T. G. Steffan, E. Steffan and W. W. Pratt (London: Penguin, 1973). Canto XI, stanza 60, line 1: p. 412.

[16] Percy Shelley, *The Letters of Percy Bysshe Shelley*, ed. Frederick L. Jones. 2 vols. (Oxford: Oxford University Press, 1964), II: p. 284.

[17] Susan Wolfson, 'Keats Enters History', in *Keats and History*, ed. Nicholas Roe (Cambridge: Cambridge University Press, 1995), p. 28.

[18] Barrett Browning to Kenyon, August 1844.

true poet'.[19] In this, the tautological accent, Barrett again adopts something of the form she means to elevate. While Keats's physical health may have been subject to forces outside his control, his poetic character has a forcefulness all its own. In this proleptic theory of poetic genius, leaning into a tragic future becomes a sign of authenticity, transforming the decorousness that her friend Jane Welsh Carlyle will attribute, sometime later, to Keats's 'want of thought for thought', into a prophecy only possible of being 'dreamed by some "animosus infans", like Keats himself'.[20] In Barrett's account, Keats is neither submissive nor effeminate, but visionary. Her portrayal is not of 'weak ego boundaries' but of powerful, 'divine' individuality: a characterization that unites Keatsian intuition and agency without the impressionability so often ascribed to negative capability.

Mysteries and Doubts: Foretelling the Poet's Death

Stereotypes about female intuition can be traced to Enlightenment distinctions between masculine reason and feminine sensitivity. In Immanuel Kant's *Observations on the Feeling of the Beautiful and the Sublime* (1764), for instance, women are naturally inclined towards 'beautiful' forms of understanding, which include sympathy, 'a stronger innate feeling' for decoration and adornment, 'good-heartedness', 'compassion', and an affinity for knowledge that comes easily, that is not 'strived' after.[21] Women are the passive receivers of that which they know; men the active pursuers, suited for '[d]eep reflection', 'long drawn out consideration', and '[l]aborious learning and painful grubbing' after knowledge that is 'useful' (p. 36). Mellor's *Romanticism and Gender* (1988) brings principled feminism and insight into the performativity of gender to an account of 'masculine and feminine Romanticism' that, nonetheless, defines its terms similarly. For Mellor, the masculine Romantic subject is self-contained and active, while feminine 'subjectivity [is] constructed in relation to other subjectivities, hence [the feminine Romantic subject] is fluid, absorptive, responsive, with permeable ego boundaries' (p. 209). Supported by Homans in 'Keats Reading Women, Women Reading Keats', the notion that Keats's passive receptiveness marks him as feminine has been variously interpreted.[22]

[19] Barrett Browning to Mitford, 26 October 1841.

[20] Elizabeth Barrett Browning to Robert Browning, 9 September 1845, Browning Letters, Baylor University Libraries Digital Collections, accessed 7 July 2018, http://digitalcollections.baylor.edu/cdm/ref/collection/ab-letters/id/2186.

[21] Immanuel Kant, *Observations on the Feeling of the Beautiful and Sublime and Other Writings*, ed. Patrick Frierson and Paul Guyer (Cambridge: Cambridge University Press, 2011), pp. 35–6.

[22] For Mellor, Keats is an 'ideological cross-dresser' whose poetry, as well as his self-presentation, transgresses the male–female binary. See 'Ideological Cross-Dressing' in

Homans's essay begins by noting how the poet Adrienne Rich interprets Keats's negative capability as a sign of a gendered allegiance, in a dialogue that is also the oft-cited twenty-first-century conversation to which I alluded above.[23] In a discussion between Rich and Barbara Charlesworth Gelpi about the feminist psychoanalyst Nancy Chodorow, Rich proposes that Chodorow's concept of women's 'so-called "weak ego boundaries"' might have something to do with Keats:

> [weak ego boundaries] might be a negative way of describing the fact that women have tremendous powers of intuitive identification and sympathy with other people. And, yes, a woman could get totally lost in that? She can lose all sense of her own ego, but that is not necessary? It might be a source of power.
> BCG: John Keats had weak ego boundaries.
> AR: Negative capability. Exactly. Any artist has to have it to some extent. … The male ego, which is described as the strong ego, could really be the weak ego, because it encapsulates itself.[24]

Rich turns the weak/strong distinction on its head, claiming that a truly stronger ego would withstand the permeability of its limits. A bounded ego, which is also, for Rich, a masculine-coded ego, 'encapsulates' itself as protection against the forces of sympathetic identification with other people.[25] As Homans interprets it, Rich and Gelpi thereby 'align' themselves with a more open, and ultimately more powerful state of mind: 'an egoless receptiveness they see as feminine'.[26] Given these distinctions, Homans is quick to point out, Gelpi's nod to Keats is apt: many of Keats's letters would appear to align him with such ego-permeable impressionability. In an 1818 letter, for instance, Keats embellishes his account of a recent bout of indolence by evocatively comparing himself to the 'feminine flower' who gets pleasure from the busy attendance of the bee (*LJK*, I: p. 232).

Although the letters shed retroactive light on Keats's clever, sometimes anxious, and often ego-driven self-reflexiveness amongst his friends, nineteenth-century observers outside of that circle would likely not have known of Keats's

Romanticism and Gender, pp. 171–212. For a response to Mellor and Homans, see Wolfson's discussion in *Borderlines*, pp. 282–3. For a discussion of Keats's *active* use of passivity, see Carmen Faye Mathes, '"Let us not therefore go hurrying about": Towards an Aesthetics of Passivity in Keats's Poetics', *European Romantic Review*, 25: 3 (2014), pp. 309–18.

23 Homans, 'Keats Reading Women', pp. 343–5.

24 Quoted in Homans, 'Keats Reading Women', p. 343.

25 Homans, 'Keats Reading Women', p. 343. For an alternative reading of Keats's embodied impressionability, see Jonathan Mulrooney, 'Keats's Avatar', *European Romantic Review*, 22: 3 (2011), pp. 313–21.

26 Homans, 'Keats Reading Women', p. 345.

private jokes. As we have seen, Barrett was well acquainted with his uneven public reception and fraught self-presentation in *Endymion*'s 'Preface', and this informs the admiring resistance with which she discusses his legacy. On the heels of Keats's death, however, Letitia Elizabeth Landon (who seems to have had access to the same materials as Barrett) offers a strong counterpoint. Neither critical nor disappointed, on 15 May 1822 Landon tells an unidentified correspondent, a Mr. Richards, that her 'admiration for Keats is greater than ever. I have read his Lamia his Endymion "that sweetest of sweet songs for ever new" with perfect ethusiasm [*sic*]'.[27] The occasion for the letter appears to have been an attempt to solicit a poem or two from Landon, following Keats's death on 23 February 1821. While she officially declines the offer, demurring, 'It would be evincing more vanity than I really possess, were I to enroll my slight expression of admiration among the bright tributes he has received from the masterspirits of the age', she nevertheless includes, against her 'rule … of never allowing my manuscripts to be read', two poems in the return envelope: 'one sonnet, and the lines to his picture'.[28] According to F. J. Sypher, the sonnet remains untraced, but attached to the archival transcript is a newspaper clipping of Landon's 'Lines on Seeing a Portrait of Keats', from the 12 September 1824 issue of *The Examiner* (p. 10). The suggestion here, of the desire to canonize Keats overcoming Landon's reticence about sharing drafts, is also the implication of Landon as a first responder in the Keats legacy debates. Alongside Percy Shelley and Byron, Landon's 'lines to his picture' sets the stage for the vision of Keats as immature genius to which Hunt, Mary Shelley, and Barrett also respond. By eulogizing an 'inward looking' Keats, whose intuitive powers let him disengage from the world, the poem also aligns acclamatory Landon with judicious Barrett, figuring a Keats whose self-contained attitude challenges Rich and Gelpi's gendered characterization of his ego as 'strong', in the sense of its feminine-coded receptiveness.

'Lines on Seeing a Portrait of Keats' is a poem about a future-haunted present, one just barely passed, for Landon, along with Keats and his melancholy prescience. Landon's ekphrastic elegy twirls round its subject, limning a spiral of 'dark curls' and heavy thoughts, which 'hang o'er' a poet who likewise bends under the weight of his own mortality. Three repetitions of 'hang(s) o'er' in the first nine lines turn innocent curls into an encircling, foregone conclusion:

> The dark curls cluster round thy graceful head,
> And hang o'er thy pale forehead, where the mind

[27] *Letters by Letitia Elizabeth Landon*, ed. F. J. Sypher (Ann Arbor, MI: Scholars' Facsimiles & Reprints, 2001), p. 10.

[28] *Letters*, ed. Sypher, p. 10.

Her visible temple hath; upon thy lip
Is throned a rich and melancholy smile,
So sad, it seems prophetic of the doom
That hangs o'er thy young life, and thine eye wears
An inward look where outward things but pass
Unnoticed: thou dost hold communion with
Thoughts dark and terrible; a blight hangs o'er
The spring flowers of thy youth; the seeds of death
Are sown within thy bosom, and there is
Upon thee consciousness of fate. The light
That lingers on thy face is as a star,
The last remaining one, a shadowy beam
Of those which have been. Ardent hopes were thine,
Dreams of the laurel and of high renown,
Ere health departed; and on thy wan lip
And hope-forsaken cheek a spirit burns,
Which will not wholly pass till in the grave.
I looked upon thee, youthful minstrel! thou
Wert like the lovely presence of a dream;
Such shapes as come when, o'er the sleeper's brain,
The memory floats of some wild, saddening tale;
And he has slept, his inmost spirit filled
With sorrow's beautiful imaginings,
Or as th' Endymion of thine own sweet song.
I look'd upon thy open brow, and felt
Almost an interest like to life in thee;
Thine influence is upon the heart; thou can'st
Awaken such sweet sympathies, we think
Of youth, of genius, gathered like the rose
In the first blushing of its purple morn;
Of a bright harp, whose chords for aye are mute,
But whose rich breathings are remembered still;
Whose tone can never be forgotten.

Landon's Keats understands his impending death. Observing the portrait,[29]

[29] The portrait in question is a mystery. Joseph Severn's miniature of Keats was exhibited at the Royal Academy in May 1819 (*LJK*, II: p. 48, n. 4). While it is possible that Letitia Elizabeth Landon saw it there (she was in Old Brompton at the time), in a 1819 letter Keats attests that, amidst the images on display, 'a drop of water in the ocean is a Miniature' (II: p. 48). Even were Landon to have visited the exhibition, her chances of seeing it and recalling it in detail several years later seem low. Grant Scott thinks Landon's poem is likely 'what John Hollander calls a "notional ekphrasis", or a verbal representation of an

she sees in him a 'consciousness of fate': knowledge that 'the seeds of death / Are sown within [his] bosom'. For Landon, as for Percy Shelley, Hunt, Barrett, and others, this myth of Keats's ever-dying youth shaped a life and its poetry. In *Adonais*, Shelley suggests that the specter of death hovered closely enough that it drained an essential quality from Keats's life: the 'youngest, dearest one has perished / The nursling … who grew / Like a pale flower … / … fed with true-love tears' (lines 46–50). Keats's failure to ripen, Shelley intimates, is both a physical and poetical affliction. Replaced by a flower of ghostlike color and sentimental appetite, the nursling poet was never fated to mature, but to sip palely on unrequited love.

Landon's 'pale forehead' recalls Shelley's 'pale flower'; yet, even as she encourages the myth of Keats's ever-dying youth, Landon does not judge him harshly for it. Instead, she finds in the portrait's highlights and shading an animating incandescence: a 'light', a 'shadowy beam', or a 'spirit' that 'burns' and illuminates the poet like a dream of himself. Rich with 'sorrow's beautiful imaginings', this vision of Keats is also a vision of Endymion, another beautiful dreamer: Landon likens the portrait to 'Endymion of thine own sweet song'. Collapsing the distinction between poet and poetic character, Landon feels their 'influence … upon the heart' as 'sweet sympathies' 'Awaken' in her. Newly energized by the fantasy, she offers another, curlicue figure, one that is neither a delicate coiffure nor a vision of 'doom', but rather an emblem of 'youth, of genius, gathered like the rose'. Here, twining petals turn encircling death into a budding renewal, casting Keats not as 'pale flower' but as vital one. The 'seeds of death' blossom into the flower of legacy, one whose petals coil together what will become the twin tenets of Keats's affirmative reputation: youth and genius. Intuition here impels a creative melancholy that becomes a form of agency, allowing Keats to turn 'sorrow's beautiful imaginings' into a legacy that 'can never be forgotten'. Landon's poem therefore offers the suggestion of a connection between Keats's intuition about death and his poetic ego, or between prescience and legacy building.

In 'Lines', intuition about death is generative. Landon establishes Keats's foreknowledge as productive of the introverted mindset of a literary genius, whose ambitions were grand: 'the laurel and high renown'. Motivated by this desire for poetic accolades, his impending mortality compels Keats to pursue, self-interestedly, his poetry. Yet, it is Landon's (female) speaker—approaching her subject with a perspective recognizable as a kind of negative capability—who

imagined work of visual art'. As Susan Wolfson pointed out to me, an earlier version of Landon's poem was published in *Literary Gazette* on 15 May 1824, and its portrayal of Keats contains some notable differences, strengthening the notion that the portrait is a fiction. For their help in my pursuit of answers to this question, many thanks to Wolfson, Scott, Beth Lau, David Latané, and Julie Watt.

receives impressions from Keats's verse. Inward-turning Keats remains bounded by the poem's encircling imagery, including the 'gathered' rose, which is a figure both delicate and self-contained. Thus Landon's suggestion of a fragile but 'encapsulated' ego fits Rich and Gelpi's definition of masculine-coded *weakness*, not feminine-coded strength, and in so doing Landon upends the revisionary characterization of Keats's ego as strong, feminine-coded, and open.

Egotistical Decline: 'that strong excepted soul'

While neither Barrett nor Landon was likely to have known about negative capability *per se*, a combination of Keats's reputation and poetry does seem to have suggested links between the sensitivity they associate with Keats and his foresight about his own death. According to Barrett, Keats's genius goes unrecognized because of his inability to self-aggrandize, but his true poetic nature grants him insight about his death. Similarly, Landon sees Keats's 'consciousness of fate' reflected in his 'open brow'. Making the poet's 'weak ego-boundaries' responsible for empathic understandings uniquely available to women, however, appears only later. For Rich and Gelpi, women's ways of being in the world are keyed to a negatively capable psychology of creativity-inducing receptiveness. That this understanding hangs on negative capability's formulation of artistic inspiration through the openness made possible by not knowing ('being in uncertainties, Mysteries, doubts') disrupts the potential through-line from nineteenth-century women to those of the present day. While it seems clear that, even before negative capability was an available referent, the threads of Keats's sensitivity and intuitive powers were already spinning together, the characterizations of Keats's intuition and egotism from Landon and Barrett are nevertheless extremely limited in their ability to presage more recent interest in the female subject and the psychology of negative capability.[30]

Yet there is a final sally to be made. If taking control of one's life and posthumous reception is a proto-feminist cause, then Landon and Barrett apply themselves to its realization on Keats's behalf. There is a pattern of encircling imagery that runs through Landon's, Barrett's, *and* Rich and Gelpi's accounts, which might be seen to protect Keats from censure. Reading backwards Rich and Gelpi's male 'encapsulated ego' onto Landon's 'inward turn' illuminates a Keats whose egotism has nothing to do with passivity: it would be weak, yes,

[30] The gendering of negative capability as feminine (and even feminist) by Rich and Gelpi reflects instead changing conceptions of gender. This in turn helps explain the terminological slipperiness that undergirds this supposed alliance, and which Wolfson casts as a dismaying elision: Rich 'miss[es] the male definition of negative capability ("Man of Achievement") and never note[s] that Keats's attitude towards women of genius, and views, and achievement … was hostile' (*Borderlines*, p. 282).

but in the sense of strongly masculine-coded. While our current interpretations of impressionable Keats might not square with this assessment (Jonathan Mulrooney's Spinozist reconsideration of Keats's 'camelion poet' letter, for instance), the nineteenth-century women's desire to give posthumous Keats choice and agency might also have necessitated drawing borderlines around him.

For Barrett (now Browning) in 1856's *Aurora Leigh*, canonizing a Keats who remains unable, egotistically speaking, to canonize himself means redefining the relationship between youth and poetic power.[31] Through the perspective of the verse novel's eponymous speaker, Barrett Browning allies Keats with other well-established poets, including the decidedly more thunderous Byron:

> By Keats's soul, the man who never stepped
> In gradual progress like another man,
> But, turning grandly on his central self,
> Ensphered himself in twenty perfect years
> And died, not young,—(the life of a long life,
> Distilled to a mere drop, falling like a tear
> Upon the world's cold cheek to make it burn
> For ever;) by that strong excepted soul,
> I count it strange, and hard to understand,
> That nearly all young poets should write old;
> That Pope was sexagenarian at sixteen,
> And beardless Byron academical,
> And so with others. (lines 1003–15)

Here the 'excepted soul' reinforces Keats's extraordinariness and establishes him firmly within the English literary canon. Alongside Pope and Byron, Keats is one whose writerly maturity exceeded his physical age, perhaps owing to wisdom that is innate (found in his 'central self') rather than gained, Wordsworth-like, through 'gradual progress'. Similar to Landon, the inward cast of the young poet's mind signals his capacity for profound poetic insight.

At the same time, from Aurora Leigh's perspective, that 'nearly all young poets' 'write old' is curious; Keats's exceptionality throws into relief the oddity of such widespread poetic maturity. Rather than similarities of upbringing or experience, she suggests, these young poets must share an attunement to the suprasensible. Whether 'in trance, to attain to clairvoyance' or through a 'melancholy' divine inspiration (lines 1017, 1021), Leigh describes poetic mindsets that map easily onto Keats's 'ensphered' creative life. Of course,

[31] Elizabeth Barrett Browning, *Aurora Leigh*, ed. Kerry McSweeney (Oxford: Oxford University Press, 2008).

such fantastic perceptibility is also tenuous. For Leigh, it does not take much for lived experience to sully the 'vision'. Like Hunt, and like Barrett in her earlier letters, Leigh resolves this quandary not by elevating the poets' literary achievements but by collapsing the distinction between poetry that is good and poetry that is true: 'I wrote / False poems, like the rest, and thought them true. / Because myself was true in writing them' (lines 1023–4). Those poets, such as Keats, who are true to themselves, she claims, can write bad verse that still counts as true poetry.

For Barrett Browning, the simultaneous elevation of Keats and depreciation of his poems reveals the interpretive space that such an approach to his legacy offered. By allowing readers to mourn the legacy that *might have been*, should a poet as exceptional as Keats have matured, the 'strong excepted soul' uncouples his legacy from any momentary, personal disappointment in his poetry. Moreover, and without explicitly declaring Keats in possession of foreknowledge about his death, the speculations about what makes a true poet in *Aurora Leigh* acquaint the two sides of its story. Where Keats's encapsulated egotism and prophetic–poetic powers collide, his juvenile poems transform, becoming the imperfect literary outputs of a creative life perfectly 'distilled'. The characterization of a Keats in possession of his own life rather than as the pitiable object of the winds of chance depends upon tragic foresight. Thus his intuition becomes a way forward, a means of positioning him as a 'strong soul' amongst the strong egos of the age.

Considered alongside the famously caustic negativity of Keats's early reception, the accounts of Mary Shelley, Barrett, and Landon reveal the admiring resistance that shapes their approaches to his legacy and to the legacy-building projects of others. Landon, the least overtly critical of the three, offers the first connection, in 1822/24, between Keats's tragic foresight and the forms and functions of his poetic ego, towards a discussion of what recent scholars identify as his feminine-coded, negatively capable way of being in the world. Yet if the openness Landon imagines presages that allegedly feminine trait, the 'weak ego boundary', then the extent to which intuition and impressionability together shape Keats's reception later in the century should reveal his lack of masculine-coded egotism. Instead, granting Keats power over the life he has left to live, Barrett's letters of the 1840s and her later poem *Aurora Leigh* depict the poet as wise beyond his years, contemplative of his own death, and preternaturally talented. The 'ensphered' life, like the 'inward turn' and the 'encapsulated ego', protects itself against outside forces, but is also generative: a space in which to 'distill' a perfectly lived creative life.

Part Two

'examplified throughout': Forms of Negatively Capable Reading

Chapter Five

Negatively Capable Reading

Cassandra Falke

It is difficult to define the kind of knowledge one gains from literature. A reader may encounter new concepts that facilitate the organization of future knowledge or new facts that affect the perception of history, but these forms of learning do not seem to capture what is most meaningful about a reading experience. Through the reading of science or history or philosophy we acquire forms of knowledge that are certain, explicable, and sharable, but what we learn from literature calls for another way of speaking. The knowledge literature gives is ineffable, experienced as an event. Bounded by the stability of the text and the contingency of a reader's circumstances, an act of reading nevertheless opens an infinity within these limits, like the infinity between zero and one.

In order to enable a way of talking about this ineffable, experiential knowledge, this essay juxtaposes the writings of contemporary phenomenologist Jean-Luc Marion and romantic period poet John Keats. As unlikely as this pairing may seem, both Keats and Marion offer concepts that clarify the means through which reading grants knowledge that exceeds certainty. As Marion says, some 'kinds of knowledge' could be

> described as noncertain, but should not be considered as *un*certain, because the indetermination here plays the role of a *positive* qualification of that which is to be known. … In a word, certitude sometimes constitutes an *obstacle* to the true knowledge of certain phenomena.[1]

Literature's knowledge is noncertain. A predeterminative expectation that a work could grant its readers only factual or conceptual knowledge would be

[1] Jean-Luc Marion, *Negative Certainties*, trans. Stephen E. Lewis (Chicago, IL: University of Chicago, 2015), p. 206. Emphasis in the original.

the sort of obstacle that Marion describes. And yet scholars and readers still lack a vocabulary for discussing the noncertain knowledge that literary readers receive. Keats recognized this when he proposed the term 'negative capability' to describe the capacity poets have to let themselves be overwhelmed by the otherness of the work they are creating. Shakespeare, he says, exemplifies this capacity because he is a man who 'is capable of being in uncertainties, Mysteries, doubts, without any irritable reaching after fact & reason' (*LJK*, I: p. 193). Such a capacity allows a certain recognition that some insight has been achieved without needing to define that insight in a determinative way. Christina Gschwandtner points out that Descartes's concept of *intuitus* provides an important precedent for Marion's noncertain knowledge.[2] Marion himself gestures toward Augustine and Kant as precursors (pp. 42, 6). I would like to suggest that the concept of negative certainty also has an unrecognized precedent in romantic literature and that Keats's articulation of negative capability provides the most explicit example.

By using Shakespeare as his example of negative capability, Keats hints that it might be a quality that creators of art alone can obtain, or that they can develop negative capability to an extent that readers or viewers of art never can. After all, ten months after his contemplation on negative capability, Keats returns to the question of porous selfhood and creativity and develops the idea of the 'camelion Poet' (*LJK*, I: p. 387) with no mention of a 'camelion' reader. Nevertheless, he writes that negative capability is an attribute of 'a Man of Achievement especially in Literature' (*LJK*, I: p. 193), which suggests a broader category of person than just poets. If tolerance for mystery in a reader or viewer is also a form of negative capability, then perhaps it can be expanded through encounters with art in which the viewer or reader lets him or herself be overwhelmed by the intense experience that a work offers. Although many critics have assumed that negative capability is possible for both the creator and receiver of a work of art, Marion's phenomenological language makes it possible to describe with greater precision the characteristics of what might be called a 'negatively capable reader'. The remainder of this essay explores negative capability in reading in three stages. The first introduces two phenomenological concepts that Marion has articulated—saturated phenomenality and negative certainty. The second considers Keats's description of negative capability in light of the vocabulary these concepts provide. The final section turns to two of Keats's poems—'On First Looking into Chapman's Homer' and 'This living hand'—and shows how they exemplify and invite negatively capable reading.

[2] Christina Gschwandtner, 'Marion and Negative Certainty', *Philosophy Today*, 56: 3 (2012), p. 365.

Marion's Phenomenology and Overwhelming Acts of Reading

A collection of responses to his work published in 2007 confidently asserts that Jean-Luc Marion is 'unarguably ... the leading figure in French phenomenology'.[3] Ian James credits him with 'redefin[ing] the terms of philosophical debate in France in the wake of deconstruction and the 'death of the subject'.[4] To a large extent, this recognition is based on Marion's description of saturated phenomenality. Nevertheless, literary scholars are not broadly familiar with Marion or the idea of saturated phenomenality. Since it provides a way of describing an event of reading without imposing the limitations of certainty, the concept of saturated phenomenality offers a great deal of (as yet) untapped potential. Marion began defining the concept in the 1990s, but published his most complete exploration of the term in France in 2001. In 2002, it appeared in English as *In Excess: Studies in Saturated Phenomena*. Marion has returned to the concept in several works since, emphasizing the everydayness and 'The Banality of Saturation' in an essay of that title from 2007. He explores the implications of saturated phenomenality for subjectivity in *Being Given* (1997, trans. 2002) and *The Erotic Phenomenon* (2003, trans. 2007).

Marion explains that phenomenology has traditionally taken account of only two of the three possible combinations of intuition and intentionality that make up our phenomenal experience of the world. 'Intuition', within phenomenology, refers to the givenness of experience, that which appears to perception, whether it be a physically present object such as a cup of coffee or an imaginatively present intuition, like the cup of coffee I wish I had but do not. 'Intentionality' refers to the manner of attention that a perceiver turns toward intuition and can be characterized in a variety of ways, including by its intensity, duration, dispersion among multiple phenomena, and conceptual assumptions that shape intuition's manner of appearing. Marion points out that phenomenology has traditionally investigated either phenomena in which intuition fails to fill the intentionality turned toward it, sometimes called 'common-law phenomena', or phenomena in which intuition perfectly fills intentionality, an occurrence most easily recognizable in mathematics. In contrast to both common-law phenomenality and the rarer phenomena in which intuition and intentionality exhaust each other, Marion draws attention to phenomena in which what is given overwhelms the intentionality we turn toward them. These phenomena, he says, saturate our intentionality with intuition. They dazzle us, overwhelm us and leave us changed.

[3] Kevin Hart, ed., *Counter-Experiences: Reading Jean-Luc Marion* (Notre Dame, IN: University of Notre Dame Press, 2007).

[4] Ian James, *The New French Philosophy* (Cambridge: Polity, 2012), p. 18.

Saturated phenomena are not rare, but may go unnoticed if the perceiving subject fails to admit the excess of experience that a saturated event offers. All objects, Marion suggests, offer themselves to be experienced as events, and to the extent that they are, we experience them as saturated. Our intention could never adequately contain an accurate prediction of how they would unfold, and our memory, the intentionality we turn to them after the event, can never recapture everything an event offered. Clearly some events are more fully saturated than others, and likewise some events of reading are more fully saturated than others, but literary texts always offer in themselves the possibility of a high level of saturation because of their hermeneutic richness. When welcomed by a reader, the event of reading can be transformative in that it expands the reader's capacity to take in future experiences by enriching the intentionality available for them.

In developing the concept of 'negative certainty', Marion finds a way to think about these phenomena as unconditional, categorically unknowable and yet secured in their possibility by the fact that they are unfolding all the time. These are phenomena that one 'sees only by first responding to them' (p. 188) because we have to open ourselves to their temporally bound phenomenal appearing according to the conditions set by the phenomena themselves. Even though we cannot say with certainty *what* we learn after reading, viewing, or hearing a work of art, if we were open as readers or viewers to being in the mystery of a work then, after seeing or reading a work, we do know that our future experiences will be predicated on having already experienced the expansion of horizons brought about by that prior encounter with art. Marion's *Negative Certainties* (2010, trans. 2015) contends that saturated phenomena demand that we rethink the epistemological assumptions underlying our search for objective or certain knowledge. Because experiences of art, or love, or even simply the experience of embodiment defy our ability to think about them categorically, they cannot be known certainly. Nevertheless, these experiences do give us knowledge, and in fact they are the experiences that contribute most to the processes of our developing selfhood.

This selfhood, for Marion, is never static and never bounded but always porous with respect to the world. He shies away from even using the words 'subject' or 'self' because they suggest an observable object where none is to be found. This experience of the self that we name selfhood has a fuzzy, in-process lack of definitiveness as one of its defining characteristics, particularly since we recognize it changing through the very process of contemplating it. Marion contends, however, that the 'indefinition of man does not remain undecided and anonymous' (p. 50). He experiences himself through an awareness of the horizon of intentionality that circumscribes the world in every direction as he beholds it. One's self 'is inscribed and developed within the horizon opened by its assignation' (p. 50). This horizon alters as it takes in new experiences. This mobile, outward-looking self becomes the model of negative certainty more generally for Marion. To whatever extent we can be aware of that wavering edge of our perceptive horizons, we can be certain that there is a great deal beyond that horizon.

The negatively certain awareness of something beyond the self's horizon cannot be described using the language of conceptual construction or objective observation because whatever lies just outside a self's horizon will enter it as a phenomenon that, in being experienced, alters the horizon of our perception and gains visibility in reference to other experiences that are themselves non-objective. The self's recognition of a new experience—be it a new physical perception, imaginative flight, or cognitive assimilation—cannot be understood outside of its relationship to the horizon of the perceiving self or its relationship to the other perceptive events that shape its appearing. An act of reading literature exemplifies negative certainty by exposing the boundaries of a reader's horizon even as it reconfigures that horizon. Their essentially temporal nature and tendency to strike us a little differently with every reading draw attention to the non-objective status of reading events. They make us aware of the process of the self's reconfiguration. We can always say that we have never thought about 'x' the way that reading 'z' made us think about it, except that after we have read 'z' that ceases to become true. I had never thought of cricket-song as earth's unceasing cold weather poetry until I read 'On the Grasshopper and the Cricket', and now I can never not have that thought.

Viewing reading as a saturated phenomenon that leads to negative certainty has implications for acts of interpretation that follow the reading experience as well as for the development of readerly habits over the course of a life. First of all, this view of reading implies an infinity of interpretive possibilities without suggesting that all interpretations are valid. The fact that a text imposes on a reader its own positively definable boundaries eliminates some interpretive possibilities. 'On First Looking into Chapman's Homer' is a sonnet, for example, a fact that can be granted more or less priority but never interpreted away. Even so, the interpretive significance of this fact will vary with every act of reading. One time the form's importance may seem to lie in the balance it allows Keats to achieve between his descriptions of reading pre- and post-Chapman. Another time, the rhythmic expectations it sets up may stand out, emphasizing the soft syllables that do not quite assert themselves as iambs. As Keats writes to Reynolds in April of 1817, with each reading some passage must 'come rather new to' a reader 'continually … notwithstandg that we read the same Play [or poem, or novel] forty times' (*LJK*, I: p. 133). The infinite hermeneutical possibilities of a reading act spring forth from within the limits set by the text itself, but spring forth unpredictably nonetheless. This rich potentiality is part of their phenomenal richness.

A second implication of reading for negative certainty is that this openness to half knowledge has to become habitual, otherwise the 'irritable reaching after fact & reason' will reassert itself. If we recognize the presence of so many other interpretive options, any interpretation arrived at necessarily constitutes the kind of 'half knowledge' that Keats says Coleridge could not be content with. The elder poet, Keats writes, 'would let go by a fine isolated verisimilitude caught from the Penetralium of mystery, from being incapable of remaining content with half knowledge' (*LJK*, I: pp. 193–4). A negatively capable reader has to best Coleridge in this, and remain content with 'uncertainties, Mysteries, doubts'. There is a danger here that openness could become mere lethargy. Not reaching after fact and reason could become not reaching at all. The concept of intentionality helps clarify the certainty that a negatively capable reader would reach for, even in the midst of the knowledge that it is unachievable. He will try to expand his intentionality to accommodate all that is offered by a work of art. After many such efforts, he will be all the more certain that his intentionality could never expand to accommodate all of what is intuitively offered in a reading, but the intentionality he turns toward a work will gradually have grown greater. Keats captures this paradox when he writes in a letter to George and Georgiana one year after his negative capability letter: 'The more we know the more inadequacy we discover in the world to satisfy us' (*LJK*, II: p. 18).

Negative Capability and Everyday Saturation

At the beginning of the negative capability letter Keats uses the language of obliteration and intensity that also characterizes Marion's description of saturated phenomenality. Keats laments that Benjamin West's *Death on the Pale Horse*, which he had seen two days before, offers 'nothing to be intense upon; no women one feels mad to kiss; no face swelling into reality'. Keats recounts viewing the painting ready to be overwhelmed. He describes wanting the painting to demand something from him as a viewer—an attentive intensity, a longing to kiss, an accommodation within reality. He continues, saying that 'the excellence of every Art is its intensity, capable of making all disagreeables evaporate, from their being in close relationship with Beauty & Truth' (*LJK*, I: p. 192). 'Disagreeables' might include anything from worries about what a viewer or reader might do after viewing/reading to petty critiques of an artist's formal accomplishment, but they are dispelled as we receive the intensity of a great work. The 'evaporation' of these disagreeables indicates that Keats approaches a work of art ready for the work to take over and alter the intentionality he turns toward it. He not only recognizes but also celebrates saturated phenomenality.

The thought that saturated phenomena might surround us is inspiring. Keats, like Marion, suggests that every day offers opportunities to receive gifts that overwhelm our capacity to take them in. A 'nap upon Clover engenders ethereal finger-pointings', and 'the leaves whisper' lines of poetry. For Keats, reading literature always opens an infinity of imaginative and interpretive possibilities. In 1818, two months after he has defined negative capability, Keats imagines that one could 'read a certain Page of full Poesy or distilled Prose' and 'wander with it, and muse upon it, and reflect from it, and bring home to it, and prophesy upon it, and dream upon it—untill it becomes stale—but when will it do so? Never' (*LJK*, I: p. 231). The list of possible things a reader can do with a page of literature suggests habits that can expand the negative capability Keats celebrates. The poem he includes in the same letter addresses directly what a reader should not do. The lyric speaker is a Thrush who seems to say 'O fret not after knowledge—I have none / And yet my song comes native with the warmth' (I: p. 233). The thrush's receptivity overflows with song, just as Keats pictures his own reception of the morning and its songs overflowing into the poem itself. The song and the poem become acts of receptivity as much as creation. That receptivity, however, is not passive. It wanders, muses, brings home, prophesies, and dreams. It pursues open-ended acts of receptivity and readerly co-creation without foreclosing the possibility of what will arrive by expecting 'knowledge'.

Keats's proliferation of ways one could think about a page of literature and his openness to thrushes, naps, and leaves result from his appreciation of the event-ness of everyday life. Neither leaf nor poem is approached as an object. The distinction between object and event is never absolute. It arises from an act of interpretation that we engage in following a temporally structured encounter with a something. The something—the leaf or poem—can be interpreted in its event-ness with attention to the temporality and contingency of our encounter with it, or it can be conceptually pocketed away as an object. If something that normally appears as an object surprises us, then the event-ness of the object's appearing is more likely to stand out. The leaves' whispering, for example, may awaken Keats's awareness of the event of hearing them because leaves do not always whisper. Even so, Keats's tendency to list possible ways for the givenness of everyday phenomena to break through to him suggests that if the leaves had not whispered to him something else would have. What we wonder at in an event is always to some extent the unexpectedness of its arrival (even if we expected something, like a visit from a friend), but Keats proposes the possibility that we might cultivate the expectation that something unexpected will arrive. With a work of literature, readers decide to create an event through the work by reading it, but make choices before, during, and after the reading that delimit the event-ness of the reading act. In choosing, with Keats, to not only 'reflect from' a work of literature but also wander with and dream upon it, readers can develop the habit of active receptivity that allows new uncertain knowledge to unexpectedly arrive.

A work may surprise a reader into awareness as the leaves surprise Keats with their whisper. Surprise is one of the most common and most recognizable ways in which works of literature overflow the intentionality we turn toward them. Being surprised, we become aware of a work's event-ness. We can also almost describe the event-mental character of what has happened (it surprised me when …), but most of what arises in an event of reading cannot be so easily described without recourse to the language of a work's object-ness. If a line pleases us unaccountably, we typically try to account for it as soon as we begin to describe the event of reading it. In his definition of negative capability, Keats seems to suggest that we might leave it unaccounted for. An event of reading a line will, like all saturated events, remain definitively unaccountable, but a negatively capable reader will only try to account for the event to the extent that that account can testify to all it leaves out. 'On First Looking into Chapman's Homer' exemplifies one significant way to describe an event of negatively capable reading by presenting the reading it describes as indescribable—as vast as the Pacific and as surprising as a new planet.

Lyricizing Negative Capability

Negatively capable reading provides opportunities for criticism—to be less sure of itself, to focus on opening up rather than discounting readerly possibilities—but it also poses a problem. A critic whose work must unfold in stages of logically appreciable argument employing clarifying concepts will struggle to describe the event of reading in a way that reflects the tolerance of mystery that distinguishes negative capability. Whatever it is that inspires a critic's longing to write about a work will normally be lost as that description is crimped and corseted into an academic argument. Keats allows that readers, even critical readers, dream when he says that anyone hoping for a 'pleasant life' could read a page a day and 'dream upon it' (*LJK*, I: p. 231), but he reserves for poets the ability to recount a dream, 'For Poesy alone can tell her dreams' (*PJK*, p. 478). Criticism cannot meet demands for conceptual clarity and also recount a negatively capable reader's acts of dreaming upon and wandering with a text. A critic who hopes to encourage negatively capable reading among others can, at best, articulate the concepts that allow for such a form of reading to be recognized and valued, and then point out the ways that a work invites itself to be experienced. It will then be up to the reader to accept or reject that invitation. In the final section of this essay, I briefly consider two poems that seem to issue particularly strong invitations to negatively capable reading. As both of them are short, I quote them in full.

> Much have I travell'd in the realms of gold,
>   And many goodly states and kingdoms seen;

  Round many western islands have I been
Which bards in fealty to Apollo hold.
Oft of one wide expanse had I been told
  That deep-brow'd Homer ruled as his demesne;
  Yet did I never breathe its pure serene
Till I heard Chapman speak out loud and bold:
Then felt I like some watcher of the skies
  When a new planet swims into his ken;
Or like stout Cortez when with eagle eyes
  He star'd at the Pacific—and all his men
Look'd at each other with a wild surmise—
  Silent, upon a peak in Darien. (*PJK*, p. 64)

In 'On First Looking into Chapman's Homer', Keats contrasts two forms of reading, one that puts the intentionality of the reader in the dominant position, and one that subordinates the reader's intentionality to the intuition offered by the reading experience. Lines 1–6, with their language of free passage from one literary realm to the next, suggest that the will of the reader is in control of where he wanders. He is free to move round western islands and see new kingdoms as he likes. Nothing has arrested his attention sufficiently to make him stop. The foregrounded language of quantity ('much') and directionality ('round') couples with the language of political empowerment to portray the reader's world as one that he has obtained mastery over, at least sufficient mastery to know how to go where he likes with Apollo's approval. But the tone changes in lines seven and eight.

Line seven parallels line one sonically for the first four words ('Much have I travell'd', 'Yet did I never'). The syntax here is identical until the parallel words 'travell'd' and 'never', a pairing which prioritizes the similar sounds in the middle of each word over syntactic similarity. 'Never' shifts the focus from the quantity of experience that the reader/speaker has had to all the experience that he has yet to wander into. The sense that he is in control of the reading experiences available to him falls away. 'Breathe', as Emily Rohrbach notes, shifts the poem's focus toward direct physical experience, a shift that has epistemological implications.[5] That shift marks the beginning of the poem's emphasis on contingency rather than the pursuit of mastery over one's own experiences. After line seven, the language of spatial navigation ('round', 'expanse') gives way to temporal language ('Till', 'Then', 'When', 'when'). This alters the poem's power dynamic, as time is not, like realms and islands on a map, something one can navigate. It happens *to* us. The temporal focus of the

[5] Emily Rohrbach, *Modernity's Mist: British Romanticism and the Poetics of Anticipation* (New York: Fordham University Press, 2016), p. 62.

poem's second half draws attention to the factors outside of a reader's control. The passing of time is given, and a literary text's control of the reader's time is one way that it expresses intentionality toward us. Temporality is part of a literary work's counter-intentionality. The last six lines of Keats's sonnet focus almost exclusively on the reader's yielding of his own intentionality to make way for the experiences that reading Chapman's Homer offers, an experience that, as a saturated phenomenon, he could not anticipate beforehand, cannot adequately capture in the present, and will not be able to fully re-enact through memory afterwards.

Both of the similes for reading—watching the sky for a new planet or discovering a new expansive sea—evoke experiences of saturated phenomenality. Even if an astronomer were watching the skies intentionally for a new planet, he or she could not anticipate the sight itself, not only because the angle, color, or brightness expected might have been wrong but more profoundly because such an experience startles the observer with his or her own insignificance and lack of control in the world. The watcher *can* only watch. Similarly, although Cortez is portrayed as 'eagle-eyed', he is reduced to staring and silence when confronted with his belated view of the Pacific. Cortez, his men, and the watcher of the skies have their intentionality directed toward that which surprises them. New planets and new seas do not surprise them with something they did not expect. They surprise them with something that their expectations prove inadequate to contain. The reader implied by these two similes likewise reaches for and opens Chapman's Homer with a general expectation of what could be found there, but the event of reading that takes place, like the unrulable ocean or unrulable sky, breaks through the expectations he had to overwhelm him with its intuitive givenness.

The givenness of the event of reading, as presented in this sonnet, evokes images associated with the sublime, that territory of aesthetic experience experienced first as unknowable and uncontainable. Skies, seas, and mountains, all present here, consistently function as allegories for the vastness of what escapes or surprises an observer's perceptive attention in period descriptions of the sublime.[6] The concept of saturated phenomenality does not contradict the concept of the sublime, but in fact radicalizes it. For Marion, there is no after-the-fact metacognitive reconciliation of a sublime experience to reason as there is for Kant (p. 88). Keats's poem, explicitly hinting at a Marionian radicality, closes with no Kantian reconciliation to reason. The planet is a new planet, which cannot be described according to characteristics other than its

[6] Immanuel Kant, *Critique of Judgement*, ed. Nicholas Walker, trans. James Meredith (Oxford: Oxford University Press, 2007), p. 86; Edmund Burke, *A Philosophical Enquiry into the Origins of the Sublime and the Beautiful*, ed. David Womersley (London: Penguin, 1998), pp. 102, 114.

novelty. Keats uses the word 'ken', which is etymologically related to the Old English verb 'cennan' (to make known). It swims into his field of awareness without him exerting his will. It makes itself known, or to put it in phenomenological terms, the intuition acts, and the intentionality receives. And after that reception, there is no further comment on the planet that might position it securely within the sky-watcher's conceptual apparatus. The lack of reason-driven conclusion is even more apparent in the second simile. Although the line does fill out a full pentameter of beats, it is visibly shorter than all the other lines, hinting that there is nothing more one can say. It ends by describing the position of the men, offering no claim to try to describe or rationalize the Pacific. Their surmise is wild and silent.

The final poem that I will consider does not describe an act of negatively capable reading as 'Chapman's Homer' does, but addresses the reader directly and demands such an act. By imagining the possibility of speaking from eternity to a mortal reader, 'This living hand' draws its poignancy from the ultimate limits of horizonality, which is the temporal bound of our life and the spatial bound of our body.

> This living hand, now warm and capable
> Of earnest grasping, would, if it were cold
> And in the icy silence of the tomb,
> So haunt thy days and chill thy dreaming nights
> That thou would wish thine own heart dry of blood,
> So in my veins red life might stream again,
> And thou be conscience-calm'd. See, here it is—
> I hold it towards you. (*PJK*, p. 503)

Without hands and without sight, this poem bids the reader imagine the warmth of a grasp, the chiasmic touch that Merleau-Ponty uses to describe the paradox of our situatedness in the world, where we both feel and feel that we are felt. As one hand grasps another, it is both tangible for the other hand and touching. We can be aware of both phenomena, but not focus on them both simultaneously: 'Through this crisscrossing within it of the touching and the tangible, its own movements incorporate themselves into the universe they interrogate'.[7] The transition between these two simultaneous and co-dependent phenomena come to stand, in Merleau-Ponty's late essay, for the interaction that a subject has with the world more broadly. We know ourselves to be feeling the touch of the world in the intuition granted us, and also understand that we touch the world, that it makes room for us. For

[7] Maurice Merleau-Ponty, *Maurice Merleau-Ponty: Basic Writings*, ed. Thomas Baldwin (London: Routledge, 2004), p. 251.

Keats the grasping hand dramatizes the possibility of two people transitioning between feeling and being felt by the other, where one could even go so far as wishing one's 'own heart dry of blood', so that the other might pulse again with 'red life'.

The temporality of the poem opens into eternity within the boundaries of the first line's 'now' and the last line's present tense 'hold'. That eternity, from which one could haunt or be dreamt of, posits an intuitive excess that intentionality can never accommodate. In picturing the possibility of an unknowledgeable longing reaching toward the still living narratee to be received, Keats is explicitly working in the realm of impossibility. The claim that he makes on the narratee, that she would wish her heart dry, functions not as a possibility to be enacted or denied but as a gesture toward the communicative power of impossibility itself. Jonathan Culler states clearly the poem's demand on readers:

> We fulfill [its] icy prediction, not by seeking actually to sacrifice our lives that Keats might live, but by losing our empirical lives: forgetting the temporality which supports them and trying to embrace a purely fictional time in which we can believe that the hand is really present and perpetually held toward us through the poem.[8]

In fulfilling that prediction, no facts are revealed, no new concepts formed. The images are grotesque or absurd if they are literally imagined. Consequently, what the poem describes does not add, through fiction, a new possibility to the non-fictional world in the way some novels do. Nothing that can be called certain knowledge passes from imagined speaker to actual reader, and yet reader after reader feels the touch of the poem the way one feels the touch of another hand grasping. It is an intersubjective mediation like that grasping of hands in that one feels oneself both reaching and being reached for. But the other subject here is not another human subject at all, but a text. It would be easy to throw up one's hands in the face of this little lyric and say, 'I don't know why it has this pull on me—it's a mystery', and glorify the tolerance of that mystery in the name of negative capability. But to do so would be to push the poem's outstretched hand away. The effort to reject 'irritable reaching after fact & reason' should not exclude 'be[ing] intense upon' the poem. The concept of negative certainty helps clarify that, in a negatively capable reader's reading, the certainty that the poem has made a claim on you and that you must respond is its own intense kind of knowledge.

[8] Jonathan Culler, *The Pursuit of Signs: Semiotics, Literature, Deconstruction* (Ithaca, NY: Cornell University Press, 1981), p. 154.

Appropriating Keats

This brief attempt to appropriate Keats, anachronistically, into phenomenology contributes to a long tradition of appropriating Keats that exemplifies the negative capability of readers who are attracted to his work. Keats's readers accommodate his ways of thinking and reinterpret it as their own in a way not unlike Shakespeare's allowing himself to be taken over by the developing voice of Lear, or Keats's allowing himself to be taken over by Shakespeare's writing. Adrienne Rich, for example, has identified negative capability as a capacity that all artists must have but that women especially manifest.[9] Eloise Knapp Hay reads negative capability as related to negative theology in the Christian tradition.[10] Sharon Todd connects it to Buddhism.[11] Li Ou's statement that 'negative capability has become part of the general education' in 'literature' might be somewhat optimistic.[12] Nevertheless, the broad cultural currency of the term negative capability, at least within literary studies, testifies to the lasting resonance of Keats's idea. Constant reinterpretation, however, also risks emptying the term of any specific content. If the term negative capability becomes too capacious, it ends up duplicating more general concepts such as 'receptivity' or 'imagination'.

In describing negative capability using phenomenological terminology, my goal has not been to expand the term as much as to tease out its implications for one activity—reading—more completely. The concepts of intentionality, intuition, saturated phenomenality, and negative certitude provide a vocabulary for discussing a phenomenon that most literary readers are familiar with, but that has proven difficult to describe. Andrew Bennett observes that Keats's persistent concern with the possibilities of knowing makes him a kind of epistemologist, but an odd kind, an anti-epistemological one. He defines an epistemologist as 'the kind of person that seeks to know, really to know, what it is like to know, what it is like really to know, and in particular to know that one can know'. He goes on to define Keats as the opposite of this person. What Keats is, he claims, 'or wants to be, is the sort of person … who wants

[9] Adrienne Rich, 'Three Conversations', in *Adrienne Rich's Poetry*, ed. Barbara Charlesworth Gelpi and Albert Gelpi (New York: Norton, 1975), p. 115. See also Susan Wolfson, *Reading John Keats* (Cambridge: Cambridge University Press, 2015), p. 144; and Anne K. Mellor, *Romanticism and Gender* (New York: Routledge, 1993), p. 24.

[10] Eloise Knapp Hay, *T. S. Eliot's Negative Way* (Cambridge, MA: Harvard University Press, 1982).

[11] Sharon Todd, 'Experiencing Change, Encountering The Unknown: An Education In "Negative Capability" In Light Of Buddhism And Levinas', *Journal Of Philosophy Of Education*, 49: 2 (2015), pp. 240–54.

[12] Li Ou, *Keats and Negative Capability* (London: Bloomsbury, 2009), p. 19.

to know, really know, what it is like not to know'.[13] Through the concept of negative certainty, Marion provides a phenomenological vocabulary that recognizes this certainty in not knowing as itself a kind of knowledge. Through the concept of saturated phenomenality, he articulates the process by which negative capability becomes an enabling form of knowledge.

[13] Andrew Bennett, *Ignorance: Literature and Agnoiology* (Manchester: Manchester University Press, 2009).

Chapter Six

Knowledge's 'gordian shape'

Keats and the Disciplines

Kurtis Hessel

Disciplinarity was unkind to John Keats, and the review was its bludgeon. The literary field, elite reviewers, and other poets famously responded to the incursions of an 'uneducated and flimsy stripling' into their midst by attacking his medical training and education.[1] His previous professional commitments, unrefined by medical celebrity and ungilded by a reputation for scientific genius, encouraged critics rhetorically to undermine his poetic legitimacy. Attacking Keats's education, John Gibson Lockhart (under the pseudonym 'Z') wrote disparagingly that both Keats and Leigh Hunt 'write about Apollo, Pan, Nymphs, Muses, and Mysteries, as might be expected from persons of their education' (Z, p. 275). Nicholas Roe argues that these reviews waged a proxy war in the literary press against the politically threatening models of dissenting education embodied in Keats's Enfield School: 'it was Keats's unusual educational background, above all, which served as a focus for [Lockhart's] animosity'.[2] Lockhart dismissed Keats to the apothecary's toiling anonymity: 'It is a better and a wiser thing to be a starved apothecary than a starved poet; so back to the shop Mr John, back to 'plasters, pills, and ointment boxes', &c'. (Z, p. 276). This is a disciplinary dismissal; even if Lockhart subtextually disregards Keats on the basis of the young poet's radical politics, he explicitly claims that Keats's problem is that he lacks the right sort of expertise.[3]

Keats responded by redoubling his commitment to maintaining porous boundaries between medical and poetic practice. Critics have spoken

[1] Z [John Gibson Lockhart], 'Review of *Endymion*', in *Keats's Poetry and Prose*, ed. Jeffrey N. Cox (New York: Norton, 2009), p. 274.

[2] Nicholas Roe, *John Keats and the Culture of Dissent* (Oxford: Clarendon Press, 1997), p. 23.

[3] On the association between the medical profession, radical politics, and dissenting academies see Roe, *Culture of Dissent*, pp. 160–81.

voluminously about how Keats's medical training emerges in his poetry.[4] His characterization of the poet as 'A humanist, physician to all men' in *The Fall of Hyperion* fuses his two professional pursuits (Canto I: line 190). Indeed, as Roe maintains, Keats's responses to the critical drubbing of *Endymion* indicate that he considered his apothecary training and his poetry as intertwined (pp. 168–9). For instance, in an 1819 letter to his brother, Keats wrote, 'I have been at different times turning it in my head whether I should go to Edinburgh & study for a physician', going on to suggest that should he fail in that role it would not be because of an incapacity for the work but because of a distaste for the need to charge fees as a healer (*LJK*, II: p. 70). Later he would remark in a letter to Charles Brown about the *Lamia* volume, 'This shall be my last trial; not succeeding, I shall try what I can do in the Apothecary line' (II: p. 298). Important to note is Keats's assurance that, having left medicine, he could return to it—poetry would not distract from or undermine his medical attainments; in fact, it likely strengthened them.

Though critics have thoroughly attended to the echoes of Keats's medical training in his published poetry, they have not considered the effect of his era's epistemological organization, with its professions and its growing disciplines, on his poetics. In part, this inattentiveness arises from the dispersed and unsystematic character of Keats's theoretical statements, appearing as they do amongst the letters. In this essay, I argue that the concept of negative capability participated doubly in the period's increasingly disciplinary organization of knowledge: it both arose from the plurality of Keats's professional commitments and also served as a conceptual bridge among disciplines. After situating several of Keats's most poetically theoretical letters in a multi-disciplinary context, I turn to reading Keats's *Lamia* as a test case for his vision of negative capability, and I explore how the poem's allegorical dimensions contribute to preserving an experimental space in which Keats brings together diverse species of knowledge. Viewed within the context of the period's proliferating arts and sciences institutions, negative capability and Keatsian allegory both become tools for imagining the reconciliation of different schools of thought.

4 In addition to sources cited throughout this essay, see Donald C. Goellnicht, *The Poet Physician: Keats and Medical Science* (Pittsburgh, PA: University of Pittsburgh Press, 1984) on Keats and the medical sciences. On Keats and Romantic brain science see Alan Richardson, *British Romanticism and the Science of the Mind* (Cambridge: Cambridge University Press, 2001), pp. 114–50, and on the poet's indebtedness to climatological notions of disease see Alan Bewell, *Romanticism and Colonial Disease* (Baltimore, MD: Johns Hopkins University Press, 1999), pp. 161–93.

Negative Capability amid the Arts and Sciences

To fully engage with Keats's concept of negative capability we must consider the intellectual milieu within which it circulated, not in an exclusively literary context but in one influenced by the arts and sciences institutions. Romantic-era writers and audiences witnessed a transformation in the organization and dissemination of scientific and philosophical knowledge in society. The eighteenth century had been characterized by epistemological fluidity: the 'man of science' dabbled in experimental pursuits. His natural philosophical method did not constrain the objects of his scrutiny: he might ponder the geological age of the earth over breakfast, but spend the evening musing on the constituent principles of air, seeking to bait arcane substances like phlogiston out of hiding. Joseph Priestley, for instance, would have used some of the same glassware to construct the Leyden Jars for his electrical experiments that he later used to trap gases in his chemical experiments. Travelers in the enlightenment 'Republic of Letters' could credibly traverse its diverse domains, drawing together the discrete arts and sciences (not so alienated then) that now structure our universities.[5] Louisa Calé and Adriana Craciun extrapolate from this characteristic a fruitful 'disorder' that we might draw upon in contradistinction to our own more rigidly hierarchical systems of knowledge.[6]

Nevertheless, scholars have long recognized the protracted foreclosing of such possibilities, positioning the end of the Republic of Letters at the close of the eighteenth century. Clifford Siskin broadly situates 'the simultaneous advent of modern disciplinarity ... and modern professionalism' during the late eighteenth and early nineteenth centuries.[7] More recently Jon Klancher has pointed to the role the prominent London Arts and Sciences institutions played in proliferating an epistemological model predicated on a 'matrix' of recognizably distinct arts and sciences.[8] Klancher describes the ambivalent transfiguration that fields of knowledge underwent as the century turned: on the one hand, practitioners of discrete arts and sciences sought to realize the systematic completeness of their intellectual pursuits, rendering them logically enclosed and 'autonomous'. By this logic Wordsworth could stake out in the 1802 preface to *Lyrical Ballads* the separate and opposed claims to

[5] On the enlightenment Republic of Letters' downfall see Paul Keen, *The Crisis of Literature in the 1790s: Print Culture and the Public Sphere* (Cambridge: Cambridge University Press, 1999), pp. 25–131.

[6] Louisa Calé and Adriana Craciun, 'The Disorder of Things', *Eighteenth-Century Studies*, 45: 1 (2011), p. 1.

[7] Clifford Siskin, *The Work of Writing* (Baltimore, MD: Johns Hopkins University Press, 1998), p. 2.

[8] Jon Klancher, *Transfiguring the Arts and Sciences* (Cambridge: Cambridge University Press, 2013), p. 1.

specialized knowledge of the 'poet' and the 'man of science'. At the center of this claim for separate spheres lay a growing professional rivalry. According to Catherine Ross, some degree of disciplinary antagonism was inevitable, given that poets and philosophers would have to compete for 'affirming audiences' drawn from the same 'polymathic public'.[9] As a result, 'a rivalry ensued that became the catalyst for both groups to initiate the delineation and emphasis of their differences' (Ross, p. 24). Nevertheless, as Klancher's work makes clear, such enclosures within the cultural field of knowledge were by no means complete. He emphasizes that transfiguring the arts and sciences also involved a 'lateral movement' that 'figured the arts and sciences rather as entangled, intermediated, confusing, contingent, messy, disorderly' (p. 18). Effectively, this means that even as disciplines strategically coalesced around stabilizing nomenclatures or regularized sets of practices, they nevertheless remained interwoven.[10]

Understanding the arts and sciences as at once interconnected and also straining towards separation requires attending to complex sets of ideas and material practices. Historically, fields coalesced at different rates; for instance, chemistry and the life sciences achieved their recognizably modern form significantly later than physics.[11] To get an idea of this epistemological shift's slow development, consider, for instance, that the impulse towards intellectual specialization had to be legitimized before it could be made a common disciplinary prerogative. According to Robin Valenza, it was Scottish enlightenment thinkers such as Adam Smith and Dugald Stewart who first expressed the notion that specialization was central to human intellectual life: 'Both Smith and Stewart treat intellectual specialization as a natural consequence of the division of labor, arising from no intentional human wisdom, but rather from propensities inborn in the species itself' (p. 12). I want to stress that this philosophical development was intrinsic to every eventual disciplinary designation, even if it cannot be said entirely to constitute disciplinarity itself.

Yet while many professions increasingly yearned for disciplinary enclosure during this period, the practice of medicine, the object of young John Keats's study, more than any other field, exposed in practice the quixotic nature of seeking autonomy for a field of knowledge. Medical practitioners marshalled expertise from across the spectrum of scientific research, and formal training at

[9] Catherine Ross, '"Twin Labourers and Heirs of the Same Hopes": The Professional Rivalry of Humphry Davy and William Wordsworth', in *Romantic Science*, ed. Noah Heringman (Albany, NY: SUNY Press, 2003), p. 24.

[10] Alice Jenkins describes 'the twin pulls toward spread and containment of information' in *Space and the 'March of the Mind'* (Oxford: Oxford University Press, 2007), p. 7. On the period's complicated engagement with disciplines see Jenkins, *Space*, pp. 80–112.

[11] Robin Valenza, *Literature, Language, and the Rise of the Intellectual Disciplines in Britain, 1680–1820* (Cambridge: Cambridge University Press, 2009), pp. 7–8.

Guy's or any of the other teaching hospitals (mandatory for licensure after the 1815 Apothecaries Act) exposed one to diverse schools of knowledge. Students attended lectures on chemistry, medical practice, materia medica, medical botany, and anatomy. Indeed, medicine as a profession straddled the division between art and science; it could not boast the mathematical precision of a science such as physics, given its reliance upon anatomy and chemistry, which were themselves only partially systematized. Neither was it clear that doctors acted first as scientists or as social agents; as Hermione De Almeida writes, romantic-era doctors perceived medicine as 'at once humanitarian philosophy and practical art for knowing life'.[12] Brittany Pladek informs us that doctors who failed to cure disease because of medical science's imperfections turned instead to assuaging pain: 'instead of a failure, the doctor who could not cure was a humanist, his palliative attendance a shining example of professional sympathy'.[13] Pladek describes how pervasive this role as comforter was during the period, which increasingly lauded medical professionals' humanist credentials. Not only, then, did medicine bear the marks of being both a science and an art (that is, an ordered collection of commonplace best practices), it also took up both scientific and humanistic practices and prerogatives.

John Keats responded to this epistemological schematic, which organized knowledge as a matrix of permeable fields. Indeed, Keats was conscious of the era's proclivity towards specialization and insistent that such categories not be lasting or intellectually exclusive. An 1818 letter to John Hamilton Reynolds describes the interaction between his medical and poetic activities:

> Were I to study physic or rather Medicine again,—I feel it would not make the least difference in my Poetry; when the Mind is in its infancy a Bias is in reality a Bias, but when we have acquired more strength, a Bias becomes no Bias. Every department of knowledge we see excellent and calculated towards a great whole. (*LJK*, I: 276–7)

Here 'departments of knowledge', mental 'infancy', and 'bias' are linked—Keats describes a proclivity towards specialization that he at least partially stigmatizes. He degrades narrow thinking, naturalizing it as a stage in human development. But he expects that with 'strength of mind' comes a more capacious kind of thinking oriented towards 'a great whole'. In fact, he puts forth a developmental narrative that valorizes the expansion of knowledge: 'an extensive knowledge is needful to thinking people—it takes away the

12 Hermione De Almeida, *Romantic Medicine and John Keats* (Oxford: Oxford University Press, 1991), p. 34.

13 Brittany Pladek, '"Soothing Thoughts": Romantic Palliative Care and the Poetics of Relief', *European Romantic Review*, 23: 3 (2012), p. 405.

heat and fever; and helps, by widening speculation, to ease the Burden of the Mystery' (I: p. 277).

Of course, the well-known 'Mansion of Life' passage from later in this letter reimagines Keats's 'departments of knowledge' framework, and the overlap between these two frameworks suggests that while Keats ultimately seeks to expand knowledge by connecting it to the universal he is not entirely averse to the era's newly developing matrix of arts and sciences. The architectural metaphor at the center of the passage (quoted in full below) indicates a compartmental logic:

> I compare human life to a large Mansion of Many Apartments, two of which I can only describe, the doors of the rest being as yet shut upon me—The first we step into we call the infant or thoughtless Chamber, in which we remain as long as we do not think—We remain there a long while, and notwithstanding the doors of the second Chamber remain wide open, showing a bright appearance, we care not to hasten to it; but are at length imperceptibly impelled by the awakening of the thinking principle—within us—we no sooner get into the second Chamber, which I shall call the Chamber of Maiden-Thought, than we become intoxicated with the light and atmosphere, we see nothing but pleasant wonder, and think of delaying there for ever in delight: However among the effects this breathing is father of is that tremendous one of sharpening one's vision into the heart and nature of Man—of convincing ones nerves that the World is full of Misery and Heartbreak, Pain, Sickness and oppression—whereby This Chamber of Maiden Thought becomes gradually darken'd and at the same time on all sides of it many doors are set open—but all dark—all leading to dark passages—We see not the ballance of good and evil. We are in a Mist—*We* are now in that state—We feel the 'burden of the Mystery'. (*LJK*, I: pp. 280–1)

As in the passage on the 'departments of knowledge', Keats first posits a naïve stage of unthought: in the mansion allegory this is 'the infant or thoughtless chamber, in which we remain as long as we do not think', and in the departments framework it is the mind 'in its infancy [when] a Bias is in reality a Bias' (I: p. 277). Next follows, in the mansion allegory, the 'Chamber of Maiden-Thought', where poets experience and inhabit 'the Burden of the Mystery' (I: p. 281). This period in thought represents a kind of interminable middle, an endless present that has no clear analog in the departments framework. However, the departments framework does finally promise to ease this burden by 'widening speculation' to achieve 'an extensive knowledge' beyond 'departments' (I: p. 277). Superimposing these two formulations reveals that the 'Chamber of Maiden-Thought' is at once characterized by murk—the indistinctness of Keats's allegorical description—and by an epistemology structured around 'departments' or disciplines. Indeed, knowledge in this stage is dim precisely because it is compartmentalized: at any given point, we dwell within an epistemological territory that limits our understanding of the world by occluding those of its features not relevant to our current concern. From this intersection, I take Keats to be arguing that dwelling with specialized knowledge, accepting the truth proscribed by departments, prevents a deeper awareness of the world.

Cast in this light, Keats's famous commitment to 'negative capability' takes on new significance once set amidst the diverse territories of the arts and sciences matrix. I argue that negative capability provides a way to navigate between types of knowledge for Keats, an aid that facilitates 'widening speculation' without effacing specialization. It is not a negation of systematic thought, but an openness to the intermedium between thought systems. Keats neither sought to escape nor to abolish departments, only to recognize their fitness to 'a great whole' (*LJK*, I: p. 277). As the capacity 'of being in uncertainties, Mysteries, doubts, without any irritable reaching after fact & reason' (I: p. 193), negative capability seems situated within the darkened 'Chamber of Maiden-Thought', which I have characterized as at once obscure and compartmentalized. Keats celebrates, here, a person's capacity to rest within one discursive or epistemological territory while remaining open to 'Mystery', the murkiness that at once encloses that way of knowing and houses other contiguous 'departments'. Mystery therefore functions as an ether—the medium of knowledges. Importantly, the indistinctness of Mystery does not efface the heterogeneity of knowledge. Forgetting or rejecting Mystery would involve a disavowal of that heterogeneity and an attempt to expand a single system of thought to contain the cosmos. Coleridge's public commitment to metaphysics looks like just such an attempt to construct a master-system, which is why Keats posits him as the antithesis of negative capability; to use Keats's terms, Coleridge appears to want to expand a single 'department' until it encompasses all knowledge, rather than to 'widen speculation' by embracing the diversity of knowledge. This is why Keats's call to be 'content with half knowledge' isn't anti-intellectual: such contentment merely indicates an author's having recognized the limitation of his current intellectual sphere and embraced it as an opportunity to explore the mystery of other ways of knowing.

Being content with incomplete knowledge would have been a valuable skill for Keats to cultivate during his medical training. As a patchwork of scientific pursuits, medical practice inevitably failed to articulate itself as a completely autonomous field. Furthermore, human bodies were and remain mysterious objects of scrutiny. Keats's own lecture notes indicate the field's incompleteness. We might consider, for instance, that he took notes on a lecture that listed five separate explanatory theories for blood's coagulation without resolving upon one as most probable. My point is that negative capability was not, for Keats, solely a literary quality; it was a characteristic that more broadly went to form 'a Man of Achievement'. That it is instrumental 'especially in Literature' does not make it exclusively so (*LJK*, I: p. 193). Perhaps, here, we find a medical precursor for poetic negative capability: apothecary training involved holding in suspension multiple types of knowledge and also entertaining competing scientific theories.

Gordian Capability

Keats's *Lamia* offers a poetic test case for this view of negative capability, inviting as it does allegorical interpretations that posit its investment in multiple scientific discourses. The lamia herself stands in for several distinct sciences; at the same time, she figures the very process by which natural phenomena become ordered into disciplines. Marjorie Levinson claims of *Lamia* that it is 'the closest thing we have in the Romantic repertoire to a scientific poem', by which she means that in it Keats undertook the most methodical, and in that sense scientific, analysis of the processes of his own poetic production.[14] Other commentators have extended this line of thought, offering readings that highlight different sciences. For Denise Gigante the lamia represents the unruly energy of eighteenth-century vitalism; she is 'a central instance of Romantic monstrosity whom Keats positions explicitly against Newton's mechanically organized rainbow'.[15] Dometa Wiegand Brothers reads in the celestial forms adorning the lamia's scales an astronomical vision: she is 'a galaxy', or 'the universe embodied'.[16] Stuart Sperry, in an early instance of such reading, argued that the lamia's transformation 'resembles nothing so much as the effects of a violent chemical reaction'.[17] Life sciences, astronomy, chemistry: critics have found in *Lamia*, and in the poem's excoriation of its exacting philosopher Apollonius, traces of a litany of epistemological domains.

These discrete disciplines share critical space in the poem without appearing at odds because, as I maintain, in *Lamia* Keats explores, at a more fundamental level, how discrete types of knowledge form and negate each other. Levinson argues that the poem operates by linked tactics of division and abstraction. Her analysis finds in the monetary form the ultimate symbol towards which

[14] Marjorie Levinson, *Keats's Life of Allegory, the Origins of a Style* (London: Basil Blackwell, 1988), p. 28.

[15] Denise Gigante, *Life: Organic Form and Romanticism* (New Haven, CT: Yale University Press, 2009), p. 210.

[16] Dometa Wiegand Brothers, *The Romantic Imagination and Astronomy* (New York: Palgrave Macmillan, 2015), pp. 111–12.

[17] Stuart M. Sperry, *Keats the Poet* (Princeton, NJ: Princeton University Press, 1994), p. 302.

Keats's poem tends, with the lamia coming to signify an emptied-out and exchangeable commodity. I would posit that these processes—division and abstraction—serve equally well to characterize the forces that increasingly produced seemingly discrete disciplines (and indeed, money as an institutional pursuit often motivated public arts and sciences institutions to publicize knowledge in a disciplined fashion). Yet disciplinary designations in the arts and sciences generally proved barely capable abstractions, drawing together as they did a complicated mix of contradictory theories, unsettled nomenclatures, incompatible practices, and unreliable apparatuses. Of course, the real world these disciplines described was undifferentiated and in fact hostile to such tidy system-making, a truth to which Keats's medical experience would have attested. In what follows, then, I show that Keats's poem embraces the generative potential of 'departments' as a means of intensifying the scrutiny of natural phenomena, while nevertheless maintaining the need for a capacious and multivalent view of knowledge.

In her serpentine form, the lamia embodies the natural world's undifferentiated character, uniting, as she does, incommensurable contrarieties. Her being affronts the natural philosopher's categories. She compiles diverse aspects of the animal kingdom, bridging the divide between predator and prey—she is 'Striped like a zebra, freckled like a pard'—and even crossing different classes; since she is 'Eyed like a peacock' she contains birdlike attributes along with her mammalian and reptilian ones (Part I: lines 49–50). Not merely terrestrial, she is 'full of silver moons' that compound the night sky with her animal vivacity; yet the night does not exclusively predominate in her pattern, as her 'rainbow-sided' nature also sees a daytime glory splayed in chromatic brilliance across her body (I: 51, 54). The rainbow itself is a colloquy of natural and human aspects—sunlight, vapor, vision, humanity, belief, covenant, God. Indeed, bearing God's covenant she nevertheless evokes a complicated spiritual nature: she is 'at once' perhaps a pagan 'elf, / Some demon's mistress, or the demon's self' (I: 55–6). This potential pandemonium bespeaks a complex moral nature—she embodies a spectrum of good and evil. That she is a 'gordian shape' suggests the permanence of this condition (I: 47). Over the poem's course, she will be twice untangled, but that she is described as a knot famously impossible to untie suggests the persistence of her undifferentiated shape even after her transformation. In this respect, the serpent lamia signifies an immense and undifferentiated nature. While in this state, she can 'muse / And dream … / Of all she list, strange or magnificent', traversing as a wandering thought the supernatural and natural worlds from Elysium to Corinth (I: 202–4). She, the serpent, coextends fully with the cosmos—a vaster object than human knowledge could hope to comprehend.

Her transformation unfolds as a process of division and arrangement; each portion of her gordian self gets reordered into units of epistemological similarity—that is, units pertaining to various sciences. Her transformation begins as bodily, so an anatomist's attentiveness characterizes its opening lines: 'her elfin blood in madness ran / Her mouth foamed … / Her eyes in torture fix'd' (I: 147–8, 150). Next we learn that her eyes 'Flash'd phosphor and sharp sparks, without one cooling tear, / The colours all inflam'd throughout her train' (I: 152–3), which suggests, as Stuart Sperry has noted, the combustive effects of a chemical experiment. Soon 'A deep volcanian yellow took the place / Of all her milder-mooned body's grace; / And, as the lava ravishes the mead, / Spoilt all her silver mail, and golden brede' (I: 155–8), alluding to objects of geological scrutiny. A final turn notes that this metamorphosis 'Made gloom of all her frecklings, streaks and bars, / Eclips'd her crescents, and lick'd up her stars', hinting at an astronomical cataclysm (I: 159–60). Physiology, chemistry, geology, astronomy: the lamia's disordered and diverse aspects, which had been thoroughly intermixed, come to rest over this transformation's course in compartmentalized groups of between two and three lines in length. These lines' enjambment, and the syntactic piling up of images, evinces a residual connection among these 'departments', but the lamia's aspects have, during the course of this transformation, nevertheless been sorted. As I noted above, critics have variously taken up these distinct sciences in readings of *Lamia*, but have stopped short of recognizing that Keats depicts here the very process by which individual disciplines form.

The fruitful possibilities of division come to characterize the lamia in her human form, as focused specialization enables new kinds of learned intensity. She is, though, 'Not one hour old, yet of sciential brain / To unperplex bliss from its neighbor pain; / Define their pettish limits, and estrange / Their points of contact, and swift counterchange' (I: 191–4). Her brain's 'sciential' nature invokes the systematic quality of her specialized training in 'the lore / Of love' (I: 189–90). Her focus is singular. For her, love is a science, as seemingly autonomous as the popular chemistry of the Royal Institution.[18] Her method involves division: unperplexing, defining limits, estranging points of contact. The lamia can induce pure pleasure and dispel pain. She has enclosed an area of expertise, dividing it from 'the specious chaos' of undifferentiated human experience (I: 195). That singularity of focus allows her to develop an intensity of pleasure otherwise unattainable. The lyric voice describes her in superlative terms: she is at once 'A virgin purest lipp'd' and knowledgeable about love 'to the red heart's core' (I: 189–90). These descriptors suggest that her schooling in love runs the gamut from chaste to erotic pleasures, and indeed, Lycius's total enthrallment, achieved without direct supernatural enchantment—she

[18] On the specialization of popular chemistry and its relationship to the period's literary lectures see Kurtis Hessel, 'The Romantic-Era Lecture: Dividing and Reuniting the Arts and Sciences', *Configurations*, 24: 4 (2016), pp. 501–32.

wins him 'with no more awe than what her beauty gave' (I: 338)—affirms her command of her subject.

Intensity, in this instance, is the fruit of compartmentalized thinking. The lamia's 'sciential brain' makes her a better lover, gives her greater command of her erotic discipline, and allows her to focus on her goal, pleasure, extricating and isolating it from pain. In this sense, division is not unequivocally pernicious; in fact, it trains the departmental practitioner to attend to minute details, to cultivate effective protocols, to be precise. Medical man that he was, Keats could hardly dismiss the improvements that scientific thinking had conferred upon medicine. For an important appraisal of intensity, it is worth returning to the negative capability letter. Early in that letter Keats asserts that 'the excellence of every Art is its intensity, capable of making all disagreeables evaporate, from their being in close relationship with Beauty & Truth' (*LJK*, I: p. 192). Intensity narrows focus, makes 'all disagreeables evaporate', in contradistinction to the 'widening speculation' that eases 'the Burden of the Mystery' (I: p. 277). Furthermore, through intensity—that is, the piercing focus that follows from scientific thinking—one approaches more closely to 'Beauty & Truth'. This approach is as diverse as the arts and sciences matrix itself. Keats remains committed to honoring the capacity of individual departments, through increased intensity, to produce great good. That this paean to intense focus appears in the same letter with the concept of negative capability suggests that Keats saw these two impulses as co-implicated. He perceived that half-knowledge and intense knowledge balanced each other.

Division becomes anathema, for Keats, only when it grows single-minded or destructive. We may be tempted to read the famous passage recounting the effects of the 'touch of cold philosophy' as an absolute warning against the divisive characteristics of all scientific or philosophical scrutiny (*Lamia*, II: 230). In other words, we might be tempted to consider this an anti-scientific poem. But the lamia's own fruitful 'unperplexing' complicates such a view, and argues for the possibility of a worthwhile form of division. This verb, while implying a disentangling of complicated strands, clarifies rather than marring. It separates to enable greater degrees of productive focus upon the disentangled parts. By contrast, 'cold philosophy' 'unweaves' the rainbow, an act of aesthetic unmaking that cannot be undone. Apollonius's character signals, in many respects, the selfishness and singularity of his particularly destructive version of philosophy. As he enters the temple he laughs, 'As though some knotty problem, that had daft / His patient thought, had now begun to thaw, / And solve and melt:—'twas just as he foresaw' (II: 160–2). Here the image of the lamia as problematic knot returns; she is the object of his philosophy's penchant for 'unweaving'. Even more significant, however, is what the line suggests about Apollonius's intellectual method: he does not seek to discover new truths through experimentation, but rather to confirm what he already knows. This Corinthian sage seeks only to expand his own philosophy, not truly to increase the breadth of his knowledge by embracing epistemological diversity. Apollonius is an epistemological tyrant, a dogmatic refuser of negative capability.

Ultimately, the most egregious ill recounted in the passage on cold philosophy is its tendency to expand a single species of knowledge into a totality. More execrable than its unweaving of the rainbow is philosophy's attempt to 'Conquer all mysteries by rule and line' (II: 235). Seeking to conquer 'mystery' is tantamount to aspiring to eclipse all forms of knowledge outside one's own narrowly proscribed department of thought. Apollonius, it seems, 'would let go by a fine isolated verisimilitude caught from the Penetralium of mystery', rather than allow his pupil to escape the narrow constraints of his intellectual influence. In this sense, *Lamia* is a poem that advocates a particular version of negative capability: one that does not begrudge the usefulness of intense focus, but which maintains the need for openness to other ways of understanding the world.

Departments of Allegory

As a fable about the formation of distinct types of knowledge, and one that poetically overlays diverse departments while addressing a Romantic-era readership newly retrained to disciplinary thinking by the public arts and sciences institutions, Keats's *Lamia* also reinvents allegory for the world of disciplines. There is, of course, a tradition of reading Keats in terms of allegory. A letter of 1819 to George and Georgiana Keats invites this attention in the assertion that 'a Man's life of any worth is a continual allegory' (*LJK*, II: p. 67). Drawing upon this quotation, Marjorie Levinson's seminal *Keats's Life of Allegory* offers a poignant use of the trope to explain Keats's relationship to his economic circumstances. According to Levinson, Keats's poetry served as 'a parodic reproduction of the social restrictions that marked Keats as wanting: unequipped, ineffectual, and deeply fraudulent' (p. 6). Her conceit makes of his poetry an allegory of his life, particularly highlighting his poverty and exclusion from literary history and community. Keats's use of allegory, however, demands a more overdetermined sense of the trope: Keats is not pushing for a view of human life that discovers its meaning in some single extrinsic and totalizing system of meaning; rather, he refers to the plurality of interpretive lenses that people bring to bear upon life, and the diverse types of knowledge that go to forming a human 'of any worth'. In reconditioning allegory to suit it to multiple modes of thought, as he does in *Lamia*, Keats adapts the trope to the arts and sciences matrix. His statement points to allegory's capacity to mediate among varieties of human experience.

That Keats was cognizant of the epistemic shift his society was undergoing seems apparent, and he also clearly understood the imagination to be a means of accommodating this social change. *Lamia* itself evinces a concern with epistemic shifts. The poem's opening lines set the scene with reference to a sequence of mythological paradigms (a conceit the poem shares with the Hyperion poems):

> Upon a time, before the faery broods
> Drove Nymph and Satyr from the prosperous woods,
> Before King Oberon's bright diadem,
> Sceptre, and mantle, clasp'd with dewy gem,
> Frighted away the Dryads and the Fauns
> From rushes green, and brakes, and cowslip'd lawns,
> The ever-smitten Hermes empty left
> His golden throne, bent warm on amorous theft. (I: 1–8)

Jeffrey N. Cox describes how these lines 'call attention to the outmoded beliefs and fictions of "old Romance"' in the interest of discovering 'a new eroticized romance, with *eros* not as a power of dubious enchantment but as a means of connecting with the physical world'.[19] He builds this reading into his argument that a broader trajectory organizes the three romances—*Lamia*, *Isabella*, and *Eve of St. Agnes*—in Keats's 1820 volume. This passage from Greek to Italian to British models 'plots a cultural movement from the classical past through the Christian middle ages to the present' (pp. 56–7). Convinced of the centrality of this historical development for Keats's thinking, I suggest that his description of passing mythopoetic systems, in light of my above reading of negative capability, also signifies the passage of epistemic systems. In other words, Keats announces in these opening lines a concern with how people think, which over the course of the poem develops into an engagement with how they organize knowledge into disciplines.

In addition to offering a new form of romance, therefore, *Lamia* also suggests a new theory of allegory, one consonant with a growing world of departments. As Theresa Kelley has argued, the empiricist philosophy of the eighteenth century gave rise to a crisis for allegorical representation. However, Kelley challenges the traditional view, which holds that the period's rhetorical rejection of allegory hinged on its perceived inferiority to realistic modes of representation. She contends instead that 'allegory survive[d] after the Renaissance, against pressures that ought to have done it in, by making border raids

[19] Jeffrey N. Cox, '*Lamia*, *Isabella*, and *The Eve of St. Agnes*, Eros and Romance', in *The Cambridge Companion to Keats*, ed. Susan J. Wolfson (Cambridge: Cambridge University Press, 2001), pp. 57–8.

on the very categories that [had] been presented as its contraries: realism, mimesis, empiricism, and history'.[20] These 'border raids' suggest a shifting ground for allegory—as a conceit it came to serve a mediating function. In an intellectual milieu increasingly organizing knowledge into types, allegory provided a way of accounting for their separateness, contiguity, and overlap, hence *Lamia*'s multiply-signifying title character.

Allegory invites critical attention for its tendency to foreground the process of signification in its representations, which has historically led commentators to speculate on its epistemological function. Paul de Man describes allegory as 'dryly rational and dogmatic in its reference to a meaning that it does not itself constitute'.[21] According to de Man, this transparent signification rendered allegory anathema to Romantic thought, which preferred the mystifications associated with the symbol. Gordon Teskey moves beyond de Man's focus on the linguistic function of allegory, positing for the trope a deeper metaphysical significance: 'the very word *allegory* evokes a schism in consciousness—between life and a mystery, between the real and the ideal, between a literal tale and its moral—which is repaired, or at least concealed, by imagining a hierarchy on which we ascend towards truth'.[22] At the heart of the 'psychological work' allegory does is a persistent splitting, what Teskey calls 'instrumental meaning': in allegory, the drive to meaning is a wedge that cleaves the undifferentiated natural world, manifesting a division between vehicle and tenor analogous to that between subject and object. Teskey's innovation is not to see allegory as a simple species of representation in which meaning is secondary to or follows from an opaque narrative but to reconceive it as a literary practice in which meaning is the 'creative exertion of force' that produces the difference between the word as written and an occluded 'other' significance (p. 5).

Keats's allegorical practice in *Lamia* is new insomuch as it accommodates this aspect of allegory to the growth of the intellectual disciplines. In *Lamia*, modern disciplines exert their influence upon allegory, and allegory reciprocally provides a means of imagining the contiguous relation of discrete (and seemingly autonomous) modes of thought. Much like with the formation of disciplines, allegory involves the articulation of difference and hierarchy out of an undifferentiated and unmanageable other. Teskey argues that in allegory 'the object on which the force [of meaning] is exerted belongs to a realm that is intolerably "other"'—nature, in other words—and that relative to this meaning that other appears as 'a chaos' (p. 6). By the early nineteenth century,

[20] Theresa Kelley, *Reinventing Allegory* (Cambridge: Cambridge University Press, 1997), p. 2.

[21] Paul de Man, 'The Rhetoric of Temporality', in *Blindness and Insight* (Minneapolis: University of Minnesota Press, 1983), p. 189.

[22] Gordon Teskey, *Allegory and Violence* (Ithaca, NY: Cornell University Press, 1996), p. 2.

any attempt to create order out of the chaos of the natural world would have had to pass through the epistemological medium of the arts and sciences.

The diversity of human knowledge can be at once maintained as separate and reintegrated in the literary space of allegory. Furthermore, there exists an intimate relationship between allegory and negative capability, which serves as the bridge concept for 'widening speculation'. It is our own critical negative capability that allows us to see the lamia as an archetype of biology *or* chemistry *or* astronomy *or* geology, while also conceding that she is exclusively none of those things (and all of them at once). Keats wrote that 'A Man's life of any worth is a continual allegory—and very few eyes can see the Mystery of his life' (*LJK*, II: p. 67). 'Mystery', we must recall, lurks at the fringes of departments. The 'continual' nature of Keats's allegory points to the constant tension between resting in half-knowledge and preparing to plunge through a doorway, down a murky corridor, and towards some new way of understanding the world. Meaning in human life constantly shifts as we traverse the diverse territories of knowledge and experience, ceding ground here and making inroads there into the mystery. In this regard, Keats anticipates Teskey's claim that 'allegory elicits continual interpretation as its primary aesthetic effect' (p. 4). But Keats's allegory is one modeled on medicine: it must accommodate competing artistic and scientific schema; it must correlate separately conceived interacting biological systems. Knowledge, no longer constructed on the syncretic principles of Francis Bacon or the enlightenment Republic of Letters, but now fracturing and fragmentary, interrupts allegory's metaphysical work. In *Lamia*, Keats offers up a modern allegory, one that signifies with a single serpentine figure at once the union of all knowledge and multiple autonomous disciplines. Allegory provides the means of holding these departments, in their completeness, in solution; negative capability builds the passages amongst them.

In the same sequence of letters that features his statement on allegory Keats acknowledges a much messier vision of human life. This comes during a moment of disillusionment at the reviews of *Endymion*, when Keats was thinking once again of returning to medicine. 'Every body is in his own mess', he tells his brother (*LJK*, II: p. 70). His disappointment whispers that lives are messes of circumstances; bodies are messes of vessels and tissues. The medical practitioner and the poet in Keats could not rest easy with such a bitter embrace of disorganization. Negative capability and allegory were means of arranging messes, intensifying scrutiny, building knowledge while maintaining the connections between types of investigation. It is in this sense, in a world increasingly characterized by intellectual plurality, that Keats offers a modern vision: one that recognizes the valuable focus that specialization brings, but that looks always in between schools of thought for the connections that enrich human understanding.

Chapter Seven

'Irritable Reaching' and the Conditions of Romantic Mediation

Jeanne Britton

In the well-known letter of December 1817, John Keats defines 'negative capability' as the ability to remain in 'uncertainties, Mysteries, doubts, without any irritable reaching after fact & reason' (*LJK*, I: 193). Somewhat surprisingly, given the careful attention paid to this letter by Keats's critics, precisely what is meant by 'irritable reaching' has been regularly overlooked. 'Irritability', like many of Keats's crucial terms, carries medical and literary significance, both of which inform the account of negative capability I offer here. In this reading, Keats's famous concept describes the literary-historical and physiological nature of the writing process itself.

Irritability was often considered the biological counterpart of sensibility. While the cultural history of sensibility explores that term's physiological and literary permutations, the cultural history of irritability, a concept that also, albeit less prominently and consistently, touches on the physiological and the literary, simply doesn't exist.[1] These circumstances are in direct opposition to two meanings that the term carried in the early decades of the nineteenth century: its association with the character of the poet, and its postulation, in eighteenth-century medicine, as the origin of muscular mobility. Keats's critics have made much of his medical training in demonstrating that scientific concepts permeate and enhance his poetic language. What I suggest is

[1] For comprehensive studies of sensibility in literary culture, see G. J. Barker-Benfield, *The Culture of Sensibility* (Chicago, IL: University of Chicago Press, 1992) and, especially for its medical sources, Anne Vila, *Enlightenment and Pathology: Sensibility in the Literature and Medicine of Eighteenth-Century France* (Baltimore, MD: Johns Hopkins University Press, 1997). George Rousseau discusses intersections between irritability and sensibility in a medical context in *Nervous Acts: Essays on Literature, Culture and Sensibility* (New York: Palgrave Macmillan, 2004), pp. 229–33. See also Ildiko Csengei, *Sympathy, Sensibility and the Literature of Feeling in the Eighteenth Century* (New York: Palgrave Macmillan, 2012).

that the medical and literary-historical meanings of 'irritability' illuminate the role of the body in poetic creativity and textual mediation, and that Keats's articulation of negative capability forges a connection between the medical and the literary that warrants particular attention.

Writing to Percy Shelley after Keats's death, Byron referred to '*that second-hand* school of poetry'.[2] Such assessments, even in the vein of praise Byron seems to adopt, have tainted Keats ever since the early criticism of his works and the branding of the Cockney school of poetry up to fairly recent assessments of Keats's 'badness'. Keats's literary inheritance did indeed come second-hand. His knowledge of the classics was primarily through translation, his experience of Greek architecture came explicitly through imperial conquest (his sonnet responds specifically to 'Elgin's marbles'), and his familiarity with visual art came through print reproductions more often than their painted originals.[3] Grant F. Scott makes the case quite clearly: 'Keats was never more interested in nature than when it was mediated through art, through the words or pictures or statuary of other artists. His best poetry is composed largely of representations of representations, meditations "on" objects or texts that are themselves reflections of other artists' creative acts.'[4]

Many of Keats's works exist as mediated renditions of his own earlier works—*Hyperion* and *The Fall of Hyperion*, and the two versions of 'La Belle Dame sans Merci' are prominent examples. These extensive remediations across individual works and the foregrounding of mediated experience throughout his poetry suggest that his oeuvre might be reassessed in light of the turn to questions of media and mediation in Romantic-era literary culture. His version of embodied aesthetics additionally promises to specify relationships between mediation, mimesis, and ekphrasis, relationships that deserve fuller scrutiny within a broad historical scope. Even more than these conspicuous features of his verse and his biography, his intense consideration of the body's imbrication in the workings of the mind, the negotiations of history, and the nature of subjectivity make him an especially useful figure in whose works we can consider the mediating forces of the responsive body and literary history. The reading of negative capability that I offer here is an initial effort in this direction.

John Guillory has claimed that mediation offers its own kinds of pleasure.[5]

[2] Lord Byron to Percy Bysshe Shelley, 26 April 1821, in *Selected Letters and Journals*, ed. Leslie A. Marchand (Cambridge, MA: Harvard University Press, 1982), p. 254.

[3] The most comprehensive critical discussion of Keats's experience of particular works of art continues to be Ian Robert James Jack, *Keats and the Mirror of Art* (Oxford: Clarendon Press, 1968).

[4] Grant F. Scott, *The Sculpted Word: Keats, Ekphrasis, and the Visual Arts* (Hanover, NH: University Press of New England, 1994), p. xi.

[5] John Guillory, 'Genesis of the Media Concept', *Critical Inquiry*, 36 (Winter 2010), pp. 321–62.

Based on this proposition, I want to consider negative capability as an articulation of momentary pleasure that is analogous to the mediated conditions of Keats's works. I argue that negative capability, in light of its physiological significance, should be understood as a goal that is briefly attained during the moments when inspiration, influence, and composition are simultaneous and when acquiescence to cultural belatedness facilitates rather than forestalls the movement of the pen across the page. Negative capability describes, then, the historical and embodied nature of the writing process itself. This view does not deny the prevalence of inadequacy, weakness, and insignificance in Keats's self-pronouncements; rather, it fundamentally reconceives the nature of poetic composition in the mode of negative capability as an experience of satisfied awareness of belatedness, susceptibility to influence, and self-articulation through mediated forms of aesthetic experience. In this way, the sense of negative capability as a mode of composition rather than a type of identity or a feature of his poetry might account for certain patterns in composition history, such as his writing of 'To Autumn' after his abandonment of 'Hyperion'. Life to Milton would be death to Keats as a writer, but it is Keats's susceptibility to that self-effacement that prompts the person-less lyric voice of 'To Autumn' and ushers in one of his greatest poems.[6]

This essay, however, has more restricted aims. Negative capability's physiological and literary-historical meanings urge us to reconsider this concept in a few different ways. First, what might it mean, in various permutations, to overcome an immediate, reflexive, bodily response? Second, in light of the physiological and gestural meaning that 'irritable reaching' invokes, we ought to reconsider the role of the hand, not only in the sense of physical immediacy, but also in its figure for indirect, or 'second-hand', mediations. Keats's pleasure in mediation during the moment of composition seems to animate the 'ghoulish' body that extends to us 'This living hand', a poem concerned with the immediacy of writing and, particularly in its manuscript version, with the presence of the hand as it writes on the page. In this poem, the paradox of contraction and extension that 'irritable reaching' suggests is recast as a haunting gesture in which the spectral speaker of these lines endeavors to 'hold' his 'capable' hand 'towards' the reader. The somatic and gestural repetitions between the letter and this poem are part of a more thorough dovetailing that this essay aims to illuminate.

In his journal letter to George and Tom Keats of late December 1817, Keats introduces negative capability between comments on Shakespeare and Coleridge. No less here than elsewhere in Keats's writing, literary history

[6] In September 1819 he writes to George and Georgiana: 'I have but lately stood on my guard against Milton. Life to him would be death to me. Miltonic verse cannot be written but it [in] the vein of art—I wish to devote myself to another sensation—' (*LJK*, II: p. 212).

weighs heavily on the aspirational poet. The concept's immediate context in the letter gestures towards the historical and poetic associations of 'irritability'. Equally, the physical movement identified by 'irritable *reaching*' emphatically invokes the medical discussion of 'irritability', a characteristic that medical discourse attributed to the muscular system. Many readers seem to have assumed that 'irritable reaching' names a dissatisfied, grumbling effort, that 'irritability' here physicalizes mental strain. Indeed it might. But, for Keats, 'irritability' had two additional echoes: a characteristic of reflexive bodily movement, and a trait of the poetic personality.

Keats invokes the term's literary sense in a number of letters, and the wide currency of 'irritability' as a physiological concept in the work of his teachers at Guy's Hospital informs the references he makes to his health in his letters. A reference to 'the "*genus irritabile*"' of poets ushers in his definition of the 'camelion Poet'; in another letter, he confesses, perhaps aspirationally, that he exhibits 'all the vices of a Poet, irritability, love of effect and admiration' (*LJK*, I: pp. 386, 414). He refers to irritation in his lecture notes from Guy's Hospital,[7] and in comments about his health—his 'nervous irritability' and being 'in so irritable a state of health'—he suggests the term's medical register (*LJK*, II: pp. 287, 129).

To say that Keats intertwines medical and literary terminology is itself nothing new, and such claims risk stating the obvious or flattening the significance of metaphor in either discourse. And yet this kind of critical work has been and promises to be especially productive in Keats studies. Critics including Alan Richardson, Hermione de Almeida, and Donald Goellnicht have enhanced our experience of Keats's language by identifying the medical connotations of terms such as 'essence', 'distill', 'intensity', and 'composition and decomposition' in his poetry and prose.[8] His poetry's profound engagement with the mechanics of chemical reaction, discoveries in neurology, and developments in physics have, in light of this critical conversation, come to be seen as sophisticated rather than, as his earliest critics would have it, sophomoric aspects of his works. De Almeida has, for example, enumerated the scientific implications of 'negative' that bear on negative capability, stressing the

[7] The reference to irritability appears in the scattered style of his lecture notes: 'Sympathy. By this the Vital Principle is chiefly supported. The function of breathing is a sympathetic action—from irritation produced on the beginning of the Air Tube affects the Abdominal Muscles and produces coughing.' *Anatomical and Physiological Note Book. Printed from the Holograph in the Keats Museum, Hampstead*, ed. Maurice Buxton Forman (New York: Haskell House Publishers, 1970), p. 56.

[8] Alan Richardson, *British Romanticism and the Science of the Mind* (Cambridge: Cambridge University Press, 2001); Hermione de Almeida, *Romantic Medicine and John Keats* (Oxford: Oxford University Press, 1991); Donald C. Goellnicht, *The Poet-Physician: Keats and Medical Science* (Pittsburgh, PA: University of Pittsburgh Press, 1984).

passive receptivity that this electro-chemical principle brings to his conception of the poetic character (pp. 288–9). The term 'irritable' promises, after similar scrutiny, to enhance and expand our understanding of negative capability.

In medical discourse, 'irritability' names a property of the muscles that determines contraction. Swiss anatomist and physiologist Albrecht von Haller defined irritability as the tendency of muscles to contract when stimulated. Sensibility, the property of the nerves, communicated the muscular response to stimuli to the brain. After Haller's mid-eighteenth-century attempt to prove the existence of irritability, nearly every medical treatise referred to this concept and its more prominent counterpart, sensibility, in some fashion. Many readers of Haller attributed more significance to irritability than Haller did himself: even the English translator of his *Dissertation on the Sensible and Irritable Parts of Animals* claims that 'irritability is the long-sought vital principle, the key to nature itself' in a contradiction of Haller's explicit warning that this principle should not be taken as the vital principle.[9] In Haller's system, irritability is an involuntary, physiological force that determines mobility, and sensibility is associated with feeling and expressive of the soul. According to Haller, an irritable body part 'becomes shorter upon being touched', and a sensible body part that is touched communicates with the soul.[10] The reception of his terminology in later medicine blurred these distinctions, and sensibility alone came to be associated with the vital principle.[11]

Critics have stressed Keats's proximity to major advances in early nineteenth-century science. Less prominent, perhaps, but especially significant for their role in the medical history of irritability, are reinterpretations of this concept carried out by Keats's own teachers and their sources. His teacher at Guy's Hospital, Astley Cooper, refashioned his mentor John Hunter's concepts of physiological sympathy and irritability, and the Scottish physician John Brown influentially adapted Haller's distinct categories of sensibility and irritability into his more capacious concept of excitability. According to Brown, 'The blood by its quantity distends the muscular fibres of the vessels; that distention stimulates the excitability in the fibres, and produces excitement, commonly called their irritability; thus excited, the fibres contract.'[12] Eighteenth-century origins of the medical

[9] Vila, *Enlightenment and Pathology*, pp. 27–8.

[10] Albrecht von Haller, *Dissertation on the Sensible and Irritable Parts of Animals*, trans. Tissot (London: Nourse, 1755), p. 4.

[11] Robert Whytt's disputes with Haller in the mid-eighteenth century largely concern the attribution of irritability to various particular body parts. See 'Observations on the Sensibility and Irritability of the Parts of Men and other Animals; occasioned by M. de Haller's late Treatise on these Subjects' in *Physiological Essays* (Edinburgh: Balfour, 1766), pp. 127–202. Also see Csengei for a helpful description of Whytt's different types of irritability (p. 108).

[12] John Brown, *The Elements of Medicine; or, a Translation of the Elementa Medicinae*

concept of irritability continued to have traction in early nineteenth-century definitions of the term, appearing in the entry for 'irritability' in the 1810 and 1823 editions of the *Encyclopaedia Britannica*. The version of irritability that circulated within and beyond Guy's Hospital draws on the blurring of Haller's distinction between sensibility and irritability and the later conceptualization of a generally responsive principle in the human body.

The negative capability letter falls squarely within the period of Keats's conspicuous use of medical and chemical terminology in the development of his aesthetics, which Goellenicht identifies as the period between May 1817 and November 1818 (p. 53). If irritability identifies the tendency for muscular contraction, then 'irritable reaching' describes movement that combines contraction with expansion. Keats's phrase would, in this light, produce either paradox or pain. Janis Caldwell has provocatively aligned irritability's physiological meaning with negative capability's operation, arguing that this poetic ideal would require 'an active suspension of reason analogous to the voluntary effort required to abort a motor reflex'.[13] The physicality of what I take to be the instinctive, unreflective 'reaching'—which negative capability overcomes—serves to re-evaluate the embodied nature of irritability, negative capability, and mediation in Keats's works.

Beyond the term's medical meaning, irritability had also been linked to the figure of the poet since Horace, whose complaint about the fretful tribe of scribbling lyricists seeking fame is echoed in the writings of Coleridge, Byron, and Keats himself.[14] The term's literary associations complement the immediate context of negative capability's definition in Keats's letter—the assimilating character of Shakespeare as opposed to the determined objectivity that Keats

Brunonis with large notes, illustrations, and comments by the author of the original work. Trans by the author. 2 vols. (London: Johnson, 1788), vol. 1, p. 111. For a fuller discussion of John Brown's excitability as a development upon Haller's irritability, see de Almeida, *Romantic Medicine*, pp. 66–73.

13 Janis Caldwell, *Literature and Medicine in Nineteenth-Century Britain* (Cambridge: Cambridge University Press, 2004), p. 378. De Almeida, by contrast, discusses irritability in its early nineteenth-century reformulation as a kind of general susceptibility. She identifies the medical concepts of irritability and sympathy as the 'first seed for the Keatsian concepts of intensity, negative capability, and the unpoetical poetical character' (pp. 98–9) because they prioritize susceptibility to outside forces. Attentive to the discourse of sensibility and irritability during the years of Keats's medical training, de Almeida's reading implies an equivalence between irritability (as susceptibility) and negative capability that the letter's phrasing seems to contradict.

14 In the second chapter of *Biographia Literaria*, Coleridge has a section, which may refer covertly to Byron, on the supposed irritability of men of genius. Byron refers to the irritability of poets in *Don Juan*: 'But he had genius,—when a turncoat has it / The 'Vates irritabilis' takes care / That without notice few full moons shall pass it; / Even good men like to make the public stare' (Canto III, stanza 81).

attributed, however oddly, to Coleridge. Along these lines, negative capability suggests that the ideal poetic character sheds the historical stereotype of the fame-seeking scribbler. In Keats's reference to irritability, the dovetailing of the literary and the medical approximates the complexity of the poet's relationship to literary inheritance and sensory experience.

The issue of poetic inheritance has, of course, played a significant role in Keats's critical heritage. Ever since Bloom's *Anxiety of Influence* deemed Keats's comment about the strain of Milton's influence—'Life to him would be death to me'—'The motto to English poetry', Keats's stance has been alternatively recognized as a representative or anomalous case of the nature of literary influence.[15] In recent years, critics including Beth Lau and Lucy Newlyn have seen discussions of Keats's relationship to his literary forbearers as more complex negotiations of imitation, influence, and creative force that allow for alternations between agency and receptivity, alternations that themselves manifest negative capability. My argument seeks, in one respect, to bridge the space between, on one hand, Lau's claim that Keats's notions of negative capability and the chameleon poet betray a desire 'to lose his own inadequate identity in those of his creation' and, on the other, her discussion of Keats's productive relationship to poetic inheritance.[16] The mediated nature I identify in negative capability reframes a long-standing concern in Romanticism that is especially relevant for Keats: the nature of inheritance and influence. The roles that the responsive, reflexive, and controlled body might play in this question deserve fuller consideration.

The critical history of negative capability is, as other essays in this volume will also attest, extensive and expansive.[17] Within this tradition, it has been common to align negative capability with a propensity for self-effacement or, more broadly, empathy's capacity to sustain oppositions. Perhaps the most well-known claim for Keats's self-annihilating persona remains that of Paul de Man, for whom Keats 'almost succeeds in eliminating himself from his poetry altogether'.[18] There is a long history of reading negative capability as

[15] Harold Bloom, *The Anxiety of Influence: A Theory of Poetry* (New York: Oxford University Press, 1973), p. 32.

[16] Beth Lau, 'Protest, "Nativism", and Impersonation in the Works of Chatterton and Keats', *Studies in Romanticism*, 42: 4 (2003), pp. 519–39. In a similar vein, in *Paradise Lost and the Romantic Reader* (Oxford: Clarendon Press, 1993), Lucy Newlyn finds in Keats's revisions of *Paradise Lost* 'a poet who is able at once to displace and to defer to authority, who can play ambiguous games with divinity, and who caricatures Milton as the poet of absolutes, whilst plundering his text for the indeterminacies which are themselves redolent of "negative capability"' (p. 251).

[17] In *Keats and Negative Capability* (London: Bloomsbury, 2009), Li Ou offers a genealogy of the term's use after Keats and catalogs its appearances in Keats criticism.

[18] Paul de Man, 'Introduction', *John Keats: Selected Poetry*, ed. John Hollander (New York: New American Library, 1966), p. xxiii–xxiv.

an incarnation of sympathy or empathy that positions this poetic principle as a development of over a century of British associationist philosophy. More recently, negative capability has been divorced from this historical and critical tradition and recast in the vein of postmodernism's radical selflessness.[19] Alternatively, Nicholas Roe and Jonathan Mulrooney have argued for a more assertive persona in negative capability. Roe argues that negative capability names an 'assertive consciousness which is *simultaneously* assimilative and projective', and Mulrooney's insightful reading of the Keatsian 'self' emphasizes the process of becoming, rather than annihilation.[20]

In addition to being aligned with Keats's persona, negative capability has frequently been identified in the compositional, structural, or syntactic aspects of Keats's verse. Helen Vendler's intensive study of the odes reveals a compositional structure determined by the project of situating the self within patterns of indeterminacy considered characteristic of negative capability; more recently, Linda von Pfahl has argued that the process of progression, revision, and return that negative capability names also shapes Keats's compositional practice.[21] Central to the compositional, structural, and syntactic manifestations of negative capability, I argue, is its relationship to influence and mediation. The physiological and literary-historical aspects of negative capability might specify James Brooke-Smith's identification of a 'kind of Keatsian "half-knowledge", a negative capability that is experienced not as aesthetic pleasure but rather as affective dissonance' in 'mediated states of perception that fall short of fully conceptualized knowledge [and] yet nevertheless embody a dim awareness of distant political, social, and historical realities'.[22] Negative capability identifies conditions of mediation. But in order to be understood in this way, negative capability must be understood in relation to the body and, specifically, the writing hand.

Questions about mediation's limitations and possibilities have been drawing increased attention in recent years. These questions point towards fundamental issues in the nature of poetic expression insofar as the 'situation of British poetry' during the Romantic era, according to Maureen McLane, 'offers us a window onto the transhistorical condition of poetic "mediality"—the condition

[19] Jacques Khalip, *Anonymous Life: Romanticism and Dispossession* (Stanford, CA: Stanford University Press, 2009), pp. 26–64.

[20] Nicholas Roe, *John Keats and the Culture of Dissent* (New York: Oxford University Press, 1997), p. 235. Jonathan Mulrooney, 'Keats's Avatar', *European Romantic Review*, 22: 3 (2011), pp. 313–21.

[21] Helen Vendler, *The Odes of John Keats* (Cambridge, MA: Harvard University Press, 1983); Linda von Pfahl, 'The Ethics of Negative Capability', *Nineteenth-Century Contexts*, 33: 5 (2011), pp. 451–66.

[22] James Brooke-Smith, 'Remediating Romanticism', *Literature Compass*, 10: 4 (2013), p. 346.

of existing in media, whether oral, manuscript, print, or digital'. The aim of such inquiry is to study 'the means through and historical conditions under which human imagination materializes itself'.[23] It is significant that the poet's body and voice are understood as forms of media here; for David Wellberry, 'the body itself is a medial apparatus and an elaborate technology. But it is also radically historical in the sense that it is shaped and reshaped by the networks to which it is conjoined.'[24] This essay understands 'media' as a capacious concept through which Keats's aesthetic endeavors touch on the cultural mediations of the anthology (John Lemprière's *Classical Dictionary*), the linguistic mediations of translation (Chapman's Homer), and the more loosely defined media, following McLane and Wellberry, of the body and the senses. Keats's body has a hand, as it were, in the mediated forms that constitute and complicate his poetic production.

To take a new look at Keats's interaction with the conceptual parameters of mediation rather than to examine the particularities of his engagement with individual authors—Milton especially—invokes a long history of theories of intertextuality. Those theories include Renaissance *imitatio* or neoclassicism instead of focusing exclusively on Romanticism's associations with the individual creative genius. The implications of mediated literary endeavors are vastly different for Keats's own sources than they are for him, since for Keats belatedness is itself a literary inheritance. A prominent articulation of Keats's belatedness comes in the early sonnet 'On First Looking into Chapman's Homer', whose 'mediated title'[25] thrice announces the indirect experience of classical culture by admitting to glancing, for the first time, at an English translation of Greek epic. Charles Rzepka convincingly argues that the reference to Cortez extends Keats's profound interest in the theme of belatedness, of historical, linguistic, and cultural mediation.[26] This sonnet investigates forms of immediacy that arise from the pleasure of mediated experience, whether literary, linguistic, visual, exploratory, or scientific, and this poem renders the mediated nature of translated, printed poetry into the more proximate pleasures of breathy sound.

[23] Maureen N. McLane, *Balladeering, Minstrelsy, and the Making of British Romantic Poetry* (Cambridge: Cambridge University Press, 2008), pp. 6–7.

[24] David Wellberry, 'Foreword', *Discourse Networks 1800/1900*, trans. Michael Metteer and Chris Cullens (Stanford, CA: Stanford University Press, 1990), p. xiv.

[25] Daniel Pollack-Pelzner, 'Revisionary Company: Keats, Homer, and Dante in the Chapman Sonnet', *Keats-Shelley Journal*, 56 (2007), p. 40.

[26] Charles J. Rzepka, '"Cortez—or Balboa, or Somebody Like That": Form, Fact, and Forgetting in Keats's "Chapman's Homer" Sonnet', *Keats-Shelley Journal*, 51 (2002), pp. 35–75. By contrast, the most prominent argument for the sonnet's 'error' remains Marjorie Levinson's *Keats's Life of Allegory: The Origins of a Style* (Oxford: Blackwell, 1988).

Commonly set at odds against Wordsworth's egotistical poetic persona as a force of self-negation, negative capability, along with the chameleon poet, has been aligned with a conception of the poetic persona that does not account for the productive and even privileged effects of aesthetic mediation and literary-historical belatedness. The literary-historical connotations of irritability suggest close but overlooked connections between, on one hand, negative capability's irresolution and half-knowledge and, on the other hand, the much-discussed belatedness and indirectness of Keats's experience of literary history. Keats's performance of negative capability through poetic composition is a specific site for the constitution of Romantic subjectivity through self-conscious acts of mediation. His explicit engagements with the works he was often currently reading during the time of composition suggest a new model of intertextual compositional practice, of cultural inheritance that is marked not only by susceptibility but also by self-articulation.

Keats has long been seen as the aspirational poet whose working-class background, limited knowledge of foreign languages, and slipshod education persistently clouded his pursuit of poetic glory. Reading the literary-historical implications of negative capability through their resonance with physiological theory allows us to see Keats's relationship to poetic tradition as a kind of satisfaction in oppositions. Without straining after, on one hand, the 'facts' of direct aesthetic experience through a familiarity with original languages or, on the other hand, the 'reason' of unmediated cultural exposure, the negatively capable poet resists an automatic, twitching urge for immediacy and instead experiences pleasure in the mediated immediacy that poetic production must necessarily provide in this period.

Negative capability articulates Keats's sense of his own literary production: with pen in hand, while pressed by the identities of earlier poets and open to the influence of external forces, negative capability determines his active compositional mode. But after these moments of inspiration and composition pass, dissatisfaction with his belatedness returns, and the ideal of negative capability is lost. In this reading, negative capability describes both qualities of the verse, as generations of critics have argued, as well as the self-effacing character of the practicing poet, particularly during his acquiescence to literary tradition's inspiring agency. In this way, the true 'negative capability' that Levinson assigned to Keats's 'badness' might instead be seen as an adequate compensation for the impossibility of immediate literary experience in the early nineteenth century.

As an incarnation of these ideas, I look to a poem that seems to imagine what unmediated immediacy would look like. If literary mediation renders experience second-hand, is there such a thing as first-hand literary experience? Jerome McGann influentially argued that different versions of individual poems allow Keats to render his own work an original text and to produce, in the second version, a translation.[27] But in 'This living hand' the written content and writing process of a single verse fragment display negative capability at work. The poem is almost violently devoted to a fiction of bodily presence, and its meaning derives in part from its original script form (Figure 7.1).[28]

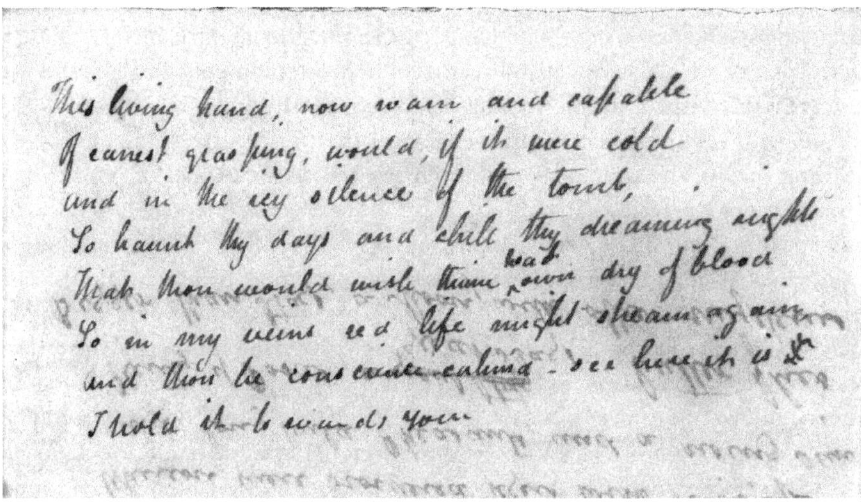
This living hand, now warm and capable
Of earnest grasping, would, if it were cold
And in the icy silence of the tomb,
So haunt thy days and chill thy dreaming nights
That thou would wish thine own heart dry of blood
So in my veins red life might stream again,
And thou be conscience-calm'd – see here it is –
I hold it towards you.

Figure 7.1: The manuscript of Keats's 'This living hand'.
MS Keats 2.29.2 (Houghton Library, Harvard University).

There is much in this poem that links to the physiological associations of negative capability—the 'capable' hand, the 'streaming blood' that invokes circulation, and the poem's final striking gesture: 'I hold [this hand] towards you.' The poem's ambiguous context makes its deixis all the more jarring. The statement 'here is my hand' is one thing on a theatrical stage but quite another in a hand-written letter. As a poem that existed only in manuscript during Keats's lifetime, the medium to which it seems to refer—handwriting—is particularly significant.

The 'hand' of the poem's first and penultimate lines can equally refer to writing and the body. In this sense, the phrase 'living hand' bestows the written word with immediacy and presence. Elsewhere in Keats's writing, hands point to the brevity and transience of human life. *The Fall of Hyperion* begins with an induction that imagines a time 'when this warm scribe my

[27] Jerome McGann, 'Keats and the Historical Method in Literary Criticism', *Modern Language Notes*, 94: 5 (1979), pp. 988–1032.
[28] MS Keats 2.29.2, Houghton Library, Harvard University.

hand is in the grave' (Canto I: line 18), and Keats describes to his brother in September 1819 the 'uneasy thought that in seven years the same hands cannot greet each other again' (*LJK*, II: pp. 208–9). The 'living hand' of this poem, especially in print, contributes to what Susan Wolfson has called the poem's ghoulishness.[29] In its printed form, its suggestion of handwriting emphasizes the mediation of print in a poem that is radically devoted, verbally and materially, to a fiction of bodily presence. But in its handwritten and unpublished form, the poem creates a more radical dissonance between the physical hand that it conjures and the written word that constitutes it. In print, the poem adds another layer of dissonance by raising the specter not only of the ghostly hand but also that of the absent handwriting. The poem's ghoulishness, then, is in part an effect of its two alternative forms of mediation: in our encounter with the poem's asserted immediacy—'see here it is / I hold it towards you'—we experience almost viscerally the mediation that both script and print instantiate.

In the movement from the manuscript poem's penultimate to its final line we witness the resurrection of the poet in the striking and reappearance of the 'I'. With the struck-through 'I' at the end of line seven, the lyric subject is first effaced—as the poem has guided the reader to imagine—and then, at the beginning of the next line, revived through the reader's projected self-sacrifice. On one hand, of course, Keats simply runs out of space on the sheet of paper. But, on the other hand, the poem's original medium of script seems to perform the resurrection of the speaking self. This striking-out and reappearance of the writing self across the break in the poetic line is central to the physiological conception of negative capability. The pleasure Keats finds in mediation during the moment of writing serves as a particularly appropriate gloss to 'This living hand'. In this poem, deixis focuses particular attention on the very moment of writing—the presence of the hand as it writes on the page.

The poem has drawn significant attention from deconstructionist camps. Following the work of de Man, critics have most commonly considered this poem through the figures of death it so vividly enacts—the deaths of the poet, the reader, and death's centrality to poetry itself.[30] Less centrally, critics have also attended to the implications of the poem's varied potential contexts—as a

[29] In *The Questioning Presence: Wordsworth, Keats, and the Interrogative Mode in Romantic Poetry* (Ithaca, NY: Cornell University Press, 1986), Wolfson describes the poem as a 'ghoulish assault on the reader' (p. 368).

[30] In *Keats, Narrative and Audience: The Posthumous Life of Writing* (Cambridge: Cambridge University Press, 1994), Andrew Bennett calls the poem 'an exemplary Romantic poem because of its explicit engagement with, and implicitly, its presupposition of, the death of its reader' (p. 12). See also Brendan Corcoran, 'Keats's Death: Towards a Posthumous Poetics', *Studies in Romanticism*, 48: 2 (2009), pp. 321–48; and Richard Macksey, 'Keats and the Poetics of Extremity', *Modern Language Notes*, 99: 4 (1984), pp. 845–84.

remnant from Keats's attempts at drama, a private address to Fanny Brawne, or a fragment unintended for public viewing.[31] The poem appears to be an attempt to achieve immediacy through what Jonathan Culler has identified as its replacement of 'a temporal presence and absence with an apostrophic presence and absence'.[32] The poem's rapid shift to informality ensures a sense of embodied presence that aligns with a rejection of formality's distance. Brendan Corcoran observes that 'The abrupt switch from the formal 'thou' to the more familiar 'you' drops any archaic pretense of social discretion for a jarring assertion of direct address and boldly embodied poetic presence' (p. 343). The two types of immediacy defined by Jay David Bolter and Richard Grusin are instructive here:

> in the epistemological sense, immediacy is transparency: the absence of mediation or representation. It is the notion that a medium could erase itself and leave the viewer in the presence of the objects represented, so that he could know the objects directly. In its psychological sense, immediacy names the viewer's feeling that the medium has disappeared and the objects are present to him, a feeling that his experience is therefore authentic.[33]

But in the case of Keats's poem, rendering immediacy is already mediated, a point that the manuscript's striking erasure of the speaking 'I' in the poem's penultimate line suggests.

Readers of Keats's letters quickly sense the urgency of his hand as it moves across paper, a point made clear in misspellings that often appear at the ends and edges of a page. With 'This living hand', the struck-through 'I' suggests, in addition to this familiar urgency, both self-effacement and otherness. What is suspended between this line and the next is the very question of identity and agency. Composition means, for Keats, a willingness to suspend subjectivity and absorb the literary identity of another, whether that 'other' is Chapman's version of Homer, Milton, or one of Keats's own poetic personae. This is the issue at the core of Keats's self-conception as a poet, an identity achieved only

[31] For an insightful overview of these contexts and their ultimate incompatibility, see Lawrence Lipking, *The Life of the Poet: Beginning and Ending Poetic Careers* (Chicago, IL: The University of Chicago Press, 1981), pp. 180–4. In *Intangible Materialism: The Body, Scientific Knowledge, and the Power of Language* (Minneapolis: University of Minnesota Press, 2009), pp. 124–6, Ronald Schleifer's reading of the poem's indexicality denies its potential contexts as well as the possibility that 'hand' might point to script.

[32] Jonathan Culler, *The Pursuit of Signs: Semiotics, Literature, Deconstruction* (Ithaca, NY: Cornell University Press, 1981), pp. 153–4.

[33] Jay David Bolter and Richard Grusin, *Remediation: Understanding New Media* (Cambridge, MA: MIT Press, 2000), p. 70.

in the act of composition, in the mediated immediacy and self-effaced agency that the hand of negative capability strains to grasp.

'Irritable reaching' suggests a paradox of contraction and extension, and this paradox reappears in this poem's haunting gesture, in which the spectral speaker of these lines endeavors to 'hold' his hand 'towards' the reader. Read through the lens of medical history, the 'irritable reaching' that negative capability overcomes raises questions about the ways that the body registers immediacy and mediacy. 'This living hand' articulates these aspects of negative capability and specifically echoes the paradoxical physiology that negative capability overcomes. To 'hold' one's own hand or that of another—say, that of a corpse or patient—allows for the same locution, as the initial description of the hand's ability to grasp (presumably another hand, that of the reader) has already made clear. Alternatively, though, the hand's warm capability also signals a resolute susceptibility to mediated, indirect forms of influence, a susceptibility that finds its articulation in a poem that pinpoints media transitions between thought, script, and print. Its perceived immediacy is a product of its mediation, and its self-effacement—in content and script—is the precondition for its existence. The 'living hand' that overcomes a tendency for 'irritable reaching' points towards new directions in media and mediality studies in the Romantic period that reinflect more traditional questions of ekphrasis, imitation, and neoclassicism with increased attention to physiology, script, and print.

Chapter Eight

'uncertainties, Mysteries, doubts'

Pluralities and the Historical Present in Keats and Hazlitt

Emily Rohrbach[1]

Why might it matter that when Keats coined his now-famous phrase 'negative capability' in 1817 he pluralized the 'uncertainties, Mysteries, doubts'—those forces of questioning with which the negatively capable mind could remain, as he put it, 'without any irritable reaching after fact & reason' (*LJK*, I: p. 193)? Reading Keats's curiously plural epistolary formulation in relation to his developing poetics, this essay proposes that Keats conceives plurality as a poetic figure crucial to accommodating the complexities of the early nineteenth-century historical moment—that is, a post-Waterloo moment caught between the rise of periodization (with an attendant urgency to name the 'spirit of the age') and the temporalities of modernity (the sense of speed and of an unknowable futurity, which made that naming all but impossible).[2] These competing pressures can be felt in the paratactic pluralities of Keats's phrase—a phrase whose very form helps multiply to an indefinite number the unknown possibilities, while the 's' sounds in Keats's expression, added to the caesural hesitations, extend the line temporally, slowing the reader down. Keatsian historical thinking begins with a slowing down and a dwelling on 'uncertainties, Mysteries, doubts'.

A Keatsian poetics of slow reading and lateral sideshadowing might not immediately bring to mind the work of a modern historian called on to record the historical dimensions of the age. But when one recalls the letter Keats wrote two years later about the shortcomings of Voltaire and William

[1] This essay includes sections from Chapter One and Chapter Three of my monograph, *Modernity's Mist: British Romanticism and the Poetics of Anticipation* (New York: Fordham University Press, 2015)—reworked for this occasion and reprinted with kind permission from Fordham University Press.

[2] For a full discussion of this intellectual history, see the Introduction and Chapter One to my monograph, *Modernity's Mist*.

Robertson's historiography (the 1819 letter on the 'vale of Soul-making'), the historiographical dimension to Keats's negatively capable, plural poetics becomes more clear. I am arguing, that is, that the dimensions of Keats's poetry we might associate with negative capability as he formulates it in 1817 are consistent with his more explicit efforts to find a way of imagining the historical present that succeeds where the methods and assumptions of enlightenment historians fail. I begin, therefore, by revisiting the 1819 letter before considering how 'To Autumn'—Keats's poem perhaps most famously accused of political escapism—engages with historiographical problems of Keats's moment in what might be called a negatively capable historical thinking. For Autumn's wind and breath move about like an elusive 'spirit of the age'. The essay concludes by turning to William Hazlitt's critical essay collection of that name, *The Spirit of the Age: Or, Contemporary Portraits*, as an example of a prose form modeling the historical thinking that Keats's negatively capable poetics envision.

'Soul-making' as Alternative Historiography

A preliminary detour through Keats's letter on the world as a 'vale of Soul-making' will help make visible the movement from poetic self-reflexivity to historical thinking that takes shape in 'To Autumn', for the April 1819 letter to George and Georgiana Keats performs the very displacement of linear progressive history that takes poetic shape in the ode's 'hours by hours'. It does so, moreover, by virtue of a self-reflexivity that becomes, we might say, simply *reflexivity*, removing from the process the notion of an unalterable consistency in essential 'selfhood'. Read in light of the 'vale of Soul-making' letter, 'To Autumn' appears in its proliferation of possibilities not only as an aesthetic thinking through of the challenges of imagining and writing the present as history in post-Waterloo England but also as itself an event that takes place through reading.

Keats's epistolary meditation on 'Soul-making' serves as an alternative to what he sees as the failures of historical discourse, as the shortcomings of Enlightenment historical narratives appear to prompt the very idea. The 1819 letter to George and Georgiana Keats vividly shifts from a discussion of the problems of trying to understand the world through William Robertson's *History of America* to a proposal for the solution to those problems: the poet's own philosophy of subject-making in the worldly, temporal making of a soul. For Keats, the world is not suited for making progress toward happiness in civilized commercial society; it is a place to learn to read the 'human heart' and to be altered by that reading, through 'proovings'. In view of the short-comings of Robertson's mode of historical discourse, Keats proposes, instead, the world as 'vale of Soul-making' (*LJK*, II: p. 103).

'I have been reading lately two very different books Robertson's America and Voltaire's Siecle De Louis xiv', Keats writes: 'It is like walking arm in arm between Pizarro and the great-little Monarch' (*LJK*, II: p. 100). However different from one another, the books are both histories of the modern period displaying a commitment to the notion of cultural progress:

> In How lementabl[e] a case do we see the great body of the people in both instances [Robertson and Voltaire]: in the first,[3] … . If [Man] improves by degrees his bodily accommodations and comforts—at each stage, at each accent there are waiting for him a fresh set of annoyances—he is mortal and there is still a heaven with its Stars abov[e] his head. The most interesting question that can come before us is, How far by the persevering endeavors of a seldom appearing Socrates mankind may be made happy—I can imagine such happiness carried to an extreme—but what must it end in?—Death … in truth I do not at all believe in this sort of perfectibility—the nature of the world will not admit of it— … . Call the world if you Please 'The vale of Soul-making'. (II: pp. 100–2)

Keats's meditation on cultural progress contradicts Robertson's and Voltaire's commitment to valorizing modern history and culture when he posits the almost random ('seldom appearing') historical appearance of a Socrates. With the measure of Keats's pulse, the historical dimensions of the present age made the prevailing historiography appear inadequate. The most overt critique centers on Robertson, with the key words 'happiness' and 'perfectibility', for underlying Robertson's historiography was the assumption of happiness as a perfectible, achievable goal. But this model and its aims—a unified social and cultural progress toward civilized happiness—struck Keats as ill-suited to the world as he found it: 'In truth I do not at all believe in this sort of perfectibility—the nature of the world will not admit of it.' Stadial progress of civilization, even if it were viable, would not reduce overall human discomfort, which only comes in new forms: 'at each stage', 'a fresh set of annoyances'.

Keats finds the guiding notion of Christian redemption even more wanting than he does philosophical history. In place of both, Keats's 'vale of Soul-making' offers alternative aims. His vale is not a place to find happiness, but 'A Place where the heart must feel and suffer in a thousand diverse ways!' Happiness is neither viable nor the most valuable aim. Keats's process of feeling and suffering that rings changes on one's subjectivity so as to make a soul replaces the telos of happiness. The world Keats proposes in an extended metaphor is a 'school' for the 'reading' of the human heart, a schoolroom reading that promises circuitous access to the (temporal) world that Robertson's

[3] Keats never returns, in the letter, to the second 'instance', Voltaire.

prose had missed. That access crucially hinges upon the singular subjectivity of what Keats here calls 'identities': 'There may be intelligences or sparks of the divinity in millions—but they are not Souls till they acquire identities, till each one is personally itself' (*LJK*, II: p. 102). Subject-making, for Keats, is a process of becoming that requires a world in which to feel and suffer, and it is *reading* that provides access to that world.

The language of 'identities', which indicates Keats's notion of the singularity or uniqueness of each soul that is made, should not lead us to think that Keats upheld any static notion of essential selfhood or that this notion of the soul is anything other than a process that makes sociality—the imagination of the social world and thus social engagement—possible. 'That you may judge the more clearly', Keats writes, 'I will put it in the most homely form possible.' Here follows the crucial formulation:

> I will call the *world* a School instituted for the purpose of teaching little children to read—I will call the *human heart* the *horn Book* used in that School—and I will call the *Child able to read, the Soul* made from that *school* and its *hornbook*. Do you not see how necessary a world of pains and troubles is to school an intelligence and make it a soul? (*LJK*, II: p. 102)

The purpose of the world, in Keats's model, is to enable one's reading of 'the human heart' and, in turn, one's alteration by that process so as to become a soul, where before there was only an 'intelligence'. This notion of an identity or soul as earned entirely in a figurative, temporal process of reading marks Keats's break not only from the discourse of Christianity, which Keats called 'vulgar superstition', but also from the idea of one's identity as originating in inherited rank or blood. The Keatsian subject is not reducible to the body or to social identity, but is also not an entirely private subject, sealed off from social experience. For Keats does not make the hornbook equivalent to one's own heart (an object possessed); rather, it is equivalent to 'the human heart', the ambiguity of which enables the concept to pivot between one's own heart (one's unique circumstances and experiences of feeling and suffering) and a broader notion of 'human' suffering in a 'world of pains'. In the kind of 'reading' Keats describes, the separation between 'identities'—between one's own heart and the hearts of others—dissolves in the capacious notion of 'the human heart'.[4] Crucially, Keats imagines this reading as a more

[4] It is perhaps worth noting in relation to the metaphor of the school that Keats attended the Enfield School from 1803 until 1811. In *John Keats and the Culture of Dissent* (Oxford: Clarendon Press, 1997), Nicholas Roe argues convincingly for the centrality of this experience to the formation of Keats's radical political views. Keats's time at Enfield

adequate means to understand man's present circumstances than what the philosophies of Scottish Enlightenment historiography could provide. What appears ostensibly as a self-reflexive turn inward, in reading the heart, turns out to mark not a separation from the world but a finer model for reading it.

Legibility, however, does not imply what Keats called 'smokeability', the notion that a text could be transparently understood once and for all.[5] No all-knowing schoolmaster appears in Keats's model. The soul is figured as what in us learns to read, but also, significantly, as what remains always a child reader. In a world of flux that defies perfect mastery, one maintains a sense of wonder—indeed, of 'uncertainties, Mysteries, doubts'—and is, as a capable reader, still able to be surprised. Unlike in progressive narrative histories that close off the potential for the unexpected, the future for Keats cannot be predicted through patterns or lessons of the past ('the nature of the world will not admit of it') or be rationally controlled, but is subject to the unpredictable alterations of nature that come through reading the heart. For 'what are proovings of [man's] heart', Keats asks, 'but fortifiers or alterers of his nature? and what is his altered nature but his soul?' (*LJK*, II: p. 103). The pluralized present participle, 'proovings', underscores the notion of an always ongoing process. It calls for an openness to the worldly, unpredictable, eternally mysterious process of altering one's 'nature' that makes a person—that makes a distinctive soul and a capable reader.[6] That openness to encountering the new or the unpredictable—an openness to something so different from previous experience that it revises one's understanding of self and world—is the kind of subjectivity that Keats's poetry so often both describes and elicits. Turning to 'To Autumn' with this notion of 'Soul-making' in view, one can start to see the poem as a kind of hornbook to the world. This is not to suggest that

was intellectually and socially rich, and this is where Keats developed voracious reading habits. Keats won books as prizes while at school, including Bonnycastle's *Introduction to Astronomy*, but he read primarily books that he borrowed from the school's library, as well as some additional books borrowed from Charles Cowden Clarke. Roe writes, 'Like everything else at Enfield School, the library was remarkable' (p. 46). If we take Keats's metaphor of 'reading' literally, that in school he was reading not only books he owned but also those that would circulate through the hands of others supports the notion of reading (of suffering and feeling in the world) as a process that is at once one's own (a private act) and social (an act that renders the reader permeable to a broader human experience of the temporal world).

[5] For commentary on 'smokeability', see James Chandler, *England in 1819: The Politics of Literary Culture and the Case of Romantic Historicism* (Chicago, IL: University of Chicago Press, 1998), pp. 395–402.

[6] Although 'reading' in the 'vale of Soul-making' letter is clearly figurative, it is not incidental that Keats witnesses, and dramatically benefits from, a historical moment of rapidly expanding print culture and rising literacy rates that made literal reading accessible in an unprecedented way.

'To Autumn' provides a solution to the world's mysteries, but that it offers a poetics of relation to the historical world, a set of figural, grammatical, and conceptual tools for reading it.

Mists, Spirit

Keats's ode self-consciously alters our sense of time, while it plays with our patterns of breathing. The course of the poem dilates the moment in a way that opens the present to multiple possibilities drawn from obscurities that the season of plural 'mists' immediately puts in play (line 1). In the opening phrase, pluralizing the word *mist*—as with 'uncertainties, Mysteries, doubts'—appears an entirely arbitrary semantic choice in 'Season of mists and mellow fruitfulness'. Rhythmically, however, making 'mists' plural immediately, insistently slows the pace of reading. Associated phonetically with mystery, 'mists' imply an impediment to clear sight and an epistemological challenge. An atmosphere of mists suggests that we cannot see what is coming—hence a further impetus to slacken pace. Loaded with monosyllabic words, the opening stanza slows the reading process down. The speaker's enjoyment of lyric delay is knowing (unlike that of the bees), and he enjoys time's slowness all the more, it seems, in light of its tentative quality, in light of the knowledge that warm days *will* cease, even if the senses for the moment suggest otherwise. Geoffrey Hartman observed in the ode 'a westerly drift like the sun', indicating that, though the perspective shifts in the course of the poem, the time of day does not significantly progress. '"To Autumn"', he wrote, 'does not explicitly evolve from sunrise to sunset but rather from a rich to a clarified dark. Closely read it starts and ends in twilight.'[7] Keats's lyrical suspension of time's progress thus is both rhythmic and thematic.

As one reads, the poem's rhythms also alter our patterns of breathing in unpredictable and telling ways, registering aesthetically the speaker's anticipation of change. Although Keats frequently enjambs lines, eliminating the space for breath at the line's end, enjambment occurs at different points in each stanza (lines 3 and 7 in the first stanza; 2, 6, and 8 in the second; 5, 6, and 9 in the third). Alterations of breathing as one reads thus occur irregularly, unpredictably. The use of caesura is equally irregular, suggesting that the poem self-consciously asks that we breathe with it. In anticipation and delay of the stanza's end, for instance, the notion of endlessly warm days is interrupted by a pause after 'cease', both rhythmically and semantically (even if by negation) bringing the sense of ending into play (10). This interruption momentarily contradicts the continuous sense of enjoyment the line has just suggested, while

[7] Geoffrey Hartman, *The Fate of Reading and Other Essays* (Chicago, IL: University of Chicago Press, 1975), p. 129.

providing a space to draw life-sustaining breath, however paradoxically, from the anticipatory sense of finitude that joins poet and reader.

A self-reflexive invocation of the poet occurs even earlier. For autumn is, we immediately learn, 'Close bosom-friend of the maturing sun; / Conspiring with him how to load and bless / With fruit the vines that round the thatch eves run' (2–4). Hearing a pun of 'maturing *son*', one might recall Keats's self-consciousness about his own poetic maturity when he wrote in the preface to *Endymion* that the poem had proceeded from a place somewhere between 'the imagination of a boy' and 'the mature imagination of a man' (*PJK*, p. 102). His relentless ambitions to become a better, more mature poet, like the Wordsworth he described in 1818 as having explored the 'dark Passages', placed him lingering before them. With this association between the 'maturing' poet's work and nature's growth processes, the season's work of 'load[ing] and bless[ing]' appears self-consciously interwoven with the poet's. Keats famously advised Percy Shelley 'that you might curb your magnanimity and be more of an artist, and "load every rift" of your subject with ore' (*LJK*, II: p. 323). In 'To Autumn', he has semantically loaded the very activity of 'load[ing]' with the poetic process of creating rich figuration. Grammatically it is, of course, Autumn who 'conspir[es] with' the 'maturing sun'. The language suggests not just the political plotting of conspiracy to which Nicholas Roe alerts us, but also, in its etymological affiliation (from the Latin *conspirare*, literally to 'breathe together'), the process of a reader's breathing together with the 'maturing sun', with the poet as maker.[8] That Keats's most memorably recalled reading experience—of Chapman's translation of Homer—took the form for him of an extraordinary event of breathing ('Yet did I never breathe its pure serene') suggests how consciously attuned to this physical, sensory aspect of reading he was (*PJK*, p. 64).[9]

To keep pace in breath, however, is still to be eluded, at least in part, by the poem's ostensible subject, Autumn, whose fruits finally cannot be contained by their overly 'plump[ed]' 'shells' (7) and 'cells' 'o'er-brimm'd' (11). This sense of Autumn's intractable excess is heightened in the second stanza, where the personified Autumn is addressed as at once obviously immediate and oddly elusive. 'Who hath not seen thee oft amid thy store?' the speaker asks rhetorically. To breathe with Keats is to sense an elusive yet immediate present and thus to open the interpretive possibility that Autumn is Keats's figure of elusiveness for the 'goings on of the world' that seemed to defy narrative control.

Breath, spirit, soul-making: If the world is to be understood not as a politically progressive history, but as a 'vale of Soul-making', then Autumn,

[8] See Roe, *Dissent*, pp. 253–67.

[9] Along these lines, in 'Ode on a Grecian Urn' the repetitions in 'More happy love! more happy, happy love!' (line 25, emphasis added) elicit the reader's 'panting' (27) akin to that of the urn's figured lovers.

its prime inhabitant for the time being, might very well be Keats's candidate for the vagaries of the 'spirit of the age' in the post-Waterloo period.[10] The second stanza shifts from the present-perfect of 'has o'er-brimm'd' (11) to the present tense, as if to underscore Autumn's immediacy, but it is also structured by the repetitions of 'Sometimes', 'Or', 'And sometimes', and 'Or', which suggest a certain slipping away in the very abundance of possible locations:

> Who hath not seen thee oft amid thy store?
> Sometimes whoever seeks abroad may find
> Thee sitting careless on a granary floor,
> Thy hair soft-lifted by the winnowing wind;
> *Or* on a half-reap'd furrow sound asleep,
> Drows'd with the fume of poppies, while thy hook
> Spares the next swath and all its twined flowers:
> *And* sometimes like a gleaner thou dost keep
> Steady thy laden head across a brook;
> *Or* by a cider-press, with patient look,
> Thou watchest the last oozings hours by hours.
> (12–22, italics mine)

These 'Or' 'And' conjunctions conjure the difficulty of pinning Autumn down in a world of diverse, evenly balanced, plural possibilities. In 'To Autumn', all possibilities appear equally plausible, even if incompatible; the speculations about Autumn's location, that is, do not improve on earlier ones in the course of the stanza, but simply add to the possibilities, defying a progressive movement of thought. Along these lines, Helen Vendler has noted the chronologically disordered presentation of processes: 'Where we would expect (in this minutely conscious poem) first reaping, then gleaning, then threshing, we find instead first threshing, then reaping, then gleaning, a sequence invented'.[11] Not only does this non-chronological sequence suggest a self-consciousness about poetic artifice; it insists on the non-progressive, lateral movement of time: 'hours *by* hours'.

In her essay 'Looking at the Stars Forever', Rei Terada writes of the post-Waterloo era: 'The idea that it is no longer possible to tell revolution and

[10] Responding to Keats's sonnet 'Great spirits now on earth are sojourning', the critic 'Z.', John Gibson Lockhart, in however irate a tone, clearly recognized Keats's poetry as contributing to debates about the 'spirit of the age' when he wrote in *Blackwood's Edinburgh Magazine* in 1817, 'Mr. Keats classes together WORDSWORTH, HUNT, and HAYDON, as the three greatest spirits of the age, and that he alludes to himself, and some others of the rising brood of Cockneys, as likely to attain hereafter an equally honorable elevation'. *Keats's Poetry and Prose*, ed. Jeffrey N. Cox (New York: Norton, 2009), p. 273.

[11] Helen Vendler, *The Odes of John Keats* (Cambridge, MA: Harvard University Press, 1983), p. 251.

restoration apart ... is more disturbing than any "failure" of revolution.' Whereas Terada observes that for Keats in *Hyperion* 'impasse is more of a solution than a problem', in 'To Autumn' the personified Autumn, as a figure for the present, gives us a different response to impasse, from the point of view of the speaker.[12] The difficulty of knowing Autumn with certainty, despite the season's visceral immediacy, creates an impasse that leads not so much to stasis as to sideshadowing—in its proliferation of simultaneous possibilities, side-by-side. Indeed, this suspension of time's forward movement, enabling the moment to dilate, seems to be a phase in the poem's larger movement of opening up that the slow delay of transforming the plural 'mists' into the upward and outward 'skies' underscores. No teleological trajectory would seem to close off the generating of yet another possible locale, a different narrative point of departure.

In addition to the way conjunctions ('Or', 'And') grammatically generate the plurality of possibilities, the stanza form Keats develops in 'To Autumn' reinforces the sense of prolonging presentness and opening up. Keats borrows from the sonnet form—a form traditionally marked by the resolution of a sestet or the closure of a rhyming couplet—to achieve something else. If the traditional English or Italian sonnet begins with the larger verse unit to develop a problem that the shorter couplet or sestet often resolves, Keats reverses this pattern, beginning his stanza with one Shakespearean quatrain followed by a modified Italian sestet (extended to seven lines). Not only does the larger verse unit come last so as to counter the traditional closure of the English couplet, but the pattern of the last seven lines is close enough to a sestet to make the (extraneous, added) penultimate line (which forms an internal, though not an ending, couplet) seem to distort the form slightly; insofar as the stanza conveys, however critically, an idea of the present as timelessness, the added line delays the pressure of temporality by putting off the stanza's end.

Whereas, in the second stanza, the speaker visualizes a number of places potentially to find Autumn—linked by 'Or' and 'And'—the final stanza focuses on listening to the multiple, distinct songs of Autumn's music, not all of them joyful. Autumn's aural tones are mixed, ranging from plaintive 'bleat[ing]' to joyful 'sing[ing]' and 'whistl[ing]' and sorrowful 'mourn[ing]', and the speaker's ear is attuned so finely to each across the landscape and sky as to suggest the acoustics of an astonishingly mobile or diffuse subjectivity.[13] With the suggestion of beginnings in 'bloom' and the several homophones of born ('borne', 'bourn'), together with shadows of winter and death (as in the

[12] Rei Terada, 'Looking at the Stars Forever', *Studies in Romanticism*, 50: 2 (Summer 2011), p. 279.

[13] Remarkably, there are no leaves in 'To Autumn', where we might expect to find visually mixed tones of color.

'wailful choir' and 'soft-dying day'), contrasts between alternatives sharpen in the language of this stanza, but they are harmonized by the musicality of the verse and the protean capaciousness of the speaker's perception.[14] There is no Wordsworthian deictic as, for example, when in 'Tintern Abbey' the speaker remarks: 'I again repose / Here, under this dark sycamore, and view / These plots of cottage-ground'.[15] James O'Rourke is, I think, right to revise Vendler's notion of an 'unmoving center from which all is seen and heard' (p. 254), by observing instead 'the stylistic effect of a pendulum-like swing' (p. 167). With no 'I' appearing in the poem, the lyric subject is less an 'egotistical sublime' than a 'thoroughfare for all thoughts' (*LJK*, I: p. 386; II: p. 213).

The landscape, too, appears a thoroughfare for 'light wind', leading Paul Fry to see the scene as 'a faintly breathing thing ... like the lungs in an interval of pain'.[16] Jonathan Bate's ecocritical reading of the poem extended this attention to the wind by putting the poem in the context of Keats's epistolary discussions of the weather's effects on his health around the time he was writing 'To Autumn'. 'The consumptive has no choice but to gape after the weather', Bate reminds us; 'Air quality is of the utmost importance for those whose lungs have been invaded by Mycobacterium tuberculosis. Keats was hurried to his death less by his reviewers, as Byron supposed, than by the weather.' In Bate's view, the ode's celebratory tone should be understood in light of the fact that the 'good summer and clear autumn of 1819 very literally gave [Keats] a new lease on life'.[17] If the 'light wind' held personal meaning for a consumptive poet who had seen both his brother and mother die from the disease, however, it also suggested a larger, shared condition of uncertainty about the forces of intellectual and social change, as the heavier-handed 'mighty winds' did in 'Sleep and Poetry':

> What though I am not wealthy in the dower
> Of spanning wisdom; though I do not know
> The shiftings of the mighty winds that blow
> Hither and thither all the changing thoughts

[14] A number of fine critics have discussed the elaborately interwoven sound patterns. See, for instance, James O'Rourke's extensive description of them in *Keats's Odes and Contemporary Criticism* (Gainesville: University Press of Florida, 1998) and Garrett Stewart's wonderful essay, 'Keats and Language', *The Cambridge Companion to Keats*, ed. Susan Wolfson (Cambridge: Cambridge University Press, 2001).

[15] Samuel Taylor Coleridge and William Wordsworth, *Lyrical Ballads: 1798 and 1800*, ed. Michael Gamer and Dahlia Porter (Peterborough: Broadview Press, 2008), p. 143.

[16] Paul H. Fry, 'History, Existence, and "To Autumn"', *Studies in Romanticism*, 25: 2 (Summer 1986), p. 218.

[17] Jonathan Bate, *Song of the Earth* (Cambridge, MA: Harvard University Press, 2002), p. 105.

Of man: though no great minist'ring reason sorts
Out the dark mysteries of human souls
To clear conceiving: yet there ever rolls
A vast idea before me … (lines 284–91)

Like the 'changing thoughts / Of man', the small gnats in 'To Autumn' are 'borne aloft / Or sinking as the light wind lives or dies' (28–9). Keats's concern with breathing and wind invites an intimation of mortality that alters the second stanza's emphasis on abundance; it also envisions an atmosphere of flux in which the only force against the shifting of the wind is a temporal imagination that sees the present as transient and, without access to a predictable futurity, anticipates its significance only tentatively. This temporal imagining lifts the speaker above the helpless delusions of the absorptively present-minded bees and wind-tossed gnats.

Teeming with possibilities and heterogeneous in tone, Keats's conception of the present implicitly makes the onward writing of narrative history—or at least the kinds of histories available in early nineteenth-century England—appear impossible, for the futurity that shadows the present in 'To Autumn' appears indefinite and unknowable. That sense of uncertainty renders Keats's sense of time incompatible with the assured notion of stadial progress informing enlightenment histories. 'To Autumn' is short on direct political or historical statements, and that is surely why it became the center of debate with the rise of new historicism in the early 1980s. What that lack of direct statement enables, however, is a consideration of what the distinctive *poetic* qualities of Keats's verse can say and do, providing a sense of the 'altering' self, an ordering of time and the senses, that Keats described as so crucial to approximating the shifting world—a world that political histories could not accommodate.

In view of the early nineteenth-century contest over the temporality of narrating recent history, Keats's sense of proliferating possibilities in a world of vanishing predictability, of epistemological 'uncertainties, Mysteries, doubts', makes the poem not only an event in literary history but also an event of historiographical thinking. To live in Keats's time, the poem tells us, was to anticipate an unknowable future in the midst of a present whose elusiveness—whose multiple uncertainties affording possibilities—made the narration of its significance in conventional historical forms impossible. If the spirit of the age remained elusive, how could one confidently narrate its significance in a sequential history of before and after? To what might this elusive present of scattered possibilities lead? The world 'would not admit of' the probabilistic narrative practices upon which enlightenment historians relied. Read allegorically, Keats's 'To Autumn' conceptualized an early nineteenth-century historiographical problem—the urgency and impossibility of comprehending the present as history—as the consequence of a present that did not have recourse to the past for its self-understanding, but that abounded in imagined potential scenarios and opened toward an unknown futurity. The way of reading the world offered in 'To Autumn' is not epistemological, but ethical in that the world it conceives is not subject to complete understanding. Considered as a historiographical intervention, 'To Autumn'—hornbook to the world—offers a reading of the present as multiple and de-centering, teeming and mysterious: its plural 'mists'—like the epistolary '*Myst*eries'—suggesting something missed: a historical dimension both elusive and palpable at once.

Hazlitt's Plural Spirit

If 'To Autumn' can be understood as metaphorical hornbook for the historical moment, then what might a negatively capable historiography (not just a set of poetic-conceptual tools but a historical prose narrative) of early nineteenth-century Britain look like? I propose for consideration William Hazlitt's essay collection published in 1825, *The Spirit of the Age; Or, Contemporary Portraits*, for Hazlitt's collection of prose portraits presents different ways of finding or reading (in both senses) the 'spirit of the age' in a strikingly heterogeneous collection. Forgoing the strategy of characterizing the present by tracing its narrative forward from some single, unifying origin, Hazlitt discovers traces of that spirit in the contemporary works of various living writers. Suggesting some uncertainty about how to sum it all up, these discoveries do not contribute to one coherent image of the age, but appear as seemingly incompatible possibilities. Like Keats's poetry, Hazlitt's *The Spirit of the Age* imagines history as a dynamic process and the present as a world of multiple, equally plausible possibilities, never finally solving the question of what that spirit is.

Let me begin with Hazlitt's provocative title, which already indicates some of the historical work's most significant formal and narratological aspects. Hazlitt does not comment on the choice of title directly, but six years later, in a similarly titled essay, 'The Spirit of the Age', John Stuart Mill wrote the following:

> The 'Spirit of the Age' is in some measure a novel expression. I do not believe that it is to be met with in any work exceeding fifty years in antiquity. The idea of comparing one's own age with former ages, or with our notion of those which are yet to come, had occurred to philosophers; but it never before was itself the dominant idea of any age.[18]

[18] John Stuart Mill, 'The Spirit of the Age', in *The Spirit of the Age: Victorian Essays*, ed. Gertrude Himmelfarb (New Haven, CT: Yale University Press, 2007), p. 51.

If Mill is right that this was the 'dominant idea' of early nineteenth-century Britain or Europe, the elusiveness of the age's defining qualities surely contributed to writers' prevailing preoccupation with the subject. The phrase itself points not to an object or any aspect of the material world but to an immaterial force, suggesting that, although it lacks a fully identifiable material form itself, the spirit at least potentially touches on all that exists simultaneously.

Hazlitt's subtitle—as with Autumn's possibilities, initiated by 'Or'—reinforces the notion of simultaneity when it announces a key aspect of the work's formal structure: a series of *contemporary* portraits. Whereas a history by an Enlightenment historian, or even an account of the French revolution by Helen Maria Williams, ends in a later chronological moment than it begins—whether it moves successively through grand historical periods, or in a more personal vein through days, weeks, and only a few years—Hazlitt's final 'portrait', his last entry in the collection (James Sheridan Knowles), is contemporaneous with his first one (Jeremy Bentham), as well as with those of all the other living authors who feature in the prose portrait collection. In this respect, the narrative moves in time not progressively or regressively, but laterally.

What's more, the prose portraits focus primarily on philosophers', poets', novelists', and other writers' works in relation to the present times—not on their biographies or even on the literary or cultural histories they inherit or revise. Hazlitt's *Spirit of the Age* is an insistently present-focused series of essays based on the oeuvres of a number of poets and thinkers—each assessing how we can perceive the spirit of the age in, or in relation to, their works. For example, Hazlitt writes of William Godwin, 'The Spirit of the Age was never more fully shown than in its treatment of this writer—its love of paradox and change, its dastard submission to prejudice and to the fashion of the day.'[19] In another entry, Hazlitt describes Wordsworth's genius as 'a pure emanation of the Spirit of the Age. Had he lived in any other period of the world, he would never have been heard of' (p. 203). When it comes to Sir James MacKintosh, he announces, 'The subject of the present article is one of the ablest and most accomplished men of the age, both as a writer, a speaker, and a converser' (p. 215). In addition to how the portraits appear presentist, we can see in this selection of excerpts how Hazlitt's collection comes as a group of distinct reflections, without any obvious threads that work to make the title's pluralized 'portraits' into one unified, coherent, or comprehensive portrait of the age. How does Godwin's status of most 'full[y] show[ing]' the spirit match up—or compete or contrast—with Wordsworth's as the spirit's

[19] William Hazlitt, *The Spirit of the Age: Or, Contemporary Portraits* (Grasmere, Cumbria: The Wordsworth Trust, 2004), p. 105.

'pure emanation'? Hazlitt's is a collection of balkanized contemporary histories, not a unified, grand historical narrative.

In addition to Hazlitt's present-focused selection of authors, within any given 'portrait' nothing like a chronologically organized history of a writer's career appears. Hazlitt traces the historical present neither back to the origins of British identity in the culture of Greece and Rome (as Scottish Enlightenment historians overwhelmingly do), nor back to the biographical beginnings and successive development of the individual authors on which he focuses. Rather, the painting metaphor of Hazlitt's title evokes the way in which the prose portraitist seems to assess each writer's work *at the given moment*. However much that image of a moment might suggest a past or future, in the way that a portrait subject's dress or collected objects might suggest a past experience or future ambition, it is the past or future only as embodied in that precise historical moment of becoming. All of these essays in succession describe Hazlitt's own contemporaries: all living writers, most of whom are still actively writing. That is to say, Hazlitt's critical assessments inevitably relinquish the ambition of being comprehensive representations even of these individual authors' oeuvres. As a historical narrative of the spirit of the present age, the collection unfolds in a series of simultaneous reflections on that spirit in the character or work or genius or treatment of a writer. The narrative progression thus tells a story that is not so much a linear temporal progress as it is a proliferation of simultaneities—figures of potential historical significance living contemporaneously alongside one another, reflecting the spirit of the age in various ways that do not so much cohere as accumulate, without the structure of an underlying, unifying system.

Although Hazlitt selects only a few dozen individuals, all of whom are British male writers or philosophers of some kind, the sense of incompletion that the collection courts affords the historiography multiple, simultaneously available points of contact with the spirit of the age (multiple points of entry), rather than signaling a single point of origin, such as that in Greco-Roman culture. Where, or in what, British culture originated appears less important to Hazlitt than are the various perspectives that are shaping it anew.

Hazlitt's critical esteem for heterogeneous thinking becomes clear in his very first portrait, when he disparages Jeremy Bentham for the uniformity of his accomplished philosophical thought—as tidy as it is unarresting. Assuming the principle of utility as the foundation of his moral and political reasoning enables Bentham to constantly refer his argument back to it. Regarding that unifying principle, Hazlitt observes,

> Perhaps the weak side of his conclusions also is, that he has carried this single view of his subject too far, and not made sufficient allowance for the varieties of human nature, and the caprices and irregularities

> of the human will. … Mr. Bentham's method of reasoning, though comprehensive and exact, labours under the defect of most systems—it is too *topical*. It includes every thing; but it includes every thing alike. It is rather like an inventory, than a valuation of different arguments. (pp. 92, 99)

Unlike Bentham, the author of *The Spirit of the Age; Or, Contemporary Portraits* is less a philosopher than a critic—he is, above all, a sensitive reader. He takes the work of each author on its own terms, discovering its principles and contradictions and considering how those qualities might speak to the political, social, and artistic currents of the day. In a remarkable recent study, Kevin Gilmartin similarly observes that Hazlitt's 'successive figures open up distinct arenas of contemporary public life, without yielding a comprehensive spirit of the age'; Gilmartin affirms, instead, Hazlitt's 'interest in political and historical inconsistency as a hallmark of the present age'.[20] I suggest, moreover, that the plurality of Hazlitt's vision signaled in the volume's coordinating 'Or' subtitle is key to the historiographical project of accommodating an age of inconsistencies. It is a poetic–conceptual resource that Hazlitt's volume shares with Keats's 'To Autumn' and which helps the critic realize in his unconventional essay collection a negatively capable historiography.

[20] Kevin Gilmartin, *William Hazlitt: Political Essayist* (Oxford: Oxford University Press, 2015), pp. 3, 8.

Part Three

'pursued through Volumes', Volume I: Negative Capability in Twentieth- and Twenty-First-Century American Poetry

Chapter Nine

Beyond the Great Divide

Negative Capability and Postwar American Poetics

Robert Archambeau

The poets are at war. This, at least, is what a great many American poets, along with a host of scholars and critics concerned with their work, have been saying from the middle of the twentieth century to the present day. The wars in question are internecine, directed at other poets, and other kinds of poetries. Perhaps the most famous announcement of the conflict came from the mouth of Robert Lowell, speaking after his *Life Studies* received the National Book Award in 1960:

> Two poetries are now competing, a cooked and a raw. The cooked, marvelously expert, often seems laboriously concocted to be tasted and digested by a graduate seminar. The raw, huge blood-dripping gobbets of unseasoned experience are dished up for midnight listeners. There is a poetry that can only be studied, and a poetry that can only be declaimed, a poetry of pedantry and a poetry of scandal.[1]

Thirty-five years later, the scholar Alan Golding quoted those words in his study *From Outlaw to Classic: Canons in American Poetry*, in which he claimed that the conflicts between competing groups of poets remained as fresh as ever, and that the battle for recognition and aesthetic dominance between different poetic camps had become one of the most entrenched facts of postwar American poetry.[2] Just over twenty years after Golding's book appeared, a number of American poets, under the general direction of Kent Johnson, launched the website *Dispatches from the Poetry Wars*, as if to affirm

[1] Stanley Kunitz, 'The New Books', *Harper's Magazine*, 221 (August 1960), p. 100.

[2] Alan Golding, *From Outlaw to Classic: Canons in American Poetry* (Madison: University of Wisconsin Press, 1995), p. 28.

the continued relevance of the kind of poetic turf war Lowell announced and Golding described. But beneath the turbulence of the wars between various poetic styles lies a peaceful calm, a deep consensus about the nature of poetry that has only rarely been challenged in postwar American poetry. And the name of this consensus is 'negative capability'.

What I mean is this: while the conflicts within postwar American poetry have been both numerous and substantial, very few poets have actually broken with the core precept of Keats's theory of negative capability, and those that have done so have also found themselves relegated to the poetic sidelines. Michael Theune, who notes the widespread use of the term negative capability by several generations of American poets and critics, has been struck by the malleability of the term. He notes that it contains a 'quantity of abstraction that allows the term to be applied to almost anything', and that so many 'caveats and concessions' surround the use of the term that it has ceased to be useful.[3] Theune is correct to note that various poets and critics have seen negative capability differently, often attaching it to key terms in their own thinking and recruiting it to agendas undreamed of in Keats's philosophizing. Walter Jackson Bate, for example, Keats's most prominent academic interpreter in midcentury America, articulated a version of negative capability very much in accord with the dominant mode of academic critical thought of the time. And Robert Duncan, the great counter-cultural mystic poet, found ways of connecting Keats's concept to the Gnostic spiritual traditions so important to his own poetic development. But it would be incorrect to say that the term is so flexible as to be meaningless, that it indicates no definite position in poetics. Despite its flexibility, it does, in fact, describe a definite poetic position, one increasingly widespread after Romanticism, and rather more difficult to find in earlier eras. It has, over time, become something like a climate of opinion, within which disputes are possible, but against which resistance is largely futile.

What we have from Keats regarding negative capability is brief and vague, maddeningly so for those who approach the concept without a degree of negative capability themselves, especially given the dubious textual provenance of the letter in which Keats famously expounds the idea (*LJK*, I: 191n1).[4] The negative capability necessary for achievement in poetry is found, writes Keats, 'when a man is capable of being in uncertainties, Mysteries, doubts, without any irritable reaching after fact & reason' (I: p. 193). But if we permit ourselves to reach after fact, we can say that one thing that negative capability is most definitely not is the quest for a single, definable certainty,

[3] Michael Theune, '~~Negative Capability~~: T wang dillo dee', *Jacket*, 40 (2010), accessed 7 July 2018, http://jacketmagazine.com/40/theune-keats.shtml.

[4] See also Brian Rejack's essay in this volume for a detailed accounting of the letter's textual history.

free of mystery and doubt. Such a quest did indeed inform the poetry and poetics of several earlier generations of poets, and became the dominant form of Augustan poetry in the eighteenth century. In that body of work, poetry often set out for certainty and (in W. K. Wimsatt's phrase) sought 'to sound like a statement about literary criticism, about ethics, or about cosmology'.[5] Such poetry tends not merely to reach for fact and reason, but to begin with them, and to proceed by illustrating them with a great deal of consistency and clarity. As James Sutherland put it in his classic *Preface to Eighteenth Century Poetry*, 'in the poetry of Pope and his contemporaries thought does, normally, come first, and thought remains all-important'.[6] In Pope's own words, the poet's true gift was to apprehend 'Something, whose Truth convinc'd at Sight', and then to take this self-evident truth and state it clearly, since 'Expression is the Dress of Thought'.[7]

This is not, of course, to say that Augustan poetry lacked subtlety. But subordinate poetic effects beyond the primary denotative mode tend not so much to ironize or undermine as to re-enforce the central line of the poem's reasoning. As Sutherland says:

> at its most characteristic eighteenth century poetry is rather the poetry of clear, strong statement, packed with meaning: *all* the meaning will not necessarily lie exposed on the surface, but most of it will, and any further values it has (of rhythm, texture, allusion) will normally reinforce the surface meaning. (p. 164)

The change from this pre-Romantic poetic to the prevailing post-Romantic view is profound, leading Maynard Mack to observe that the transformation is nothing less than a movement from the notion of a 'poetry of statement' to the opposition 'poetry *or* statement'.[8] The degree to which Keats's articulation of the idea of negative capability plays a causal role in the transformation is a larger question than can be addressed here, but it is certainly symptomatic of the change.

The ideal of the poet as someone 'capable of being in uncertainties, Mysteries, doubts', rather than making a clear statement of an already apprehended truth,

[5] W. K. Wimsatt, *Hateful Contraries: Studies in Literature and Criticism* (Lexington: University of Kentucky Press, 2014), p. 151.

[6] James Sutherland, *A Preface to Eighteenth Century Poetry* (Oxford: Oxford University Press, 1970), p. 164.

[7] Alexander Pope, *Essay on Criticism*, ed. Alfred S. West (Cambridge: Cambridge University Press, 2014), pp. 70–1.

[8] Maynard Mack, *Collected in Himself: Essay Critical, Biographical, and Bibliographical on Pope and Some of His Contemporaries* (Newark: University of Delaware Press, 1982), p. 38.

underlies the majority of mid-twentieth-century American thinking about poetry. It is as present in the then-dominant academic tradition as it is the confessional movement, and in the outsider tradition of the New American Poetry. So pervasive are the various versions of negative capability that when a poet–critic such as Yvor Winters breaks with the poetics of negative capability he forfeits his place in the dominant tradition and becomes, in the eyes of many, a marginal crank. Despite the apparent cacophony of competing poetic sects, the center of negative capability is virtually everywhere in midcentury America, its circumference visible nowhere—except possibly in the hills of Palo Alto, where Winters taught at Stanford.

The dominant midcentury tradition, sometimes referred to as academic poetry, was indeed dominated by academics, often poet–critics associated with the New Criticism, such as John Crowe Ransom and Allen Tate. The New Criticism drew heavily on Keats. Cleanth Brooks's *The Well-Wrought Urn*, arguably the most prominent articulation of New Critical poetics, takes its title from Keats's 'Ode on a Grecian Urn', and Jasper Bernes is right to claim that Brooks was 'working from Keats's notion of negative capability' when he 'asserts in *The Well-Wrought Urn* that a successful poem is a structural edifice of paradoxically harmonized oppositions and tensions'. The goal of Brooks's New Criticism, says Bernes, was to 'take full measure of such paradoxes without violating them or making what is not meant to be rational conform to the principles of logic'—that is, to remain in uncertainties without a reaching, irritable or otherwise, after reason.[9] As Brooks put it in *The Well-Wrought Urn*, the language of all true poetry is 'the language of paradox'.[10] Against the Augustan tradition's emphasis on a central thesis, supported by various figures of speech and poetic techniques, Brooks maintained that poetic 'imagery and rhythm are not merely the instruments by which this fancied core-of-meaning-which-can-be-expressed-in-a-paraphrase is directly rendered' (p. 197). Rather, they introduce contrary and paradoxical elements, creating 'the resistance which any good poem sets up against all attempts to paraphrase it' (p. 196). The principle, it is important to note, is not presented as descriptive of a particular style of poetry, but as prescriptive for all successful poems. Like Keats, Brooks saw negative capability as a core value for poetry, not an elective or optional one.

Many New Critical precepts, with their emphases on the irreducibility of the poem to certainty or to a single rational thesis, derive from this iteration of negative capability. For example, Brooks's ideas of the heresy of paraphrase

[9] Jasper Bernes, 'New Criticism', in *American Poets and Poetry*, ed. Jeffrey Gray and Mary Balkun (Westport, CT: Greenwood, 2015), p. 437.

[10] Cleanth Brooks, *The Well-Wrought Urn: Studies in the Structure of Poetry* (New York: Harvest, 1956), p. 3.

and of irony as a principle of structure are deeply Keatsian, as is Wimsatt's idea, presented in *The Verbal Icon*, of the concrete universal. Wimsatt invokes Keats before describing how the irreducible specificity of poetry does not contribute to the development of rational argument, but 'distinguishes poetry from scientific or logical discourse'.[11] John Crowe Ransom also emphasizes poetic concreteness in a manner consistent with Keatsian negative capability. In *The World's Body*, for example, he argues for an unparaphrasable poetry, combining ideas and the world of the senses in images irreducible to conclusive certainty. 'An idea', he argues, 'is derivative and tamed. The image is in the natural or wild state, and it has to be discovered there, not put there, obeying its own laws and none of ours.' While we may think 'we can lay hold of image and take it captive', that simply isn't the case, for 'the docile captive is not the real image but only the idea, which is the image with its character beaten out of it'.[12] Particularity and concreteness join equilibrium and subtle irony among the desiderata of poetry—and the poem's structure, or prose argument, is not to take precedence over its texture, the particular connotations of its component parts.

These theories were immensely influential not only on the poems of the generation that articulated them but on the poems of many of their students—the early works of Ransom's most famous student, Robert Lowell, for example, have been seen as 'inextricably bound' to the precepts of the New Criticism.[13] They also contributed to a climate in which Keats's negative capability was reframed in a format amenable to the terms of the New Criticism. Keats's biographer Walter Jackson Bate was no New Critic, but when his monumental *John Keats* was published in 1963—the apex of the New Criticism—he described negative capability in distinctly New Critical terms. After quoting Keats's letter about negative capability, Bate says:

> we could paraphrase these famous sentences as follows. In our life of uncertainties, where no one system or formula can explain everything—where even a word is at best, in Bacon's phrase, a 'wager of thought',—what is needed is an imaginative openness of mind and heightened receptivity to reality in its full and diverse concreteness. (p. 249)

There is nothing about concreteness in Keats's letter, but a great deal about it in the New Critical thinking inspired by Keats—and a great deal more in

[11] W. K. Wimsatt, *The Verbal Icon: Studies in the Meaning of Poetry* (Lexington: University of Kentucky Press, 1954), p. 76.

[12] John Crowe Ransom, *The World's Body* (Baton Rouge: Louisiana State University Press, 1968), p. 115.

[13] James Longenbach, 'The Unfinishable Robert Lowell', *Boston Review* (June 2003), accessed 9 July 2018, http://bostonreview.net/poetry/james-longenbach-unfinishable-robert-lowell.

the poems produced under the aegis of the New Criticism. Bate's Keats was, like Bate himself, very much the product of the midcentury American literary establishment.

Within that establishment, Yvor Winters offers the most prominent, and most thorough, rejection of negative capability—a rejection that came at a great cost to his reputation. Initially considered a peer of the New Critics, Winters broke with them over the issue of the poem's paraphrasability. He came to insist upon a necessarily rational basis for poems, and rejected the ideals of paradox outlined by Brooks, Ransom, Tate, and others. His *In Defense of Reason*, for example, eviscerates Keats's 'Ode on a Grecian Urn'—the very poem that inspired Brooks's theories of paradox and irony—for its uncertainty and 'incomprehensibility'.[14] Moreover, he attacks Keats's 'Ode to a Nightingale' precisely because of its persistence in uncertainty and lack of clearly defined, reasoned motives. 'As an act of moral contemplation', writes Winters, 'the poem is incomplete and may even be misleading and dangerous' (pp. 50–1).

Brooks, Ransom, and others associated with the academic tradition were merciless with Winters. Winters, having provoked them with statements such as 'many poems cannot be paraphrased and are therefore defective', was dismissed by the establishment, as were those few young poets who strictly followed Winters' doctrines.[15] Randall Jarrell, for example, wrote this assessment in his essay on poetic obscurity:

> Is Clarity the handmaiden of Popularity, as everybody automatically assumes? How much does it help to be immediately plain? … [T]he poems of the students of Yvor Winters are quite as easy to understand as those which Longfellow used to read during the Children's Hour; yet they are about as popular as those other poems (of their own composition) which grave Alice, and laughing Allegra, And Edith with golden hair used to read to Longfellow during the Poet's Hour. If Dylan Thomas is obscurely famous, such poets as these are clearly unknown.[16]

This is not so much refutation as condescension, and became part of a climate of opinion marginalizing Winters.[17]

[14] Yvor Winters, *In Defense of Reason* (Denver, CO: Swallow, 1947), p. 476.

[15] Robert Von Hallberg, 'Yvor Winters', in *American Writers: A Collection of Literary Biographies, Supplement Two, Part Two*, ed. A. Walton Litz (New York: Scribner's, 1981), p. 804.

[16] Randall Jarrell, 'The Obscurity of the Poet', in *American Poetic Theory*, ed. Carl Perkins (New York: Rinehart, 1972), pp. 307–8.

[17] For a fuller discussion see Robert Archambeau, *Laureates and Heretics: Six Careers in American Poetry* (Notre Dame, IN: University of Notre Dame Press, 2010), pp. 26–31.

Yvor Winters notwithstanding, to break with the academic tradition in midcentury American poetics was not necessarily to break with the idea of negative capability. It was often a matter of breaking with concepts the academics had associated with Keats's idea. When, with *Life Studies*, Robert Lowell turned away from the elaborate paradoxes and ironies of his early poetry, he maintained his admiration for what he called 'the large unhurried gravity of negative capability'.[18] Should anyone tell Lowell that the self-centeredness of his newfound confessionalism was a barrier to the negative capability that Bate said entailed 'negating one's own ego' (p. 249), Lowell had good critical authority to help him refute his critic. No less a figure than Lionel Trilling declared, 'negative capability, the faculty of not having to make up one's mind about everything, depends upon the sense of one's personal identity and is the sign of personal identity'.[19] Ego and negative capability were, it seems, compatible.

The confessional Lowell may have been an apostate from the academic tradition, but others were heretical through and through. As the editor Donald M. Allen said of the poets from beyond the academic mainstream he'd collected in his landmark 1960 anthology *The New American Poetry: 1945–1960*, they had all 'shown one common characteristic: a total rejection of all those qualities typical of academic verse'.[20] But the differences between Allen's New Americans and the academics he decried were never so total as Allen supposed. An essential belief in negative capability bound them together despite their many differences.

Charles Olson, one of the most notable of the poets collected in Allen's anthology, sometimes speaks of negative capability in terms not too far removed from the New Critic's version of the concept, linking it, as they did, to the concrete.[21] In the 1958 essay 'Equal, That Is, to the Thing Itself', Olson imagines Keats's thoughts the night before he wrote to his brothers about negative capability: 'all that irritable reaching after fact and reason won't do', writes Olson in Keats's voice, 'I don't believe in it. I do better to stay in the condition of things. No matter what it amounts to, mystery confusion doubt, it has a power. It is what I mean by *Negative Capability*.'[22] The linkage of

[18] Robert Lowell, *Robert Lowell: Interviews and Memoirs*, ed. Jeffrey Meyers (Ann Arbor: University of Michigan Press, 1988), p. 295.

[19] Lionel Trilling, *The Moral Obligation to be Intelligent: Selected Essays*, ed. Leon Wieseltier (Evanston, IL: Northwestern University Press, 2009), p. 249.

[20] Donald M. Allen, ed., *The New American Poetry, 1945–1960* (New York: Grove, 1960), p. xi.

[21] For another reading of Olson's engagement with negative capability, see Eric Eisner's essay in this volume, in which he draws out surprising affinities between Olson and Walter Jackson Bate.

[22] Charles Olson, 'Equal, That Is, to the Real Itself', in *Collected Prose*, ed. Donald Allen,

negative capability with attention to concrete things—a linkage never made explicit by Keats himself—stayed with Olson. Almost a decade later we find him contrasting the 'irritable reaching after fact and reason' with attention to 'the condition of things themselves', and declaring the thing itself central to poetry, with its 'self-existence, without reference to any other thing'.[23]

Elsewhere, though, we find Olson invoking Keats and negative capability to justify a kind of poetry that looked very different from the academic tradition informed by the New Criticism. Olson quotes Keats's negative capability letter, along with a passage of Heraclitus, as an epigraph to *The Special View of History*, a prose collection compiled from notes for the lectures he gave at Black Mountain College in 1956. William Spanos has described the book as a call for poetry 'to be open and projective, a "forwarding"'—an articulation of the kind of ongoing serial poetic project we see in Olson's *Maximus Poems*, where there is no sense of closure or finality, no conclusiveness, except that attendant upon the poet's death.[24] In this context, Keats serves as a kind of patron saint of non-closure, of the poem as an ongoing process retaining uncertainties about both form and final statement. 'To stay in mysteries, uncertainties, doubts', writes Olson, 'is Keats's way of talking about staying in process.'[25]

One may well entertain doubts about whether Keats would have seen the connection between negative capability and the serial poem, but Olson was not alone in sensing the connection. Another of Donald Allen's New Americans, Robert Duncan, likewise invokes Keats as a sponsor of serial poetics. Duncan was very much against the Augustan notion of expression being the 'Dress of Thought', decrying how poets after Dryden would 'deliver over their art to reasonable men' rather than shroud it in mysteries that hint at, but never fully reveal, a 'momentous design'.[26] For Duncan, 'a poem moves' when the poet begins 'to feel the pattern' of ideas and images release 'the patterning they are true to, the melody they belong to. Once this feeling of a patterning begins, the work comes to one's hand; the form of the whole can be felt emerging in the fittingness of each passage'. When this happens he finds he is 'no longer thinking or proposing ideas but working *with* them' (p. 31).

When Duncan feels the form of the whole, though, we mustn't confuse this with his having arrived at certainty about how things will conclude. In Duncan's eclectic, largely Gnostic mysticism, the whole in unavailable to

Benjamin Friedlander, and Robert Creeley (Berkeley: University of California Press, 1997), p. 120.

[23] Charles Olson, *Human Universe and Other Essays* (New York: Grove, 1967), pp. 117, 6.

[24] William V. Spanos, 'Charles Olson and Negative Capability: A Phenomenological Interpretation', *Contemporary Literature*, 21: 1 (Winter 1980), p. 48.

[25] Charles Olson, *The Special View of History* (Berkeley, CA: Oyez, 1970), p. 42.

[26] Robert Duncan, *Fictive Certainties* (New York: New Directions, 1985), p. 45.

us in time: 'I take the truth of things to be the truth of their belonging to [a] form of forms', he writes, 'having its completion in the end of time and space, surely beyond my individual comprehension' (pp. 37–8). He believes all creation—whether it be a poem or the universe itself—'to be in process as evolution and revelation of Itself, and the meaning of the parts, the meaning of all definitions, to be posited finally in a totality of resonances' (p. 38). We are always approaching revelation, but its truth is to be withheld from us until an apocalyptic moment beyond history, outside of space and after the end of time. The poetic projects written under the aegis of this mysticism include Duncan's ongoing series *Passages*, which takes on ever-richer meanings and resonances without closure. And the great predecessor of this 'adventure of not knowing' is Keats. For Duncan, it is only after we put to rest the clarity of the Augustans that a poetic of incompletion and uncertainty—'the notion of Negative Capability, Keats called it in poetry'—returns (p. 46).

Poetic schools and movements continued to proliferate among American poets younger than the academics and the New Americans—but beneath the diversity it is striking to note how pervasive the belief in negative capability remains. We see it evoked, for example, to justify both the poetry of the American Surrealist movement that came to prominence around 1970, and the work of the Language poets that emerged a few years later.

Like its European and Latin American namesakes, American Surrealism—whose more prominent figures include James Tate and two former poets laureate, Mark Strand and Charles Simic—grants an important role to chance. Simic, for example, writing in 1992 about his early collaborative work with Tate, says:

> Tate and I collaborated on some poems in the following manner: We'd take a word or a phrase and then we'd turn ourselves into a 'pinball machine of associations', as Paul Auster would say. For example, the word 'match' and the word 'jail' would become 'matchstick jail'. At some point we'd stop and see what we had. We'd even do a bit of literary analysis. We'd revise, free-associate again, and watch an unknown poem begin to take shape. At some moments we felt as if we were one person.[27]

A few years after Simic and Tate's experiments with chance, Simic linked chance with Keats's negative capability in the essay 'Negative Capability and Its Children'. Here, Simic quotes Keats on the persistence of uncertainty in negative capability, then argues that in a world conscious of concentration camps and other modern calamities we must return to Keats and ask 'are we

[27] Charles Simic, *The Life of Images: Selected Prose* (New York: HarperCollins, 2015), p. 46.

capable of being in anything *but* uncertainties?'.[28] When poets inspired by the New Criticism looked inside negative capability, they found irony and concreteness; when New American poets looked, they found process. Simic finds chance—a release from certainty, from ego, and from the limitations of rational statement. The techniques deployed in pursuit of negative capability vary, but the end remains the same: to remain in uncertainties, mysteries, and doubts, to avoid reaching after fact and reason.

Few poetic movements have seemed as resolutely anti-Romantic as the Language poetry associated with figures such as Charles Bernstein, Bruce Andrews, Ron Silliman, and Susan Howe. The most significant critical proponent of Language poetry, Marjorie Perloff, has even written that it was 'opposition to [the] romantic paradigm that prompted the theoretical discourse of Language manifestos in the first place'.[29] The poets themselves, though, seem to grant a Keatsian exception to any policy of anti-Romanticism—even when, like Silliman, they claim 'one of the most important aspects of this writing [Language poetry] … is that it is anti-romantic, anti-mystical and anti-lyric'.[30]

Whatever his reservations about Romanticism generally, Silliman invokes Keats's idea of negative capability in much the manner Charles Simic does—as a principle of composition. Referencing poet Jack Spicer's notion of the muse as a radio broadcast from Mars, Silliman describes his method as 'negative capability or listening for the Martians … nothing will cause the poem to go dead faster than setting out to write "about" X'—instead of dressing thought in expression in the manner of an Augustan, the poet has to allow for uncertainty, happenstance, chance. 'The writer', Silliman continues, 'has to be open to anything coming into the poem.'[31]

With other Language poets, though, negative capability appears less as a principle of compositional technique than as a description of the state in which they hope to leave the reader of their poems: it becomes less a creative than a hermeneutic precept. Consider Bernstein's comment on negative capability and interpretation:

> I don't think I manage to achieve as many different interpretations as I might like. I'm very much limited by what makes sense to me, because

[28] Charles Simic, 'Negative Capability and Its Children', in *Claims for Poetry*, ed. Donald Hall (Ann Arbor: University of Michigan Press, 2000), p. 399.

[29] Marjorie Perloff, 'Language Poetry and the Lyric Subject: Ron Silliman's Albany, Susan Howe's Buffalo', *Critical Inquiry*, 25: 3 (Spring 1999), p. 433.

[30] Ron Silliman to Susan Howe, 7 December 1985, Susan Howe Papers, Mandeville Special Collections Library, University of California, San Diego.

[31] Ron Silliman, 'An Interview with Ron Silliman', *Double Room*, 6 (Fall 2005/Winter 2006), accessed 9 July 2018, www.webdelsol.com/Double_Room/issue_six/Ron_Silliman.htm.

> of this horribly mistaken but nonetheless ongoing concern for the poem to sound right. I have a desire for an infinitely negative capability and yet I am always coming upon very concrete forms of stabilization, characterization, that makes patterns in respect to one another.[32]

Elsewhere, Bernstein reaffirms this sense of negative capability as a principle of structuring—or unstructuring—poetic works so as to render them open to plural interpretive possibilities. He praises Louis Zukofsky's objectivist epic *A*, for example, in terms derived from Keats. The poem is laudable for avoiding 'recourse to a single thematic or syntactic underpinning to create unification' and therefore is 'exemplary of a genuine negative capability' (p. 361). The uncertainty, here, is not so much to be cultivated within the poet's sensibility as passed on from him to the reader. But whether it is, as in Simic's case, cultivated within the poet, or passed on from him to the reader via a kind of hermeneutic undecidability, negative capability underwrites a whole range of different poetries in the generation coming after the academics and New Americans.

In 2006 the poet Tony Hoagland declared the 'predominant Poem of Our Moment' to be a 'skittery' thing, 'fast-moving and declarative, wobbling on the balance beam between associative and dissociative, somewhat absurdist, and, indeed, cerebral'.[33] It was, in short, the Elliptical poem, so named by poet–critic Stephen Burt eight years earlier. Burt had named John Ashbery as the greatest precursor to Elliptical poetry, a master whose influence is 'everywhere, ramifying still'.[34] When we look at Ashbery's poetics, we find that both he and his critics describe his work as a poetry of negative capability. And when we look at Elliptical poetry, we find that it is not just Ashbery but, through his influence, Keats, who is everywhere, ramifying still. We find, that is, negative capability at the heart of the dominant school of contemporary American poetry.

At the beginning of the first full-length study of John Ashbery's work, David Shapiro declares Ashbery's talent 'beautifully negative, in the line of Keats's grandest remarks on the Negative Capability of the poet who does not reach out after dogmatic uncertainties'.[35] Ashbery, he continues, 'like Stevens, is master of those who know they do not know' (p. 2). Other critics have echoed

[32] Charles Bernstein, *Content's Dream: Essays 1975–1984* (Evanston, IL: Northwestern University Press, 2001), p. 458.

[33] Tony Hoagland, 'Fear of Narrative and the Skittery Poem of Our Moment', in *Poet's Work, Poet's Play*, ed. Daniel Tobin and Pimone Triplett (Ann Arbor: University of Michigan Press, 2007), p. 165.

[34] Stephen Burt, *Close Calls With Nonsense: Reading New Poetry* (Saint Paul, MN: Graywolf, 2009), pp. 345–6.

[35] David Shapiro, *John Ashbery: An Introduction to the Poetry* (New York: Columbia University Press, 1979), p. 1.

the observation, with one going so far as to say of Ashbery's *Self-Portrait in a Convex Mirror*, 'uncertainty, vagueness, the tentative, the barely perceptible … . This is negative capability and then some'.[36] Ashbery himself has called negative capability a 'valuable asset' for those seeking to understand his work, and he uses Keats's term in his poetry.[37] In one passage from the poem 'From Such Commotion', Ashbery speaks of his own negative capability:

> …the whole damn ocean
> is there, up for review, for us. It's just
>
> that we don't understand. It's my negative capability acting up
> again. Well, I'm within my rights.
> It's like apples and pears, or oranges and lemons,
> what I always say.[38]

How to interpret this? Part of it seems obvious enough: the ocean, present for us, eludes our understanding, but we aren't troubled by it—it is, the speaker asserts, 'within his rights' not to understand it. His ability to be in uncertainties, mysteries, and doubts is, it seems, beyond doubt. Were this all we had, we'd be in possession of a statement of the poetics of uncertainty that is remarkably certain of itself. But it's not all we have: we're given a simile or, rather, two of them. What's it like to have one's negative capability acting up? Firstly, it's like 'apples and pears', perhaps the most famous phrase from cockney rhyming slang. The term literally means 'stairs'—but it is difficult to know what it means for negative capability to be somehow like stairs. Is negative capability to be understood as means of ascent? If so, to what? Or a means of descent? Or is it the codedness of the slang that is important, with negative capability somehow a secret language for the initiated? It's impossible to say, and we are forced into a position of uncertainty. We may enter the spirit of negative capability and accept the uncertainty, or we may grow irritable (as readers of Ashbery have been known to do) and reach after something definite, like fact or reason. But we haven't even entered into the poem's larger ambiguity, because there's another simile to address. 'Oranges and lemons' would seem to be parallel to 'apples and pears', but it refers not

[36] Maureen McClane, 'In Retrospect', *Critical Mass* (11 September 2009), accessed 9 July 2018, http://bookcritics.org/blog/archive/in_retrospect_maureen_n._mclane_on_john_ashberys_self_portrait_in_a_convex_/.

[37] John Ashbery, 'Houses at Night: Erica Wright Interviews John Ashbery', *Guernica* (8 February 2008), accessed 9 July 2018, https://www.guernicamag.com/interviews/houses_at_night_1/.

[38] John Ashbery, 'From Such Commotion', in *Wakefulness* (New York: Farrar, Straus and Giroux, 1999), pp. 14–15.

to cockney rhyming slang but a different kind of language—the traditional English nursery rhyme. The most common form of the relevant rhyme is:

> Oranges and lemons,
> Say the bells of St. Clement's.
>
> You owe me five farthings,
> Say the bells of St. Martin's.
>
> When will you pay me?
> Say the bells of Old Bailey.
>
> When I grow rich,
> Say the bells of Shoreditch.
>
> When will that be?
> Say the bells of Stepney.
>
> I do not know,
> Says the great bell of Bow.
>
> Here comes a candle to light you to bed,
> And here comes a chopper to chop off your head![39]

Understanding how 'oranges and lemons' are like negative capability is a tricky business. The words are presented as the statement made by the bells of a church, but it is unknown which church the rhyme refers to: both St. Clement's Danes and St. Clement's Eastcheap are plausible, since wharves where citrus was unloaded were located near both churches. Perhaps, then, negative capability is like words connected with uncertain reference—but one feels one might be reaching. The lines take on further ambiguity, since the meaning of the whole rhyme is unclear—it has been interpreted as referring to child sacrifice, to public executions, and to the marital travails of Henry VIII.[40] The two fruit pairings both indicate that negative capability seems to be like something uncertain, but precisely what, and how, is shown to be unknowable—twice. The poem enacts the uncertainty of which it speaks.

The uncertainties and ambiguities of 'From Such Commotion' are actually much greater and far more vexed than I have made them seem, because the

[39] I. Opie and P. Opie, *The Oxford Dictionary of Nursery Rhymes* (Oxford: Oxford University Press, 1951), p. 337.

[40] Opie and Opie, *Nursery Rhymes*, p. 338.

context of the lines before and after the quoted passage make for further complications. By taking a relatively small passage out of context I have committed the sin attributed to many of Ashbery's critics by Brian McHale in his analysis of Ashbery's long poem 'The Skaters':

> [In 'The Skaters'] one encounters an intractable flux of verbal 'found objects', shifting styles and registers, teasing literary allusions and echoes, fragmentary narrative episodes and descriptive scenes. How is one to negotiate or manage such flux? Critics tend to select 'key' lines or passages, treating these as interpretative centers or 'nodes' around which to organize the heterogeneous materials of the poem. Other materials come to be subordinated in various ways (explicitly or, more often, implicitly) to these 'key' passages or are simply passed over in silence, so that the poem is reduced to a skeletal structure of points that yield most readily to a particular interpretative orientation.[41]

When one goes beyond treating certain lines in isolation as 'key' passages, one finds one either needs a great deal of negative capability to appreciate an Ashbery poem, or one abandons the poem in irritation. Like the Language poets, Ashbery invites us to use negative capability as an interpretive principle as much as a creative one.

What is true of Ashbery is true of the Elliptical poets writing in his wake. They are, says Stephen Burt, 'always hinting, punning, or swerving away from a never-quite-unfolded backstory', and, like McHale's Ashbery, 'they are easier to process in parts than in wholes'. What is more, they offer a certain 'provisionality—the sense that they might change, that nothing they say counts as final' (p. 346). 'Ellipticals', says Burt, 'love poems that declare "I am X. I am Y, I am Z", where X, Y, and Z are incompatible things' (p. 347). Elliptical poems, like Ashbery's poems, elicit the reader's negative capability. As Will Cordeiro puts it in a review of one of Burt's Elliptical poets, Susan Wheeler, 'nothing remains reliable, and the poem becomes a Rorschach blot of the reader's negative capability'.[42]

When we survey the range of different kinds of poetry that have been justified by the concept of negative capability—New Critical poems of concretion and irony; New American poems of process and mysticism; Confessional poems of individual authenticity; American Surrealist poems of chance; Language poems of hermeneutic multiplicity; Elliptical poems of

[41] Brian McHale, 'How (Not) to Read Postmodernist Long Poems: The Case of Ashbery's "The Skaters"', *Poetics Today*, 21: 3 (Autumn 2000), p. 561.

[42] Will Cordeiro, 'All That Glitters', *Jacket*, 38 (2009), accessed 9 July 2018, http://jacketmagazine.com/38/r-wheeler-rb-cordeiro.shtml.

provisionality—we may well feel sympathy with Michael Theune, who writes 'What *can't* Negative Capability attach itself to? It turns out: not much.' But must we share his conclusion, that 'doing more harm than good, Negative Capability is a term we should, and can, do without'? My answer, simply, is 'no'.

As flexible as the term has proved, justifying many techniques and allowing for emphases on both poet and reader, it has in all of the instances treated above maintained its core emphasis on unresolved doubt and uncertainty. That this is a pervasive desideratum in postwar American poetry, with few notable exceptions, ought not to be taken as a sign of the banality or emptiness of the concept. Rather, it may be seen as a sign that the core definition of what makes a poem a poem has been remarkably consistent, behind apparent diversity, for generations of American poets. That this is a historical contingency, rather than a trans-historical truth about the nature of all poetry, is clear: we need look no further than the Augustans to find a phalanx of poets who conceive of their art in terms very much at odds with the poetics of negative capability. We may take the facts—negative capability's contingency, and its current pervasiveness—as an invitation to better understand what transformed poetry between the Augustans and the postwar period (at least in America). Whether the rise of negative capability was caused by some combination of the rise of the novel, the disruption of the patronage system and the relation of poet to audience, the transformations in publishing and the reading public, or by some other factor or set of factors has yet to be ascertained. But any full understanding of the transformation and its cause is likely to involve the concept of negative capability. If we are to reach after the facts or reasons for poetry's transformation, we will have need of it.

Chapter Ten

Versions of Negative Capability in Modern American Poetry and Criticism

Eric Eisner

As Michael Theune observes, the phrase negative capability has been used so often, in so many disparate contexts, that it often feels like an empty cliché.[1] Yet the fact the phrase so commonly appears as mere platitude does not mean it must always work that way: at other times, the concept can be deployed with quite specific local meanings, in differential tension with its significance in other contexts. In other words, while writers at times go to 'negative capability' for a hit of feel-good fuzziness, the phrase elsewhere emerges as the ground of more sharply marked contestation. As the concept travels along multiple itineraries through modern and recent poetry and criticism, it moves in tandem with particular versions of Keats, in connection with particular histories of Keats-reception, and in relation to specific discursive, disciplinary, and institutional configurations. Though in the space I have here I cannot hope to map these itineraries in any kind of comprehensive way, I aim in what follows to locate a few orientation points within this terrain through a comparative look at three individually rich takes on negative capability.

I begin by briefly reviewing important mid-twentieth-century formulations of negative capability by two towering figures operating in what would seem opposite institutional circumstances: the Harvard scholar Walter Jackson Bate and the poet and Black Mountain College figure Charles Olson. While Bate's writing on negative capability has been widely influential, Olson is also a key origin point for the concept's currency within experimental poetics specifically. Despite the vast difference in the terms through which these writers understand negative capability, however, there are also surprising similarities in the aims with which each mobilizes the concept within the scene of pedagogy

[1] Michael Theune, '~~Negative Capability~~ T wang dillo dee', *Jacket*, 40 (2010), accessed 7 July 2018, http://jacketmagazine.com/40/theune-keats.shtml.

and within the postwar intellectual scene more generally. Adrienne Rich's complex negotiation with Keats in her 1986 elegy 'In Memoriam: D.K.' comes at negative capability from a quite different angle. Engaging a queer (and queering) tradition of Keats-reception, the poem tests and critiques the ideas Bate and Olson both advance of negative capability as 'virtue'.

Walter Jackson Bate

Any time after the mid-1960s, when people say negative capability they often—but *not* always—mean something like 'Walter Jackson Bate's negative capability'. One of a line of prominent Harvard Keatsians also including such figures as Douglas Bush, David Perkins, and Helen Vendler, Bate addressed negative capability in Bergsonian terms in his Harvard college thesis, written under Bush's supervision and published as *Negative Capability: The Intuitive Approach in Keats* in 1939. But the most consequential discussion has been his chapter on negative capability in his classic 1963 biography.[2] There, Bate glosses negative capability as 'an imaginative openness of mind and heightened receptivity to reality in its full and diverse concreteness' (p. 249). This formulation immediately suggests the tensions between imagination and concrete reality, between what we perceive and what we half-create, that Keats's letters and poems are at pains to explore. Bate's negative capability reconciles these tensions by locating the imagination and concrete reality on the 'common ground' of 'living process'.[3] His discussion in *John Keats* follows John Dewey's treatment in *Art as Experience* of the dichotomy between embodied, intuitive experience, 'a life of Sensations', and the disembodied artificiality of what Keats called 'consequitive reasoning' (*LJK*, I: p. 185) (Bate indeed reports he first encountered the phrase 'negative capability' reading Dewey as a high school student).[4] Rejecting a separation of the aesthetic and everyday life, Dewey turns to animal life and instinctive energy as the ultimate source of art, taking as a key text Keats's identification 'of the attitude of the artist with that of the live creature',[5] epitomized in Keats's absorption in the 'alertness of a Stoat' (*LJK*, II: p. 80). Dewey's organicist philosophy aims to restore the participation of art, artist, and audience in a concrete, living reality of developmental process and growth from which we are more typically separated by the abstraction, rationalization,

[2] Walter Jackson Bate, *John Keats* (Cambridge, MA: Belknap Press of Harvard University Press, 1963), pp. 233–63.

[3] Stuart M. Sperry, *Keats the Poet* (Princeton, NJ: Princeton University Press, 1973, 1994), p. 31.

[4] Bate, 'The Endurance of Keats', in *The Persistence of Poetry: Bicentennial Essays On Keats*, ed. Robert M. Ryan and Ronald A. Sharp (Amherst: University of Massachusetts Press, 1998), pp. 54–6.

[5] John Dewey, *Art as Experience* [1934] (New York: Penguin, 2005), pp. 32–3.

and compartmentalization engendered by the structures of industrial capitalism. Negative capability here figures the movement from fragmented, rationalized, dispersed cogitation to integral 'experience', a moment in time possessing 'its own individualizing quality and self-sufficiency' (p. 37).

As readers have often noted, Bate makes negative capability into a hinge concept connecting ideas Keats explores across many different letters in 1817–19. His decisive move is to connect the 'openness' and 'receptivity' of negative capability fundamentally with the poet's gift for 'sympathetic imagination', his 'adhesive purchase of mind'—the 'camelion' poetics through which, by 'negating one's own ego', one enters vicariously into the experience of another.[6] Bate can so collapse these different elements of Keats's thinking because he positions Keats within a longer tradition of eighteenth-century 'psychological criticism' developing through Hazlitt, formulating this tradition in Coleridgean terms as an effort

> to describe and justify confidence in the imaginative act—an act whereby sensations, intuitions and judgments are not necessarily retained in the memory as separate particles of knowledge to be consulted one by one, but can be coalesced and transformed into a readiness of response that is objectively receptive to the concrete process of nature and indeed actively participates in it. (p. 239)

Bate leans hard, as many commentators do not, on the fact that Keats's lines about negative capability take place within a discussion of aesthetic reception—*art's* capability of 'making all disagreeables evaporate' through its intensity, the 'sense of Beauty' which for the artist 'obliterates all consideration' (*LJK*, I: pp. 192, 194). He thus understands negative capability not only as a psychological posture in relation to ideas (a tolerance for ambiguity, a preference for intuition over reason, or an open-ended emphasis on process rather than completion), but in terms of the *act* (even a leap) of aesthetic perception.

This allows Bate to frame negative capability in surprisingly active terms. He acknowledges that the 'openness' and 'receptivity' associated with negative capability remind us of Keats's fascination with idleness and passivity (p. 250). But for Bate these are passing moods, and connected more to virtues of patience and attentiveness than to a dubious indolence: downplaying 'uncertainties, Mysteries, doubts', Bate recasts negative capability as a nervy 'readiness of response' (p. 239). 'For a "great poet" especially', Bate sums up,

> a sympathetic absorption in the essential significance of his object (caught and relished in that active cooperation of the mind in which

[6] Bate, *John Keats*, pp. 253, 249.

> the emerging 'Truth' is felt as 'Beauty', and in which the harmony of the human imagination and its object is attained) … 'obliterates' the act of 'consideration'—of deliberating, analysing, and piecing experience together through 'consequitive reasoning'. (p. 249–50)

Bate's energetic prose echoes in its rhythms the capable activity he imagines. 'Relish' is a striking word, with its appetitive, sensual overtones; Bate uses it just after to describe the 'Chaucerian relish of character' with which Keats observes personality types (p. 255). The poet's 'sympathetic absorption' in the object becomes here a figure for the biographer's 'relish' of character as well, and for the reader's, in a series of transferences in which the biographer, his subject, and the reader reflect each other in their capacity for 'sympathetic absorption' and their sense of activity.

This version of Keats chimes tellingly with Bate's particular pedagogy. Bate's approach is to present his students with examples of admirable character whose 'greatness' involves both a willingness to tolerate imaginative extremes and a recognition of a 'common humanity', an empathetic capacity. In his lectures, Bate not only tries to foster in his students an imaginative connection to these authors, but brings them to life in his teaching through a kind of sympathetic projection. Helen Deutsch mentions the famous lecturer's skill in conjuring the spirit of Samuel Johnson, also the subject of one of his biographies; 'according to legend', she reports, he 'left his own deathbed to perform the death of Johnson'.[7] One obituary for Bate reports student testimony that 'when Bate lectured at Harvard on the harrowing fantasies and nightmares of the great lexicographer … it was as if their teacher had momentarily become Dr. Johnson'.[8] Though he did less lecturing on the Romantics, Bate's biography similarly dramatizes Keats's capacity for sympathetic identification.

Grant Scott describes Harvard Keatsians such as Bate as using the 'virility' of *their* Keats to counter the 'powerful and persistent myths' of Keats either as '"pale flower"' (à la *Adonais*) or 'Cockney poetaster, vulgar and effeminate'.[9] If, as Susan Manning proposes, an idea of Keats's characterlessness makes him an exciting and troubling figure for nineteenth-century readers, Bate makes Keats into a certain type of solid character—vital, humanistic, sympathetic, at once literary and earthy, emphatically no soft esthete.[10] Among the many later twentieth- and twenty-first-century poems that stage Keats as character in these terms, Thom Gunn's sonnet 'Keats at Highgate' (1982) is especially

[7] Helen Deutsch, *Loving Dr. Johnson* (Chicago, IL: University of Chicago Press, 2005), pp. 14, 48.

[8] Mark Krupnick, 'Obituary: Walter Jackson Bate', *The Guardian* (1 August 1999), par. 3.

[9] Grant Scott, 'Introduction: Tabloid Keats', *European Romantic Review*, 6: 1 (1995), p. v.

[10] Susan Manning, *Poetics of Character: Transatlantic Encounters, 1700–1900* (Cambridge: Cambridge University Press, 2013), pp. 88–121.

interesting in the way it confirms the link between a version of masculinity and the venturesomeness of Bate's negative capability, while shifting Keats out of the heteronormative context of the Harvard Keatsians. Concerned with questions of class, male sexuality, and the male body, the poem resonates suggestively with Gunn's description elsewhere in the same volume of cruising for sex on Hampstead Heath. Remembering Coleridge's verdict on meeting Keats— '"Loose, [...] slack, and not well-dressed"'—Gunn imagines how, after listening to Coleridge's 'talk talk talk', Keats 'sauntered back / Homeward in his own state of less dispersed / More passive consciousness':

> —passive, not slack,
> [...]
> He made his way toward Hampstead so alert
> He hardly passed the small grey ponds below
> Or watched a sparrow pecking in the dirt
> Without some insight swelling the mind's flow
> That banks made swift. Everything put to use.
> Perhaps not well-dressed but oh no not loose.[11]

This 'cheerful' Keats is nonetheless a scrapper, 'alert' as a stoat, 'everything put to use' as the sonnet's taut form resourcefully organizes its materials, the end rhymes balancing 'flow' and compression. Like Bate's biography, the poem advertises a vicarious access to Keats's experience and proposes the embodied Keats as a figure for richness of experience. But negative capability need not pull us back in this way to an embodied Keats, or into the vicarious experience of subjectivity. To see the distinctiveness of the move Bate makes, it is useful, then, to consider alternatives. Recalling James Russell Lowell's insistence on the remarkable capacity of Keats's imagination for identification 'with the momentary object of its contemplation', Virginia Jackson suggests that nineteenth-century readers might have stressed the object-hood of the object here as we now do not.[12] In other words, in contrast to Bate, they imagined a going-out of self generative of object-effects rather than subject-effects for the speaker or reader (pp. 206–8). In a more formalist vein, the 'negation of ego' Bate describes subtends a notion of poetic impersonality, selfhood dissolving into or by form, that works against the sense of embodied character Bate presents as so vital.[13] Instead of a way to implant the subject more fully in

[11] Thom Gunn, *Passages of Joy* (London: Faber, 1982), p. 40.

[12] Virginia Jackson, 'Thinking Dickinson Thinking Poetry', in *A Companion to Emily Dickinson*, ed. Martha Nell Smith and Mary Loeffelholz (Malden, MA: Blackwell, 2008), p. 206; Lowell, quoted in Jackson, p. 206.

[13] Jackson sees Vendler as operating from a premise that lyric reading is essentially a kind of vicarious identification with the thought-process of the poet in composing the poem—a

nature or the real, negative capability becomes a way to lose the self in art (though, for Paul de Man, for example, this may constitute a route to the real by negative means).[14]

Or consider the poet Lyn Hejinian's discussion of the operation of mind she calls 'doubt'. Hejinian comments that what she intends by 'doubt' is 'not entirely unlike what Keats called "negative capability"', but the margin of daylight between the concepts is instructive—and I highlight her emphasis on 'doubt' because, compared to mystery and uncertainty, it is the element most frequently dropped, I think, in iterations of negative capability (which often tend to their own kind of certainty).[15] As in a long philosophical tradition, 'doubt', for Hejinian, operates in the space between our thought and the world: it is connected at once to our desire 'to join words to the world—to close the gap between ourselves and things' and to our anxious recognition of 'the incapacity of language to match the world', a 'doubt or anxiety' which 'permits us to distinguish our ideas and ourselves from the world and things in it from each other' (p. 56).[16] In *My Life*, she aligns doubt with the motive quality of 'restlessness': 'Restlessness is a form of doubt as well as a form of curiosity', an (irritable?) impatience that keeps us moving.[17] Hejinian's doubt is a form of affirmation: operating in tandem with 'curiosity', it describes a form of 'care' and acknowledgment of things in the world, an 'affirmation of our deepest reason, the one that tells us that things and our experiences of them count', without assimilating them to sameness.[18] 'Doubt' allows for 'co-reality' or 'encounter' without coalescence, so that what phenomena have in common—their happening to happen together—is recognized not as a shared ground of 'process' but as a form of 'dilemma', precisely 'in doubt' (pp. 346–7, 351).

mode Jackson sees as a commonplace and for which Keats has become the signature (pp. 207–8). I see Vendler as tacking between a more depersonalizing formalism and the kind of ethically inflected sympathy with the embodied, experiential Keats presented by Bate. On Vendler, negative capability, depersonalization, and formalism see Robert Kaufman, 'Negatively Capable Dialectics: Keats, Vendler, Adorno, and the Theory of the Avant-Garde', *Critical Inquiry*, 27: 2 (Winter 2001), pp. 354–84.

14 Paul de Man, 'Introduction to the Poetry of John Keats' (1966), in *Critical Writings 1953–1978*, ed. Lindsay Waters (Minneapolis: University of Minnesota Press, 1989), pp. 179–97.

15 Lyn Hejinian, *The Language of Inquiry* (Berkeley and Los Angeles: University of California Press, 2000), p. 351.

16 Peter Nicholls discusses Hejinian's 'doubt' in 'Phenomenal Poetics: Reading Lyn Hejinian', in *The Mechanics of the Mirage: Postwar American Poetry*, ed. Michel Delville and Christine Pagnouelle (Liège: Liège Language and Literature, 2000), pp. 245–8.

17 Lyn Hejinian, *My Life* (Los Angeles: Green Integer, 2002), p. 59.

18 Hejinian, *Language*, p. 351.

Charles Olson

While Bate was in Cambridge popularizing one version of negative capability, Olson was expounding his own thinking about Keats and negative capability in his writing and in his teaching at the experimental Black Mountain College, where he worked from 1951 to 1956. Olson's fellow poet Robert Duncan later recalled the negative capability passage from Keats's letters as a text 'Olson insisted on at Black Mountain until it must have been memorized'.[19] Where Bate sees Keats's thought as developing out of eighteenth-century tradition, Olson views Keats as marking a radical break with the subject-centered itinerary of Western thought from Socrates to Romanticism: with the concept of 'negative capability', he declares, 'Keats, without setting out to, had put across the century the inch of steel to wreck Hegel, if anything could'.[20] Olson wants a poetics that keeps pace with, and incorporates, developments in atomic physics, cybernetics, advanced mathematics, and the social sciences: notions of relativity, uncertainty, the continuous universe, the interchangeability of matter and energy, 'feedback' in systems, the concept of the field. If Olson seeks, as Peter Middleton argues, to have poetry capture some of the glamor these scientific and social scientific discourses held at midcentury, then by positioning Keats as *anticipating* these discoveries, he restores poetry not only to an exchange among disciplines but to pride of place among them.[21]

Olson's 'Equal, That Is, to the Real Itself' (1958) is ostensibly a review of a new book on Herman Melville but really an argument for the new way of seeing reality opened (in Olson's view) by Keats, recognized by Melville, and formalized in projective geometry and new mathematics. The review begins by recounting the story told in Keats's negative capability letter as a kind of ur-scene of the revolution in modern thought:

> John Keats, walking home from the mummers' play at Christmas 1817, and afterwards, he'd had to listen to Coleridge again, thought to himself all that irritable reaching after fact and reason, it won't do. I don't believe in it. I do better to stay in the condition of things. No matter what it amounts to, mystery confusion doubt, it has a power, it is what I mean by *Negative Capability*. (p. 120)

[19] Robert Duncan to Denise Levertov, 12 January 1961, *The Letters of Robert Duncan and Denise Levertov*, ed. Robert J. Bertholf and Albert Gelpi (Stanford, CA: Stanford University Press, 2004), p. 271.

[20] Charles Olson, *Collected Prose*, ed. Donald Allen and Benjamin Friedlander (Berkeley: University of California Press, 1997), p. 120.

[21] Peter Middleton, *Physics Envy: American Poetry and Science in the Cold War and After* (Chicago, IL: University of Chicago Press, 2015), pp. 101–3.

The 'condition of things' is an ongoing, non-teleological process, with the emphasis as much on *historical* as on natural process. Olson connects a Heraclitan notion of temporal flux with concepts of relativity, the interchangeability of matter and energy, and the space–time continuum advanced in twentieth-century physics. For Olson, this means a renewed recognition of humanity's 'physicality': 'man' is 'a thing among things' in a reconceived universe where 'nothing was now inert fact' and 'reality was without interruption' (p. 121).

Presenting the poem as action or enactment rather than representation or description, a mode of 'work[ing] in open', Olson's manifesto 'Projective Verse' describes the activity of the poem as 'energy transferred from where the poet got it ... by way of the poem itself to, all the way over to, the reader'.[22] Olson borrows the concept of the 'field' from physics and the social sciences for a notion of field composition in which elements in a poem, like entities in the world, are understood as particles in a field of forces, acting on one another: 'what *is*, is no longer THINGS but what happens BETWEEN things' (*Prose*, p. 138). In his important poem 'The Kingfishers' Olson borrows (as Sherman Paul has observed) the language of negative capability along with the language of cybernetics to frame both the idea of continuity within constant change and the approach to thinking it:[23]

> And what is the message? The message is
> a discrete or continuous sequence of measurable events
>   distributed in time
> [...]
> is change, presents
> no more than itself
>
> And the too strong grasping of it,
> when it is pressed together and condensed,
> loses it
>
> This very thing you are[24]

As Olson writes in 'The Human Universe', again echoing Keats's negative capability, 'There must be a way which bears *in* instead of away, which meets

[22] Charles Olson, 'Projective Verse', in *Twentieth-Century American Poetics: Poets on the Art of Poetry*, ed. Dana Gioia, David Mason, and Meg Schoerke (New York: McGraw Hill, 2004), p. 174.

[23] Sherman Paul, *Olson's Push: Origin, Black Mountain, and Recent American Poetry* (Baton Rouge and London: Louisiana State University Press, 1978), p. 22.

[24] Charles Olson, 'The Kingfishers', in *The Collected Poems of Charles Olson*, ed. George F. Butterick (Berkeley and Los Angeles: University of California Press, 1997), p. 90.

head on what goes on each split second, a way which does not—in order to define—prevent, deter, distract, and so cease the act of, discovering' (*Prose*, p. 158).

Dispensing (he hopes) with dichotomies of subject and object, body and soul, his language emphasizes the body's immersive participation in the 'condition of things'. For Olson, Keats is again the forerunner here. 'Projective Verse', endorsing a poetics of breath, process, and the body, kicks off with Keats's protest against the 'egotistical sublime', taken up again in the manifesto's closing formulation of 'objectism', 'the getting rid of the lyrical interference of the individual as ego, of the "subject" and his soul' (pp. 174, 179–80). The interface between the body and the world is not the eyes (as in Bate) or the soul, but the physical boundary of the skin: 'What happens at the skin is more like than different from what happens within' (*Prose*, p. 162).

It is tempting simply to set up Olson and Bate as foils for each other. This is the line taken by William Spanos in his Heideggerian reading of negative capability in Olson's poetics, where Bate's discussion of negative capability stands in for what Spanos describes as a New Critical embrace of the unified subject he sees Olson's poetics as deconstructing.[25] But such a too-neat opposition between the traditionalist and the radical experimentalist also obscures significant parallels that have to do with each thinker's place in a shared midcentury intellectual discourse. It is worth noting that the two have intriguing overlaps in their intellectual formation: Olson was a graduate student in the new program in American Studies at Harvard around the same time Bate was getting his undergraduate degree at the university, and the intellectual climate at Harvard is crucial to them both. More directly, they share an important 'touchstone' in the work of the philosopher Alfred North Whitehead, a mentor to Bate at Harvard starting in the 1940s and a thinker with whose work Olson engages centrally starting in the mid-1950s. When Bate talks about concrete process in his negative capability chapter, he refers to Whitehead's process philosophy repeatedly. To see Bate simply as rehearsing a kind of formalism misses the way he and Olson are engaged with similar midcentury ideas of a holistic universe not of substance but of continuous process.

Beyond these connections, 'Keats' and negative capability fill an important symbolic role for both writers in figuring a desired identification of cultural authority and 'common life' in response to a certain form of professionalism in the academy, and to forms of loss and abstraction in twentieth-century culture more widely. Though Spanos aligns Bate's thinking about negative capability with that of New Critics such as Cleanth Brooks, Bate differentiates

[25] William V. Spanos, 'Charles Olson and Negative Capability: A Phenomenological Interpretation', *Contemporary Literature*, 21: 1 (Winter 1980), p. 43.

his humanism strongly from what he sees as the distortively professionalized, over-specialized discourse of the New Critics. In Bate's 1982 essay 'The Crisis in English Studies', a controversy-sparking salvo bemoaning the apparent undermining of a coherent curriculum by deconstruction, women's studies, gay studies, and other supposed 'fads', New Criticism appears as one form of 'trivially specialized expertise' within English departments in a trend that begins with the philological research of the earlier twentieth century.[26] Common to all these movements, in Bate's view, are a rigidity of method and disciplinary insularity (imitative of the sciences) producing 'self-imposed limitations through *specialization*' (p. 49; emphasis Bate's). His plea is for an approach that is '*frankly eclectic*' (his emphasis), grounded in 'commonsense, the essence of which is to be able to keep in mind several things at once', that attends to literature as presenting 'the *whole* experience of life—historical movements and also the individual's dilemmas in choice of values' (p. 53). For Bate, this demands a return to the Renaissance ideal of 'humane letters', an ideal that for him expresses itself in part in a freedom of range across disciplinary boundaries, and that is embodied in a 'man of letters' tradition exemplified by figures from Hazlitt to Edmund Wilson (pp. 47–53).

At Black Mountain College, an institution founded with the idea of putting Dewey's educational philosophy into practice, there is a somewhat conceptually parallel move to connect art and life, though expressed, of course, in opposite terms of wild experiment, a deliberate attack on the institutional norms of the traditional university. This spirit is embodied in Olson's own flagrant disciplinary eclecticism, his investigations across the sciences, anthropology, history, and philosophy. Again, this is not to lump Bate's traditionalism together with Olson's postmodernism; I imagine Bate would be at least amused and Olson probably horrified by the suggestion. Yet, as different as they are, Bate and Olson push against some of the same targets, and with some of the same means.

Indeed, in her analysis of the institutional coordinates of Olson's career, Libbie Rifkin shows how, as Olson goes about 'forging his avant-garde poetic career in a climate of inchoate anxiety over masculine authority and cultural centrality', he adopts a variety of conflicting stances towards 'professionalism'. If Olson positions the poet as bohemian outsider against the 'emasculated' (Rifkin's term) academic professional—a 'clear neuter' (Olson's words) engaged in arid specialization and concerned solely with professional advancement—Olson simultaneously, Rikfin argues, vies competitively for (masculinized) scholarly authority and professional reputation in the way he adopts the language of multiple academic disciplines.[27] As Rifkin elsewhere observes, if

[26] Walter Jackson Bate, 'The Crisis in English Studies', *Harvard Magazine* (September–October 1982), p. 53.

[27] Libbie Rifkin, *Career Moves: Olson, Creeley, Zukofsky, Berrigan, and the American*

Olson is 'a precursor to [David] Simpson's "academic postmodern"', whose interdisciplinary license appears as an 'institutionally buttressed amateurism', at the same time 'Olson's projective poet is on a continuum with the old-style man of letters, an interdisciplinary pioneer whose poaching license has a long literary history' (p. 24). This last is the lineage Bate claims for himself in figures such as Hazlitt.

As Stephen Voyce has recently described, Olson's aim of 'working in open' applies not only to his poetics but to the day-to-day practice at Black Mountain, where crossings between disciplines, open-ended process, and an improvisatory approach to art-making and to just making do with available resources form the anti-institutional ethos.[28] One sees the attractiveness of Olson's take on negative capability as a guiding concept for Black Mountain practice generally. But these models in Olson's work and his institutional vision are also derived in part, Middleton suggests, from Olson's experience as a graduate student in Harvard's then-new interdisciplinary History of American Civilization program (p. 143). Others, such as Robert Motherwell, also served as conduits of ideas between Harvard departments and Black Mountain. In institutional terms, the distance between the experimental Black Mountain College and the encampment of Harvard Keatsians in many respects could not be wider, but in other ways it looks smaller than one might think.

If Bate's pedagogical charisma involves a capacity for channeling long-dead authors in riveting performance, however, Olson's pedagogical charisma is dependent on his performing himself in the moment, the bodily enactment of what Lytle Shaw calls 'events of Olson-in-process', 'proposing a kind of excess connectivity, a continuous epiphanic breakthrough that must be experienced in real time'.[29] This is hyperbolized in Olson's legendary, or notorious, performance at the 1965 Berkeley Poetry Conference, where he talked—and drank—on stage for hours, until the reading/lecture was shut down. Trotted out as a kind of elder to the poetry scene, he interrupts himself, philosophizes extemporaneously, spins yarns, taunts audience members, and pushes back aggressively when restive listeners ask him to just read a poem, snapping, 'a poet, when he's alive, whether he talks or reads you his poems is the same thing'.[30]

Avant-Garde (Madison: University of Wisconsin Press, 2000), pp. 33–4; Rifkin quotes 'clear neuter' from Olson's 'Letter for Melville 1951' in *Collected Poems*, p. 239.

[28] Stephen Voyce, 'Alternative Degrees: 'Works in OPEN' at Black Mountain College', in *After the Program Era: The Past, Present and Future of Creative Writing in the University*, ed. Loren Glass (Iowa City: University of Iowa Press, 2016), pp. 85–104.

[29] Lytle Shaw, *Fieldworks: From Place to Site in Postwar Poetics* (Tuscaloosa: University of Alabama Press, 2013), p. 65.

[30] Charles Olson, *Muthologos: The Collected Lectures and Interviews*, ed. George F. Butterick (Berkeley, CA: Four Seasons, 1978), Vol. 1, p. 111.

Is this bodily enactment of a poetics of process a performance of negative capability or its opposite? That it might be, uneasily, both at once is suggested by the terms in which Rifkin and Barrett Watten independently comment on Olson's poetics. Watten cleverly describes the disconnected, all-encompassing mode of Olson's *Maximus* poems as 'a nonstop irritable reaching after everything' (quoted in Shaw, p. 62). The quip suggests something telling about the lineage of the performance Olson puts on at Berkeley: in this scene, the endlessly talking, digressive Olson is not Keats but *Coleridge*, the sage of Highgate (though, to be fair, that gives his audience the chance to play Keats). In Rifkin's telling, the performance at Berkeley takes the risk of extreme forms of openness—openness of disciplinary borders, but also 'of professional etiquette, social mores, and, most important, ego boundaries' (p. 26). Following Olson's own usage, we might call this openness a kind of enactment of negative capability. But, suggestively, Rifkin alludes to Keats a few pages later in describing Olson's high-stakes performance as 'his brand of egotistical sublimity' (p. 29). It's as if negative capability is pushed so far here it turns into its opposite, a domineering design on the audience—or, perhaps of necessity, the performance of negative capability succeeds and fails at once.

Adrienne Rich

Both Bate and Olson present negative capability as a virtue—a valuable posture or practice, even an admirable quality of character. But what if it is *not* a good thing? Adrienne Rich's moving 1986 elegy for her friend David Kalstone, 'In Memoriam: D.K.', engages Keatsian negative capability from a position of skepticism, and in a way that indirectly speaks back to the gender politics of the ways Bate and Olson construct Keats. Though in the brief discussion that follows I concentrate on Rich's elegy as individual poem, I want to suggest that its negotiation with negative capability has connections with Rich's poetics generally and the particular place she occupies in the literary field. The poet Cathy Park Hong has recently written about returning to Rich's work after largely steering clear of it as an MFA student.[31] She describes a general allergy to Rich's writing in MFA programs based on its perceived lack of negative capability: 'I thought about the word commitment. This is a word that rarely comes up in workshop. Instead, there is this word: play ("the play of words in this line ... "). In workshop, we have been raised on a diet of negative capability. Lines should quiver with equivocation' (par. 9). Hong deftly finds a way to locate uncertainty in Rich's poetry still, noting that it is

[31] Cathy Park Hong, 'Memories and Thoughts on Adrienne Rich', in *Harriet: A Poetry Blog, Poetry Foundation* (June 2016), accessed 15 December 2016, https://www.poetryfoundation.org/harriet/2016/06/memories-and-thoughts-on-adrienne-rich/.

not as if 'her words are reducible or inflexible in her anger. There is certainty in her uncertainty, resolve in her ambivalence' (par. 12). My reading of the engagement with Keats in 'In Memoriam: D.K.' detects a similar tacking between ambivalence and resolve.

If Rich's work stands in tension with negative capability as play or equivocation, Rich is on record as endorsing Keatsian negative capability as 'intuitive identification'. In an oft-cited 1970s conversation with Barbara Gelpi, Rich argues, with Nancy Chodorow's psychoanalytic work in mind, that women's 'so-called "weak ego boundaries"' translate into 'tremendous powers of intuitive identification and sympathy with other people'.[32] Gelpi replies, 'Keats had weak ego boundaries', to which Rich responds: 'Negative capability. Exactly. Any artist has to have it to some extent' (p. 115). This feminizing of Keats and of negative capability has had an important afterlife in Romanticist discussions of Keats and gender. In Margaret Homans's influential essay 'Keats Reading Women, Women Reading Keats', she picks up on Rich and Gelpi's comments, but she sees Keats as markedly defensive about the possibility that he, or his poetics, might be read in the feminizing terms Rich and Gelpi develop.[33] Homans highlights the complex gendering of 'receptivity' in the passage from a letter to John Hamilton Reynolds of 19 February 1818 that Bate also connects to negative capability:

> The f[l]ower I doubt not receives a fair guerdon from the Bee—its leaves blush deeper in the next spring—and who shall say between Man and Woman which is the most delighted? Now it is more noble to sit like Jove than to fly like Mercury—let us not therefore go hurrying about and collecting honey-bee like, buzzing here and there impatiently from a knowledge of what is to be arrived at: but let us open our leaves like a flower and be passive and receptive—budding patiently under the eye of Apollo and taking hints from every noble insect that favors us with a visit— (*LJK*, I: p. 232)

As Homans emphasizes, Keats rewrites passive receptivity as masculine, Jove-like capability and command even as he appropriates female receptivity (and 'delight').

Keats's letter seems to me very much on Rich's mind in the opening stanzas of the elegy for the poet and critic Kalstone, who died of complications of AIDS:

[32] *Adrienne Rich's Poetry*, ed. Barbara Charlesworth Gelpi and Albert Gelpi (New York: Norton, 1975), p. 115.

[33] Margaret Homans, 'Keats Reading Women, Women Reading Keats', *Studies in Romanticism*, 29 (1990): pp. 341–70.

A man walking on the street
feels unwell   has felt unwell
all week, a little   Yet the flowers crammed
in pots on the corner: furled anemones:
he knows they open
burgundy, violet, pink, amarillo
all the way to their velvet cores
The flowers hanging over the fence: fuchsias:
each tongued, staring,   all of a fire:
the flowers   He who has
been happy oftener than sad
carelessly happy   well oftener than sick
one of the lucky   is thinking about death
and its music   about poetry
its translations of his life

And what good will it do you
to go home and put on the Mozart Requiem?
Read Keats?   How will culture cure you?
Poor, unhappy
unwell culture   what can it sing or say
six weeks from now, to you?[34]

As James Najarian points out, Keats's presence in the poem is overdetermined. Najarian reminds us that Keats and Mozart are both types of the genius who dies too young; Keats's illness shadows the poem's thinking about AIDS and infection.[35] If 'death and its music' recalls 'To Autumn', as Langdon Hammer has noticed, Keats is arguably already present from the very start of the poem in the floral catalogue aligning an absorption in beauty—art, poetry, flowers, or male bodies—and a kind of passive openness or receptivity with a dangerous 'carelessness'.[36] This is of course a very different version of Keats from what we have seen in Bate and Olson, though, as noted earlier, it is a tradition against which their own, muscular versions of Keats are to some degree positioned.

Keats's language gives Rich the resources to launch, in the next stanza, an extraordinary affirmation:

[34] Adrienne Rich, 'In Memoriam: D.K.', in *Later Poems: Selected and New, 1971–2012* (New York: Norton, 2013), pp. 190–1.

[35] James Najarian, *Victorian Keats: Manliness, Sexuality, and Desire* (New York: Palgrave Macmillan, 2002), p. 15.

[36] Langdon Hammer, 'Art and AIDS; or, How Will Culture Cure You?', *Raritan*, 14 (Winter 1995): pp. 103–18.

> Give me your living hand If I could take the hour
> death moved into you undeclared, unnamed
> —even if sweet, if I could take that hour
> between my forceps   tear at it like a monster
> wrench it out of your flesh   dissolve its shape in quicklime
> and make you well again
>   no, not again
> but still ... (pp. 190–1)

As Rich at once echoes and counters Keats's fragment 'This living hand', she reconfigures Keats's haunting drama of guilt, aggression and potential reciprocity into a differently arranged exchange between selves. The gesture of Rich towards Kalstone is one of love and also an impulse to pull him back (like Orpheus and Eurydice) or steer him through to safety (like parent and child): but the insistence is on her friend's 'living' hand. The turn to iambic meter in the alexandrine line after the metrical irregularity of the earlier stanzas confers an urgency, and the demand is at once an expression of anger at the hand's unavailability and a recognition that, though the hand is gone forever, it is fully present to thought with no trace of the uncanniness that characterizes Keats's fragment. Thus the traditional elegiac trope of consolation is rejected and reworked into an expression of what Jahan Ramazani has called Rich's 'anti-elegiac' position—which Ramazani characterizes by quoting Kalstone's characterization of Rich as a poet of 'fierce optimism'.[37]

Hammer's analysis of Rich's poem is the best I have encountered. He shows the remarkable complexity, born of deep ambivalence, in the metaphors through which Rich imagines death moving into her friend's body and then fantasizes about her own wrenching it out:

> The metaphor fixes the 'undeclared, unnamed' origin of infection in a moment of 'carelessly happy' sex ... . She calls that hour 'a monster' not so much although, as because, it was also a 'sweet' time: the horror Rich expresses arises both from the irreversibility of HIV infection and from the sexual form of its transmission. The irreversibility of HIV and its sexual transmission connect infection, in this case, with human conception—only it is death, not life, that gay male sex breeds. (par. 7)

As Hammer notes, though, when Rich describes her desire to wrench infection from Kalstone's body with her 'forceps' 'she is not reversing, as much as repeating, the penetration of the body that signifies death in this poem' (par. 8).

[37] Jahan Ramazani, *The Poetry of Mourning: The Modern Elegy from Hardy to Heaney* (Chicago, IL: University of Chicago Press, 1994), p. 311.

What I want to add to Hammer's suggestive reading is the observation that these two scenes of penetration (the sexual encounter imagined as transmitting the virus, and the angry fantasy of wrenching the virus out) are themselves set up by the movement of Keats's voice into the body of Rich's poem. (This line of transmission also operates through Tennyson's elegy *In Memoriam A.H.H.* [1850], in which Keats's presence is also felt.) The openness to the precursor poems (Keats's and Tennyson's) thus parallels and anticipates the life-affirming and life-threatening forms of openness Rich explores in her poem, forms which her work holds to be life-affirming and life-threatening at once: the openness of bodies or minds to each other, to desire, to death. The poem, we might say, moves towards negative capability and repels from it. It does not want to cede the right to anger, or the right to want to reach for hard fact.

Given the cluster of Keatsian allusion in the poem it is possible to hear in the poem's ending ('no, not again / but still ... ') a link with yet another Keats poem, the sonnet 'Bright Star' ('No—yet still stedfast, still unchangeable, / ... / Awake for ever in a sweet unrest, / Still, still to hear her tender-taken breath, / And so live ever—or else swoon to death') (*PJK*, p. 328). The 'still' in Rich's poem pushes back against the death-bound mythology of Keats's sonnet, in which swooning to death and living 'ever' in an 'unchangeable' 'sweet unrest' are like two sides of the same coin.[38] In Rich's poem, 'no, not again / but still ... ' acknowledges the harsh facts: Kalstone is dead and gone, his voice stilled. In 1986, he could not be well 'again', there was no going back—no wishing could make him still well, or still alive. Yet Rich's 'but still' also registers a stubborn resistance to this logic. She holds herself open towards Kalstone even after the possibility of reciprocity is definitively ended, even fully aware of the finality of his death. The poem's final ellipses mark, I think, the kind of stance Hong has in mind when she describes Rich's 'certainty in her uncertainty, resolve in her ambivalence': a negatively capable critique of negative capability, we might say.

Rich's poem operates in the space between selves, but neither posits those selves as wholly separate nor arraigns them through a rhetoric of mutual understanding or communion. While, like Bate, she draws on Keats's thinking about vicariousness and sympathy, here vicarious feeling connects to vulnerability, to a dangerous permeability of self, to a simultaneous commitment to and sense of distance from the other, to love and hostility at once. In Hejinian's terms, the relation between self and outside appears as 'a border under pressure of doubt'. The poem tarries with difficult and intractable facts and trails off in

[38] Compare Rich's use of Keats in her 1974 poem 'To a Poet' (addressing a female contemporary, probably Anne Sexton), taking up a similar cluster of imagery; see the discussion in Barbara Johnson's 'Apostrophe, Animation, and Abortion', *Diacritics*, 16: 1 (Spring 1986), pp. 28–47.

uncertainties and doubt, but, unlike some versions of 'negative capability', we are not in the mode here of suspension or reverie, nor of 'process' or flow. This is a poem of impatience, urgency, and frustration as well as of imagination. Its final ellipses mark the insistence of a limit as much as they hold thought open.

CHAPTER ELEVEN

'giddily off into the unknown'

Negative Capability and Naturalism in Elizabeth Bishop's Poetics

Arsevi Seyran

> Art shews us nature, divested of the medium of our prejudices. It divides and decompounds objects into a thousand curious parts, which may be full of variety, beauty, and delicacy in themselves, though the object to which they belong may be disagreeable in its general appearance, or by association with other ideas.[1]

When Elizabeth Bishop read 'Lines Composed a Few Miles above Tintern Abbey' in her 1963 copy of William Wordsworth's poetry, she jotted down an excited 'Oh!?!' upon underlining the words 'Nature never did betray / The heart that loved her'.[2] The marginal note seems to capture two different reactions, surprise and skepticism, while also gesturing toward that utterance's combination of spontaneity and reflection. In this sense Bishop's note calls to mind the epiphanic 'oh!' (line 36) of the speaker from 'In the Waiting Room', Bishop's seven-year-old persona who suddenly conceptualizes her own presence in the world (while dutifully reading through *National Geographic*), and then just as quickly questions the truth of her awakening.[3] In Wordsworth Bishop seems to have looked for a similar kind of self-mirroring, and, from Robert Pinsky to Charles Rzepka, many critics have thus explored the affinities between the

[1] William Hazlitt, 'On Imitation', in *The Collected Works of William Hazlitt*, ed. A. R. Waller and Arnold Glover, 12 vols. (London: J. M. Dent, 1904), I: p. 74.

[2] Located at the Houghton Library at Harvard University.

[3] Elizabeth Bishop, *Poems* (New York: Farrar, Straus and Giroux, 2011), pp. 179–81. The young narrator's recognition of herself is rapidly followed by a questioning: '*Why* should you be one, too?' (i.e. 'an Elizabeth / ... one of them' (lines 62, 60–1)). A similar doubt thus seems to quickly ensue when Bishop identifies with Wordsworth's praise of nature's loyalty.

two poets. When Pinsky suggests that Bishop writes 'seemingly restrained, yet relaxed sentences, startlingly flexible in practice, … educated but not pedantic',[4] one remembers Wordsworth's endeavor 'to bring [his] language near to the real language of men'.[5] Both poets used plain language, both had a proclivity for the epiphanic. Both turned to the natural world for understanding and naturalized the characters they explored. Rzepka quotes Bishop's own statement: 'I find I'm really a minor female Wordsworth—at least, I don't know anyone else who seems to be such a Nature Lover.'[6] Indeed, Bishop seems to have wanted to identify with how 'Nature never did betray / The heart that loved her'; yet her approach is more that of a naturalist and comes much less from a stance of 'the wordsworthian or egotistical sublime' (*LJK*, I: p. 387). And though there is no record of Bishop's own discernment of her Keatsian tendencies,[7] it may be worthwhile to revise her ties to the Romantics and rethink her love of nature not through Wordsworth but through Keats's negative capability. Whereas Wordsworth recollects emotion in tranquility, replicating the originary 'spontaneous overflow of powerful feelings' (p. 175), Bishop effaces her emotion and her self in her poetic process; she contemplates the object. In her work the human ego is absent. Pinsky explains, in likening her to William Wordsworth, that

> it is the war of the poet to work on the world of things and people as much as that world works on her. Seeing and describing the world, and making her own cartography from the English language, she makes the world and language her own. From her native self, she sends forth mutations. (p. 7)

I suggest that Pinksy's reading invites a small revision—in regard to the word 'war' in particular—since Bishop's art triggers not 'mutations' of *herself* but a transfer into different selves as a result of relentless, meticulous concentration. The precise drive of this concentration is to dispel that 'war', not to engage in it. The aim of it is a version of negative capability. Even when her voice proceeds in the lyric I, but especially when it does not, Bishop speaks from outside

[4] Robert Pinsky, 'The Idiom of a Self: Elizabeth Bishop and William Wordsworth', *American Poetry Review*, 9: 1 (January/February 1980), p. 8.

[5] William Wordsworth, 'Preface', in Samuel Taylor Coleridge and William Wordsworth, *Lyrical Ballads: 1798 and 1800*, ed. Michael Gamer and Dahlia Porter (Peterborough: Broadview, 2008), p. 184.

[6] Quoted in Charles Rzepka, 'Elizabeth Bishop and the Wordsworth of *Lyrical Ballads*: Sentimentalism, Straw Men, and Misprision', *Romantic Circles Praxis Series* (November 1999), par. 1, accessed 9 July 2018, https://www.rc.umd.edu/praxis/lyrical/rzepka/bishop.html.

[7] The negative capability letter in Bishop's copy of Keats's letters at the Houghton Library, for instance, is completely unmarked.

her own selfhood, taking on the voices of a series of different characters with diverse beings, which can be thought of as examples of what Samuel Taylor Coleridge calls 'the I representative'.[8] With that in mind, in what follows I aim to explore Bishop's attainment of that peripheral status, contending that negative capability is an ingrained part of her process of composition, and that, further, she attains this capability through a Darwinian naturalism, a connection discussed below via her famous 'Darwin letter'. Her relation to the natural world and its processes occurs not through a Wordsworthian, fully present self; if we are to find the poet as 'Nature Lover' in Bishop's work, it is to Keats that we must turn.

I am not the first to suggest negative capability in Bishop's process of writing. In one of the first published studies on Bishop, Anne Stevenson wrote about her much admired older friend Elizabeth that she is

> indefatigably curious to explore the textures of her environment to which, like Keats, she responds with a 'negative capability'. She is able to see without making judgments, to investigate without having to fix her identity by taking sides … . She is a poet whose imagination is excited by what Archibald MacLeish has called the 'arable world'—the world of sensations, vision, appetite—to which power in a social sense is largely indifferent. The mind that apprehends this world often slips through the coarser nets of faction and in some bewilderment wonders what all the fuss can be about.[9]

In 2006 Stevenson confessed to being 'embarrassed by the sketch [she] offered to Twayne in 1965'.[10] However, her remarks on the personal letters she received from Bishop as being 'far beyond anything [she] was in those days capable of assimilating' indicate a more general sense of regret about her youth and relative naiveté, and should not discount her more particular comment about Bishop's negative capability. To add, the roots of Stevenson's 1965 claim are traceable to a particular letter that Bishop wrote her in 1964:

> Dreams, works of art (some), glimpses of the always-more-successful surrealism of everyday life, unexpected moments of empathy (is it?), catch a peripheral vision of whatever it is one can never really see full-face but that seems enormously important. I can't believe we are wholly irrational and I do admire Darwin! But reading Darwin, one admires the

[8] Samuel Taylor Coleridge, *Lectures 1808–1819: On Literature*, ed. R. A. Foakes, 2 vols. (London: Routledge and Kegan Paul, 1987), I: pp. 148–9.

[9] Anne Stevenson, *Elizabeth Bishop* (New York: Twayne Publishers, 1966), p. 47.

[10] Anne Stevenson, *Five Looks at Elizabeth Bishop* (Tarset: Bloodaxe Books, 2006), p. 12.

> beautiful solid case being built up out of his endless heroic observations, almost unconscious or automatic—and then comes a sudden relaxation, a forgetful phrase, and one feels the strangeness of his undertaking, sees the lonely young man, his eyes fixed on facts and minute details, sinking or sliding giddily off into the unknown. What one seems to want in art, in experiencing it, is the same thing that is necessary for its creation, a self-forgetful, perfectly useless concentration. (quoted in Stevenson, *Bishop*, p. 66)

By now known as 'the Darwin letter', this text has received the attention of several Bishop scholars, but the reference to Darwin as a route to extrapolating Bishop's negative capability has not been taken up, perhaps because, except for the rare Wordsworth comparisons, she tends not to be linked with the Romantics. Even Stevenson writes that 'in her poems, every one of which is a work of art, Elizabeth Bishop stands apart from life at the very moment she engages with it. In this respect her attitude is "Classical" as opposed to "Romantic"' (p. 75). For my own purposes, whether Bishop's attitude can be categorized as 'Classical' or 'Romantic' does not alter her poetics, which regardless renders a likeness between her and the Darwinian 'lonely young man, his eyes fixed on facts and minute details, sinking or sliding giddily off into the unknown'. This figure is (or can be) the poet resigned but awake in what Keats calls 'the Penetralium of mystery', and moreover 'capable of being in uncertainties … doubts without any irritable reaching', struck with beauty (or intensity, or gusto) so much that he is, in fact, absorbed by it, and thus blinded to his own subjective considerations (*LJK*, I: p. 194, 193). Truth then follows of its own accord. 'The excellence of every Art is its intensity', Keats writes earlier in the negative capability letter, 'capable of making all disagreeables evaporate, from their being in close relationship with Beauty & Truth' (*LJK*, I: p. 192). If worldly unpleasantness is accompanied by a 'momentous depth of speculation', this can 'bury its repulsiveness', and perhaps offer a kind of solace and sudden truth through art, which might be considered a significant aim of negative capability (*LJK*, I: p. 192).

Given the antinomic nature of that 'Penetralium', if a poet is to have negative capability he will endure the 'disagreeables' that are so often his material, thus allowing them to coexist until from such opposites an intense truth may arise. For this he must give up all traces of his ego and replace it with 'the poetical Character itself', which, less than a year after the negative capability letter, Keats explains to Richard Woodhouse as

> that sort distinguished from the wordsworthian or egotistical sublime; which is a thing per se and stands alone) it is not itself—it has no self—it is every thing and nothing—It has no character—it enjoys light

> and shade; it lives in gusto, be it foul or fair, high or low, rich or poor, mean or elevated—It has as much delight in conceiving an Iago as an Imogen. What shocks the virtuous philosop[h]er, delights the camelion Poet. It does no harm from its relish of the dark side of things any more than from its taste for the bright one; because they both end in speculation. A Poet is the most unpoetical of any thing in existence; because he has no Identity—he is continually in for—and filling some other Body— (*LJK*, I: p. 387)

This 'speculation' is not meant to induce ultimate resolutions; yet, within the flux of it, there is a possibility of momentary revelation—of dismissing 'philosophy' to allow the poet's self to 'sink into' an impressionable beckoning of nature so that it might, if it wishes, mark him with some impossible-to-plot, surprise Truth.[11] Being thus marked by nature and its creatures, the poet is no longer himself. In affirming this lack of motive in Keats's poetic process, David Luke points to his letters:

> Keats never indulged in the sort of public manifesto about poetry that many of his contemporaries did because the paradox of his 'sense of Beauty' is that it nearly 'obliterates all consideration'. Which is to say that it nearly 'obliterates' all attempts at formulation. This is why he inserts his ideas on the subject in the 'scraps & patches' of expendable personal letters. And this is why those 'scraps & patches', to quote Trilling, 'have an interest which is virtually equal to that of their writer's canon of created work'.[12]

Bishop worked similarly: she is another letter-writer of exceptional merit, whose individual ideas were not in the poems but in the 'scraps & patches' of her letters. She confessed to Anne Stevenson upon an attempt to read Wittgenstein: 'I'm not too good at "ideas", you know—it's like being tone-deaf. I try, with the best will in the world—but after a few minutes of philosophy—or economics—I find that my ears have closed up just the way the capivaras' ears do when they dive into the Amazon'.[13] It is not that Bishop was incapable of

[11] In many of his letters Keats describes things as pressing themselves upon him. The letter to Woodhouse quoted above includes this memorable passage: 'When I am in a room with People, if I ever am free from speculating on creations of my own brain, then not myself goes home to myself: but the identity of everyone in the room begins to to press upon me that, I am in a very little time annihilated' (*LJK*, I: p. 387).

[12] David Luke, 'Keats's Letters: Fragments of an Aesthetic of Fragments', *GENRE*, 2 (Summer 1978), p. 223.

[13] Elizabeth Bishop to Anne Stevenson, 5 December 1964, Elizabeth Bishop Papers, Washington University Libraries, St. Louis.

understanding 'ideas'; rather she was more taken by flux than static formulation. In an interview from 1977 she notes, 'I am an observer, and one of the things I like to observe is nature. I love zoology. I should tell you that I do not like to talk about literature.'[14] Like Keats, Bishop did not philosophize systematically. Though at times judgmental in her letters, she was staunchly against categorization, and her poetry differed greatly from her letters, as can be said of Keats. Further, it was a 'sense of Beauty'—Keats's path to truth—that invited her to 'speculation'. As Darwin studied natural life, a certain curiosity beckoned her to objects worth studying, often very ordinary ones like fish, moose, and gas stations, which made her fresh, seamless 'study'-from-scratch even more profound. Bishop focused as a scientist or medical student focuses, but in the poet's case without any aim of resolution. In most of her work nature itself (which includes nature with marks of human presence, too) navigates the poem, not the poet. And because nature offers observation without ultimate answers, as Stevenson puts it, 'only a very few of [Bishop's] poems achieve conclusions that do not either imply or directly raise abstract questions. Often ... things simply continue in their cloud of unknowing'.[15]

So what does the process of creating a 'cloud of unknowing' look like? One place to begin is with Jack Stillinger's well-known formulation of what he calls 'a basic Keatsian structure', one which shares much with Bishop's poetics:

> Characteristically, the speaker in the Romantic lyric begins in the real world (A), takes off in mental flight to visit the ideal (B), and then—for a variety of reasons, but most often because he finds something wanting in the imagined ideal or because, being a native of the real world, he discovers that he does not or cannot belong permanently in the ideal—returns home to the real (A'). But he has not simply arrived where he began (hence A' rather than A at the descent). He has acquired something—a new understanding of a situation, a change in attitude toward it—from the experience of the flight.[16]

In Bishop's poetry a similar pyramidal pattern ensues. This is why in her Darwin letter she claims that there is not a 'split' in 'the role of consciousness and subconsciousness in art'.[17] Darwinian 'endless ... observations' build a 'beautiful solid case' in a way that is 'almost unconscious or automatic—then

[14] George Monteiro, ed., *Conversations with Elizabeth Bishop* (Jackson: University Press of Mississippi, 1996), p. 77.

[15] Stevenson, *Five Looks*, p. 112.

[16] Jack Stillinger, 'Introduction: Imagination and Reality in the Odes of Keats', in *Twentieth Century Interpretations of Keats's Odes*, ed. Jack Stillinger (Englewood Cliffs, NJ: Prentice Hall, 1968), p. xvii.

[17] Stevenson, *Bishop*, p. 66.

comes a sudden relaxation', which is a momentary closeness to truth. Bishop's yielding to her subconscious during her observations is what enables the rise to Stillinger's 'B' in her poetry where consciousness has receded. That yielding (the arrival at 'B' through an accumulation of observations) can perhaps be thought of as the achievement or starting point of negative capability. While the poetic process is similar in Keats, there is also an important difference: what makes Keats a Romantic is the attempt to move to that higher realm, whereas Bishop's 'B' is hardly ever higher or 'ideal'; rather, her realms mostly encompass 'actual places solidly perceived and situated'.[18] Bishop does not aim to leave Stillinger's 'actual world'. In her own act of negation and transport she tends to move either to a realm of matter-of-fact defamiliarization or that of rhetorical questions, thereby creating what she refers to as 'the always-more-successful-surrealism of everyday life'.[19] The effect is one of quiet unsettling.

That sense of uncanny familiarity is precisely what the poet and the naturalist hope for as they embark on the 'build[ing]' of 'a beautiful solid case'. To elucidate, Zachariah Pickard writes that 'natural history depends on the leap from the concrete seen to the abstract imagined'.[20] He continues (while quoting from James Paradis): 'The natural historian needs to move between "a concrete landscape, full of distinct, palpable organic forms, and an abstract physical scheme", to be "alternately at the center of the whole and at its distant periphery"'.[21] 'Palpable' is a word that shares kinship with Stevenson's reference to Archibald MacLeish's 'arable land'. And a 'concentration' on the 'palpable', 'arable' 'natural appearances of objects' is what allows gusto to be brought forth. John Keats is fascinated with this word, as we know, upon reading it in William Hazlitt, who describes it as

> [the] power or passion defining any object. It is not so difficult to explain this term in what relates to expression (of which it may be said to be the highest degree) as in what relates to things without expression, to the natural appearances of objects, as mere colour or form. In one sense, however, there is hardly any object entirely devoid of expression, without some character of power belonging to it, some precise association with pleasure or pain: and it is in giving this truth of character from the truth of feeling, whether in the highest or the lowest degree, but always in the highest degree of which the subject is capable, that gusto consists.[22]

[18] Stevenson, *Five Looks*, p. 111.
[19] Stevenson, *Bishop*, p. 66.
[20] Zachariah Pickard, 'Natural History and Epiphany: Elizabeth Bishop's Darwin Letter', *Twentieth-Century Literature*, 50: 3 (Fall 2004), p. 276.
[21] Pickard, 'Natural History and Epiphany', p. 276.
[22] William Hazlitt, 'On Gusto', in *The Collected Works of William Hazlitt*, I: p. 77.

And since 'there is hardly any object entirely devoid of expression', a careful, slow accretion of details can bring forth the object's own expressed truth. Bishop, as Keats encourages, gives herself to the object of contemplation in her vista with an eye for gusto. As Pickard agrees, the poet's conscious mind begins by focusing on 'facts and minute details', and the unconscious mind follows behind with that 'sudden relaxation', the feeling of 'sinking or sliding giddily off into the unknown' (p. 281). It is when her conscious mind has built enough of the factual staircase that her giddy grasp of gusto renders the poet ready to yield to her subconscious, which then takes over the poem and, navigating it through the unknown, leads to a momentary nearness of Truth. As Bishop says, 'There is no "split"; the ascent and descent happen smoothly'.[23] Further, just as the conscious and subconscious are not split, neither are pain and pleasure. Thus Hazlitt underlines gusto's 'precise association with pleasure or pain', and we know that Truth is not in fact always Beauty, but that approaching its near-presence is beautiful. And, as poetical character 'does no harm from its relish of the dark side of things any more than from its taste for the bright one' (*LJK*, I: p. 387), William Blake's 'Opposition is true Friendship' paves the way for a negatively capable poetics. The 'arable land', with its rain and shine, invites the naturalist to build 'from a set of minute observations, depicting the visionary moment that comes from "a self-forgetful, perfectly useless concentration" on the things of the world'.[24]

But not for the fainthearted is the at times simultaneous duality of an Iago and Imogen. Endurance is a key word in Keats's life's work; a certain relentlessness against the odds is one more pivotal quality that he shares with Bishop. As Pickard writes, 'crucial to Bishop's aesthetic is a unique combination of perseverance and mystery: perseverance of observation that leads mysteriously to epiphany'. And furthermore, 'the Darwin letter is about ... the relationship between the process of empirical observation and the gift of vision or epiphany'.[25] With a poet who has negative capability, that gradual accretion of observations can lead to gusto, which nature can offer authentically if the poet holds up a mirror to it in the right angle and concentrates on his palpable view as opposed to his own views. As Luke sums it up, 'Keats considers "Negative Capability" a mode of wisdom which equates endurance with the momentum of a certain creative energy in the face of uncertainty or futility' (p. 222). That 'endurance' fits the test of suffering in both Keats's and Bishop's aesthetics, both poets having gained their intellectual openness and stamina partly from having had to fend for themselves in the world against various hardships, which Keats has said is necessary

[23] Stevenson, *Bishop*, p. 66.
[24] Pickard, 'Natural History and Epiphany', p. 279.
[25] Pickard, 'Natural History and Epiphany', p. 279.

'to school an Intelligence and make it a soul' (*LJK*, II: p. 102). And not too far from a similar Darwinian openness is Keats's background in medicine, which, as is often suggested, has a role in informing the detailed descriptions in his craft.[26] Until Bishop was 'taken up' by Marianne Moore she was contemplating a move to Boston, where, likewise, 'she thought for a while of studying medicine'.[27] If she had not been taken under Moore's wing she might have also trained to be a physician. That is a small detail, no doubt, added only to suggest that Bishop has in common with Darwin and Keats a penchant for the scientist's magnifying-glass-approach to the 'arable land'. Pickard argues that 'Darwin's vision is not ... an imaginative reaction to the visual presence of the real world' (p. 276). It is not an emotion recollected in tranquility. Rather, it is a gradual accretion of observed details through which a subconscious synthesis blossoms. Hence, I situate Elizabeth Bishop's poetics where Darwin's naturalism and Keats's negative capability merge. The former enables and sustains the latter.

'Nothing in this world is proveable', Keats writes to Benjamin Bailey in March 1818 (*LJK*, I: p. 242); in a similar manner he writes to George and Georgiana in September 1819: 'The only means of strengthening one's intellect is to make up ones mind about nothing—to let the mind be a thoroughfare for all thoughts' (*LJK*, II: p. 213). This brings us closer to truth, even if without guaranteeing it. What makes the process worthwhile, all the same, can perhaps be addressed through Schiller's 'play impulse', when 'seeing acquires an absolute value for' the poet if 'he is already aesthetically free'.[28] Schiller explains:

> Admittedly the speed with which certain characters pass from sensations to thoughts and to resolutions allows the aesthetic temper which they must necessarily hurry through in this time to be barely, if at all, perceptible. Such natures cannot long tolerate the condition of indeterminacy, and press impatiently for a result which they do not find in the condition of aesthetic boundlessness. With others, on the other hand, who find their enjoyment more in the feeling of the whole faculty rather than any individual action of it, the aesthetic condition displays itself over a much wider surface. (p. 102)

[26] See, for instance, Hermione de Almeida's discussion of 'Ode on a Grecian Urn' in *Romantic Medicine and John Keats* (Oxford: Oxford University Press, 1991), where she writes: 'The Romantic physician was charged to invoke his trained eye and penetrating vision to read beneath the smooth surfaces of an otherwise healthy body the yet-to-be-manifest signs of corroding disease [...] Poet and physician look thus at elusive mortal life as it is stilled and made accessible within the confines of an immortal Grecian urn' (p. 127).

[27] Stevenson, *Bishop*, p. 55.

[28] Friedrich Schiller, *On the Aesthetic Education of Man* (New York: Dover, 2004), p. 126.

That 'condition of indeterminacy' can be thought of as synonymous with negative capability, and here Schiller venerates it. The energy of 'play' within 'aesthetic boundlessness' is already equivalent to a certain kind of emerging wisdom, even if it never fully realizes its potential truth.

What remains to be assayed is how the play impulse benefits the aesthetic process, where naturalistic accretion is transformed by way of negative capability into not a resolution but a sudden glimpse at truth. According to Keats, 'Poetry should be great & unobtrusive, a thing which enters into one's soul, and does not startle it or amaze it with itself but with its subject' (*LJK*, I: p. 224). This requires, indeed, as complete an effacement of the self as possible—not 'mutations' or altered versions of the same 'sole self'. Like Keats, Bishop was open to 'play' and the necessary yielding of herself in the act of surmise. As Stevenson reveals: 'In 1948 ... Bishop singled out for praise Moore's ability "to give herself up entirely to the object under contemplation, to feel in all sincerity how it is to be it". Being "it" for Bishop meant knowing instinctively how not to confuse "it" with herself.'[29] But there is more to this knowing than 'instinct'. Bishop accrues. So many of her poems are long, built up in Bishop's yielding rather than paring them down as many other modernists do. In a similar vein, Darwin in his *Autobiography* refers to himself as 'a complete millionaire in odd and curious little facts'.[30] He is a collector of nature's every tidbit; he surmises 'by accretion', as Pickard puts it, suggesting that 'the phenomena that natural history seeks to explain are "hidden from the senses" because they take place over "magnitudes of space and time that human physiology [is] not equipped to apprehend"' (p. 275). Consequently, through the accumulation of individual momentary acts of perception, the naturalist can find a path to what truths there are hidden in nature. 'No single reported fact is of use, but through what Bishop calls the 'almost unconscious or automatic' process of observation, a substantial enough body of material develops, and the natural historian can synthesize and extrapolate'.[31] As Darwin does, then, Bishop synthesizes her gradually accrued observations in the seamless switch from consciousness to subconsciousness as she lets Truth come to her. A similar synthetic process seems to describe how Keats suddenly comes up with the idea of negative capability in the first place: 'I had not a dispute but a disquisition with Dilke on various subjects; several things dovetailed in my mind, & at once it struck me' (*LJK*, I: 193). Hence, the notion of 'negative capability' itself ensued from a negatively capable process where the accretion of 'several things' 'at once' gave way to epiphany, even if without resolution or further elaboration.

[29] Stevenson, *Five Looks*, p. 76.

[30] Quoted in Pickard, 'Natural History and Epiphany', p. 281.

[31] Pickard, 'Natural History and Epiphany', p. 275.

In the remainder of this essay, I turn to several of Bishop's poems in order to briefly demonstrate her method of accretion and its connection with negative capability. Her 1964 'Filling Station', for instance, moves from the sudden exclamation—the first line of the poem, 'Oh, but it is dirty!'—to a perceptive description of the gas station in a surprisingly new, albeit not exactly pleasant way. The accretion is traceable as a naturalist's inventory. 'This is what we have here!' the poet seems to declare: 'several quick and saucy / and greasy sons', 'a dirty dog', 'a big hirsute begonia'.[32] The reader is asked to ascend a set of stairs to gusto, without being supplied with any meaning or intent—not taking wing at all, but climbing up on foot—only to arrive at the near-absurd final question, 'Why, oh why, the doily?' We witness the people and objects in the poem; we briefly forget ourselves in imagining them, and at the end comes the revelation that 'Somebody loves us all'. This poem, as many others by Bishop, is the lovechild of realism and its encounter with Fancy. That the poem's effect is to leave the reader displaced is not Bishop's own demand. There is no Wordsworth to guide our thinking in 'Filling Station', no meditation involving a forceful self. Rather, the poem gives us a feeling and a riddle-like revelation, and this is achieved through an objective accretion of detail that slides the poet into the unknown, from which she returns to point 'A' with a question in the guise of an epiphanic statement (the 'somebody' of the final line implies the question, *who* loves us all?).

Another poem that couples a naturalist 'study' with the poet's self-effacing negative capability is 'The Moose'. Bishop is known as a painterly poet, and much of the present here is described with gusto. Here, the narrator is on a bus and first records her view from the window of 'a lone traveller' who 'gives / kisses and embraces / to seven relatives / and a collie supervises'. That voice then continues compiling its inventory as the bus starts moving, taking note of all the views that arise, as 'sweet peas cling / to their wet white string / on the whitewashed fences; / bumblebees creep inside the foxgloves, / and evening commences'.[33] We move with the narrator's eye: 'On the left ... a ship's port lantern'. Then 'a woman climbs in' to the bus and exchanges pleasantries with the driver. The bus moves forward; we see: 'Moonlight', 'the New Brunswick woods, / hairy, scratchy, splintery'. We hear: 'Snores. Some long sighs', and then 'A dreamy divagation / begins in the night, / a gentle, auditory, / slow hallucination'. This oneiric wandering seems to function as an invitation to the narrator's subconscious, too. But '—Suddenly, the bus driver / stops with a jolt'. After four pages of detailed accretion in sharp, economical sestets, our communal epiphany with the narrator enters in the form of a moose, 'Towering, antlerless, / high as a church, / homely as a house / ... grand,

[32] Bishop, *Poems*, p. 125.

[33] Bishop, *Poems*, p. 190.

otherworldly'. As we glance at the moose comes the realization that we have been seeing for ourselves for so long that we have forgotten completely the poet's presence. And then we arrive at the epiphanic question, 'Why, why do we feel / (we all feel) this sweet / sensation of joy?' Therein lies the poem's momentary brush with truth. Within the question there is a revelation that is reached by an accretion of observations: 'We feel / this sweet / sensation of joy' upon the creature's appearance. And in this truth there is an effervescent beauty that stops the passengers in their tracks, though the poem's negative capability bans any resolutions to arise, and the bus merely drives forward.[34]

Yet another example of Bishop's negative capability at work can be seen in 'The Fish', where the poet's 'precepts about telling the truth in a poem of letting "what happened" guide its development, and particularly of looking "long and long" at something until you are able to give yourself up "entirely to the object under contemplation" are all wonderful in evidence'.[35] Stevenson here quotes partially from an interview with Wesley Wehr, in which Bishop seems almost to boast:

> I always tell the truth in my poems. With The Fish that is exactly how it happened. It was in Key West and I did catch it just as the poem says. That was in 1938. Oh, but I did change one thing; the poem says he had five hooks hanging from his mouth, but actually he only had three. I think it improved the poem when I made that change. Sometimes a poem makes its own demands. But I always try to stick as much as possible to what really happened.[36]

In this poem we witness the quasi-scientific, highly close study of that fish, 'battered and venerable / and homely', through a voice deprived of identity.[37] That voice records the 'brown skin hung in strips / like ancient barnacles', but only imagines the fish's 'coarse white flesh / packed in like feathers, / the big bones and the little bones, / the dramatic reds and blacks / of his shiny entrails'. She 'stare[s] and stare[s] / and victory fill[s] up / the little rented boat' until the 'unknown' slides us 'giddily' to where 'everything / [is] rainbow, rainbow, rainbow!'—an epiphany of the equivalence of 'Truth' and 'Beauty', though again without affirmative resolution.[38] If, then, there are to be no resolutions, what might be the value of adhering to truth in poems born from negative capability, like 'Filling Station', 'The Moose', and 'The Fish'? To speculate,

34 Bishop, *Poems*, p. 193.

35 Stevenson, *Five Looks*, p. 78.

36 Monteiro, *Conversations*, p. 42.

37 Bishop, *Poems*, p. 43.

38 Bishop, *Poems*, p. 44.

yielding to truth could be a means of expanding it. If one does not approach 'fact' with an 'irritable reaching' but calmly and without ego or personality, it is possible that visible truth breeds, or beckons, invisible truth—even if the latter is to come in small, momentary, and uncertain packets. Similar to 'The Fish', 'the "Ode to a Nightingale" was written, Charles Brown tells us, after Keats had sat in their Hampstead garden for two or three hours one morning listening to a nightingale'.[39] There is a more heightened apostrophic imagination at work in Keats's poem than in Bishop's; she is even more resigned and thus less fanciful and more studious. But the experiences informing composition seem very similar. Like Bishop, Keats ultimately 'trade[s] the visionary for the naturalized imagination', as Stillinger puts it, 'embracing experience and process as his own and man's chief good'.[40] Be it moose, fish, or nightingale in view, then, Bishop's and Keats's processes of writing stem from a naturalist's act of astute observation, which is followed by his or her 'sliding giddily off into the unknown' through Fancy and the medium of negative capability—that is, 'on the viewless wings of poesy'. If 'a dreamy divagation / begins in the night' of Bishop's 'The Moose', in Keats's ode we witness the ending of that 'gentle, / auditory, slow hallucination'. And dovetailing that fall is the question 'Was it a vision, or a waking dream?' which feels perhaps more somber than the ones posed by Bishop in the poems discussed in this essay. Keats's lack of resolution upon his brush with truth is arrived at somewhat less 'giddily'. Even so, both poets slide down the apex of that pyramid, along with the reader, into a glimpse of still-uncertain truth.

[39] Helen Vendler, 'The Experiential Beginnings of Keats's Odes', *Studies in Romanticism*, 12: 3 (Summer 1973), p. 592.

[40] Stillinger, 'Introduction', p. 2.

Chapter Twelve

'Darkling I listen'

Jorie Graham and Negative Capability

Thomas Gardner

Jorie Graham has turned to Keats's notion of negative capability throughout her career. She takes Keats's departure from 'consequitive reasoning' and pivot toward a state 'capable of being in uncertainties, Mysteries, doubts, without any irritable reaching after fact & reason' as a template for charting how one opens the mind or soul to what she calls the world's rich silence in order to linger in it and inhabit it more fully (*LJK*, I: pp. 185, 193). In this essay I trace a history of her various attempts to spell out new ways the imagination might move forward in response to Keats's suggestive comments. Her focus on sensation and the body in developing her take on negative capability offers a window onto the new forms of attention and approach to the world that contemporary poets have developed, as well as the increasingly dark spiritual and linguistic crises that have driven those inventions. Graham arrives, in her four most recent full-length collections, at an extended articulation of these Keatsian issues, exploring how the body responds in the face of uncertainty and doubt, and how foregrounding that embodied situation creates a new form of listening crucial to fully inhabiting the world.

In an interview she did with Mark Wunderlich more than twenty years ago, for example, she notes that in order to preserve 'my silence, my not-knowing (which is, of course one's greatest resource) … I need certain things to remain secret from my own conceptual intellect'. Preserving silence, she continues, ensures 'that larger quotients of "not-knowing" are involved in that sensation we call "understanding"—as well as pleasure in that sensation (Keats would call it "negative capability", of course)'.[1] Keeping the conceptual intellect momentarily

[1] Mark Wunderlich, 'The Glorious Thing: Jorie Graham and Mark Wunderlich in Conversation', Academy of American Poets (website), accessed 9 June 2018, https://www.poets.org/poetsorg/text/glorious-thing-jorie-graham-and-mark-wunderlich-conversation.

at bay, she argues, allows one to develop a notion of understanding that folds 'not-knowing' into knowing. She labels that openness to not-knowing 'negative capability'. In a discussion with me in 2002 about Emily Dickinson's stanza 'A Color stands abroad / On Solitary Fields / That Science cannot overtake / But Human nature feels', from 'A Light exists in Spring', Graham extends this notion of stepping momentarily away from the conceptual intellect:

> [Dickinson is] not trying to say, 'You cannot overtake, you must feel.' She's saying there are certain activities that you will be drawn to called 'overtaking'—interpretation, naming, immediately going to the conceptual intellect with which to grasp the world—and there is a negatively capable activity in which you undergo the poem and arrive at sensations that only the—as it were—writing of the poem can get you to.[2]

Holding yourself in uncertainty without irritable reaching after fact and reason, then, undergoing the struggle, gives you more of, for example, the light that exists in spring. It folds not-knowing into knowing. In a 2006 interview with Hila Ratzabi, Graham returns to these ideas, arguing that by temporarily stilling the mind's irritable reaching a poem can open up, in both poet and reader:

> an other part of one's sensibility ... able to linger longer in uncertainty, and feel, sense, intuit, associate, analogize sensorially rather conceptually. ... From such a condition, such a negative capability, one can allow the matter of a poem—its activity, place, action, imagery, indwelling occasion—room to act upon one before one acts upon it. ... Lingering is essential—loitering as Whitman calls it—for allowing ... paradoxical complexities to be fully entertained and given voice.[3]

In each of these interviews, Graham insists that holding oneself in mystery or not-knowing without irritable reaching opens both reader and writer to being acted upon and changed by the world or occasion attended to and voiced.

'Scirocco', a poem from Graham's second book *Erosion* (1983), identifies the different qualities of these two approaches to the world and can stand as an initial illustration of how the poet envisions these two approaches working together.[4] It is set in the rooms Keats rented at 26 Piazza di Spagna in

[2] Thomas Gardner, *A Door Ajar: Contemporary Writers and Emily Dickinson* (New York: Oxford University Press, 2006), p. 200.

[3] Hila Ratzabi, 'Nothing Mystical About It: An Interview with Jorie Graham', Jorie Graham (website), accessed 11 June 2018, http://www.joriegraham.com/interview_ratzabi_2006.

[4] I will refer to the following Graham texts in this essay: *Erosion* (Princeton, NJ: Princeton University Press, 1983), *The End of Beauty* (New York: Ecco, 1987), *The Errancy*

Rome, quite deliberately calling into play the ideas set forth in the negative capability letter. Graham begins the poem by describing the scirocco wind, outside Keats's window: 'working / the invisible. / Every dry leaf of ivy / is fingered, // refingered' in its grip. She calls this wind 'the nervous spirit / of this world'—an embodiment of the conceptual intellect that 'must go over and over / what it already knows' in its attempt to unveil what is not yet visible (p. 8). But, she adds, there is another side to this spirit, which she links to the grapes outside the same window which 'soften / till weak enough / to enter // our world' (p. 9). Somehow, she asserts, they work together: the wind, touching and touching, and the grapes, 'which are nothing, / which break in your hands' (p. 11). The relation between the weakening grapes and the insistent wind is not spelled out yet, but already we see that the mind coming to a halt—the wind dropping, as the poem goes on to suggest—is what prompts this early version of negative capability's boundary-dissolving openness to uncertainty and mystery.

'Vertigo', from *The End of Beauty* (1987), Graham's third book, more fully develops this movement from mastery to openness and introduces—better, it discovers in the act of writing—an emphasis on the body's role in feeling or intuiting its way into a fuller sort of understanding growing out of not-knowing, not holding in one's hands. This focus on the body is one of Graham's distinctive turns on Keats's formulation, an emphasis that will be deepened and challenged as her books progress.[5] The poem begins with a

(Hopewell, NJ: Ecco Press, 1991), *Swarm* (New York: Ecco Press, 2000), *Never* (New York: HarperCollins, 2002), *Overlord* (New York: HarperCollins, 2005), *Sea Change* (New York: HarperCollins, 2008), and *PLACE* (New York: HarperCollins, 2012). Extracts from *Erosion*, by Jorie Graham, copyright © 1983 by Jorie Graham, courtesy of Princeton University Press; extracts from *The End of Beauty*, by Jorie Graham, copyright © 1987 by Jorie Graham, courtesy of HarperCollins Publishers; extracts from *Region of Unlikeness*, by Jorie Graham, copyright © 1991 by Jorie Graham, courtesy of HarperCollins Publishers; extracts from *The Errancy*, by Jorie Graham, copyright © 1997 by Jorie Graham, courtesy of HarperCollins Publishers; extracts from *Swarm*, by Jorie Graham, copyright © 1999 by Jorie Graham, courtesy of HarperCollins Publishers; extracts from *Never*, by Jorie Graham, copyright © 2002 by Jorie Graham, courtesy of HarperCollins Publishers; extracts from *Overlord*, by Jorie Graham, copyright © 2005 by Jorie Graham, courtesy of HarperCollins Publishers; extracts from *Sea Change*, by Jorie Graham, copyright © 2008 by Jorie Graham, courtesy of HarperCollins Publishers; extracts from *Place*, by Jorie Graham, copyright © 2012 by Jorie Graham, courtesy of HarperCollins Publishers.

[5] Keats scholars past and present have discussed negative capability with respect to embodiment. Walter Jackson Bate, for instance, in *John Keats* (Cambridge, MA: Harvard University Press, 1963), in his reading of the concept notes that it requires not only 'imaginative openness of mind', but also 'heightened receptivity to reality in its full and diverse concreteness' (p. 249). In his chapter on negative capability in *Keats the Poet* (Princeton, NJ: Princeton University Press, 1973), Stuart Sperry glosses Keats's concept as such: 'The way to insight was to allow oneself to be led, to let the poetic process determine

figure on the edge of a cliff, looking at the world below and celebrating the conceptual reach of the mind as a kind of power, exulting in 'the sheer drop of its intelligence'. A bird lifted in a thermal and then frozen in a downdraft provides an opportunity for the mind to display its drives: 'the stages of flight, broken down, broken free, / ... *Parts*, she thought, *free parts*, watching the laws / at work, *through which desire must course* / seeking an ending, seeking a shape' (p. 66). A sudden shift in the wind frees the bird, however, its 'properties / no longer knowable', and momentarily brings the conceptual fingering of the world to a halt, softening or weakening it. What follows, as the speaker experiences in her body a kind of vertigo-laden uncertainty, is a series of questions about movement and ownership and point of view that become increasingly frantic and less grounded as the world below slips free from the speaker's grasp and she is overtaken by a kind of charged inner sickness:

> Oh it has vibrancy, she thought, this emptiness, this intake
>   just prior to
> the start of a story, the mind trying to fasten
> and fasten, the mind feeling it like a sickness this wanting
> to snag, catch hold, begin, the mind crawling out to the edge
>   of the cliff
> and feeling the body as is for the first time—how it cannot
> follow, cannot love. (p. 67)

This 'vibrancy' just before the 'start of the story' when all possibilities are alive and active is Graham's version of the emptiness negative capability opens up. Irritable reaching isn't so much put aside as it comes up short, finding nothing to finger and clutch. And what takes its place? The body that 'cannot / follow, cannot love' what it cannot reach. And here the poem stops, as if the body vibrantly alive, deeply aware of its limits, is what still must be investigated. It is with the body, this poem suggests, that we inhabit uncertainties, mysteries, and doubts, but what imaginative shape the body's engagement with the world will take remains to be seen.

its own direction and to create afresh its network of sensations and perceptions' (p. 64). More recently, Jonathan Mulrooney in 'Keats's Avatar', *European Romantic Review*, 22: 3 (2011), notes that negative capability tends to be read as a 'psychological quality', whereas his reading 'call[s] attention to the physical dimension of experience Keats describes, and more specifically to the unmisgiving connection he draws between a seemingly free-floating subjectivity and the sensations of the body' (pp. 313–14). Lastly, Susan Wolfson in *Reading John Keats* (Cambridge: Cambridge University Press, 2015), situates negative capability by contrasting Keats's and Wordsworth's poems, focusing specifically on the younger poet's greater deployment of sympathetic embodiment (pp. 14–19). Graham, I suggest, takes the implicit focus on the body in Keats's original formulation and extends it further.

Graham begins to focus on the awakening body's ability to inhabit uncertainty in her fourth book, *Region of Unlikeness* (1991). 'Fission' is a forceful example. The poem is set in 1963, the poet reliving—in the present, with occasional shifts into past tense to remind us she is looking back—a turning point in her life. The speaker is thirteen, in a movie theater in Rome, where she grew up, watching a movie with her father. The film is Kubrick's *Lolita*, and the poem begins with the famous scene in which Lolita lowers her heart-shaped shades and glances up. Humbert Humbert looks down: 'Tick tock. It's the birth of the mercantile / dream (he looks down). It's the birth of / the dream called / *new world* (looks down). She lies there. A corridor of light filled with dust / flows from the booth to the screen' (p. 3). With the glance, Lolita moves out of unmarked existence and into time. Story begins, the dream called buying and selling commences. Discovery is in the air. The projector's long corridor of light fingers and refingers the world it holds before us; it establishes the laws 'through which desire must course', as 'Vertigo' put it. And then a fascinating thing happens: the houselights come on, the sound is cut, a man runs down the aisle calling for everyone's attention, but the movie continues playing: 'I watch the light from our real place / suck the arm of screen-building light into itself / until the gesture of the magic forearm frays, / and the story up there grays, pales—' (p. 4). That is to say, story frays and weakens but continues, even as the theater's skylight is opened and an even deeper erasure occurs: 'whiting the story out one layer further // till it's just a smoldering of whites / where she sits up. And her stretch of flesh / is just a roiling up of graynesses, / … some *likeness* in it but not particulate, / a grave of possible shapes called *likeness*' (p. 5).

What is awakened when the desiring, story-telling mind—the conceptual intellect—is weakened but not brought to a halt? What was it like to be held in its still-flickering, vertiginous space? Graham explores what awakens there in a single extraordinary sentence, shifting from past to present tense. I've excerpted it here in order to give some sense of its sweep:

> Where the three lights merged:
>   where the image licked my small body from the front, …
>
>   where the long thin arm of day came in from the top
> to touch my head,
>
> …   —undressing something there where my
>   body is
> though not my body—
>   where they play on the field of my willingness,

> where they kiss and brood, ...
>
> —there
> the immobilism sets in,
> the being-in-place more alive than the being. (p. 7)

What awakens is the body—newly aware of itself, touched, licked, willing, and alive. And immobile, which is to say halted in place, outside of story, no longer anticipating a future, no longer linked to the past. And then, something else: what we might call writing itself, or thinking, newly aware of itself as a charged, risky, luminous act, awakens. To move forward would be to choose, to act, to sort one possibility from another, to gain and lose:

> the velvet armrest at my fingers, the dollar bill
>
> in my hand,
> *choice* the thing that wrecks the sensuous here the glorious
> here—
> that wrecks the beauty,
> choice the move that rips the wrappings of light, the
> ever-tighter wrappings
>
> of the layers of the
> real: what is, what also is, what might be that is,
> what could have been that is ... (p. 8)

Her body knows both the cost of moving forward, the confident mind having been undone and the sensuous, uncertain flarings of possibility swirling all around, but it also knows the cost of doing nothing. 'Don't move', she whispers to her younger self, 'don't / wreck the shroud, don't move—' (p. 8). But you have to move, you have to finger the layers, for to refuse to choose is to die and leave the world shrouded and dead. The body, then, free of the conceptualizing mind, is where the unfolding of uncertainty Keats pointed her to will be fought out: the body on the edge of movement and story. The body on the edge of a cliff. What to do with the body will take several books to articulate.

The Errancy (1997) tries to answer. The poems push over and over into the exhausted space where the mind's hold on things has weakened or run its course and where story has been whited out. But, if to stay there is to stay dead and shrouded, what other action might follow? How to make something out of the body's suddenly charged awareness of itself? 'The Scanning' is a powerful attempt at an answer. It begins with a couple driving down the interstate, on a long trip: 'After the rain there was traffic behind us like a long kiss'. Scanning the radio dial is this poem's version of the mind at the edge of its cliff 'trying to fasten and fasten' or 'likeness' on a screen having been reduced to a 'roiling up of graynesses': 'the bands of our listening scan / the bands of static, / seeking a resting point, asymptotic, listening in the hiss / for the hoarse snagged points where meaning seemingly / accrues: … / … hoping for a place to stop' (p. 7). But the possibility of such an arrival has seemingly passed. The mind's irritable reaching comes up empty. Exhausted, they pull off the interstate and stop, the mind's forward motion temporarily set aside. This is a familiar moment in many Graham poems, as is the series of questions that beset her. What follows the mind's collapse? How do we make sense of emptiness?

> What shall we move with
> now that the eye must shut? What shall we sift with
> now that the mind must blur? What shall we undress the veilings
> of dusk with,
> what shall we harvest the nothingness with,
> now that the hands must be tucked back in their pockets[?]
> (p. 8)

It's one thing to set the irritably reaching hands aside, but what follows? What new aspect of one's sensibility is awakened there, and what might it uncover?

There is no immediate answer. Instead, the speaker walks away from the car and down by a nearby river, where a huge flock of geese, along the bank, begins to stir at her presence: 'A mess of geese. Unperfectable. A mess / of conflicting notions… . / what the whole madness led to' (p. 9). All 'shoulder and waddle', 'groping their armless way', the geese are what the world feels like when the mind has tucked its hands into its pockets—moving, murmuring, many-sided, faintly ridiculous. It's what the thirteen-year-old in a movie theater was awakened to and what the figure on the edge of the cliff became newly aware of. But here, that new world feels almost absurd. How to move into uncertainty when it takes such an ungainly form? The speaker's brain stirs, 'extend[ing] its sugared fingertips. / Itching so to create something new' (p. 9). But nothing comes. And then this:

> Then *here* and *here*, a freckling of the light,
> as where parts curdle up
> to fetch a whole—and the birds lift up—
> and from the undulant swagger-stabs of peck and wingflap,
> collisions and wobbly runs—out of manyness—
> a molting of the singular,

> a frenzied search (unflapping, heavy) for cadence, and then
> cadence found, a diagram appearing on the air, at arctic
> heights (pp. 9–10)

She suddenly finds herself with something to do, using her body to take the world in, alive again between the freeway and the diagrammed sky: '[below the flock] the freeway lustrous with accurate attention— / above us now, the sky lustrous with the skeleton of the dream of reason—look up!— / … the winged volumetrics chiseling out a skull / for a dream' (p. 10). The death of the dream of reason, that is to say, chisels out a new space to work and dream in. It is a space only the body can fill. The body, which cannot follow and cannot love, can, by means of the imagination which successfully lingers in uncertainty, lift and molt and soar.

Swarm (2000), which follows, is a desperate swerve of a book. It still asks about the work the body might do to inhabit mystery and uncertainty once irritable reaching has been put aside, but this time, instead of looking up to a larger sort of freedom, it looks below, to something smaller and smaller. It asks if one can more fully awaken to the world through diminishment and silence, through pulling back from self-assertion and story. In the first poem in the book, '*from* The Reformation Journal', Graham's speaker details all she intends to turn aside from: 'My throat is an open grave. / I hide my face. / I have reduced all to lower case. / I have crossed out passages. / I have severely trimmed and cleared. / Locations are omitted. / Uncertain readings are inserted silently' (p. 3). That is to say, she will attempt to speak by means of the grave of her throat—recall 'Fission''s grave of likeness—without showing her face. She will speak below the level of an identifiable self, welcoming uncertainty and trimming most marks of location. Thoreau speaks in *Walden* about getting lost in the woods, calling attention to new ways of perceiving awakened by such a state, and celebrating the discovery there of 'the infinite extent of our relations'.[6] *Swarm* seems deeply aware of this passage. What the poet hopes to find, in this lost area of 'anguish' where the mind is not able to 'adjust', is some small shard of language or self, something that one can trust to move forward with and to offer as love: 'Give me the glassy ripeness in failure / Give me the atom laying its question at the bottom of nature / … that we be founded on infinite smallness' (pp. 4–5). Infinite smallness, she proposes, might open up infinite relations. Such thinking produces a poetry of erasure or elimination, but one that is, at the same time, also surprisingly bodily. Might it be possible to use the hands not to reach, irritably, but to sift through fragments, to undo the old way of moving through the world: 'Burn all the letters. / Look in the ashes with both hands. / Finger in there for any

[6] Henry David Thoreau, *Walden* (New York: Library of America, 1991), p. 139.

bits intact. / Wrist-deep / in the fine grains, so cold, / feel further round for fragments / for any last unburnt / piece of / the crashing of mind' (p. 25). Or might one use the hands to keep the fragments apart and charged, powerful and unstoried, potentially infinite in their relations, embracing mystery: 'So that I'm writing this in the cold / keeping the parts from finding the whole again / page after page, unstitched, speaking for sand' (p. 89).

Graham's four most recent books form a kind of sequence in which, after the retreat of *Swarm*, she returns to the physical world, but now with her words deeply chastened and bewildered, convinced that such a broken, bodily language, 'saturated with situation', might be a primary tool in regaining a world that we have lost. Irritable reaching is put aside, in many of these poems, by composing *en plein air*, the poet trying to record her senses' engagement with particular, ever-shifting plays of light and shadow or waves and shoreline, exhausting the mind, which cannot keep up. *Never* (2002), the first of these books, begins with a remark Keats made to Charles Brown upon first viewing the scenery of the Lake District: 'How can I believe that? Surely it cannot be?' The statement hangs over all four books—first, as an expression of being overwhelmed by the world's beauty and mystery, but second, as a statement about our inability to believe in a physical world at all, as news of its eventual disappearance begins to creep into and then dominate our imaginations. How the body responds in the face of that uncertainty and doubt becomes the central issue of these books and offers a last spin on Keats's letter.

In *Never*, the problem is simply that the moment passes—'I cannot of course come back. Not to this. Never. / It is a ghost posed on my lips. Here: never' (p. 3). The mind of course doesn't want to acknowledge this, and a number of the poems struggle against 'the mind's insistent coming back and coming back … / … The death of / uncertainty. The song that falls upon the listener's *eye*, / that seeks the sleek minimum of the meaningless *made*' (p. 13). The speaker of these poems fights the death of uncertainty by putting herself in a position where the eye can't keep up, can't make a sleek, stable form out of the world's continual movement. Here, for example, is a portion of 'Dusk Shore Prayer' where language has been almost overwhelmed by its need to constantly revise and add to its notations:

> The creeping revelation of shoreline.
> The under-shadowed paisleys scripting wave-edge down-
>   slope
> on the barest inclination, sun making of each
>   milelong wave-retreat
> a golden translucent forward downgoing,
> golden sentences writ on clearest moving waters,
> moving their meaninglessness on (not *in*) the moving of the

waters
(which feels tugged) (the rows of scripting
[even though it's a trick] adamant with
self-unfolding) (wanting the eye to catch and take
dominant final-hold, feel the thickest rope of
waterlipped
scripting
to be a producing of a thing that speaks [to whom
one does not know, but a true speech])—to believe this truly,
not in metaphor—
to put it in the blank in which one *sees*,
... And never to be
emptied by the wound of meaning.
The gash of likeness. The stump interpretation.
Spelled from the living world. (p. 31)

One hesitates to attempt to trace such an intricate descriptive act, but perhaps we can gain something by the attempt. As waves wash up the shoreline and retreat, their thin, pulling-back layers, shadowed by the retreating sun into paisley-like droplet patterns, seem a kind of scrolled-out writing, 'golden sentences' of the last light written on the surface of the 'downgoing water'. What might they mean? How might one read them, their 'meaninglessness' written 'on (not *in*)' the moving water? That first revision sets off a series of attempts to keep up with the moving water: the water 'feels tugged'; the golden sentences of the declining light across those waters feel 'adamant' in their intention to unfold something; so much so that, even though one knows 'it's a trick', one's eye feels drawn to 'catch' and 'take hold' of the 'thickest rope' of that scripting as if it were 'a thing that speaks'; giving play to that Keatsian desire to 'believe' that the world is speaking not 'in metaphor' but as a 'living thing'; a desire rising all the more intensely to the surface because of the acknowledgment that the world moves and moves and never arrives, its speech 'never to be / emptied by the wound of meaning'. Such a notation, I would suggest, is the body which cannot follow, cannot love speaking into uncertainty: brackets within parentheses, and restless lines extending and reforming, breaking off at unexpected intervals in tumbling, indented columns.

These are poems as much about language as about the world, the speaker thrilled but at the same time baffled by this headlong release of language. 'Gulls', in fact, seems to describe words and fluid movements at the shoreline almost simultaneously: 'The wind swallows my words one / by / one. The words leaping too, over their own / staying. / Oceanward too, as if being taken / away / into splash—my clutch of / words / swaying and stemming from my / saying' (p. 28). What comes across is the impossibility of describing at all.

Her words madly attempt to still and respond but in fact testify to a world in which 'Nothing is coming back the way it was' (p. 38). Wallace Stevens would call this 'form gulping after formlessness', her words testifying to the vibrancy of emptiness as they are washed to and fro by what they cannot hold:

> Preferring to be dissolved to
> designation,
> backglancing stirrings,
> wedged-in between unsaying and
> forgetting—
> what an enterprise—spoken out by
> me as if
> to *still* some last place, place becoming even as I speak
> unspeakable— (pp. 28–9)

These poems would seem to be recordings of attempts to hold oneself in unspeakability without an irritable reaching after fact or reason.

Overlord (2005), however, takes a darker, more literal approach to the disappearance of place. It is as if the emptiness before the start of the story that previous books had been drawn to is now re-imagined as the thought that, after global warming and climate disaster, there is no ongoing story any more to enter. What these poems wonder is if it is still possible to approach and inhabit such an emptiness through the body. The book begins with a memory from grade school, before she 'became lost' ('a different life. / One where you can go back'), of being sick at home and somehow hearing, in that state, her name called by a teacher and 'absent' being spoken into the room. This was the moment when the possibility of living a life outside of the body dawned on her

> I don't know if I cried out,
> but they came running up to see what was wrong.
> This is what is wrong: we, only we, the humans, can retreat from ourselves
> and not be
> altogether here.
> We can be part full, only part, and not die. We can be in and out of here, now,
> at once, and not die. The little song, the little river, has banks. We can pull up
> and sit on the banks. We can pull back
> from the being of our bodies, we can live in a
> portion of them, we can be absent, no one can tell. (pp. 2–3)

This is the problem she attempts to address in *Overlord*. Is it possible to enter and use her body again, in the face of an emptiness which declares we can't go back again to an unbroken story, to a world fully present? One of the ways she tries to regain her body in this blank space is through a series of pre-dawn poems she calls 'Praying', dating the attempts and, not unlike trying to record the sliding layers of incoming water and sunlight on the beach, recording her uncertain words in a notebook beside her in the darkness. She is uncertain about who she addresses as well as the state of the world:

> I don't know where to start. I don't think my face
> in my hands is right. Please don't let us destroy
> Your world. No *the* world. I know I know nothing. I know I
> can't use you like this. It feels better if I'm on
> my knees, if my eyes are pressed shut so I can see
> the other things, the tiniest ones. Which can still escape
> us. (p. 24)

This posture—eyes shut, in the dark, pressed down against the cold floor, refusing to reach after fact and reason—gives her her body back, as a recording instrument: 'here I can feel the whole crushing / emptiness on my back. Especially on my shoulders' (p. 24). It roils up the issues of language, gets it lost, and moves it out into uncertainty:

> But here, I did this other thing
> Again. (Here) (I write the open parenthesis, press my face,
> try again, then lift, close) (then this clause to explain)
> (to whom?) (always wanting to be forgiven) (not seen)
> (no)—See,
> it is already being lost here, the channel is filling
> in, these words—ah—these, these—
> how I don't want *them* to be the problem too, there are
> so many other obstacles, can't these just be a part of
> my body, look (put my head down again)(am
> working in total dark) (maybe this will not be
> legible). (pp. 24–5)

What these attempts at prayer do, I think, is allow her to move out into the world, despite the Keatsian uncertainty and doubt she feels about its continuity. In this attempt, for example, when she finally opens her eyes to the first glimmers of light, she feels able to embrace its uncertain progress: 'when I open my eyes I see two white lines, / vertical, incandescent, I will keep all the knowledge / away I think, I try to think, I will keep / the knowing away, the lines seem to come out of nowhere' (p. 26). In another attempt, she wrestles with her most loved approaches to the world seeming oddly privileged and almost irrelevant: 'O Lord what do I do with the great desire to praise.

/ The frenzied joy of detail. The fullness of / existence I feel in *contradiction*' (p. 81). Such awakenings make her more raw, more attentive, more fully an inhabitant of doubt and uncertainty. But the way is hard. 'Impressionism', a poem at the midpoint of the book, recording impressions of Omaha Beach, brings us into this uncertain, open area in a shockingly direct way. The poet notices a young girl in a white frock with puffed-up sleeves standing very still on a small bridge over an inlet and eventually wanders over to investigate. She seems a picture of calm and peace, holding a string suspended into the water. The poet asks what's on the string. And the girl draws up a horror—a bleached-out turkey leg with eleven crabs attached, wildly feeding, immediately dispatched by the child with a hammer, 'the leg/thigh leaking all over the faded grayed-out planks', other hands suddenly materializing 'out of the nowhere to which I am / now sent. / There's no way back believe me. / I'm writing you from there' (p. 57). We fall with her into a 'nowhere' from which there is no way back to life, or story, or a trust in the ongoingness of things. We're nowhere, suspended in immobilism.

Sea Change (2008), the darkest of these four books, extends that sense of disconnection and makes it global. Its title suggests the total transformation of the world, as in the use of the phrase 'suffering a sea-change' in *The Tempest* and *The Waste Land*, but even more literally in the destructive changes to the earth's seas as the climate shifts. These are poems increasingly convinced that the 'future is a superfluity I do not / taste' (p. 20). What is the 'wild unstoppable rumor' of the soul to do with such an insight, 'look[ing] all the way to end of / your gaze' and coming up blank? (p. 39). Can one really hold oneself in a negativity this deep? 'Root End' powerfully poses the problem, thinking of 'The desire to imagine / the future' as 'Walking in the dark through a house you know by / heart'. At first, you move calmly through darkened rooms that you assemble and make coherent by responding to shifts in temperature on the side of your face or taking in the difference between various silences. Oh, you think, 'the mind knows our place so / deeply well—you could run through it—without fear—even in this total dark' (p. 48). You belong. But then she brings herself to a halt and asks, what 'if you make yourself think of it', the way the roads outside the house, 'everywhere going only forward', actually spread and thin out and end, leading nowhere: 'root-ends then nothing, thinnest trailings of / all' (p. 49)? What is she to do with her body, her imagination, in this blank uncertainty? With the knowledge that 'my species is ill, the / end of the world can be imagined' (p. 34).

Her answer is sad but fascinating. She will speak from within this knowledge. That is, she will speak 'as the sensation of what is coming places its shoulders on the whole horizon', internalizing that sense of an ending and using that stranding knowledge to make this moment all the more precious, uncertain, hard to 'believe in'. 'I peer back through this time to / that one', she writes—that one in which it will be lost and no longer imaginable: 'You will not believe it / when the time / comes. Also how we mourned our dead—had / ample earth, took time, opened it, closed / it' (p. 55). Imagining the world *for* the future, as if it were already lost, gives her body something to do, makes the wonder of the present moment all the more charged and uncertain, saturating it with the knowledge of being lost and never to be returned to: 'there are sounds the planet will always make, even / if there is no one to hear them' (p. 56). Or this: 'there is something I must / tell you, you do not need existence, these words, praise be, they can for now be / said. That is summer. Hear them' (p. 21). Or this, spoken to the imagined reader, from a position of infinite smallness:

> I have begun the action of beauty again, on
> the burning river I have started the catalogue,
> your world,
> I your speck tremble remembering money, its dry touch, sweet strange
> smell, it's a long time, the smell of it like lily of the valley
> sometimes, and pondwater, and how
> one could bend down close to it
> and drink. (p. 16)

Those sounds the planet will always make, even if no one is there to hear them, seem to be what drive her most recent book, *Place* (2012). It's a book about listening, as if, by now, even eyesight is associated with irritable reaching. Maybe there is no future, but there is still work to do, these poems suggest, listening into a silence which may be all the future offers. 'Sundown', the first poem in the book, turns back, 'for no reason', and discovers, almost inadvertently, in the image of a man on a horse galloping toward her on the beach, a suggestion that, somewhere in her world, the past still moves confidently into the future. The hoof prints left behind seem to record that passing energy and call her out into it, a call she responds to by closing her eyes and moving forward, listening with her entire body:

> and when I shut my eyes now I am not like a blind person
> walking towards the lowering sun.
> the water loud at my right,
> but like a seeing person
> with her eyes shut
> putting her feet down
> one at a time
> on the earth. (p. 5)

Sound seems to call on the body's full engagement in a way that sight does not. It calls out to her, uncertainly, from silence and must be embodied by the imagination in order to be known. For example, in 'Cagnes Sur Mer 1950' the sound of her mother's voice draws her back into her past and, as she unfolds it, sensual detail by sensual detail, she finds herself returning to this world's silence—'here from there again' (p. 6)—but charged and changed by what she has discovered. In a sense, she wants to be like the dead tree she celebrates in another poem, 'still-being-here in this small apparently silent multitudinous world of / infinite yearning and / killing', following its lead and stating: 'I will not listen for / song anymore. I will / listen for how the dark comes-on', until 'the holy place shuts, baggy with evening, and here it is / finally night / bursting open / with hunt' (pp. 26, 28). Many of the poems begin with sounds in the dark breaking the silence and calling out to her, inviting her into a charged world in which 'The human does not fit in' (p. 55). For example, 'End' begins with an autumn day, deep fog, and the sounds of chains and hinges, some sort of swinging gate with a 'sound like stringed / instruments from / some other culture' (p. 23). The fog becomes a stage set she must take in by listening and attempt to enter—is it a neighbor working a gate as he moves a herd of cows? The mysterious sound becomes a call: 'I / hear over the / chewing [an] out of tune torn string but once it made / music it might still make / music if I become a new way of / listening, in which / above all, / nothing, I know nothing'. The empty space beyond her reach is 'blank but in it is an / appeal, a ruined one, reduced, listen:' (pp. 24–5). That blank calls all of her senses to work together to become a charged, new way of listening.

Knowing nothing is the space Graham's poems have always moved toward, but it has taken a series of books for her to arrive at the ability to embrace the looming absence of a future this calmly: 'there will be no more: no more: not enough to go around: no more around: no / more: love that' (p. 31). That calmness is perhaps Keats's strongest presence in her work. 'Message from Armagh Cathedral, 2011' demonstrates both the call of silence and her response. Walking through a cathedral in Northern Ireland, she discovers a stone carving, 'large as an infant, / hundreds of / pounds, triangular / body which ends at / waist, swaddled by / carvings, 3000 years / old' (p. 76). Its silence 'speaks', insisting first on its distance and otherness—*what are you to me*, it says—but gradually offering other details that draw the poet in. Most intriguing is the statue's silver arm, an artificial limb mirroring that of the king the statue was based on. The poet 'listens' by helping it hold its arm on: 'Three hands, same / size, where I clasp yours, where I cover it, where I hold your arm on you / with you' (p. 77). It's a powerful image for how the imagination embraces what is missing, how it moves out into uncertainty. 'How shall we be whole', her gesture asks. 'Who / will make the missing part' (p. 78). As the poet draws closer, touching her fingers to the statue's mouth and drawing words, in a sense, out of its silence, she 'hears' a new sound. The story of a soldier, losing his arms in an explosion set off in a basket of fresh laundry, comes to her. Just at the moment he reached down to touch the laundry, overcome by a memory of a row of shirtsleeves drying on a line in Indiana, 'all blowing one way', he heard, in the 'tiny rhythm in the flapping sleeves', the sound of 'feet all running on dirt as fast as possible away from / this place' (p. 79). His brothers, his uncle, his father—if only he had turned his head in the direction they were pointing, Graham's soldier thinks, he might have turned with them and run. It is not too much to say that, as Graham reaches into and handles the uncertain silences yawning all around us, she too intends to sound a warning. She too wants to speak before it is too late. Such are the occasions these poems inhabit and call us into, to be acted upon.

Part Four

‘pursued through Volumes’, Volume II: Adaptations, Appropriations, Mutations

CHAPTER THIRTEEN

Negative Capability in the Twenty-First Century and Romantic Self Annihilation in Philip Pullman's *His Dark Materials*

Suzanne L. Barnett

By now nearly everyone is familiar with Keats's musings on what he calls—precisely once—'negative capability' and that concept's sporadic unspooling over several letters written in 1817 and 1818. The idea has both demonstrated remarkable critical endurance and become so popular that poet and essayist Mary Ruefle has lamented its omnipresence that approaches near meaninglessness:

> those words have become like a sickness unto death for me. As often as I have used them myself, I wish there were a moratorium on them for a decade, so overused are they, so bandied about that they have come to mean just about any thing one wants them to, especially a bebop version of *Be Here Now*, or a diffusive religious awe in which the poet wanders, forever in a stupor.[1]

Similarly, Dan Simmons (a science fiction writer perhaps best known for his Keats-influenced *Hyperion Cantos*[2]) refers to negative capability as 'old hat, of course, drained of most of its vitality by high school English teachers' and claims that, based on his 'visits to colleges and writing classes, there certainly seems to be no lack of Negative Capability on campuses these days—classrooms and curricula fairly reek of it. John Keats could not have imagined an annulment of self so complete and devastating.'[3] However, despite its alleged

[1] Mary Ruefle, 'On Fear: Our positive capability', *Poetry*, 200: 3 (June 2012), pp. 277–90.

[2] These include the novels *Hyperion* (1989), *The Fall of Hyperion* (1990), *Endymion* (1996), and *The Rise of Endymion* (1997) and three short stories: 'Remembering Siri' (1983), 'The Death of the Centaur' (1990), and 'Orphans of the Helix' (1999).

[3] Dan Simmons, 'Shapeshifters and Skinwalkers: the Writer's Curse of Negative Capability', *Journal of the Fantastic in the Arts*, 8: 4 (1997), pp. 400, 405.

ubiquity, a precise definition of negative capability has remained elusively protean since 1817, vacillating between a sort of synonym for 'empathy', to radical uncertainty, to the hallmark of what Simmons calls—adopting language from the end of Keats's negative capability letter—a writer 'who obliterates all consideration beyond the sense of Beauty' (p. 411). My intention in this essay is to suggest the ideas underlying some of the twentieth- and twenty-first-century appropriations of negative capability and how that critical tradition is reflected and ultimately challenged with a radically different reading of negative capability in Philip Pullman's *His Dark Materials* trilogy (1995–2000).

Pullman has repeatedly acknowledged his philosophical debt to romantic literature; even the epigraph to the final book, *The Amber Spyglass*, is a quotation from William Blake's *America a Prophecy*. *His Dark Materials* is a sprawling, 1100-page young adult trilogy that takes place in a vaguely steampunk yet magical world parallel to ours, one embroiled in a crisis over a substance called Dust, which the Magisterium (Pullman's sinister representation of organized religion) associates with the 'dark principle', the sin of the Fall into knowledge.[4] Dust constitutes the invisible aura that settles on people after adolescence and is described in the first book, with a none-too-subtle nod to Blake, as 'physical proof that something happened when innocence changed into experience' (p. 327); naturally, the oppressive Magisterium wants to control and ultimately eliminate what they view as 'an emanation from the dark principle itself ... something bad, something wrong, something evil and wicked' (*GC*, pp. 85, 247). The second half of the trilogy includes a 'war on heaven' in which the forces aligned with Dust, joy, and knowledge clash against the repressive Magisterium and its murderous, Blakean 'Priests in black gowns' who bind 'with briars' mankind's 'joys & desires'.[5] One rebellious character declares that there will be 'No kings, no bishops, no priests. The Kingdom of heaven has been known by that name since the Authority first set himself above the rest of the angels. And we want no part of it. ... We intend to be free citizens of the *Republic* of Heaven' (*AS*, p. 188; italics mine). The phrase 'Republic of Heaven' recurs as the final words of the final book, and it is a profoundly romantic idea that would not seem out of place in the works of Blake or Percy Shelley. However, it's not exactly what we expect alongside Keatsian negative capability, especially if we accept the critical

[4] The first book of the trilogy was released as *Northern Lights* in the UK in 1995 and as *The Golden Compass* in the United States in 1996. Citations throughout refer to the boxset, Philip Pullman, *His Dark Materials Trilogy: The Golden Compass, The Subtle Knife, and The Amber Spyglass* (New York: Random House, 2003). Abbreviations indicating references to individual volumes are as follows: *GC* for *The Golden Compass*, *SK* for *The Subtle Knife* (1997), and *AS* for *The Amber Spyglass* (2000).

[5] 'The Garden of Love', lines 11–12.

tradition which equates Keats's concept with empathy. Pullman's reading of negative capability—which I argue comes to us through a Blakean and Shelleyan negotiation of selfhood as an obstacle on the path towards both creation and revolution—actually goes against the grain of many twentieth- and twenty-first-century critical readings of Keats's ubiquitous concept. While the trajectory of negative capability and associated concepts that I offer below suggests that, in both popular and critical readings, 'doubt' gives way to 'patience' before it eventually arrives at 'empathy', Pullman returns in *His Dark Materials* to a renewed skepticism about the role of the self in poetic creation.

When we wonder 'who owns negative capability'—as the editors of this collection did in a recent panel at the North American Society for the Study of Romanticism—we can consider a vast and often contradictory storehouse of allusions and applications.[6] It has appeared recently in discussions of climate change, in political philosopher Roberto Unger's theories of false necessity and formative context, and, in a development that aspiring apothecary Keats might have appreciated, within the emerging field of narrative medicine.[7] It lends its name to an independent press founded in 1981 in Mobile, Alabama and its associated journal, and dozens of poems entitled 'Negative Capability' or works that reference it have appeared in print in the last few decades alone, as well as collections of critical essays, at least one play, and several songs and albums from contemporary music ranging across a variety of genres.[8] As Ruefle and Simmons grumbled, negative capability has become so firmly entrenched in popular culture that in Woody Allen's 1979 film *Manhattan* Dianne Keaton's character claims that a featureless steel cube 'was perfectly integrated, and it had a marvelous kind of negative capability', and viewers read that obfuscation as cultural shorthand for critical jargon. Li Ou notes that by the 1980s negative capability had become so commonplace that it began to appear in criticism of authors other than Keats (as in William V. Spanos's 'Charles Olson and Negative Capability' or Beth Lau's 'Jane

[6] The panel 'Who Owns Negative Capability?' was presented at *Romanticism & Rights*, the twenty-third annual meeting of the North American Society for the Study of Romanticism held in Winnipeg in August 2015. An early version of this paper was presented on that panel, and I thank the editors for including this expanded version here.

[7] Deborah Lilley, 'Theories of Certain Uncertainty: Climate Change and Negative Capability', *symploke*, 21: 1–2 (2013), pp. 97–108; Roberto Unger, *False Necessity: Anti-Necessitarian Social Theory in the Service of Radical Democracy* (London: Verso, 2004); Terence E. Holt, 'Narrative Medicine and Negative Capability', *Literature and Medicine*, 23: 2 (Fall 2004), pp. 318–33; Delese Wear, 'Toward Negative Capability: Literature in the Medical Curriculum', *Curriculum Inquiry*, 34: 2 (Summer 2004), pp. 169–84.

[8] For a list of many examples of negative capability appearing in contemporary poetry, music, and elsewhere, see this volume's companion website: keatslettersproject.com/negativecapability.

Austen and John Keats: Negative Capability, Romance and Reality')[9] and became 'part of the general education of literature, beginning to enjoy a more or less established status'.[10] In recent years, negative capability has even wound its way into legal scholarship. In *A Modern Legal Ethics: Adversary Advocacy in a Democratic Age*, Yale Law School professor Daniel Markovits posits a framework for legal ethics that emphasizes the lawyer's passivity and invokes negative capability as a model for client engagement.[11] According to W. Bradley Wendel, Markovits claims that:

> The lawyer's role must, therefore, be constructed in such a way as to maximize the possibility for affective, transformative participation in the political process, which at the retail level primarily occurs through adjudication of litigated disputes. It follows that a lawyer ought to be a kind of conduit to participation, enabling clients to be as directly involved as possible. In order to do this, a lawyer must possess the virtue of 'negative capability'. 'Negative capability' means effacing one's own personal beliefs about the justice of the causes of one's clients, serving literally as a mouthpiece for clients' positions.[12]

In Markovits's permutation, then, negative capability means that an individual becomes a mere 'conduit', a belief-less 'mouthpiece' for his or her client. And, in a different legal context, intellectual property law expert Barton Beebe argues that 'Trademark law is arguably the most difficult of the intellectual property laws to contemplate [...] because it requires a form of what John Keats called "negative capability", the capability, more specifically, to think through the consumer and see the marketplace only as the consumer sees it.'[13] Or, in other words, What Would John Keats Buy?

What many of these recent invocations of negative capability have in common is their assumption that one's ability to be 'in uncertainties, Mysteries, doubts, without any irritable reaching after fact & reason' results in empathy,

[9] William V. Spanos, 'Charles Olson and Negative Capability: A Phenomenological Interpretation', *Contemporary Literature*, 21: 1 (Winter 1980), pp. 38–80. Beth Lau, 'Jane Austen and John Keats: Negative Capability, Romance and Reality', *Keats-Shelley Journal*, 55 (2006), pp. 81–110.

[10] Li Ou, *Keats and Negative Capability* (New York: Bloomsbury, 2009), p. 19.

[11] Daniel Markovits, *A Modern Legal Ethics: Adversary Advocacy in a Democratic Age* (Princeton, NJ: Princeton University Press, 2008).

[12] W. Bradley Wendel, 'Methodology and Perspective in the Theory of Lawyers' Ethics: a Response to Professors Woolley and Markovits', *The University of Toronto Law Journal*, 60: 4 (Fall 2010), p. 1016.

[13] Barton Beebe, 'Search and Persuasion in Trademark Law', *Michigan Law Review*, 103: 8 (August 2005), p. 2022.

or, to put it another way, that the absence of a firmly rooted selfhood necessarily leads to more visceral connections with other people or the ability to see the world from their perspectives (*LJK*, I: p. 193). In 'The Locked Room', the third episode of the first season of the HBO noir drama *True Detective*, negative capability is quietly invoked as a reason for Matthew McConaughey's character Rust Cohle's remarkable ability to coerce confessions from suspects by exuding empathy until they practically beg to confess their crimes. When asked for his secret, Cohle demurs: 'Oh, I never really found it that hard. You just look at somebody and think like they think, negative capability.'[14]

After this episode aired, armchair literary critics took to Twitter to register their outrage that the show had misread (or, in the words of one user, 'f****ed up')[15] Keats's theory, that negative capability was not the same thing as empathy. For example, Keats scholar Richard Marggraf Turley tweeted that the reference failed to distinguish between negative capability and Keats's later notion of 'chameleon identity'.[16] However, the twentieth- and twenty-first-century understanding of negative capability as a virtual synonym for 'empathy' is so firmly entrenched that the *Oxford English Dictionary*'s current definition suggests absolute parity: '*negative capability, n.* (Keats's term for) the ability to accept mystery and uncertainty rather than trying to rationalize it, regarded as a quality of a creative artist; (now also, more generally) empathy.'[17] One of the earliest associations of negative capability with empathy occurs in Claude Lee Finney's 1936 study, which identifies negative capability as radical empathy and unbiasedness. Finney attempts to develop negative capability into a fully fledged philosophical system, 'an interpretation of Shakespeare's humanism in the light of English empiricism' that was 'inspired' by Hazlitt.[18] He even goes so far as to claim that Keats associates 'the principle of egotism' with 'the principle of evil' (p. 580). But previous invocations of negative capability—going all the way back to early mentions in the *Edinburgh Review* in 1849 and *Macmillan's Magazine* in 1860[19]—emphasized doubt, not empathy. In Aubrey de Vere's *Edinburgh Review* discussion of Richard Monckton Milnes's *Life, Letters, and*

[14] 'The Locked Room', *True Detective*, HBO (26 January 2014). Television.

[15] Madhu Pawar (@Madhu_020), 'writer(s) f****d up Keats's concept of negative capability. When I heard it I was like that's not what it means', Twitter, 14 March 2014.

[16] Richard Marggraf Turley (@RMarggrafTurley), 'True detective s01 e03 @ 33.44m reference to Keats's negative capability. Superb script, but wrong use of neg cap to mean chameleon identity', Twitter, 26 February 2014, 3:36 p.m.

[17] 'negative, adj., adv.2, and int', *OED Online*, Oxford University Press, June 2016. Web. 5 July 2016.

[18] Claude Lee Finney, *The Evolution of Keats's Poetry* (Cambridge, MA: Harvard University Press, 1936), p. 478.

[19] David Masson, 'The Life and Poetry of John Keats', *Macmillan's Magazine*, November 1860, pp. 1–16.

Literary Remains of John Keats (1848)—the first collected publication of Keats's letters—the critic mentions negative capability for what is most likely the first time in print outside of Milnes's volume:

> His mind had itself much of that 'negative capability' which he remarked on as a large part of Shakespeare's greatness … . There is assuredly such a thing as philosophical doubt, as well as of philosophical belief: it is the doubt which belongs to the mind, not to the will; to which we are not drawn by love of singularity, and from which we are not scared by nervous tremours; the doubt which is not the denial of any thing, so much as the proving of all things …[20]

For de Vere, the key to negative capability lies in one's ability to be in uncertainty, mystery, and especially doubt; this ability does not necessarily involve empathy or serving as a self-less conduit for poetic inspiration.

Arguably the first critic of Keats to pay more than passing attention to the letters (in his Oxford lectures published in 1909), A. C. Bradley associates negative capability with patience and calm acceptance: 'a man, and especially a poet, must not be in a hurry to arrive at results, and must not shut up his mind in the box of his supposed results, but must be content with half-knowledge'.[21] John Middleton Murry's *Keats and Shakespeare* (1925) connects negative capability with the moral qualities of tolerance and forgiveness and identifies it as 'that quality that Christ pre-eminently possessed'.[22] In a chapter entitled 'Negative Capability' in *John Keats* (1963), Walter Jackson Bate glosses the concept as: 'an imaginative openness of mind and heightened receptivity to reality in its full and diverse concreteness. This, however, involves negating one's own ego.' Bate also claims in *Negative Capability: The Intuitive Approach in Keats* (1939) that the negatively capable poet 'will not only tolerate but unhesitatingly welcome the obliteration of himself by the life around him, and, with the truth thus gained, rest content'.[23]

[20] From an unsigned review (later attributed to Aubrey de Vere) of Tennyson's *The Princess* (1848), *The Poetical Works of Percy Shelley* (ed. Mary Shelley, 1847), and *Life, Letters, and Literary Remains of John Keats* (ed. R. Monckton Milnes, 1848) in *The Edinburgh Review*, 90 (July 1849), pp. 427–8.

[21] A. C. Bradley, *Oxford Lectures on Poetry* (London: Macmillan and Company, 1911), p. 235.

[22] John Middleton Murry, *Keats and Shakespeare: a Study of Keats's Poetic Life from 1816 to 1820* (Oxford: Oxford University Press, 1925), p. 48.

[23] *John Keats* (Cambridge, MA: The Belknap Press of Harvard University Press, 1963), p. 249. *Negative Capability: The Intuitive Approach in Keats* (New York: Contra Mundum Press, 2012), p. 27. Bate's is the first critical work on Keats to feature negative capability in its title and the first monograph on the concept. The second, Li Ou's *Keats and Negative*

Other key twentieth-century readings include Lionel Trilling's association of negative capability with Keats's 'heroism' (1951),[24] Aileen Ward's brief mention of a 'tolerance for ambiguity',[25] Stuart Sperry's 'state of perpetual *indeterminacy*',[26] and Anne K. Mellor's association of negative capability with 'feminine' empathy. By the time the term is essentially canonized by its inclusion in the first edition of *The Norton Anthology of English Literature* in 1962 it had already, as the Norton editors drily note, 'accumulated a heavy body of commentary'.[27]

In 1993 *The New Princeton Encyclopedia of Poetry and Poetics* cross-references 'negative capability' with 'empathy and sympathy', further cementing the *OED* definition that appears in *True Detective*'s descriptions of Rust Cohle's interrogation techniques.[28] In another example, in 'Reflections on Teaching Playwrighting [*sic*] in the Schools' Jonathan Levy explicitly equates negative capability with sympathy: 'Sympathy, in the sense I mean it, is the ability to get out of one's own shoes and into the shoes of others. It is a quality close to what Keats called "negative capability". A novelist or poet *may* have this ability. A playwright *must* have it.'[29] But 'empathy'—both the word and the idea—are even newer additions to the English language than negative capability. 'Empathy' made its way to English from German philosophy (by way of the ancient Greek *empatheia*) in 1895. The familiar *OED* definition of 'empathy' as 'the ability to understand and appreciate another person's feelings, experience, etc.' dates to only 1946. A slightly different, earlier definition (now considered rare) of empathy as 'the quality or power of projecting one's personality into

Capability, offers a thorough 'overall picture' (p. x) of critical and theoretical approaches to the idea.

24 Lionel Trilling, introduction to *Selected Letters of John Keats* (New York: Farrar, Straus and Young, 1951), p. 1. Trilling later reprinted his introduction to this volume as an essay entitled 'The Poet as Hero' in *The Opposing Self: Nine Essays in Criticism* (New York: Viking Press, 1955).

25 Aileen Ward, *John Keats: The Making of a Poet* (New York: The Viking Press, 1963), p. 161.

26 Stuart Sperry, *Keats the Poet* (Princeton, NJ: Princeton University Press, 1973), p. 245.

27 M. H. Abrams, ed., *The Norton Anthology of English Literature* (New York: Norton, 1962), p. 1275.

28 *The New Princeton Encyclopedia of Poetry and Poetics* (Princeton, NJ: Princeton University Press, 1993), pp. 824–5.

29 Jonathan Levy, 'Reflections on Teaching Playwrighting in the Schools', *The Journal of Aesthetic Education*, 26: 3 (Autumn 1992), p. 105 (italics in original). Simmons makes a similar claim that negative capability 'remains … a required precursor to empathy in life and in art' (p. 402) because it 'allow[s] the best of writers to become skinwalkers and shapeshifters and to create characters more real and memorable than many of the living, breathing human beings we meet in our lifetime'; he then blames a lack of negative capability for the two-dimensionality of so many characters in contemporary speculative fiction (p. 414).

or mentally identifying oneself with an object of contemplation, and so fully understanding or appreciating it', was coined only in 1909.[30] So, as the idea of empathy itself developed in the late nineteenth and early twentieth centuries in the Anglophone world, it is perhaps not surprising that the spongy concept of negative capability was carried along with it—and colored by it—in the modern era.

Into this lineage Pullman's novels situate themselves with respect to negative capability largely through his main characters' abilities not to empathize but to eradicate completely any sense of their individual identities. The protagonist of *His Dark Materials* is Lyra, a feral and headstrong girl who gains possession of a rare object called an alethiometer, or 'truth meter'. She alone is able to 'read' the mysterious alethiometer, and eventually we find that when she 'empties her mind' and enters the trancelike state of alethiometer-reading she is accessing the knowledge of Dust, that Dust is actually conscious nanoparticles that superstitious people once named 'angels'. In order to read the alethiometer and communicate with Dust Lyra must hold the pictures on the alethiometer 'in [her] mind without fretting at it or pushing for an answer' (*GC*, p. 112), or enter a state that another character, Dr. Mary Malone, associates explicitly with negative capability: 'Shadows [what Mary calls Dust] are particles of consciousness ... you can't see them ... . Unless you put your mind in a certain state. You have to be confident and relaxed at the same time. You have to be capable—Where's that quotation ... ' (*SK*, p. 78). Mary then retrieves and reads from her handwritten copy of the negative capability letter, and throughout the rest of the trilogy 'the poet Keats' is invoked as the champion of alethiometer-reading and, eventually, as the model for how another character, Will, can wield a second tool, the Subtle Knife, which can slice doors between worlds. Will is told that 'it's not only the knife that has to cut, it's your own mind. ... Lyra ... knew this process. So did Dr. Malone, so did the poet Keats, whoever he was, and all of them knew you couldn't get it by straining toward it' (*SK*, pp. 161–2). Throughout *His Dark Materials*, Pullman develops a version of negative capability that is reminiscent of meditation, the i-Ching (which also figures into the plot), or viewing autostereograms, those aggravating 'hidden sailboat' pictures that one cannot look *at* but must look *through* so that the true image surfaces from a mass of meaningless blobs. It is about letting the self dissolve and taking action through inaction. As Lyra puts it: 'I just make my mind go clear and then it's sort of like looking down into water. You got to let your eyes find the right level, because that's the only one that's in focus' (*GC*, p. 152). Lyra and Will use negative capability to acquire knowledge—of the present and future, of other worlds, and ultimately of their own sexuality. In Pullman's

[30] 'empathy, n.', *OED Online*, Oxford University Press, June 2016. Web. 5 July 2016.

neo-romantic rewriting of *Paradise Lost*[31] Lyra is Eve, Will is Adam, and Mary is the serpent whose story about marzipan and sense memory opens for Lyra a 'rich house with all of its doors open and all its rooms lit' (*AS*, p. 396), an image possibly inspired by another notable phrase from a Keats letter: the 'Mansion of Many Apartments' (*LJK*, I: 280).[32] Lyra and Will do bring knowledge into the world with their 'fall' into joyous sexuality, and it is knowledge gleaned from allegedly 'sinful' Dust.

What Pullman describes when Lyra reads the alethiometer or Will wields the Subtle Knife is actually the *opposite* of empathy; it is self-annihilation, or the complete dissolution of one's ego so that a higher power (Dust, destiny, or doom, as it were) can fill the empty space, much like the ecstasy experienced by Bacchantes who dance and drink so that their selves can dissolve and make room for the god who suffuses them. When in *The Fall of Hyperion* the poet is careful to distinguish himself from 'all mock lyrists, large self worshipers' (Canto 1, line 207), Keats contributes to a long romantic tradition of rejecting entrenched selfhood—what he calls in his 'camelion Poet' letter the 'wordsworthian or egotistical sublime'—in favor of a model that inspires Pullman's reading of negative capability as anti-empathy, a reading which directly contradicts so many twentieth- and twenty-first-century readings of an inherently, even characteristically empathetic, negative capability.[33] The 'camelion Poet', according to Keats, 'is not itself—it has no self—it is every thing and nothing—it has no character ... a Poet is the most unpoetical of any thing in existence; because he has no Identity' (*LJK*, I: 387). Keats's apparent skepticism about the poet's identity as anything but a conduit through which poetry must flow not only influences Pullman's twenty-first-century version of 'the poet Keats' as the advocate for selfless access to truth but also echoes his contemporaries Blake's and Shelley's philosophies of selfhood as a fundamental problem that stands between mankind and paradise. Thus Pullman's reading of negative capability brings into sharper relief the radical idea of selfhood it implies and its closeness with the thinking of the more typically recognized radicals, Blake and Shelley.

[31] The title of the first book of the trilogy, *The Golden Compass*, is a reference to Book 7 of Milton's *Paradise Lost*: 'He took the golden compasses, prepared / In God's eternal store, to circumscribe / This universe, and all created things' (lines 225–7).

[32] Pullman's description of Lyra's epiphany as such: 'She felt as if she had been handed the key to a great house she hadn't known was there, a house that was somehow inside her, and as she turned the key, she felt other doors opening deep in the darkness, and lights coming on' (*AS*, p. 396).

[33] This is what Mark Lussier—in 'Self-Annihilation/Inner Revolution: Blake's "Milton", Buddhism, and Ecocriticism', *Religion & Literature*, 40: 1 (Spring 2008), which shows the parallels between Blakean self-annihilation and Buddhism—calls, without explicit reference to Keats, 'negative consciousness': 'Self-annihilation functions, in Blake, Buddhism, and Ecocriticism alike, as the method for inner revolution, an evolutionary state of freedom from the self-victimizing tendencies of the sovereign self' (pp. 43–4).

Blake, for example, proposes his view of the dangers of selfhood most explicitly in *Milton: a Poem in Two Books* (1804–1810), in which the opposing forces of self and other, forgiveness and egocentricity, coalesce in a vision of humanity redeemed by means of self-annihilation. Milton seeks to correct the errors of his mortal life with his spirit's descent into the sexual, temporal world and his face-off with his selfish specter, Satan, then chooses to annihilate himself rather than his foe. His moment of self-recognition is also a reversal, a resolution to correct his errors and a realization of how this change can occur:

> I will go down to self annihilation and eternal death.
> Lest the Last Judgment come & find me unannihilate
> And I be seiz'd & giv'n into the hands of my own Selfhood.
> ....
> I in my Selfhood am that Satan: I am that Evil One!
> He is my Spectre! in my obedience to loose him from my Hells
> To claim the Hells, my Furnaces, I go to Eternal Death.
> (plate 14: lines 22–4, 30–2)

In this pivotal moment in *Milton*, the titular character achieves epiphany by recognizing his mistaken reliance on his own entrenched sense of self and, refusing any longer to engage in dualistic obligation with his foe, Satan, acknowledges that the Laws of Eternity dictate that 'each shall mutually / Annihilate himself for other's good' (38: 35–6). Anticipating a Last Judgment in which he is found unworthy and finally comprehending both his need for reintegration with his Emanation and the necessity of confronting his Satanic spectre, Milton realizes that 'self annihilation and eternal death' are the only means by which these goals may be achieved. The cover illustration for *Milton* depicts the nude Milton having removed 'the robe of the promise' and, as he strides forth into a swirling mist with his right hand outstretched (echoing Blake's plea for inspiration to descend 'down the Nerves of my right arm'), his hand breaks his own name in two as a symbolic step towards this vital self-annihilation. Milton eventually understands that it is counterintuitive to fight Satan aggressively—to do so only reinforces the self-versus-other conflict that contradicts the notion of forgiveness that is Jesus—so he sacrifices himself: '… I come to Self Annihilation; / Such are the laws of Eternity that each shall mutually / Annihilate himself for others' good, as I for thee' (38: 34–6). By annihilating himself, Milton will indirectly accomplish his goal of annihilating Satan, for Satan is Milton's own selfish nature that cannot survive such selflessness. But, by formulating his confrontation as an act of love ('for others' good, as I for thee'), he avoids the violence and self-righteousness he condemns in Satan's false churches and instead embraces the example of Jesus.

Blake's general attitude of profound distrust towards the process of self creation—the desire of the individual will to construct meaning, to possess the other, to accumulate power—is one shared by Percy Shelley, who also uses selfhood and, often, the idea of self annihilation to discuss sexual dynamics, political dissent, critiques of philosophy or theology, and the function of the speaking 'I'. By the end of *Milton*, individual actions have achieved far-reaching effects; Milton's reintegration with Ololon will herald the Human Harvest in much the same way that the reunion of Prometheus and Asia ushers in paradise in Shelley's *Prometheus Unbound*, a reunion initially barred by Prometheus' participation in a Hegelian opposition with Jupiter similar to that between Blake's Milton and Satan. Whereas for Blake this is a religious objective, with a union with Jesus and the Divine principle as the ultimate goal, Shelley uses this idea to promote his political aim of a transformed world in which all selves are one, all hierarchical and oppressive social and political systems are leveled, and 'None frowned, none trembled, none with eager fear / Gazed on another's eye of cold command / Until the subject of a tyrant's will / Became, worse fate, the abject of his own' (Act III, Scene iv, lines 136–40). Just as Milton recognizes that he must not attack Satan, since to do so would perpetuate a cycle of violence, Prometheus cannot overcome Jupiter aggressively; like Asia's and Panthea's agency-less descent into Demogorgon's realm, Jupiter's fall must happen not due to any action of Prometheus's but rather from the latter's refusal to continue to assert his individual will. This idea of selfishness as a barrier to both human happiness and political revolution recurs repeatedly in Shelley's verse, from the Dionysiac desire that the west wind will 'be thou me, impetuous one' (line 62) to the 'Hymn''s speaker's acknowledgment that Intellectual Beauty has made him 'fear himself' (line 84), to Hope's selfless sacrifice in *The Masque of Anarchy*.

Like Shelley's Hope, Lyra must sacrifice herself, though she forgoes not her life but her happiness when she voluntarily separates from Will in order to keep open the window that allows the ghosts of all the worlds' dead to leave the gloomy nothingness of the Underworld and become 'part of everything alive again' (*AS*, p. 286). She enacts a similar sacrifice when she breaks her elemental bond with her daemon, Pantalaimon, in order to perform the *katabasis* to the land of the dead that ultimately frees those ghosts from eternal stagnation. Also like Prometheus or Milton, Lyra can only change the world if she does so unconsciously; in *The Golden Compass*, the witch Serafina Pekkala relates a prophecy about Lyra: 'She is destined to bring about the end of destiny. But she must do so without knowing what she is doing, as if it were her nature and not her destiny to do it' (*GC*, p. 271). Lyra is able to annihilate her selfhood and read the alethiometer while she remains in a state of Blakean innocence, when she does not have to *try* to do so, but once she discovers her sexuality and Pantalaimon 'settles' into his permanent form of a pine marten, she finds that she can no longer slip into the state of negative capability that allowed her to gain knowledge so effortlessly. She is told at the end of the trilogy that she might, through a lifetime of rigorous study, teach herself what had once come so naturally, but she would never again be able to empty her mind and look *through* the alethiometer into absolute truth. Most grown-up minds, Pullman implies, are simply too cluttered and self-conscious to access a process so inherently destructive of the individual consciousness.

On the final page of *The Amber Spyglass*, Pantalaimon and Lyra—still mourning Will's return to his version of Oxford and their permanent separation—reflect on the fall of the Authority (who, like Jupiter in *Prometheus Unbound*, collapses with more whimper than bang) and the dissolution of the Kingdom of Heaven. Lyra reiterates that each individual must build the Republic of Heaven themselves, wherever they are, but that 'no one could [build it] if they put themselves first' (p. 464). With what might be an intentional pun, Pullman ends the trilogy with Lyra smarting over her sacrifice but recognizing that she had to forfeit Will—and her own will—in order to be a true citizen of the Republic of Heaven. Pullman's foregrounding of negative capability and 'the poet Keats, whoever he was' as key elements of the trilogy's vision of both political and religious revolution returns a Blakean, Shelleyan, and ultimately radical significance to negative capability, a concept that has so often been read, as noted above, as a purely aesthetic exercise in poetic creation. By returning negative capability to its self-annihilative, romantic roots, Pullman diverges from many twentieth-century readers of Keats who argue that negative capability separates definitive 'knowledge' from Keatsian 'truth'. It is noteworthy yet perhaps unsurprising that Pullman's books have been the targets of numerous boycotts and protests by those who argue that the books peddle radicalism and atheism disguised as fantasy to impressionable young readers, that, despite the talking bears and magic, the trilogy might radicalize tots to real-world political action and skepticism about religious orthodoxy.[34]

[34] According to the American Library Association's annual 'Banned/Challenged Books List', *His Dark Materials* was the second most challenged title in the United States in 2008 and the eighth most banned or challenged in the decade 2000–2009; the reasons most frequently invoked, according to the ALA, are 'political viewpoint, religious viewpoint, violence'. See 'Top 100 Banned/Challenged Books: 2000–2009', *American Library Association* (website), accessed 14 September 2018, http://www.ala.org/bbooks/top-100-bannedchallenged-books-2000-2009. In an interview with *The Guardian*, Pullman claimed to be 'very glad to be back in the top 10 banned books' and added that 'the power of organised religion is very strong in the US, and getting stronger because of the internet'. As Pullman notes in the same interview, the trilogy's profile was raised by the release in December 2007 of a big-budget film version of *The Golden Compass* (starring Nicole Kidman and Daniel Craig), and many reviews of both the film and books condemned them as 'atheism for kids' (according to Bill Donohue, president of the Catholic League and organizer of many of the protests). See Ed Pilkington, 'Children's writer

The version of negative capability in this avowedly Keats-influenced young adult series has more in common with romantic self-annihilation than it does with many recent and contemporary readings of negative capability as essentially empathetic; for Pullman, being negatively capable means turning off one's self-consciousness entirely, not tuning it into another's, and therein lies the potential for both political and religious revolution.

Philip Pullman ranked second on US banned books list', *The Guardian*, 30 September 2009, accessed 14 September 2018, https://www.theguardian.com/books/2009/sep/30/american-library-association-banned-books.

CHAPTER FOURTEEN

Negative Capability in Psychoanalysis

Keats and Retroactive Judgment in Bion, Freud, Lacan, and Milner

David Sigler

In formulating his celebrated idea of negative capability, John Keats found 'a medium for speculative thinking and critical formulations that are now part of our vocabulary', as Susan J. Wolfson explains.[1] Yet what is implied by that vocabulary, and that medium, have not always been stable. We tend currently to believe, as Li Ou says, that: 'To be negatively capable is to be open to the actual vastness and complexity of experience, and one cannot possess this openness unless one can abandon the comfortable enclosure of doctrinaire knowledge.'[2] But that sense of the term only became fully entrenched after about 1970, following the publication of Walter Jackson Bate's *Criticism: The Major Texts*, as Li notes (p. 16). And Basic Books was at the same time publishing *Attention and Interpretation* (1970), a book by the British psychoanalyst Wilfred Bion, which appropriated and adapted Keats's concept for the psychological disciplines. Bion transformed the concept of negative capability in lasting ways, even while literary scholars, seldom reading Bion, have tended to remain wedded to Bate's understanding of the term.

Romanticists have at times treated negative capability as a proto-psychoanalytic concept. For Joel Faflak, negative capability is at once Keats's strategy for mitigating the terrifying gender ambivalence located everywhere in his poetry and a term for the poet's engagements with the unconscious dimensions of philosophy, such that Keats's poetry 'establish[es] a dialogue with ... the radical otherness of the unconscious' as it 'traces the dark anthropomorphism of the subject within the theater of its other subjectivities' to

[1] Susan J. Wolfson, *Reading John Keats* (Cambridge: Cambridge University Press, 2015), p. xi.

[2] Li Ou, *Keats and Negative Capability* (London: Bloomsbury, 2009), p. 2.

create 'the distinctly heterogeneous and dark empiricism of the Romantic psychoanalytic scene'.[3] Emily Rohrbach sees negative capability as Keats's way of keeping open an 'anticipatory sense of possibilities' through 'multiple figurations', an attitude which she associates with Jacques Lacan's discussions, in *Écrits*, of the future anterior.[4] Even Walter Jackson Bate—someone hardly associated with psychoanalytic literary criticism—paraphrases Keats's letter in Freudian terms.[5] Thus we can say that Romanticists have oftentimes suspected negative capability of having a psychoanalytic dimension. Yet Keats's psychoanalytic inclinations aspire, as Faflak rightly observes, '*beyond* the Freudian ken of a therapeutic cure' (p. 230). Adapting Keats's form of psychoanalysis interminable into the less-than-Dionysian world of late twentieth-century clinical psychoanalysis—that is, to develop negative capability as a matter of analytic technique—took Bion's audacious re-reading of Keats's familiar if enigmatic letter.

In the final chapter of *Attention and Interpretation*, Bion offers recommendations for analysts attempting to arrive at diagnoses when a patient's words are inconsistent or overly detailed. He proposes negative capability as a way to get beyond such impasses and so to better attend to the specificity of a patient's emotional register.[6] Negative capability would go on to anchor Bion's theory of vertices and offer a way for clinicians to approach his key concept of 'O' (discussed below) in practical terms. Thus negative capability, supposedly a talent applicable, according to Keats, 'especially in Literature', began the most prominent phase of its moonlighting within psychoanalytic theory and clinical practice. The psychoanalytic engagement with Keats reveals unexpected facets of negative capability—specifically, its processes of deferral and retroaction—and enables us to better grasp Keats's continuing influence on contemporary psychoanalysis.

In the hopes of giving literary scholars a view of the clinical world of negative capability, this essay traces the theoretical hybridizations and fusions that prompted Bion to adapt Keats's concept for psychoanalysis and takes stock of how the concept is currently used within it. It suggests that negative capability has had a longer and wider psychoanalytic provenance than Bion's followers usually acknowledge, looking at predecessors such as Sigmund Freud, Jacques Lacan, and Marion Milner to consider psychoanalysis as a negatively capable science. The essay proceeds in three stages:

[3] Joel Faflak, *Romantic Psychoanalysis: The Burden of the Mystery* (Albany, NY: State University of New York Press, 2008), pp. 203, 229.

[4] Emily Rohrbach, *Modernity's Mist: British Romanticism and the Poetics of Anticipation* (New York: Fordham University Press, 2016), pp. 60, 62, 5–6.

[5] Walter Jackson Bate, *John Keats* (Cambridge, MA: Harvard University Press, 2009), p. 249.

[6] Wilfred R. Bion, *Attention and Interpretation* (London: Karnac Books, 1984), p. 185.

first, it explains why Bion needed Keats, conceptually, as he developed his theory of O and how this has led to Keats's continuing presence as a mascot of sorts within Bionic psychoanalytic circles; second, it traces Bion's thinking through key antecedent texts by Freud and Lacan, who were major influences on Bion and likely affected his reading of Keats, so as to account for the idiosyncrasies of Bion's understanding of negative capability and specifically its retroactive interpretive structures; third, it considers Milner's work, equally indebted to Keats but differently, as an important predecessor to Bion, offering her engagement with negative capability an alternative way of positioning the concept within psychoanalysis. This last phase of the argument is important because the explicit alliance between psychoanalysis and negative capability began, as far as I know, in the 1930s with Milner's work, even as psychoanalysts today tend to attribute the impulse for Keats appreciation to Bion. What Bion pioneered was a way to make negative capability a matter of analytic craft—a 'capability' of the analyst's rather than the impossible object of its psychoanalytic investigations. This essay, then, presents Milner and Bion as alternative forms of negative psychoanalytic capability, even if the former's Keatsian investigations have been overshadowed somewhat by the latter's.

A Draught of Vintage for O

The psychoanalytic tradition has since its earliest days sought strategies for interpreting, or refraining from interpreting, silence and absence, and has been ever eager to recognize the limits of its knowledge. One thinks of Freud's 'navel of the dream', the Lacanian Real, or Slavoj Žižek's recovery of the 'known unknowns' that attend American political discourse.[7] The Bionic equivalent of such concepts is 'O'—meaning psychic origin or the ungraspable thing-in-itself. O is something that any process of investigation would be unable to reach, irritably or otherwise, for the simple reason that 'O' designates unknowability *per se*. Hence, like Lacan's Real or Freud's dream-navel, O is graspable only by its effects. As Bion explains:

> I shall use the sign O to denote that which is the ultimate reality represented by terms such as ultimate reality, absolute truth, the godhead, the infinite, the thing-in-itself. O does not fall in the domain of knowledge or learning save incidentally; it can be 'become', but it cannot be 'known'. (*Attention*, p. 26)

[7] Sigmund Freud, *The Standard Edition of the Complete Psychological Works of Sigmund Freud*, trans. James Strachey, 24 vols. (London: Hogarth Press, 1964), IV: p. 111, n.1; Slavoj Žižek, *Iraq: The Borrowed Kettle* (London: Verso, 2005), pp. 9–10.

Yet, as Joan Symington points out, not every analyst is ready to 'become' O. Negative capability becomes, then, a strategy: 'How do these experiences of becoming O happen? … This is why Bion talks about negative capability'.[8]

The concept O allowed Bion to separate memory from the unconscious, making psychoanalysis less of an act of retrieving buried material and more of an encounter with unknowability itself. In this way, it performs a function analogous to Freud's triad of conscious–preconscious–unconscious. But Bion goes much further than Freud in that direction, taking very seriously the idea that memory is to be eschewed. The analyst must endeavor not to remember anything about the patient even after years of treatment together, making each session effectively the first one. He outlined such a strategy as early as 1967 in his aphoristic article 'Notes on Memory and Desire'. There, without yet any reference to Keats, Bion was honing a capacity for blankness that he hoped could eliminate the temporality of the psychoanalytic session: 'Every session attended by the psychoanalyst must have no history and no future.' To this end, he advises his colleagues to 'not remember past sessions' and to disregard the patient's words in the session itself: 'The supposed events must not be allowed to occupy the mind.' To help the analyst 'cultivate a watchful avoidance of memory', Bion advises, 'notes should be confined to matters which *can* be recorded', such as the list of daily appointments. The analyst must be blank and transitive, because: 'Out of the darkness and formlessness something evolves.'[9] The article proved controversial, with one respondent worrying that the article 'seems provocatively nihilistic of all that we have learned as psychoanalysts', and a second responding that 'the contradictions are so obvious'.[10] Bion, responding to these concerns, simply said that: 'my views have "evolved"'.[11]

Bion was concerned that 'desires interfere, by absence of mind when observation is essential, with the operation of judgment'.[12] Listening without memory or desire is a form of hard-won mindfulness. Yet what it demanded rendered psychoanalysis utterly separate from ordinary forms of listening, approaching inhumanness and leading to the sorts of commonsense reactions mentioned above. As Bion's student André Green explains: 'Observation shows

[8] Joan Symington, 'O', *Psychoanalysis Downunder* 7B (2007), accessed 9 July 2018, http://www.psychoanalysisdownunder.com.au/issues/8/papers/108.

[9] Wilfred R. Bion, 'Notes on Memory and Desire', *The Psychoanalytic Forum*, 2: 3 (1967): p. 272.

[10] John Lindon, 'Response to Bion's "Notes on Memory and Desire"', *The Psychoanalytic Forum*, 2: 3 (1967): p. 274; Avelino González, 'Response to Bion's "Notes on Memory and Desire"', *The Psychoanalytic Forum*, 2: 3 (1967): p. 277.

[11] Wilfred R. Bion, 'Notes on Memory and Desire: Author's Response', *The Psychoanalytic Forum*, 2: 3 (1967): p. 280.

[12] Bion, 'Notes', p. 272.

us that some patients (as well as many analysts) do not tolerate the state of uncertainty, mystery, or doubt'.[13] Even analysts influenced by Bion find that exercising negative capability is 'no easy matter', because, as William Betts notes, 'Bion's technical recommendations are radical … . What is required is nothing short of an inner emotional ascesis that can open out into a new and unsuspected field of inquiry.'[14] Yet others, more skeptical of this platform, allege that Bion uses negative capability as 'a kind of shorthand' whenever he 'needs to note something enigmatic about the capacity of the mind'.[15]

Since 1970, a host of practicing psychoanalysts, mainly those influenced by Bion, have contended that negative capability is absolutely central to psychoanalytic theory to an extent that one might have imagined would be reserved for key concepts like the unconscious, free association, or the Oedipus complex. Bionic psychoanalysts have called negative capability 'the definitive "essence" of psychoanalysis' and 'the sort of idea that is a guiding principle, a fount of inspiration, and, as such, it is not to be argued with but simply to be known or recognized, … [as] everything else revolves around it'.[16] William Betts refers to 'negative capability, [as] something that I consider fundamental to the psychoanalytic process'; Meltzer, whose work was especially influential in this regard, attributes negative capability even to babies, who apparently show us, through 'the capacity to tolerate a passionate relationship with the world … . [that] a passionate relationship is full of uncertainty and that uncertainty is a great stimulus to thought'.[17] Child psychologist Martha Harris hopes that, by 'forging goals for ourselves and for our clients', 'we might achieve that state of negative capability or readiness to receive and think about a patient's projections'.[18] O. D. H. Blomfield goes yet further, even wildly so, in associating negative capability primarily with Freud and Kant rather than

[13] André Green, 'The Primordial Mind and the Work of the Negative', in *W.R. Bion: Between Past and Future*, ed. Franco Borgogno, Silvio A. Merciai, and Parthenope Bion Talamo (London: Karnac Books, 2000), p. 122.

[14] William Betts, 'Negative Capability', *Psychoanalysis Downunder*, 7B (2007), accessed 9 July 2018, http://www.psychoanalysisdownunder.com.au/issues/8/papers/106.

[15] Adam Phillips, *Promises, Promises: Essays on Psychoanalysis and Literature* (New York: Basic Books, 2002), pp. 22–3.

[16] O. H. D. Blomfield, 'The Essentials of Psychoanalysis', *Australian and New Zealand Journal of Psychiatry*, 27: 1 (1993), p. 91; Meg Harris Williams, *The Aesthetic Development: The Poetic Spirit of Psychoanalysis: Essays on Bion, Meltzer, Keats* (London: Karnac Books, 2010), p. 43.

[17] Donald Meltzer, 'New Considerations on the Concept of the Aesthetic Conflict', in *Psychoanalysis and Art: Kleinian Perspectives*, ed. Sandra Gosso (London: Karnac Books, 2004), p. 217.

[18] Martha Harris and Esther Bick, *The Tavistock Model: Papers on Child Development and Psychoanalytic Training*, ed. Meg Harris Williams, rev. ed. (London: Karnac Books, 2011), p. 48.

especially with Keats, saying: 'If, in some global catastrophe, all the literature on psychoanalytic theory and therapy were lost, it could be reconstituted provided there remained some awareness of the possibility of a discipline of intersubjectivity based on "Negative Capability". ... [but] if this should be lost, all is lost' (p. 96). Bion's work even inspired the eminent psychoanalyst Meg Harris Williams to write a larger psychoanalytic investigation of Keats's poetry, entitled 'Keats: Soul-Making', from her clinical perspective, declaring Keats 'the greatest of the Romantic poets' for his 'determination to see beauty as truth'.[19] Thus negative capability becomes the secret key to psychoanalysis and its purpose for existence, as well as the principle from which all of its other teachings can be derived. All of which is to observe that, through Bion's enthusiastic recommendation, a Romantic poet's private correspondence has today become the basis of a vital and currently flourishing psychoanalytic technique.

Adam Phillips, charmingly skeptical of this tradition, posits that: 'It is indeed instructive how few analysts seem to have been in a state of negative capability about Keats's formulation of negative capability. It is repeated like a mantra as though the poet's words were themselves beyond interpretation' (p. 27). I too am wary of what I often intuitively perceive to be simplistic readings of Keats, but I suspect that such wariness might cause me to miss an opportunity to consider the unpredictable ways that an aesthetic concept can flourish in a new form and unexpected setting. To a Romanticist an article such as 'Keats: Soul-Making' might seem a distressingly naive work of poetic interpretation—though it is likely, I am aware, analogous in its results to a literary scholar's writings about contemporary psychoanalytic theory—but it also signals the continuing importance of poetry within the psychological sciences. Yet the outpouring of affection for Keats from clinical quarters has not much influenced the actual study of the poet *qua* poet, probably because, as Mary Jacobus notes, 'Bion has been comparatively neglected by literary critics.'[20] This seems like a missed opportunity to me.

As Jacobus observes, 'Bion's way with his psychoanalytic constructions is to read them aslant, against the grain of their received meaning' (p. 201), and such is just what happened to and for negative capability in, and in the aftermath of, *Attention and Interpretation*. Finding an alliance between Keats and Freud, Bion actually goes so far as to say that: 'any [psychoanalytic] session should be judged by comparison with the Keats formulation'.[21] Yet a contradiction

[19] Meg Harris Williams, 'Keats: Soul-Making', in *Psychoanalysis and Art: Kleinian Perspectives*, ed. Sandra Gosso (London: Karnac Books, 2004), p. 267.

[20] Mary Jacobus, *The Poetics of Psychoanalysis: In the Wake of Klein* (Oxford: Oxford University Press, 2005), p. 204.

[21] Bion, *Attention*, p. 125.

ensues in this rush to judgment, in that one is supposed to judge an analytic session by its propensity for 'being in uncertainty'. Bion resolves it in two ways, one related to the object of the inquiry and the other to its temporality. For Bion success in analysis is not revelatory, as it sometimes could be for Freud, but rather involves willingly descending into something necessarily and by its nature uncertain, namely O. Then, in temporal terms, Bion makes negative capability into a kind of retroactive judgment.[22] It is, for Bion, the learned ability to 'lay low' while information is gathered, leaving interpretation for later.[23] Negative capability is, in Bion's hands, the deferment of interpretation rather than a learned comfort with the limits of one's curiosity.

'Portion'd to a giant nerve': Freud, Lacan, and the *Project for a Scientific Psychology*

Consequently, negative capability began to take on a temporality distinct from anything described in Keats's 1817 letter. In Bion's view, an analyst exercises negative capability by waiting, and also waits to exercise it. This is ironic because Keats sees negative capability as a matter of immediacy and suddenness: it leads to phrases like 'at once it struck me' and 'dovetailed in my mind'; it 'overcomes' and 'obliterates' thought; it tests itself, moment by moment, against temptation. Bion's take is almost exactly the opposite: negative capability is the willingness to eschew epiphany and postpone interpretation. Bion, in effect, celebrates the ability to shift from 'mystery' to the later pursuit of that mystery 'through Volumes'—that is, Bion celebrates the same Coleridgean traits that Keats defines negative capability against.

How did negative capability become, for Bion, a practice of deferment? Primarily it was because he was reading Keats's letter through a perspective shaped by Freud, and especially Lacan's interpretation of Freud. Bion seems to be fusing Keats's insights with the enigmatic concept of *Nachträglichkeit*, or deferred action, as theorized in Freud's *Project for a Scientific Psychology*. Freud wrote the *Project* in an intense burst of activity in 1895 before abandoning the manuscript and even attempting to destroy it. Primarily a theory of nerves and neurons, the text remained unpublished and generally unknown for more than half a century. It was first published in 1950 and translated into English in 1954. Freud's presentation of deferred action in the *Project* is limited to a brief discussion of 'Emma', a patient who couldn't go into shops

[22] Friedrich-Wilhelm Eickhoff, 'On Nachträglichkeit: The Modernity of an Old Concept', *The International Journal of Psychoanalysis*, 87 (2006): p. 1464.

[23] Parthenope Bion Talamo, 'Laying Low and Saying (Almost) Nothing', in *W.R. Bion: Between Past and Future*, ed. Franco Borgogno, Silvio A. Merciai, and Parthenope Bion Talamo (London: Karnac Books, 2000), p. 23.

alone for fear of being mocked by the shopkeepers. Emma had earlier in life been groped in a candy shop, an event which became debilitating only when, as an adult, other shopkeepers, including one she had slept with, had laughed at her clothes. Explains Freud:

> Here we have the case of a memory arousing an affect which it did not arouse as an experience, because in the meantime the change … had made possible a different understanding of what was remembered. Now this case is typical of repression in hysteria. We invariably find that a memory is repressed which has only become a trauma by *deferred action*. (*SE*, I: p. 356)

The essence of the concept is that superficial similarities can tie otherwise unrelated events together, retroactively rendering earlier events traumatic by affiliation with later ones. Freud would return to the concept occasionally, most notably in the Wolf Man case, in which deferred action would become the mechanism of the primal scene. But because the *Project* was unpublished for so long, and because *Nachträglichkeit* had no consistent translation, deferred action would only gradually become a recognized concept within psychoanalysis, and it remains 'impossible to trace its use' comprehensively.[24]

The importance of the *Project* for psychoanalysis, and especially for Bion, rests primarily on three sessions of Lacan's *Seminar II*, held between 26 January and 9 February 1955. There, Lacan, repeatedly upbraiding his psychoanalyst students for not knowing the then-little-known text intimately, chapter and verse, highlights the importance of the word *Nachträglichkeit* in Freud's manuscript. Lacan's remarks there (and in his Rome Discourse of 1953) made the word, now rebranded as '*après coup*', into a major psychoanalytic concept worthy of inclusion, for instance, in Jean Laplanche and J. B. Pontalis's seminal dictionary of psychoanalytic terms (p. 111).[25] Lacan's disquisitions, through volumes, upon Freud's early text seem to have pointed Bion toward an interpretation of Freud receptive to Keats and negative capability. Deferred action suggests that events, as they occur, don't yet have significance, and even as they are recounted in psychoanalysis they may not yet have their significance, and thus a Bionic attitude toward the unknown, where one analyzes in abeyance, becomes indispensible. In Lacan's 1950s work, then, we find the seeds that would bequeath psychoanalysis its Keatsophilia.

[24] Jean Laplanche and J. B. Pontalis, 'Deferred Action', in *The Language of Psycho-Analysis*, trans. Donald Nicholson-Smith (New York: Norton, 1973), p. 111.

[25] Jacques Lacan, *Écrits: The First Complete Edition in English*, trans. Bruce Fink (New York: Norton, 2006), pp. 265–6, nn. 8, 9; Jacqueline Hamrit, 'Nachträglichkeit', *PsyArt: An Online Journal for the Psychological Study of the Arts* (2008), accessed 9 July 2018, http://psyartjournal.com/article/show/hamrit-nachtrglichkeit.

Lacan sees the *Project* as Freud's first attempt to theorize consciousness, an attempt bound to fail because Freud had yet to discover the unconscious.[26] Lacan holds that Freud solved this problem five years later, in the *Interpretation of Dreams*, by introducing a 'temporal dimension' to his work.[27] It is this same temporal dimension that Bion adds to Keats in order to make negative capability a psychoanalytic concept. The extent to which Lacan's ideas influenced Bion's remains a matter of critical debate, but increasingly scholars are finding points of convergence between them, and most agree that Bion and Lacan did influence each other to some degree.[28] Lacan became interested in Bion's work during the 1940s and met with Bion on a postwar study trip to England.[29] Bion imported deferred action into negative capability, transforming its temporality and making it relevant for analytic practice. In so doing, he also turned deferred action into the analyst's strategy rather than a patient's. Bion would call this 'listening to listening', a concept based on Freud's *Nachträglichkeit*.[30] Through the influence of Freud and Lacan, Bion came to see being in uncertainty as a counterintuitive negative phase in a dialectical process of interpretation that ironically depends on the subsequent reinterpretation and judgment of that uncertainty, effectively undoing it. At the same time, Bion leans upon Keats to authorize his own willingness to exceed Freud's own 'Recommendations for Analytic Technique' in accepting the deferred action of analytic interpretation.

Likely inspired by Bion's reclamation of the concept, several psychoanalysts in recent decades have, in writing for a largely clinical readership, recognized negative capability in Freud.[31] Freud never wrote about Keats or negative capability, but his recommendations for analytic technique can seem to depend

[26] Jacques Lacan, *The Seminar of Jacques Lacan, Book II: The Ego in Freud's Theory and in the Technique of Psychoanalysis, 1954–1955*, ed. Jacques-Alain Miller, trans. Sylvana Tomaselli (New York: Norton, 1988), p. 117.

[27] Lacan, *Seminar II*, p. 118.

[28] Richard E. Webb and Michael A. Sells, 'Lacan and Bion: Psychoanalysis and the Mystical Language of "Unsaying"', *Theory & Psychology*, 5: 2 (May 1995): pp. 195–215; Julia Borossa, Catalina Bronstein, and Claire Pajaczkowska, eds., *The New Klein-Lacan Dialogues* (London: Karnac Books, 2015); Laura Etchegoyen, 'Panel Report: The Analyst's Response to the Effects of the Transference: On Lacan and Bion', *The International Journal of Psychoanalysis*, 91 (2010): p. 399.

[29] Lacan, *Seminar II*, p. 94. See also Elisabeth Roudinesco, *Jacques Lacan: Outline of a Life, History of a System of Thought*, trans. Barbara Bray (New York: Columbia University Press, 1997), pp. 173–5.

[30] Haidée Faimberg, 'Whom Was Bion Addressing? "Negative Capability" and "Listening to Listening"', in *W.R. Bion: Between Past and Future*, ed. Parthenope Bion Talamo, Franco Borgogno, and Silvio A. Merciai (London: Karnac Books, 2000), pp. 88, 89.

[31] See Betts, 'Negative Capability' and Blomfield, 'The Essentials of Psychoanalysis'. Betts calls negative capability 'a quality that Sigmund Freud, and other innovative psychoanalysts have possessed', and Blomfield argues that Freud developed free association and free-floating attention as methods to achieve negative capability (pp. 91–2).

upon the concept intuitively. This is especially so in the *Papers on Technique*, where he advises analysts to be more like surgeons—Keats's profession, incidentally—by listening without sympathy to perform an inhuman blankness. 'I cannot advise my colleagues too urgently to model themselves during psychoanalytic treatment on the surgeon', he says, 'who puts aside all his feelings, even his human sympathy, and concentrates his mental forces on the single aim of performing the operation as skillfully as possible.' Freud warns against any 'state of mind' devised 'to achieve' a particular goal, saying that 'the analyst should be content with' just doing his or her job (*SE*, XII: p. 115). 'The doctor should be opaque to his patients and, like a mirror, should show them nothing but what is shown to him', he says (*SE*, XII: p. 118). 'The justification for requiring this emotional coldness in the analyst', Freud continues, 'is that it creates the most advantageous conditions for both parties: for the doctor a desirable protection for his own emotional life and for the patient the largest amount of help' (*SE*, XII: p. 115).

Anticipating Bion, Freud also suggests that we defer psychoanalytic interpretation:

> It is not a good thing to work on a case scientifically while treatment is still proceeding—to piece together its structure, to try to foretell its further progress, and to get a picture from time to time of the current state of affairs, as scientific interest would demand … . The most successful cases are those in which one proceeds, as it were, without any purpose in view, allows oneself to be taken by surprise by any new turn in them, and always meets them with an open mind, free from any presuppositions. (*SE*, XII: p. 114)

Psychoanalysis, then, channeling Keats, obliterates all consideration. Given this situation, Freud recommends 'swinging over', meaning committing to the lack of any steady commitment: 'The correct behavior for an analyst lies in swinging over according to need from the one mental attitude to the other', he says, 'in avoiding speculation or brooding over cases while they are in analysis, and in submitting the material obtained to a synthetic process of thought only after the analysis is concluded' (*SE*, XII: p. 114). He prizes a limber mind and advises an interpretive delay. Yet Freud, in framing variability of technique as itself a firm set of 'correct behaviors', introduces an ironic tension between form and content that would also characterize Bion's work on the vertices. As Betts observes of Bion's emphatic endorsement of Keats:

> These rules [of analytic procedure] must be obeyed all the time. One might ask, Is this negative capability? The positing of rules that must be obeyed implies an absolute certainty, and certainly sounds like trying at

> it. On the other hand, the content of the rules are undeniably endorsing negative capability. This is a paradox. (Betts)

Bion went further than Freud in insisting upon an inhuman relationship with the patient, scrubbed of any vestige of sympathy or even recognition, as a way to combat transference. The reward, in Bion, for such contentment with half knowledge is the establishment of the vertex, which is Bion's term for the point of view formed when the analyst suspends any point of view.

In *Attention and Interpretation*, Bion emphasizes Freud's own negative capability, which he sees as bestowing an artificial blindness. It is, he says, the secret by which Freud was able to shine 'the piercing shaft of darkness [which] can be directed on the dark features of the analytic situation' (p. 57; see also p. 43). The absence of light becomes, for Bion, a positive entity with its own impossible physics, the 'piercing' nature of which establishes the very foundation of psychoanalytic reason. Resisting expectations for revelation, enlightenment, or illumination, Bion sees Freud as a literal dark interpreter, who, through negative capability, defies optics. Further, Bion justifies his appropriation of negative capability through reference to Freud, suggesting that 'Freud's theories approximate' what Keats directly acknowledges (p. 125). Keats, then, is for Bion the true father of psychoanalysis. Bion rethought psychoanalysis along these lines—as the learned exercise of a 'shaft of darkness' eliminating the analyst's capacities for illumination, which depends upon the analyst's ability to suspend any sense of the analysand:

> How, then, are we to 'observe' and 'record' the patient's state of mind? Since I wish to discuss this but do not know the answer, I shall say 'by F'. Freud said that he had to 'blind myself artificially to focus all the light on one dark spot'. This provides a useful formulation for describing the area I wish to cover by F. By rendering oneself 'artificially blind' through the exclusion of memory and desire, one achieves F. (pp. 57–8)

This advice would anchor Bion's enthusiasm for Keats to psychoanalysis by way of Freud, especially the Freud of deferred action, the *Project for a Scientific Psychology*, and Lacan.

The aesthetic component that Keats thus imports into psychoanalysis, though, complicates analytic interpretation at a practical level. Poets can settle for being evocative, 'the sense of Beauty overcom[ing] every other consideration'; psychoanalysts, on the other hand, being necessarily '*consequitive reason[ers]*', have a practical need to identify discursive and interpretive pathways, exploitable in concrete terms (*LJK*, I: 194, 185). Interpretations are their stock in trade. If an analyst were to accept that the basis of clear judgment is no judgment, they would have little choice, in practical terms, but to adopt a model of deferred interpretation, as they will ultimately be called upon to deliver something; furthermore, they need to communicate their methods and interpretations to other practitioners at the levels of teaching and publishing. Negative capability is thus much harder for an analyst than for a poet to sustain. One can see, then, how a concept such as 'vertex' has 'advantages clear' for Bion.[32] He had found a practical way to hybridize psychoanalysis and Keats via *Nachträglichkeit*, making deferment and retroaction part of the negatively capable analyst's toolbox. The aesthetic dimension of the concept was imported with the rest, and has left its trace on subsequent analytic formulations. Donald Meltzer, for instance, couches (the very un-Lacanian concept of) 'ego strength' in aesthetic and Keatsian terms:

> In seeing this as a tormenting uncertainty about the interior qualities of the aesthetic object, it becomes possible to express the idea of ego strength as negative capability. When the dimension strength/weakness becomes thus observable in its operation and not merely construed from its consequences, we seem to move to a new level of precision in clinical observation (and self-scrutiny).[33]

Further, Meltzer, writing with Williams, uses negative capability to theorize 'the aesthetic conflict', something visible, they say, even in psychotic patients: 'Toleration of this conflict, which is the heart of the matter of ego strength, resides in the capacity that Bion, after Keats, has called "negative capability"'.[34] We can trace a line from Lacan's interest in the poetics of psychoanalysis to Bion's aesthetic engagements, the practical clinical considerations that attend these, and consequently a variety of contemporary analytic approaches.

Milner's Blank Amazements

A generation before Bion, Marion Milner found her own applications for Keats's negative capability, understanding the term as a strategy for resisting masculinist scientific discourses rather than, as it would be for Bion, a period of active and attentive information gathering. Written in the long aftermath of A. C. Bradley's *Oxford Lectures on Poetry*, which made negative capability a fashionable topic within British literary culture,[35] Milner developed a form

[32] Bion, *Attention*, p. 58.

[33] Donald Meltzer, 'The Compartments of the Internal Mother', in *Psychoanalysis and Art: Kleinian Perspectives*, ed. Sandra Gosso (London: Karnac Books, 2004), pp. 223–4.

[34] Donald Meltzer and Meg Harris Williams, 'Aesthetic Conflict: Its Place in the Developmental Process', in *Psychoanalysis and Art: Kleinian Perspectives*, ed. Sandra Gosso (London: Karnac Books, 2004), p. 189.

[35] Li, *Keats and Negative Capability*, pp. 10–11.

of psychoanalytic inquiry into negative capability alternative to Bion's and at least as fascinating, though less influential today. With a singular writing style that muddied distinctions between psychoanalytic theory, cultural criticism, and creative nonfiction, Milner pursued psychoanalysis as a literary art, and vice versa. Her freely associative memoir of 1937, *An Experiment in Leisure*, which was published under the pseudonym Joanna Field, investigates desire, sexism, scientific and religious knowledge, the division between humans and non-human animals, the role of literature in modern culture, and the ways that psychoanalysis might address these questions. Milner repurposes Keats's admiration for Shakespeare into a powerful critique of gendered knowledge production, finding in Keats the seeds of a feminist counterhegemonic discourse. This aspect of Milner's work brings her closely in line with the ways that Romanticists, such as Anne K. Mellor, Joel Faflak, and Rachel Schulkins, have seen negative capability as Keats's instrument for gender experimentation.[36]

Idiosyncratic and adventurous thinkers both, the contrast between Milner and Bion could not be more pronounced. While Bion endeavored to eliminate the analyst's memory from the analytic equation, Milner makes memory—her own, in particular—the foundation of every other kind of analytic work: 'I decided to begin by comparing memories', she explains.[37] And, while Bion would align himself with Keats in an effort to elaborate upon Freud, Milner enlists the poet to help her articulate a form of psychoanalysis quite resistant to Freud's model. She dispenses altogether with the concept of repression, for instance, supposing that there is nothing irretrievable about unconscious material.[38] *An Experiment in Leisure* pursues free association as an assortment of connected memories and notions, which Milner considers interesting in their own right, not because they indicate any gap in discourse or reveal repressed material. Throughout the text, she tests her innovative self-analyzes against the wisdom of Keats's letters (pp. 68, 91, 121).

Where Bion aligns with Milner, beyond their basic mutual interest in negative capability as a trait in the analyst, is their mutual conviction that negative capability is an unnatural feat. One must train the mind, painstakingly, into it. Such requires vigilance and discipline: 'my method', she explains, only worked 'if I kept strict enough watch on the wanderings of my mind' (*Experiment*, p. 40). Calling the blankness associated with negative capability 'my inner fact', she explains that, despite her attempts to 'submit myself to this inner fact … I could only very rarely do it' (p. 41). Milner quotes Keats's

[36] Anne K. Mellor, *Romanticism and Gender* (New York: Routledge, 1993), p. 174; Faflak, *Romantic Psychoanalysis*, pp. 201–7; Rachel Schulkins, *Keats, Modesty, and Masturbation* (Farnham: Ashgate, 2014), pp. 5–8.

[37] Marion Milner, *An Experiment in Leisure* (New York: Routledge, 2011), p. xliv.

[38] Maud Ellmann, 'New Introduction', in *An Experiment in Leisure*, by Marion Milner (New York: Routledge, 2011), p. xxxv.

letters frequently, maintaining, despite the experimental nature of her text, that its insights 'were only new for me'; and that her text merely reveals how, through free association, centuries-old literary insights 'have been proved upon our pulses' (p. xlv). Employing another literary metaphor, she describes her psychoanalytic investigations as the 'Odysseys of the weak', bringing a sense of epic scale and ambition to her personal memories and reflections (p. 97). Her text in general is exquisitely literary in its inclinations, offering tribute at various points to John Donne, William Blake, Samuel Taylor Coleridge, and Henrik Ibsen, as well as Homer and Keats. These male authors become experts in describing female experience and offer a way to find an alternative to the superciliousness of androcentric discourses such as science and psychoanalysis.

In an early critique of the phenomenon now known as 'mansplaining', Milner condemns scientific discourse as a marker of male privilege: 'In listening to the man and woman in the street discussing world affairs, particularly the man, I noticed how often he would lay down the law about problems the facts of which he could not possibly know. And I thought that much of so-called science did the same.' Using a textbook she remembers from school to illustrate her point, Milner faults scientific discourse for lacking negative capability. The confusion she felt in reading the unidentified textbook was obviated once she grasped that the science of the matter actually wasn't clear and that the textbook had been trying to cover that up rhetorically: 'if only the book had frankly said that here our knowledge of the facts was inadequate, what a lot of worry it would have saved me', she observes. 'Real science', she says, identifying Blake as a practitioner of such, 'must also be ready to forego the pleasures that fancied certainty gives' (pp. 104–5). Women, in Milner's account, are by necessity experts in this art: 'many women had potentially the "no identity" that Keats was so aware of, but quite unconsciously, not becoming aware of it and learning to trust its emptiness' (p. 157). Negative capability is thus, for Milner, the solution to a central epistemological problem. In recounting her struggles in mastering psychoanalytic theory, Milner relates that, after some attempts to grasp the unknowable, she began to wonder if it might not be more productive to formulate those failures as their own principle, an epistemological end unto themselves. Negative capability, she suggests, can help us locate a middle ground between ignorance and 'fancied certainty'—it can teach scientific discourses, including psychoanalysis, how to be vulnerable and attune them to 'the everchanging truth of experience' (pp. 106–7). The capability is, in Milner's view, a mark of civilization, of maturity, or what Kant would call Enlightenment.[39]

[39] Immanuel Kant, 'An Answer to the Question: "What Is Enlightenment?"', in *Kant's Political Writings*, ed. Hans Reiss, trans. H. B. Nisbet (Cambridge: Cambridge University Press, 1970), pp. 54–60.

The lesson of Keats, explains Milner, is self-annihilation, which can be attained in 'a single moment of raw lived experience' (pp. 148–9). Milner's chief example of negative capability is her feeling the unity of a large crowd at a bullfight, which was 'one moment of complete blank extinction, a plunge into nothingness' (p. 108).[40] The annihilation stems from inside of oneself and becomes a violent, even horrifying, fantasy. Milner describes an 'alien' burrowing through her body, violently literalizing Keats's 'Penetralium':

> Is this the losing of oneself, the self-forgetfulness that so many hunt after? ... Once I was revolted at the ichneumon fly grub that ate its way through the living caterpillar's body, an alien thing taking its pleasure recklessly. But now I'm glad, glad to be possessed, possessed by something that has no consideration for my good. (p. 24)

Not only must one accept the inconsiderate alien force, she argues, but one must also develop an 'emotional relation' to it: 'To be capable of being in uncertainties, mysteries, doubts ... what did this involve? Certainly it involved a definite emotional relation to the unknown, to the *x* factor; it involved a willingness to face destruction, for the unknown may always contain hidden sources of disaster' (pp. 104–5). Her words 'definite' and 'certainly' are striking here, suggesting a firm commitment to the '*x* factor' even in the absence of any knowledge about it. 'I had learned I must accept the blankness' of negative capability, Milner says, ironically (given Keats's reservations) identifying Coleridge as her model for how to do it (pp. 141–2).

By presenting negative capability as a parasite, Milner subversively aligns the concept with childbearing and, then by extension, women's experience. Hence the usefulness of Keats to her project: she is seeking to theorize life, she says, from a poet's position, because poets have ever been marginalized in hegemonic structures—meaning that they can usefully account for women's experiences (p. 98). Choosing, it seems, to ignore the 'Man of Achievement' aspect of Keats's letter, she sees in negative capability a valorization of blankness and weakness useful to combat women's social and, she thinks, biological predicament: 'Was it possible that the only ultimate safety, the only "eternal life", was to be an emptiness that could revive the power of the strong, and with it fashion some new thing—in fact, to be within the mind what a woman is in childbearing?'[41] It is a complex set of metaphors, leaving Keats as a theorist of an innovative and fertile emptiness modeled on the struggles of motherhood. Keats has much to offer feminism because he is a poet: 'surely he can give us power to live more effectively', she enjoins

[40] For Milner's account of the bullfight, see *Experiment in Leisure*, pp. 82–9.

[41] *LJK*, I: p. 193; Milner, *Experiment in Leisure*, p. 98.

her reader, and can show us how to challenge or even guide 'the armies of organized knowledge' (p. 98).

Although today she is cited less frequently than Freud, Lacan, or Bion, Milner's contribution to psychoanalysis is profound. Her deep engagement with Keats and negative capability models a mode of academic discourse that could and should be transformative to current discussions of negative psychoanalytic capability. Whereas Bionic analysts can tend to treat Keats as a seer for the ages, a teller of timeless truths, Milner presents Keats as part of a politicized counterdiscourse, one with its own long literary history, poised to challenge the exclusions enforced within patriarchal epistemologies. Milner's relation to negative capability, though deeply respectful of Keats's idea, is less confidently admiring than Keats is with Shakespeare and less worshipful than Bion is to Freud and Keats. She recognizes the immensity of Keats's achievement but presents negative capability as a harrowing ordeal to undergo, one that requires discipline and training, but that could understand epistemic violence and the experiences of those marginalized by it. By seeing negative capability as an effect of power/knowledge, instead of as a trait constitutive of genius, she is able to turn Keats's idea against the 'men of Achievement' it was meant to identify. It thus can help us find ways to mitigate, as a matter of retroactive judgment, some of Keats's worship of genius, Lacan's aggressive scientism, and Bion's cultivated mysteriousness, bringing us closer, ultimately if backhandedly, to Freud's hesitant and self-effacing modalities. Keats scholars have seen negative capability as an 'intellectual and aesthetic through-line' of Keats's work, 'part of a cluster of ideas with complex antecedents and successors'.[42] Milner seems poised to act both as forgotten antecedent and next iteration of negative psychoanalytic capability, sitting uneasily beside the Lacanian and Bionic analytic traditions by her willingness to take seriously the challenge that literary thought might present to the psychoanalytic tradition.

[42] Wolfson, *Reading*, p. 18; Li, *Keats and Negative Capability*, p. x.

Chapter Fifteen

Zen and the Art of Negative Capability

Anne C. McCarthy

> Zen has a similar style: contradictoriness, crazy wisdom, based on the fact that things both exist and don't exist at the same time—relative and absolute truths. You don't need to drill a hole in your head in order to get enlightened. You can hold several ideas in your mind that are contradictory without freaking out, Keats's negative capability. Sure, you can reach out to 'fact and reason', as long as it isn't an aggressive insistence, irritability motivating the reaching for fact. That's my opinion.[1]

> What *can't* Negative Capability attach itself to? It turns out: not much.[2]

This essay explores the uses of negative capability and other 'Keatsian' ideas in the discourse of twentieth- and twenty-first-century Buddhist modernism. The term 'Buddhist modernism' indicates, as David McMahan explains, 'a modern hybrid tradition with roots in the European Enlightenment no less than the Buddha's enlightenment, in Romanticism and transcendentalism as much as the Pali canon, and in the clash of Asian cultures and colonial powers as much as in mindfulness and meditation'.[3] Although a longstanding

[1] 'Spontaneous Intelligence: Interview with Allen Ginsberg', *Tricycle Magazine* (Fall 1995), *Tricycle.org*, accessed 19 November 2016, https://tricycle.org/magazine/spontaneous-intelligence/.

[2] Michael Theune, '~~Negative Capability~~ T wang dillo dee', *Jacket 2*, 40 (2010), par. 4, accessed 7 July 2018, http://jacketmagazine.com/40/theune-keats.shtml.

[3] David L. McMahan, *The Making of Buddhist Modernism* (New York: Oxford University Press, 2008), p. 5.

scholarly consensus holds that 'Buddhism' is a textual invention of Western imperialism that reached its height in the nineteenth century and that its canon was, in essence, created by Western scholars who translated and interpreted Asian texts in order to construct an 'authentic' or 'classical' Buddhism, usually in ways that minimized or rejected the experience of Buddhist practitioners in Asia, Buddhist modernism recognizes the 'agency of Asian Buddhists as cocreators of modernist versions of their traditions'.[4] Within this broad context of exchange and hybridity, I am specifically interested in the way that the 'Romantic' concept of negative capability functions in cross-cultural discussions of Zen principles, enabling the multi-directional dynamic of 'surprising recognition', a term I borrow from Eve Kosofsky Sedgwick. The resonance between negative capability and Buddhist ideas such as emptiness and the dropping away of self makes sense on a kind of affective level, '[a]s if'—Sedgwick suggests—'the template of truth is already there inside the listener, its own lineaments clarified by the encounter with a teaching that it can then apprehend as "true"'.[5] When Allen Ginsberg glosses negative capability as the ability to 'hold several ideas in your mind that are contradictory without freaking out', he not only offers an entertaining Beat Movement redefinition of Keats's concept, he also uses Keats's phrase as the hinge between Beat practice and the 'crazy wisdom' of the Zen master. He gestures implicitly to the historical development of Buddhist modernism, which among many Westerners 'came to be interpreted largely in language derived from Romanticism'.[6] It is possible, of course, to debate the efficacy and even the legitimacy of this associational chain—each term could be both defended and critiqued. Yet the fact that this association exists at all testifies, in my mind, to broader processes of recognition that operate on conceptual and practical levels.[7]

[4] McMahan, *Buddhist Modernism*, p. 21. See Philip C. Almond, *The British Discovery of Buddhism* (Cambridge: Cambridge University Press, 1988), for a canonical account of the Western invention of Buddhism. For an overview of the specific cultural exchange between British Romanticism and Buddhism, see Mark Lussier, 'Colonial Counterflow: From Orientalism to Buddhism', in *Interrogating Colonialism: Contextual Approaches and Pedagogical Practices*, ed. Diane Long Hoeveler and Jeffrey Cass (Columbus: The Ohio State University Press, 2006), pp. 90–106. For a more recent consideration of the roles of genre and literary form in the creation of the Buddhist canon by both Western and Eastern authors, see Sebastian Lecourt, 'Idylls of the Buddh': Buddhist Modernism and Victorian Poetics in Colonial Ceylon', *PMLA*, 131: 3 (May 2016), pp. 668–85.

[5] Eve Kosofsky Sedgwick, *Touching Feeling: Affect, Pedagogy, Performativity* (Durham, NC, and London: Duke University Press, 2003), p. 165.

[6] McMahan, *Buddhist Modernism*, p. 119.

[7] See also McMahan, who argues that, 'The way a tradition is reconfigured in a new cultural context has much to do with what seems attractive, repulsive, or anomalous about it from the perspective of the tacit understandings and social practices of the dominant

Stephen Batchelor, one of the most prominent figures in Buddhist modernism and an advocate for a secularized, philosophically oriented Buddhism, draws extensively on Romantic concepts in his published work and dharma talks. In the preface to his *Verses from the Center: A Buddhist Vision of the Sublime*, Batchelor juxtaposes Buddhist descriptions of emptiness with extracts from Keats's letters about the chameleon poet and negative capability. The way Batchelor tells it, what Keats identifies as 'when a man is capable of being in uncertainties, mysteries, doubts, without any irritable reaching after fact and reason' is a more or less exact description of 'a Ch'an/Zen practice in which the meditator settles into a state of perplexity' that gives rise to questions that can be addressed only through 'a living, on-going *response*, which, traditionally, is often expressed as spontaneous verse, song and poetry. Transposed to a Buddhist context', Batchelor concludes, '"negative capability" succinctly captures the tension between the *negative* quality of emptiness which allows the *capability* of creative and empathetic responsiveness.'[8] In many ways, this is a remarkably straightforward reading of the 'tension' in the term; it would not be out of place in more traditional literary discussions. What interests me, however, is Batchelor's insistence on what we might characterize as the 'Zen of' negative capability and, more broadly, his use of Romantic literature to absorb and 'transpose' the religiosity of the Buddhist tradition. The hybrid concept of the 'Buddhist sublime' that responds to the 'tragic excess of human life' and its contingency (p. 48) thus weaves together accounts of emptiness from Buddhist writers in many different traditions (Dogen, Shantideva, Hui-Neng, and others) with a concept of sublimity that comes from Keats and Coleridge.

Batchelor's claims are fundamentally aesthetic, rather than historical or philosophical. They are rooted in a practice of poetry that seeks, as Keats puts it in the 'Ode on a Grecian Urn', to 'tease us out of thought' (*PJK*, p. 373; line 44). Aesthetic recognition obviates certain questions of historical influence and 'authenticity': Ginsberg and Batchelor do not invoke negative capability in order to 'prove' that Keats experienced Buddhist-style enlightenment or to show that such enlightenment may be achieved by reading his works or attempting to imitate his mental practices. However, over the past several decades, attempts have been made to articulate both historical and conceptual connections between Romanticism and Buddhism in general

tradition—that is, what *resonates*. … [T]he way a new cultural form succeeds or fails depends not only on its explicit theoretical formulations but also on a rather inarticulate *feeling* of whether it can make intuitive sense in terms of a culture's pretheoretical understandings and social practices' (p. 15).

8 Stephen Batchelor, *Verses from the Center: A Buddhist Vision of the Sublime* (New York: Riverhead Books, 2000), pp. 45–6.

and Keats and Zen in particular.[9] Among the many modernizations undertaken after the Meiji Restoration in 1868 was the translation of English and American literature into Japanese. The Romantic poets in particular (Wordsworth, Coleridge, Byron, Percy Shelley, Keats, and Walter Scott) were introduced to Japanese readers through Naotaro Nakamura's translations of Samuel Smiles' *Self-Help*, which was highly influential on Meiji-era culture.[10] The poetry of Keats came to the attention of Japanese writers and intellectuals in the 1890s and was influential on the 'Japanese Romanticism' of the period. The first major study of Keats by a Japanese scholar was Kiyoshi Sato's *The Art of Keats*, published in 1924 (Okada, pp. 80–4). Richard P. Benton argued in 1966 that Keats, based on the evidence of his poems and letters, 'achieved a genuine loss of self-identity and reached the ideal Zen state of being'.[11] In a similar vein, Satya S. Pachori sets out to 'demystify certain complex overtones in Keats's poetry, by suggesting a close relationship between Zen Buddhism and his works', attending specifically to 'the poet's state of mind while composing' the 'Ode to Autumn'.[12] Yet, these scholarly efforts that seek to understand Keats in Zen terms and, more limitedly, to understand Zen in Keatsian terms, lose in negative capability what they gain in scholarly rigor.

Recognition, however, offers a form of negatively capable historiography that operates continuously, outside of linear time, and enables the strategic juxtaposition of concepts across periods and cultures. Such movements are likely to be eccentric and unpredictable—even, perhaps, somewhat promiscuous—in their trajectories, which in turn may not be registered by traditional histories or comparative analysis. The Indian poet and scholar K. Ayyappa Paniker, for example, places Keats in a more or less equitable conversation with Nagarjuna, stating that,

[9] The most sustained recent literary critical effort to explore these connections is Mark S. Lussier's *Romantic Dharma: The Emergence of Buddhism into Nineteenth-Century Europe* (Basingstoke: Palgrave Macmillan, 2011). See also John G. Rudy, *Romanticism and Zen Buddhism* (Lewiston, NY: Edwin Mellen Press, 2004).

[10] Akiko Okada, *Keats and English Romanticism in Japan* (Bern: Peter Lang, 2006), pp. 26–7. See also Yoshikazu Suzuki, '"A candle that must melt away": Early Keats Scholarship in Japan', in *English Romanticism in East Asia*, ed. Suh-Reen Han, *Romantic Circles PRAXIS* (December 2016), accessed 9 July 2018, http://www.rc.umd.edu/praxis/eastasia/praxis.2016.eastasia.suzuki.html.

[11] Richard P. Benton, 'Keats and Zen', *Philosophy East and West*, 16: 1/2 (January–April 1966), p. 34. Stephen H. Ruppenthal offers a significant critique of Benton's view, concluding that 'Keats anticipates the Zen spirit to a remarkable degree; but in terms of the Zen tradition itself, Keats would not have been considered fully enlightened'. 'Keats and Zen Enlightenment', *Studia Mystica*, 1: 2 (1978), p. 73.

[12] Satya S. Pachori, 'John Keats and Zen Buddhism: An Eastern Perspective', *South Asian Review*, 20: 17 (December 1996), pp. 12–13.

> While there is nothing in particular binding Keats to Buddhist monastic practice, there seems to be a subliminal connection between Nagarjuna's concept of emptiness and Keats's idea of negative capability. In both there is a rejection of the irritable reaching after facts; in both there is a suspension of the logical/rational faculties.[13]

The 'subliminal connection' suspends the question of historically verifiable influence as well as the need to speculate about the specific nature of Keats's spiritual life; by opening a connection whose terms remain unarticulated, Paniker creates a space for the operations of recognition. As an invitation to a kind of comparativist practice, these sites of recognition allow glimpses of what Wordsworth called the 'something far more deeply interfused'[14] in 'Lines written a few Miles above Tintern Abbey': not a transcendent orientation, independent of experience, but an immanent substrate that expresses itself according to local conditions, remaining irreducible to any specific manifestation. While it may not result in a version of negative capability recognizable to Romanticist scholars—or, for that matter, a true account of 'Zen'—I believe the method emblematizes a negatively capable reading practice that recognizes the discontinuity of textual circulation as well as the possibility of contingent, non-binary modes of interpretation. Among other things, this kind of reading practice enables us to read in and out of established historical contexts and lineages. In the second part of this essay, I take up the example of Reginald Horace Blyth's *Zen in English Literature and Oriental Classics* as a 'negatively capable' text that pushes beyond traditional comparative frameworks in ways that are not easily classifiable.

Understanding just why this is the case, however, requires some brief historical background. Zen came to the attention of the West somewhat later than many other forms of Buddhism, and was essentially a Japanese export, disseminated through 'the proselytizing activities of Japanese apologists' and by the efforts of 'internationally minded Japanese intellectuals and globe-trotting Zen priests, whose missionary zeal was often second only to their vexed fascination with Western culture'.[15] This 'missionary zeal' on the part of certain Japanese intellectuals meant, at least ostensibly, that they were more in control of their identity and how they were perceived than the practitioners of other forms of Buddhism who came under the rule of the British Empire; at the

[13] K. Ayyappa Paniker, 'Negative Capability and "Emptiness": Keats and Nagarjuna', *New Comparison* 23 (1997), p. 101.

[14] Samuel Taylor Coleridge and William Wordsworth, *Lyrical Ballads: 1798 and 1800*, ed. Michael Gamer and Dahlia Porter (Peterborough: Broadview Press, 2008), p. 145; line 97.

[15] Robert H. Sharf, 'The Zen of Japanese Nationalism', in *Curators of the Buddha: The Study of Buddhism Under Colonialism*, ed. Donald S. Lopez, Jr. (Chicago, IL: University of Chicago Press, 1995), p. 108.

same time, it also distanced them from 'pure' Zen as it was institutionalized in Japan. The most prominent and influential of these cosmopolitan Japanese intellectuals was D. T. Suzuki, the author of dozens of books on Zen and on Buddhism more generally, most of them aimed at a Western, English-speaking audience. Suzuki has been credited with popularizing and disseminating what McMahan calls 'a hybridized Buddhist-Romantic concept of creativity and spontaneity'—the 'crazy wisdom' of the Zen master taken up by the Beat poets among others—that was not exactly a pure reflection of Zen tradition in Japan (p. 123). At the same time, many of his books presented the thesis that, while Zen was at least theoretically available to all serious practitioners, the Japanese people and Japanese culture held a privileged position in the tradition, even though Zen did not originate in Japan and was not practiced by all Japanese people. Suzuki's critics point out that, despite his stature as the preeminent representative of Japanese Zen in the United States and Europe, he and many of those other 'Japanese apologists' were very much on the fringe of the Japanese Zen establishment—if not also Japanese culture in general. They tended to be lay practitioners, rather than monastics, and the elements of the Zen tradition that they emphasized may or may not have reflected more traditional teachings.[16]

Yet, one of the reasons why Suzuki's version of Zen was so influential in the West both before and after the Second World War is that it appeared to arrive already conversant with Western intellectual and literary history. As McMahan argues, Suzuki

> was placing elements of Zen literature on a scaffolding constructed of a variety of western philosophical ideas in order to translate selected Zen ideas into that discourse. Sensing affinities between Zen and the Romantic-Transcendentalist vein of western metaphysics, Suzuki deployed its terminology to frame the issue of humanity and nature, allowing Zen to claim the broad outlines of the metaphysic and then presenting Zen themes to bring it to what he considered its fullest expression. (p. 125)

For instance, in his early work *Zen Buddhism and Its Influence on Japanese Culture* (later revised under the title *Zen and Japanese Culture*), Suzuki adopts

[16] Bernard Faure, for instance, in *Chan Insights and Oversights: An Epistemological Critique of the Chan Tradition* (Princeton, NJ: Princeton University Press, 1993), observes that 'in contrast to most Japanese native thinkers, Suzuki was relatively isolated from his own people. He left Japan and went to live in the United States, and the subsequent evolution of his thought reflects his confrontation with Western values (intellectualism) or trends of thought (Christianity, psychoanalysis, existentialism, antinomianism of the 1960s). After returning to Japan with his American wife, he earned his livelihood as an English teacher and remains on the fringes of the academic world' (p. 65).

a deliberately comparativist approach that reflects the intellectual climate of pre-World War II Japan: 'If the Greeks taught us how to reason and Christianity what to believe, it is Zen that teaches us to go beyond logic and not to tarry even when we come up against "the things which are not seen"'.[17] Although Suzuki does not invoke the concept of negative capability directly in *Zen Buddhism and its Influence on Japanese Culture*, it is possible to perceive some significant echoes even in this relatively early work, such as when he discusses *mushin*, or 'no-mindedness'. At once immobile and active, 'unconsciously conscious'—this 'appalling paradox' is the groundless ground from which both the aesthetic and spiritual practices of Zen emerge (p. 73). Here we discover echoes of the Keatsian chameleon poet, the Shakespearean artist able to suspend his entire personality and go beyond the dualism of self and other. *Mushin* or no-mindedness cannot be deliberately sought: to grasp at emptiness is still to pursue a goal, to engage in fixation and to expect that reality be something other than what it is.

Influence by recognition takes eccentric and contingent pathways. As Li Ou has observed, 'The connection of negative capability with a sober, unflinching look at the world as it is, instead of tailor-making it to one's own need, is only implied when the phrase itself is enunciated.'[18] Part of the 'ripening' of Keats's concept that Li traces in her monograph involves the role of imagination in maintaining an actively open relation to a reality that is itself contingent and sometimes paradoxical. This is one of the central ideas in Reginald Horace Blyth's *Zen in English Literature and Oriental Classics*. Published by The Hokuseido Press in Tokyo in 1942, *Zen in English Literature* is a strange, capacious book that reflects the varied cultural experience and literary investments of its author. A friend and student of Suzuki's, Blyth was born in Essex in 1898. He went to prison as a conscientious objector during World War I and took an English degree at University College London in 1923. At the urging of a Japanese classmate, he accepted a teaching position at the Japanese Imperial University in Seoul in 1924, where he began to gain an appreciation for Japanese culture and also to practice Zen. He moved to Tokyo around 1939 and was arrested and eventually interned at the end of 1941, just before the publication of *Zen in English Literature*. After the war, Blyth returned to the teaching of literature and published two multi-volume works of literary criticism and a number of editions and textbooks for Japanese students before his death in 1964.[19]

[17] Daisetz Teitaro Suzuki, *Buddhism and its Influence on Japanese Culture* (Kyoto: Eastern Buddhist Society, 1938), p. 235.

[18] Li Ou, *Keats and Negative Capability* (London: Bloomsbury, 2009), p. 4.

[19] Beyond his literary efforts, Blyth played a small but significant role as a liaison between the Japanese court and the Allied occupation forces in the aftermath of World War II. See John W. Dower, *Embracing Defeat: Japan in the Wake of World War II* (London: Allen Lane, 1999), pp. 310–13.

His four-volume work on haiku was read with enthusiasm by Gary Snyder, Allen Ginsberg, and Richard Wright.[20]

Blyth's works have been described as 'a bridge between Eastern and Western culture, enabling each to understand the spirituality of the other'.[21] But it is, at best, an idiosyncratic undertaking. Blyth had been committed since he was a young man to 'Matthew Arnold's ideal of developing one's self to the fullest, to be one's own best linguist, musician, artist, and scholar'.[22] He takes seriously Arnold's notion that criticism should draw attention to 'the best that has been known and thought', and he envisions this 'best' on a global scale, with a cross-cultural outlook that embraces not only English literature but significant parts of other European canons. The opening paragraph of the preface declares Zen both the 'most precious possession of Asia' and 'the strongest power in the world … . [F]or in so far as men *live* at all, they live by Zen. Wherever there is a poetical action, a religious aspiration, a heroic thought, a union of the nature within a man and the Nature without, there is Zen.'[23] Like many Japanese scholars of the Meiji era (and after), Blyth is passionately attached to the poetry of William Wordsworth—at least to the early poems.[24] William

[20] Historian Rick Fields relates the following anecdote about Beat activities, circa 1955: 'Kerouac, Ginsberg, Snyder and Philip Whalen, a poet who had been with Snyder at Reed, spent a lot of time … "having dinner together, or just sort of hanging around together there in the yard and writing and talking and drinking wine and having a good time", Whalen remembers. Everybody was reading R. H. Blyth's four-volume collection of haikus, and trading back and forth modern American versions of their own' (*How the Swans Came to the Lake: A Narrative History of Buddhism in America* (Boulder, CO: Shambhala, 1981), p. 214). For Blyth's influence on Wright and J. D. Salinger, see Adrian Pinnington, 'R.H. Blyth, 1898–1964', in *Britain & Japan: Biographical Portraits*, ed. Ian Nish, vol. 1 (Folkestone: Japan Library, 1994), pp. 266–7. Pinnington's essay remains one of the best sources of biographical information on Blyth that exists in English, though it is not widely available.

[21] Imamura Kyoko, 'The Integration of Eastern and Western Spirituality in Blyth's *Zen in English Literature and Oriental Classics*', in *The Force of Vision: Proceedings of the XIIIth Congress of the International Comparative Literature Association* (Tokyo: University of Tokyo Press, 1995), p. 151.

[22] Robert Aitken, 'Remembering Blyth Sensei', *Original Dwelling Place: Zen Buddhist Essays* (Upland, CA: Counterpoint, 1996), p, 26.

[23] Reginald Horace Blyth, *Zen in English Literature and Oriental Classics* (Tokyo: Hokuseido Press, 1942), p. vii.

[24] 'Among the Romantic poets', according to Okada, 'Wordsworth was the first to be popular, as his nature poetry was perceived to be congenial to the Japanese mind. He was imitated in many Japanese poems, and his principle of poetry was transferred to that of Japanese poetry. The passionate love of Wordsworth up to around 1900 was called "Wordsworth fever", which was replaced by the admiration of Byron and Shelley in the democratic atmosphere of the Taisho Democracy Era (c. 1905–25)'. She goes on to note that both Wordsworth and Keats remain popular with twenty-first century scholars of English literature in Japan (pp. 16–17).

Shakespeare, Charles Dickens, and Robert Louis Stevenson form the rest of his canon of Zen expression in English literature; Wordsworth and Shakespeare are the topics of individual chapters, as is *Don Quixote*. The seventeenth-century haiku poet Bashô is, for Blyth, the greatest of all (p. viii).[25] Haiku is the apotheosis of Zen expression—it is direct experience, unmediated by many of the trappings considered 'poetic' in Western literature. When he quotes from English poetry—which he does often—Blyth tends to look at only a handful of lines at a time, identifying glimmers of Zen insight without much regard for the work as a whole.[26]

Although one scholar cites *Zen in English Literature* as the first (and one of the only) scholarly efforts to 'probe Keats's conscious or unconscious leanings toward Zen Buddhism',[27] Blyth's attitude towards Keats is decidedly mixed. What he characterizes as 'the Way of Poetry for Keats' seems always to be 'in great danger of forgetting the real world'. The third stanza from 'Ode to a Nightingale' is characterized as 'bad poetry and bad religion', for such thinking can lead only back to the self (pp. 30–1). A similar equivocation shapes Blyth's view that

> The poems of Keats are solid blocks of poetry, those of Shelley poetical prisms and crystals, *at* which we gaze with delight, but those of Bashô and Wordsworth are windows *through* which we look with a feeling beyond joy or bliss, at the real world which we tread on, which we eat and excrete, breathe and grasp in our hands. (p. 385)

[25] By contrast, Blyth has no patience for Coleridge, whom he relegates to a 'black list, partly for insincere imitation of Wordsworth, partly for his own native lack of religion and poetry' (p. 228). Blyth finally abandons this discussion with an expression of disgust: 'Coleridge is so sickening, in poetry so vulgar, in religion so sanctimonious, that I cannot bear to give any more extracts; read also *Frost at Midnight* which is Wordsworth minus poetry' (p. 229). He is somewhat more circumspect about Coleridge later on; while he still characterizes his work as 'theological claptrap and nauseating religiosity', he elsewhere concedes, if cryptically, that 'A good haiku poet was lost in Samuel Taylor Coleridge'. Reginald Horace Blyth, *A Survey of English Literature from the Beginnings to Modern Times* (Tokyo: Hokuseido Press, 1957), pp. 244, 287.

[26] Blyth continues this work of making haiku from longer verse in a deliberate way in the first volume of his *Haiku* (Tokyo: Hokuseido Press, 1949). A section called 'Haiku in English Literature' consists of three-line extracts from a range of writers. Although these excerpts are chosen 'to approximate … a haiku form', Blyth cautions his readers that 'It does not follow that these, if translated into Japanese verse, would all be acceptable by the standards of haiku; much would be omitted as redundant and unnecessary, as too intellectual or abstract' (*Haiku*, I: p. 298). The extracts are given without attribution (which is saved for an appendix) and arranged according to the seasons. The result is something like an assemblage or found poem that brings together lines both familiar and obscure in unexpected ways.

[27] Pachori, 'John Keats and Zen Buddhism', p. 13.

It is the latter type of poetry that, because of its directness, seems to Blyth to be more aligned with Zen: it provides access to reality without itself being mistaken for that reality.[28]

Nevertheless, Blyth, like others before him, finds a koan-like potential in Keats's famous pronouncement that 'Beauty is truth, truth beauty' (line 49) at the end of 'Ode on a Grecian Urn':

> Taken unpoetically, unreligiously, the line is a manifest falsehood. What Keats meant was that the further into beauty we go, the more we make it our own, the more life is immersed in beauty, the nearer we are to reality. ... When therefore we say that religion is poetry and poetry is religion, we mean that it is so whether we realise it or not, and that from the beginning, these two being one, our distinction of Reality into Religion and Beauty is both baseless in fact and destructive to both. (p. 31)

As this comment suggests, Blyth understands reality as a complex unity, one that is fundamentally paradoxical; in turn, this structures his declaration that poetry and religion are 'one thing with two names' (p. ix). 'Truth', he writes, 'is expressible only in the form of a paradox. What is not paradoxical, is not true; is not *living, inexpressible truth*' (p. 195). Although Blyth does not explicitly invoke the phrase, it seems clear that entering fully into this inexpressible reality would require something like negative capability, whether cultivated by Zen meditation (as Batchelor suggests) or through more literary means.

Yet, if Blyth remains largely ambivalent about Keats's poetry (at least insofar as it expresses the life of Zen), *Zen in English Literature* is pervaded by what might be described as Keatsian thought or a Keatsian orientation. For instance, after quoting a lengthy extract from Dickens' *Oliver Twist*, Blyth characterizes the Artful Dodger as '"the chameleon poet that shocks the virtuous philosophers" on the bench'. He continues,

> Notice how what seems to be at first mere impudence, rises with influx of energy, into an identification of himself with the whole machinery of the Law. He attains, for [the] moment, to 'Buddhahood, in which all the contradictions and disturbances caused by the intellect are entirely harmonised in a unity of higher order'. (p. 5)

This passage demonstrates much about the 'crazy wisdom' of Blyth's methodology. He reverses the positions of poet and the philosopher from Keats's

[28] 'It is of the essence of poetry', Blyth writes in the preface, 'that it points to Something, just as (to use a favourite Buddhist simile,) the finger points to the moon. This something, though instantly recognised, is not to be defined' (pp. viii–ix).

original letter, which had declared that 'What shocks the virtuous philosop[h]er, delights the camelion Poet' (*LJK*, I: p. 386). This adaptation suggests, at the very least, that Blyth was quoting the letter from memory, but it also transforms the poet from the man able to appreciate what shocks others (as he had been for Keats), to one whose existence—like that of the Zen master—is in itself shocking. Thus Blyth connects the shocking existence of the 'chameleon poet' to the condition of Buddhahood itself. A footnote on the same page identifies the second quoted phrase as 'Prof. Suzuki's definition of Zen'. Keats remains a doubly unnamed presence in this scene of cross-cultural, syncretic reading, an absent presence—itself chameleon-like—that enables the joining of Dickens and Suzuki in a 'unity of higher order'.

The absent presence of Keats is also felt throughout *Zen in English Literature*'s chapter on Shakespeare. Blyth praises the Bard's 'absence of self, of prejudice, of moral judgements' and goes on to argue that 'this state of Zen, this God-like condition of mind does not imply absence of attraction and repulsion either in Shakespeare or the reader. It only implies lack of condemnation, lack of the apportioning of praise and blame. Good is good and bad is bad, but both are necessary—the acceptance of this is the secret of Zen, the secret of Shakespeare' (p. 427). And, we might add, is the secret of Keats and of negative capability, understood in this context as the ability to operate without recourse to a language of separation that distinguishes the self from the other—through moralizing or other means—but also without obliterating those divisions. In a later work, Blyth makes a similar negatively capable claim about Shakespeare, remarking that, 'When Shakespeare wrote *Hamlet*, he became Hamlet. This is true, but at the same time he remained Shakespeare, for without this paradoxical condition, no drama, no poetry, no *Hamlet*, is possible.'[29] In his *Survey of English Literature from the Beginnings to Modern Times*, a book that is largely aimed at Japanese students, Blyth makes the connection between Shakespeare and Keats explicit:

> It is characteristic of John Keats, 1795–1821, that we are unable to divide his poetry into classes or types. Like Shakespeare he has a wholeness, even a ripeness, in his character and his works. Besides this all-roundedness, Keats has truthfulness and sensibility. By 'truthfulness' is meant not the outward but the inward honesty. Shelley, Byron, and Wordsworth were undoubtedly more or less truthful people, but they constantly deceived themselves as to their real state of mind and motives. With Keats it is different. We feel him to be like Shakespeare again, knowing himself and knowing human nature. (pp. 295–6)

[29] Reginald Horace Blyth, *Zen and Zen Classics*, vol. 7 (Tokyo: Hokuseido Press, 1962), p. 130.

Granted, these are far from original literary-critical pronouncements, even by the standards of criticism in the 1940s and 1950s. However, the values that Blyth communicates to his largely Japanese audience—'all-roundedness', 'truthfulness', and 'sensibility'—enable another form of cross-cultural recognition. In *Zen in English Literature* Keats provides the implicit groundwork to connect Shakespeare to the principles of Zen; in *A Survey of English Literature* it is Zen itself (or, at least, Blyth's hybrid, modernist version of it) that activates the work of recognition while remaining unarticulated. Indeed, although the *Survey* is more rigorously divided by period than the earlier texts, Blyth makes use of charts and timelines that juxtapose the developments of Western and Asian literatures, producing the appearance of universality and privileging spontaneous conceptual resonance—something like Sedgwick's 'surprising recognition'—over other forms of historical and ideological influence. There are obvious dangers and blind spots in such an approach, but nothing I've read of Blyth's work or about the man himself suggests that he was using literature to escape from the history that he himself was living; rather, this seems to me to be a genuine attempt to suspend the operations of temporal logic and offer an alternative account of the circulation of 'Zen' thought that arises outside of traditional or historical lineages.

Ultimately, *Zen in English Literature* is not a conventionally rigorous work of Buddhist modernism or of literary criticism. It 'works' only to the extent that it elicits from its audience a kind of negatively capable reading practice that understands, even inchoately, that these words do not contain the sum total of a paradoxical reality. Blyth writes:

> The paradox is itself an example of what it teaches. The meaning escapes the words. Very well then, instead of further and further explanations, floundering farther and farther from Real[i]ty, let us scorn truth, turn our backs on logic, defy consistency,—and behold, the intangible is grasped, the unsayable is said. (p. 183)

To the extent that the text offers a preliminary training in either Zen or 'literary' reading, it does so by cultivating the 'no-mindedness' of Suzuki and the capability to let go of explanations and phrases when they no longer serve their purpose.

At the same time, *Zen in English Literature* remains at the center of Blyth's most lasting legacy: his friendship with Robert Aitken, one of the earliest Americans to be ordained in the Zen tradition. Aitken, like Blyth himself, was interned by the Japanese during World War II. A guard in the camp lent him a copy of *Zen in English Literature.* The two men met in person when various camps were combined in May 1944, and they remained close for the next two decades. In an essay written several decades after Blyth's death, Aitken characterizes *Zen in English Literature* as 'my "first book", the way *Walden* was the "first book" for some of my friends, the way *The Kingdom of God Is Within You* was the "first book" for Gandhi' (pp. 23–4)—perhaps what Chapman's Homer was for Keats. But the first book, while an essential starting point, can never become a resting place. Reflecting on that early encounter at the distance of several decades, Aitken comments, 'Now when I look at it, even the type looks different, far smaller in size, and the references to Zen seem less profound. But it set my life on the course I still maintain, and I trace my orientation to culture—to literature, rhetoric, art, and music—to that single book' (p. 24). *Zen in English Literature* illuminates the slippage between the idea of Zen as a culturally and historically situated set of spiritual practices and Zen as an untethered, universally available emanation of 'the active principle of life itself' (p. 2) that continues to operate, if somewhat more subtly, in Western Buddhist discourse. Batchelor's use of romantic metaphors to describe Zen meditation to Western readers or Ginsberg's ecstatic evocations of negative capability and *satori* have the ability to seem at once profoundly apt and utterly specious, even a little bit flaky. But, as Blyth remarks, 'in some ways language is wiser than the men who use it; ... often we say more than we mean, especially the poets; ... we speak more truly than we know' (p. 166). All these contentions, all these orientations and resonances, are informed directly and indirectly by an eccentric, nonlinear history. This history focuses less on the primacy of ideas than on the interchanges of recognition that, while culturally and historically situated, are not reducible to those situations—call it poetry, Zen, maybe even their différance. In view of what Blyth describes as the 'continual, continuous dilemma which we call human life', a reality that demands that we 'see the invisible, do the impossible, love the unlovable, swim on the dry land and walk on the water' (p. 184), negative capability becomes more than an aesthetic practice of 'being in uncertainties'. The moment of recognition—the moment at which someone or something becomes what they are, what they already were is also—paradoxically—the realization of negative capability.

CHAPTER SIXTEEN

Negative Capability in Dialogic Context

Walter L. Reed

> There is neither a first nor a last word and there are no limits to the dialogic context (it extends into the boundless past and the boundless future). Even *past* meanings, that is, those born in the dialogue of past centuries, can never be stable (finalized, ended once and for all)—they will always change (be renewed) in the process of subsequent, future development of the dialogue.[1]

Such is a claim made by the Russian thinker Mikhail Bakhtin in his last published essay. Its wide sweep can, of course, be applied, in theory, to any text or, in Bakhtin's preferred term, utterance of human communication. But it seems especially applicable to Keats's famous phrase 'negative capability' and to the remarkable afterlife of the formulation that suddenly came to him, 'dovetailed in [his] mind', as he reported to his brothers George and Tom, in late December of 1817 (*LJK*, I: p. 193).

There is a striking variety of meaning in the 'dialogic context' within which Keats's original phrase has taken on meaning, new and old, since then. A recent and cursory Google search shows over 800,000 'results'—references, definitions, allusions, elaborations, appropriations, even coincidental juxtapositions of the two words—as the invocation of Keats's richly paradoxical and teasingly ambiguous phrase negative capability has in recent decades gone well beyond the context of literary history. It reaches into psychoanalysis (Jungian as well as Freudian), organizational leadership studies, and the proliferating

[1] Mikhail Bakhtin, 'Toward a Methodology for the Human Sciences', in *Speech Genres and Other Late Essays*, trans. Vern W. McGee, ed. Caryl Emerson and Michael Holquist (Austin: University of Texas Press, 1986), p. 170.

mediations of new media and popular culture. Following Bakhtin's example, however, I intend to concentrate on a dialogic context within literary history. For all of his wide learning and extra-literary interest in 'speech genres' of all sorts and conditions, 'aesthetic activity', as he called it early in his career, lies at the heart of Bakhtin's thought.

Most often, Romantic and Romanticist, even Modern and Modernist, analysis and interpretation consider Keats's phrase and concept in terms of origin and influence, terms based on the idea of a singular personal expression. What did Keats himself mean? By whom was he most influenced? Whose earlier meaning is being faithfully rehearsed or divergently reformulated? And later, after the fact, whom has Keats most influenced with the formulation 'negative capability' and how faithful to his original meaning are these later invocations? Bakhtin's concept of a dialogic context, in contrast, shifts our attention from a single meaning determined or governed by the expressive intention of one person to a radically plural meaning, not only interpersonal, between or among persons, but intra-personal, within a person or a person's speech, as well. Keats is not only in dialogue with others but with the voices of others in himself as he anticipates their responses. Bakhtin conceives of meaning not as belonging to one person but as belonging to more than one.[2] Thus the meaning of negative capability is not controlled by Keats himself, nor by Hunt or Hazlitt or even Coleridge (possibly mediated by Benjamin Bailey), but exists within a dynamically shifting community of authors, in direct and indirect communication with one another, in disagreement as well as agreement, an ad hoc assemblage collectively articulating a paradox in the psychology of artistic creativity, creativity registered in the contemplative reception of readers and listeners as well as in the productive expression of an author of a work of literature. We are asked to think in terms of an expanding proliferation of contested meaning rather than a straight line of discrete semantic succession.

Thus a reframing of the discussion as it has taken place among Romanticists about the essential meaning of negative capability for Keats and other Romantic writers he knew or read—the reframing in terms of Bakhtin's capacious conception of 'dialogic context' I am proposing here—describes an unfinished, open-ended collaboration, a disquisition which is in fact a set of ongoing disputes. As I said, Bakhtin conceives of dialogism as intra-textual as well as inter-textual. In the same late essay from which my opening quotation is taken, he writes, 'I hear *voices* in all things. … Contextual meaning is personalistic: it always includes a question, an address, and the anticipation of

[2] A fuller account of this distinctive theory of language and communication is given by Michael Holquist in 'Answering as Authoring; Mikhail Bakhtin's Trans-Linguistics', *Critical Inquiry*, 10: 2 (December 1983), pp. 307–19; see especially pp. 311–12.

an answer, it always includes two (as a dialogic minimum)' (pp. 169–70). This personalism is not psychological, he says, but a 'personalism of meaning'.[3] (He devotes six pages of the early essay 'Discourse in Life and Discourse in Art' to analyzing the contextual dialogism of the single exclamation 'Well!')[4]

The dialogic context thus begins within the negative capability letter itself, which registers the contradictory internal dynamics of the phrase as well as its external engagements, the question, address, and anticipation of an answer that inform the simplest, most apparently unitary utterances, according to Bakhtin's theory of language and communication. And it continues in the report of the way this notion came to him by Keats himself in his letter to his brothers George and Tom describing his conversation with his friends Charles Dilke and Charles Brown, the famous letter in which the contradictory phrase 'dovetailed'—joined itself together like two pieces of wood at an angle to one another—in his mind. (It is not entirely clear whether he spoke the phrase aloud to Dilke and Brown or reserved it for written expression to his brothers.) It seems to continue with Keats's own letters on the topic, beforehand to Benjamin Bailey, in which the imagination is compared to Adam's dream, and afterward to Richard Woodhouse, which elaborates on the 'poetical Character' that has no identity of its own (*LJK*, I: p. 386). The dialogic context is given additional personeity (to use a coinage of Coleridge) within this set of letters alone by adducing Milton and Shakespeare, Coleridge and Wordsworth, and Iago and Imogen as instances of negative capability and its opposing character, 'the wordsworthian or egotistical sublime' (*LJK*, I: p. 387). These literary figures, creators and created, enter the conversation with a disproportionate range of possible meaning, potentially the totality of their oeuvres or dramatic roles. Which aspects of these authors, works, and characters does Keats have in mind? A direct external response to the poetical character letter then appears in Woodhouse's rehearsal of Keats's idea of the poetical character and of Shakespeare's enormous claim to possess this quality, quite a detailed and literal paraphrase offered by Woodhouse in a letter to John Taylor, apparently written that same day. In a claim often voiced by later critics, Woodhouse ventures that Keats himself possesses this distinctive 'power', as he puts it in a less overtly dialogic way, to an extraordinary degree (*LJK*, I: p. 390).

[3] I opt for the translation of this last phrase from Ann Shukman, 'M. M. Bakhtin: Notes on his Philosophy of Man', in *Poetry, Prose, and Public Opinion: Essays Presented in Memory of Dr. N. E. Andreyev* (Letchworth: Avebury Publishing, 1984), p. 247, which I prefer to McGee's less resonant 'semantic personalism'.

[4] Mikhail Bakhtin and V. N. Voloshinov, 'Constructing a Sociological Poetics', in *The Bakhtin Reader*, ed. Pam Morris (London: Arnold, 1994), pp. 165–9. The dialogic character of Bakhtin's own writings in the late 1920s, with authorship either shared with or credited to V. N. Voloshinov and others, has been a topic of lively debate in Bakhtin scholarship.

After that, since there is no record of a specific reply by the Keats brothers nor any evidence that other literary figures (with the possible exception of Woodhouse) knew of Keats's specific phrase, 'negative capability' finds itself sharing semantic space, directly or obliquely, with earlier formulations of similar notions by Romantic poets and critics such as Hunt, Hazlitt, and Coleridge, perhaps even De Quincey, some but certainly not all of whom it is clear Keats himself read or conversed with before and after he coined his paradoxical term.[5] The dialogic context expands still further when, in the broad and distanced hindsight of our own time, we perceive family resemblances between negative capability and descriptions of art and aesthetic experience put forward by German philosophers such as Kant and Schelling, whom Keats would have known only generally through the writings of Coleridge, or with artistic manifestos even further afield, such as those of Goethe and Flaubert.[6] I confess to having myself gone as far as to appropriate the phrase negative capability, along with its Keatsian opposite, the 'egotistical sublime', to describe in a larger Bakhtinian 'architectonics' those Romantic literary texts in which a self-effacing author creates and reflects upon a heroic character larger than him- or herself—or vice versa.[7] This last example may be judged a bridge too far by more empirically minded critics, but the principle of a potentially ever-expanding dialogic context within and around negative capability still stands. What Keats or Hunt or Hazlitt really meant is not the final word.

It may be helpful here to say something more about the place of Coleridge in this growing cloud of witnesses, Romantic and Romanticist. Where the influence of Hazlitt has been widely agreed upon and described in detail and the influence of Hunt has been more recently and persuasively asserted, the idea of the influence of Coleridge in general and the *Biographia Literaria*, published some six months before Keats's negative capability letter, more particularly is less well recognized. This is partly due, no doubt, to Keats's identifying Coleridge as a prime example of the lack of negative capability, 'incapable of

[5] On Leigh Hunt's influence on the phrase, see Nicholas Roe, *John Keats: A New Life* (New Haven, CT: Yale University Press, 2012), pp. 32, 185, 201. The fullest account of William Hazlitt's influence on Keats's concept is in Li Ou's *Keats and Negative Capability* (London: Bloomsbury, 2009), pp. 23–61. For the probable influence of Coleridge, see footnote 9 below.

[6] The comparisons with Kant and Schelling are offered by Frederick Burwick in 'Negative Capability', in *Romanticism: Keywords* (Chichester: Wiley Blackwell, 2015), p. 194. The correlations with Goethe and Flaubert are made by Richard Ellmann and Charles Feidelson, Jr. in *The Modern Tradition: Backgrounds of Modern Literature* (New York: Oxford University Press, 1965), pp. 10, 69–73.

[7] Walter L. Reed, *Romantic Literature in Light of Bakhtin* (New York: Bloomsbury, 2014), pp. 46–64, 148.

remaining in half knowledge', in that same letter. Nevertheless, several Keats and Coleridge scholars have pointed out two quite possible contributions from the *Biographia Literaria*—of a phrase ('negative faith') in chapter 22 and of several pages of discussion, comparing Shakespeare and Milton at the end of chapter 15.[8] The comparison of Shakespeare and Milton is especially interesting for its bearing on a wider dialogic context, beyond the tight focus of traditional literary histories and new historicisms. For Bakhtin, context and meaning are closely related—indeed, for all intents and purposes, inextricable from one another. The meaning of any verbal utterance for him is radically interpersonal and interdependent, the joint product of reception and expression considered together. The dialogic context into which an utterance is cast is not limited to direct influences or literal citations. We need not produce proof positive that Keats did in fact read (or, as likely, hear from friends such as Benjamin Bailey) this particular discussion by Coleridge of the self-effacing personality of the author in the exercise of the poetic imagination or the Proteus-like nature of Shakespeare's creativity in drama, in which he 'passes into all the forms of human character and passion' to admit him to the dialogic table.[9]

What is intriguing about including Coleridge's description of Shakespeare's dramatic imagination (he distinguishes its powerful synthetic resolution of 'the creative power, and the intellectual energy' in the plays from its weaker and more conflicted expression in the narrative poems) is the way he contrasts it with an epic imagination (though without mentioning that genre specifically) of Milton, which 'attracts all forms and things to himself (*Collected Works*, II: p. 26). For Coleridge, both of these poets are co-equal, seated on 'the two glory-smitten summits of the poetic mountain', with Milton as Shakespeare's 'compeer and not rival' (*Collected Works*, II: p. 27). One type of imagination is not superior to the other. Even if Keats arrived at his view of the singular superiority of Shakespeare without being aware of Coleridge's characterization, his deprecation of the inferior 'wordsworthian or egotistical sublime' in the later letter to Woodhouse raises the question of whether his struggle with the influence of Milton on his own poetry (most notably in his *Hyperion*, abandoned and then resumed in the mode of Dante in *The Fall of Hyperion*)

[8] For Keats's probable knowledge of the *Biographia Literaria*, see Jack Stillinger, 'Keats and Coleridge', in *Coleridge, Keats, and the Imagination: Romanticism and Adam's Dream*, ed. Robert Barth and John L. Mahoney (Columbia: University of Missouri Press, 1990), pp. 26–7; Beth Lau, *Keats's Reading of the Romantic Poets* (Ann Arbor: University of Michigan Press, 1991), pp. 72, 79–82, 104–5; and James Engell, '*Biographia Literaria*', in *The Cambridge Companion to Coleridge*, ed. Lucy Newlyn (Cambridge: Cambridge University Press), p. 67.

[9] Samuel Taylor Coleridge, *The Collected Works of Samuel Taylor Coleridge*, ed. James Engell and Walter Jackson Bate, vol. 7, 2 bks., *Biographia Literaria* (Princeton, NJ: Princeton University Press, 1983), II: p. 27.

might have led him to offer the opposition as one between Shakespeare and Keats's own Romantic contemporaries, Coleridge and Wordsworth, instead of Milton, as far as their relative achievement in literature was concerned.

Contributing further to this contextual complex of meaning is Hazlitt's lecture 'On Shakspeare [sic] and Milton', delivered and published in his *Lectures on the English Poets* in 1818 and attended by Keats, perhaps being read afterwards by him as well. Hazlitt's description of Shakespeare as 'the least of an egotist as it was possible to be' and 'nothing in himself' are clearly echoed in the famous phrases 'egotistical sublime' and 'everything and nothing' in Keats's letter to Woodhouse later that same year.[10] On the other hand, Hazlitt's praise of Milton along with Shakespeare and his observation that Milton's relationship to his characters is epic while Shakespeare's is dramatic seem to echo Coleridge's complementary formulation of the contrast, but they find no such reiteration in Keats. 'Negative capability' creates its own dialogic context, one might say; it doesn't simply appear with its meaning firmly established by Keats. What is omitted in the engagement with another's utterance can be as important to a dialogic understanding as what is included.

Pursuing Bakhtin's concept of dialogic context farther afield, however, I would like to explore in the rest of this essay what could be called a postmodern, as distinct from a Romantic or Modernist, framing of the meaning of Keats's phrase. To be sure, the stability and coherence of postmodernism as a movement or period in literary history is even less certain than the stability and coherence of 'Romanticism' or 'Modernism'. Louis Mackey has put it best, perhaps, even as he argues for the continuity of postmodernity with these earlier periods. The heritage of Kant's aesthetic philosophy, he writes,

> is preserved less faithfully in the subsequent history of philosophy than in the literary movement known as Romanticism and its successor, modernism, whence it has come to troubled rest in these latter days in that peculiar mixture of creative excess and creative self-doubt that we, not knowing what it really is, call the 'postmodern'.[11]

One of the masters of such creative excess and creative self-doubt was Jorge Luis Borges, the belated modernist who became for many an early standard-bearer of the postmodern. And among his most creative and skeptical pieces is a story, a brief critical fiction characteristic of his elegant oeuvre, entitled 'Everything and Nothing'. Given in English in the original Spanish

[10] William Hazlitt, *The Complete Works of William Hazlitt*, ed. P. P. Howe, 21 vols. (London: J. M. Dent, 1930), V: p. 47.

[11] Louis Mackey, *An Ancient Quarrel Continued: The Troubled Marriage of Philosophy and Literature* (Lanham, MD: University Press of America, 2002), p. 229.

text when it was published in Argentina, the title evokes directly the elaboration of 'negative capability' in Keats's subsequent discussion of 'the poetical Character ... [which] is not itself—it has no self—it is everything and nothing' (*LJK*, I: pp. 386–7). In this later letter, Shakespeare is again adduced as the non-judgmental poet extraordinaire by means of his characters Iago and Imogen, extremes of evil and goodness in whom the author equally delights. And God himself is mentioned in passing as the maker of this paradoxical being: the true poet has 'no identity—he is certainly the most unpoetical of all God's Creatures' (*LJK*, I: p. 387). Fastening on these incidental details and others, Borges spins an extravagant story of ultimately negative creation.

We are introduced to a non-entity not identified by name: 'There was no one inside him; behind his face (which even in the bad paintings of the time resembles no other) and his words (which were multitudinous, and of a fantastical and agitated turn) there was no more than a slight chill, a dream someone had failed to dream.' We immediately begin to suspect this is the Bard, but the protagonist is presented with a distinct lack of Romantic bardolatry. He goes off to London and becomes an actor—'that person who stands upon a stage and plays at being another person, for an audience of people who play at taking him for that person'. But this relief from 'the hated taste of unreality' only drives him, 'haunted' and 'hounded', to 'imagining other heroes, other tragic fables'. Caesar, Juliet, and Macbeth are mentioned. 'No one was as many men as that man—that man whose repertoire, like that of the Egyptian Proteus, was all the appearances of being.' (The careful reader will note that 'Proteus', from Coleridge's characterization of Shakespeare's genius without character, replaces Keats's 'camelion Poet'.) The creative capability of this reimagined figure is nowhere celebrated or even mentioned. He is hardly Keats's 'Man of Achievement'. We are told that the man eventually retired from the London stage to his birthplace and became a 'retired businessman who'd made a fortune and had an interest in loans, lawsuits, and petty usury'.[12] All we are given is the negativity, Mackey's 'creative self-doubt' in spades.

In the last and shortest paragraph of the four that make up this blatantly anti-Romantic fable, however, there is a sudden reversal of the narrative in the direction of 'creative excess': 'History adds that before or after he died, he discovered himself standing before God.' In Job-like fashion, the man complains to God about his life-long lack of identity; he wishes finally to be himself. God answers him as he answered Job, 'out of a whirlwind', but not with a grand discourse on his spectacular power as a creator like the deity from the final chapters of the biblical Book of Job—rather with a startlingly apophatic revelation of his own lack of identity. '*I, too, am not I*', God tells

[12] Jorge Luis Borges, 'Everything and Nothing', in *Collected Fictions*, trans. Andrew Hurley (New York: Penguin, 1998), pp. 319–20.

him. '*I dreamed the world as you, Shakespeare, dreamed your own work, and among the forms of my dream are you, who like me are many, yet no one*' ('Everything and Nothing', p. 320; italics in the original). The theological analogy is improbably redeemed but stood on its head. This is creative excess with a vengeance, though admittedly, as with most things in Borges and all things to do with paradoxes, it cuts both ways. The appearance of 'God' can be traced back to Keats's casual use of the proverbial phrase 'all God's Creatures' in the letter to Woodhouse, but the strange assertion 'History adds that before or after he died, he discovered himself standing before God' situates the dialogue in a realm of transcendental skepticism.

Thus the dialogic encounter staged by Borges with negative capability as elaborated by Keats is as much a challenge as an homage. And although he claimed that hearing his father read aloud the 'Ode to a Nightingale' was the most significant event in his life, Borges appears to credit a letter of George Bernard Shaw—a line asserting 'I understand everyone and everything, and am nobody and nothing'—with the original inspiration for his parable.[13] But this only goes to show that the dialogic context of an utterance is often, if not always, complex rather than simple. It is not the same as a traditional dialogue on the stage, a discourse shared among clearly labeled dramatis personae, a distinction that Bakhtin himself insisted on when claiming that Dostoevsky was a more dialogic author than Shakespeare. But the transvaluation of values, as Nietzsche might put it, in 'Everything and Nothing' suggests that in the context of postmodernism the meaning of 'negative capability' is being radically redefined. As I will show in other examples of earlier Romantic meaning reborn in this later dialogic context, the phrase might be transposed to read 'capable negativity'—or even 'the negative sublime'. The aesthetic psychology of the poet takes on a larger metaphysical burden. Nothingness eclipses plenitude.

As it happens, Julio Cortázar, Borges's fellow Argentine and follower in the Latin American literary 'boom' known as magical realism, was a devotee of Keats as well. In fact, he translated Milnes's edition of Keats's letters into Spanish early in his career and left at his death in 1984 a book manuscript of over 600 pages on the 'images' of Keats that was published in 1996. It is characterized as 'a species of dialogue where Keats would be as present as possible' rather than a critical or biographical study.[14] Cortázar ranges widely over Keats's poetic oeuvre, bringing the poetry and prose of later French poets such as Baudelaire, Valéry, and Mallarmé, as well as T. S. Eliot and Edgar Allan Poe, into the

[13] Gene H. Bell-Villada, *Borges and His Fiction: A Guide to His Mind and Art* (Chapel Hill: University of North Carolina Press, 1981), p. 245.

[14] Julio Cortázar, *imagen de John Keats*, Biblioteca Cortázar (Madrid: Alfaguara, 1996). This quotation—from the back cover, apparently by Cortázar—and the following ones are from an unpublished translation by Jacqueline Veliz but give page numbers referring to the Spanish original.

discussion as he pursues, in manifesto fashion, the question of the essential character of poetry, classic as well as Romantic. He notes the importance of Keats's letters, their 'extraordinary nature', their 'absolute spontaneity, since they were written to friends and without the slightest suspicion of further publication' (p. 479). He cites the phrase 'negative capability' from time to time, calling it at one point 'a new advance in certainty' for Keats that 'forever claims (and many years before Baudelaire!) the right to express poetic truth in a pure state, without "ergo" or intellectual concatenations' (p. 476).

Cortázar is more drawn, however, to the earlier example, often taken as a preview of 'negative capability', given in the letter to Benjamin Bailey of 22 November 1817: 'if a Sparrow come before my Window I take part in its existence and peck about the Gravel' (*LJK*, I: p. 186). Cortázar sees this as a declaration of Keats's 'feelings of identification with poetic objects' (p. 476) and returns to this notion several times in the long section of the book labelled 'Poetics'. One could argue that the identification with the hypothetical sparrow is more about Keats enjoying moments of happiness than it is about him writing poetry, but it is commonly connected, as part of the earlier dialogical context, with the discussion of negative capability in literature and the lack of identity in the poetical character. In any case, Cortázar elaborates on his understanding of negative capability as a dangerous loss of selfhood: Keats 'sees that he has no *proper self*, and in turn implies *an infinite availability of irruption in other individuals*' (p. 492). This type of poet (Keats is not the only instance of this alienation) 'is disinterested in the conceptual aspects of the thing but agonizingly interested in *being* it, [he] proceeds through irruption, by jump and affective entry into the thing' (p. 495).

It seems clear that this theory of absolute poetry, derived from Keats's total oeuvre and its perceived affinities with the work of French Symbolist poets as well as later Latin American ones, is more like the capable negativity or negative sublime of the postmodern imagination than the negative capability of the Romantic context in which Keats originally thought and wrote. But the most striking instance of this poetics in the writings of Cortázar is afforded not in his poetry, of which only two volumes were published in his lifetime, but in the short stories for which he is now best known, stories where, as Borges (who himself accepted for publication Cortázar's first piece of short fiction) observed, we are given 'a porous world in which beings intermingle; a man's consciousness may enter that of animal, or an animal's into a man'.[15]

Thus the opening of 'Axolotl', the first story in the best-known volume of his short fiction in English, *Blow-Up and Other Stories*: 'There was a time when I thought a great deal about axolotls. I went to see them in the aquarium

[15] Borges, Jorge Luis, 'Julio Cortázar, *Stories*', in *Selected Non-Fictions*, ed. Eliot Weinberger (New York: Penguin, 1999), p. 514.

of the Jardin des Plantes and stayed for hours watching them, observing their immobility, their faint movements. Now I am an axolotl.'[16] Although the dialogic connection with Keats's epistolary negative capability complex is not as explicit here as Borges's 'Everything and Nothing', the allusion to Keats's 'taking part in [the] existence' of the sparrow—on the other side of a window—cannot be accidental. As with Borges' fable of the non-identity of Shakespeare, the negative capability of Cortázar's protagonist is dark and seemingly final. By the last paragraph of the eleven paragraphs that make up the first-person narrative, the human observer is being referred to in the third person. 'He returned many times, but he comes less often now', the eerily transformed narrator reports. 'It occurs to me that at the beginning we continued to communicate, that he felt more than ever one with the mystery which was claiming him. But the bridges were broken between him and me, because what was his obsession is now an axolotl, alien to his human life' (p. 9).

Negative capability, an instance of imaginative projection and moment of empathic identification for Keats, becomes metempsychosis, a transmigration of consciousness, for Cortázar. The final consolation—again, not unlike the literal deus ex machina of 'Everything and Nothing'—is the Mexican salamander (there are, in fact, several species of this animal in the real world) 'thinking that perhaps he'—that is, the surviving human spectator—'is going to write a story about us, that, believing he's making up a story, he's going to write all this about axolotls' (p. 9). Taking part in the existence of an amphibian is more dangerous than taking part in the existence of a bird, it seems, but the ambiguity of authorship—who actually is doing the writing?—remains. Such alienating transformation and displacement are, in fact, a hallmark of Cortázar's short fiction.

Cosmopolitan, New World postmodernism continued to regenerate and refashion Keats's phrase in the writings of the North American poet Charles Olson—in fact, in the early 1950s when *imagen de John Keats* and 'Axolotl' were both written, even though, like Keats's letters, Cortázar's 'dialogue' with Keats was only known to friends and a handful of scholars until it was published several decades later. It is also worth remembering that the 'transatlantic context' of John Keats's life and work, as Denise Gigante has put it in her recent dual biography *The Keats Brothers*, antedated most of the wider British context that first emerged in England as George and Georgiana Keats continued to correspond with John after their emigration from the old monarchy to the new republic.[17]

[16] Julio Cortázar, *Blow-Up and Other Stories*, trans. Paul Blackburn (New York: Pantheon, 1967), p. 3.

[17] Denise Gigante, *The Keats Brothers: The Life of John and George* (Cambridge, MA: Harvard University Press, 2011), p. 2.

Keats was not among the poets with whom Olson was most concerned in his own innovative 'projective' verse. He did allude to Keats's 'On First Looking into Chapman's Homer' in his 'On first Looking out through Juan de la Cosa's Eyes', a poem in his *Maximus* series that turns from classical epic as translated by a Renaissance poet to the diaries of the earliest explorers of the Americas. (De la Cosa was the chief map maker for Columbus and 'became famous for drawing the *mappemunde*, or first map of the world that showed the New World'.)[18] But Olson's entry into the postmodern dialogue concerning 'negative capability' came with a series of lectures he gave in 1956 at the Black Mountain School, where he was serving as Rector, that was published shortly after his death in 1970 as *The Special View of History*.

The lectures begin with two epigraphs, one from Heraclitus—'Man is estranged from that with which he is the most familiar'—and the other from Keats—the whole section of his letter to George and Tom describing how he came upon the concept of 'negative capability'. This is unexpected philosophical company for Keats, to say the least. Olson, in fact, seems to have been the first to use the term 'postmodern', in an attempt to distinguish himself from the influential modernism of Ezra Pound. He had used it in a letter to his friend and colleague Robert Creeley in 1951, and he used it again in *The Special View of History*. 'It does need to be noted that the present is *post* the Modern', he says at the beginning of the lecture entitled 'The Topological', while in the lecture entitled 'Ethics' he claims, abandoning an extended comparison of negative capability and the role of antithesis in Hegel's dialectic, 'One could see this moment of passage here precisely the moment of Keats' insistence and rejection. And crucial to post-Modern man.'[19] Olson's most extravagant claim for Keats's concept is that it spells the end of a bleak philosophical interregnum between the sixth century B.C. and the nineteenth century A.D. as far as the history of Western thought is concerned. The only other redemptive concept Olson emphasizes is the philosophy of organism put forward by Alfred North Whitehead. One might be forgiven for thinking that this particular appropriation of negative capability sounds more like the Coleridge 'incapable of remaining content with half knowledge', than Keats himself, the poet for whom 'the sense of Beauty overcomes every other consideration' (*LJK*, I: p. 194). However, the analysis of a dialogic context is not concerned first and foremost with the faithfulness of a later utterance to the earlier one. To paraphrase Bakhtin, there is neither a first nor a last definition of such context in the development of the dialogue, only loss and renewal of meaning.

[18] Enikő Bollobás, *Charles Olson* (New York: Twayne Publishers, 1992), p. 126.

[19] Charles Olson, *The Special View of History*, ed. Ann Charters (Berkeley, CA: Oyez, 1970), pp. 43, 47.

The postmodernity of Olson's deployment of Keats is emphasized and expanded by William Spanos, who brings Heidegger, Derrida, and the postmodern 'destruction of the ontotheological tradition' into the conversation with Olson.[20] Heidegger's concept of '*Gelassenheit*', which Spanos glosses as 'letting be', is only one of many deconstructive notions that Spanos correlates with Keats's more vernacular phrase. Admittedly, the style and tone of the postmodern vocabulary is far from Keats's. Spanos writes, for example:

> It is, as Heidegger implies, this nostalgic orientation, this recuperative meta-physical perspective which sees/grasps things-as-they-are (*physis*) from after or beyond or, better, from above them (*meta*) in the name of the *logos* as center that has elevated the (distancing and disinterested) eye as opposed to the other (engaging and interested) bodily senses to privileged status as the primary and virtually exclusive agency of knowledge in the onto-theological tradition. (p. 45)

Such prose is more reminiscent of Coleridge explaining the transcendental philosophy in Chapter 12 of the *Biographia* than of Keats's lively colloquial style in his letters. To be fair, Spanos does offer a less tortuous critique of the earlier modernist interpretation of negative capability, as he characterizes it, provided by Walter Jackson Bate and New Critics such as I. A. Richards and Cleanth Brooks. And, in any case, a German phenomenologist is no stranger a bedfellow for Keats than is a Mexican salamander.

More subtle and subversive is the postmodern or poststructuralist transformation of negative capability in the critical theory and interpretation of Paul de Man. A striking deconstruction of the Keats phrase appears in de Man's Introduction to *The Selected Poetry of Keats* (1966), which was republished in Harold Bloom's Modern Critical Views series in 1985. In his entry into the larger dialogic context, de Man fastens on the phrase 'self-destroying' from *Endymion* (Book I, line 799). '"Self-destroying" is obviously used in a positive sense here, to designate the moral quality of disinterestedness', de Man acknowledges, 'yet "destroying" is a curiously strong term. The phrase is revealing, for a recurrent pattern in the poetry indicates a strong aversion to direct confrontation with his own self; few poets have described the act of self-reflection in harsher terms.'[21] De Man goes on to read this harsher phrase forward into Keats's admittedly quite positive term negative capability. After

[20] William V. Spanos, 'Charles Olson and Negative Capability: A Phenomenological Interpretation', *Contemporary Literature*, 21: 1 (Winter 1980), p. 40.

[21] Paul de Man, 'Introduction', in *John Keats: Selected Poetry*, ed. John Hollander (New York: New American Library, 1966), p. xxiii. A shorter version of this essay, entitled 'The Negative Road', is included in Harold Bloom's *John Keats: Modern Critical Views* (New York: Chelsea House, 1985), pp. 29–48.

agreeing with earlier critics that the great odes of May 1819 are a consummate realization of negative capability he insists that the last poems—'The Late Keats', as the 'Table of Contents' categorizes it—'are the unmistakable sign of a change that is so far-reaching that it requires a radical readjustment on the part of the readers' (p. xxvii). Commenting on *Lamia* and *The Fall of Hyperion* and offering a more sustained reading of the poem of October 1819 entitled 'To ———' (also known as 'The Second Ode to Fanny Brawne'), de Man insists, 'We must understand that, far from detracting from his stature, the negativity of Keats's last poems shows that he was about to add another dimension to a poetic development that, up till then, had not been altogether genuine' (p. xxvii). Indeed, these late poems negate the negative capability of the earlier odes: the meditations on the Grecian urn and to the nightingale now reveal themselves as more negative than we had suspected. These much celebrated poems 'in fact set out to destroy the entities they claim to praise; or, to put it less bluntly, the ambiguity of feeling toward these entities is such that the poems fall apart' (p. xxvii).

De Man discovers a deeper, agonizing negativity underlying the more hopeful negative capability in Keats's oeuvre. The reprinting of this introduction by Harold Bloom—minus the explanation of the divisions of the poems into 'Early', 'Middle', and 'Late' and the claim that 'the exegetic importance of the letters can be exaggerated' (p. xxxvi)—is given the title 'The Negative Road'. Negative capability for de Man is only part of the road that Keats traveled in his abbreviated life, a stage on the way to a negativity that was for the poet truly incapacitating, though salutary for interpreters, we are told, even if he himself never reached the journey's end. In effect, this is a negative capability deconstructed for the postmodern condition and turned against the supremely capable poet, many would argue, who aspired to it. Indeed, in this relatively early essay by de Man, appearing five years before the more influential essays of *Blindness and Insight*, we can see the outlines of a negative sublime rather than an egotistical one, a negative sublimity that only grew in strength and scope in de Man's brilliant and troubling literary-critical career.

Nevertheless, de Man's 'epistemic violence' and 'radical negativity', as they have been called,[22] should not be taken as the dead end or *mise en abyme* of dialogic encounters, either with Keats's widely acclaimed poetic oeuvre in general or with his modest epistolary formulations concerning 'negative capability' in particular. There is no last word, according to Bakhtin, but there is hope for semantic renewal as well as semantic destruction. 'At any moment in the development of the dialogue, there are immense, boundless masses

[22] Orrin N. C. Wang, 'Romanticism and Theory: the 1970s', *Romantic Circles BookList* (blog) (30 August 2016), accessed 24 August 2018, https://www.rc.umd.edu/reviews-blog/romanticism-and-theory-1970s-orrin-nc-wang.

of forgotten contextual meanings', he writes, 'but at certain moments of the dialogue's subsequent development along the way they are recalled and invigorated in renewed form (in a new context). Nothing is absolutely dead: every meaning will have its homecoming festival' (p. 170). Bakhtin goes beyond the Romantic and Modernist assumption that meaning belongs to one person, but he also steers clear of the postmodern counter-assertion that meaning belongs to no one at all. We can envision that his middle, neither–nor way between these two extremes—his understanding that meaning belongs to more than one person—will keep revealing more occasions for homecoming festivity within the broadest possible dialogic context, the context of human history itself that Bakhtin referred to in the last words of this last essay, enigmatically, as 'the problem of great time'.

A former Poet Laureate of the United States, Billy Collins, has recently published, in fact, a distinctly non-postmodern humorous poem with the intriguing title: 'Keats: or How I Got My Negative Capability Back'. There is no last word indeed.

Afterword

Reading *Keats's Negative Capability*

Jonathan Mulrooney

Keats's Negative Capability dwells in uncertainty. I do not mean this as a criticism, but rather as a measure of the book's attention to how negative capability has invoked so many precursors, taken on so many valences, and set in motion so many trajectories that one almost despairs of obtaining even half knowledge of what it all means. 'Almost' is an important word here, though, for through the space marked by that *almost* the book's sixteen authors mobilize their array of approaches to Keats's kerygmatic formulation. Keats, as we know, has the capacity to elicit atypical scholarly engagements. Witness, to begin, the longing that suffuses Brian Rejack's essay, when he writes of the missing original manuscript of the 'negative capability letter'. Circling around Rejack's rigorous archival tracing and productive historical speculations, there is an affect that runs something like 'if we could only find the letter ... but perhaps it is best if we don't ... but truly it would be great if we did ... '. (That Rejack recognizes this oscillation is a fundamental strength of his essay.) One notes similar desires surfacing throughout the volume, such that the insufficiency of traditional scholarly apparatus in the face of negative capability becomes a defining trait of the group's collective endeavor. The overall mood that the essays create, Romantic itself, in turn shapes the reader's thoughts on what the book must leave out because its critical object displays a palpable Keatsian elusiveness. Negative capability is rendered variously as a theatrical aesthetic mixing (Bates); a philosophical echo of Hazlitt's 'natural capacity' (Theune) or Coleridge's 'negative faith' (Reed); a named or unnamed mode of receiving the literary past (Mathes) or disciplinary past (Eisner, Hessel); a conception of the future that opens the present to its effects (Rohrbach); a foregrounding of bodily sensation (Britton, Gardner); a postmodern 'transmigration of consciousness' (Reed); a movement toward the world's concrete materiality (Seyran); a measure of its 'everyday saturation' (Falke); a clinical refusal of memory (Sigler); an unspoken parallel of Eastern *askesis* (McCarthy); a belated return to Romantic self-annihilation (Barnett); a means of mapping the progress of literary history (Archambeau). Always in the background haunting these renderings is the long-presiding figure of W. J. Bate's midcentury Keats: manly, mobile, disinterested.

On its face, the book attempts to come to terms with these multiplicities by ordering its discussion neatly into four parts: contexts, ways of reading, poetic inheritances, non-literary adaptations. But here too there is slippage. Is Carmen Faye Mathes's astute essay from part one an investigation into 'aspects of what went into making negative capability', as the editors note in the introduction, or is it an exercise in reception theory, with Barrett Browning as a case study? Is Emily Rohrbach's consideration of Keats's poetics a recognition of negative capability at work, or an instance of negatively capable scholarship? Does Suzanne Barnett's treatment of Philip Pullman situate him as an adaptor of the concept, or as one of its sharpest contemporary theorists? Is Cassandra Falke's emphasis on the creative dimension of Keatsian reading more a way of reading Keats, or more an historical naming of phenomenology *avant la lettre*? Almost fair to say (again 'almost'), that each essay in the volume could slide without disruption into another section, as these examples suggest.

It would be easy, or easier than not, to say that negative capability is all the things each of the authors in this volume argues that it is. But to do so would serve no purpose, scholarly or otherwise. Rather it may make more sense to follow the volume's lead in refusing collective comprehension in favor of experiencing what Keats calls elsewhere the 'instant feeling' that each essay evokes. The task for a reader of *Keats's Negative Capability* thus becomes making a way through sixteen well-conceived and well-written essays while following their authors' example in eschewing the certitudes that contemporary literary scholarship, particularly some versions of contemporary historicism, often circumscribe. (Again, Rejack's early uncertainties set the tone here.) To that end, I would propose that one way of reconceiving the book's arrangement—not materially but via the act of reading—would be to imagine how its concerns radiate outward from the central essay by Jeanne Britton, for Britton's essay cannily names *mediation* as the scholarly crux into which the volume as a whole attempts to make its intervention. Britton's insistence on the way that negative capability 'describes the literary-historical and physiological nature of the writing process itself' hits on something indispensable in any approach to Keats, whether it be materialist, phenomenological, psychological, formalist, or whatever. Read outwards through this prism, the volume manifests its concern with mediation as a repeated recognition, first, of Keats's insistence on the relation between the embodied mind and a material world incorrigible to human imagining and, second, of Keats's ongoing belief that *reading* is nonetheless (or consequently) an indispensable human activity. (The world as the heart's hornbook, etc.) Negative capability, that is—be it action or indolence, state of mind or state of body, mode of perception or mode of unknowing—marks the space or fissure or temporal gap between human consciousness and the world. In another way of putting it, the at-once originary and final unknowability of what could be called in psychoanalytic terms 'the Real'—or, following David Sigler's engagement with Wilfred Bion, the 'O'—prompts the imaginative dispositions that negative capability names.

Kurtis Hessel's cogent historical account of Keats's disciplinary mobility can provide a first example of how such a reading might bring some of the book's most seemingly disparate essays together. Situating negative capability as a response to shifts in professional knowledge formations in nineteenth-century medicine, Hessel's engagement is a straightforward excavation of the institutional, which is to say disciplinary, conditions under which Keats plied his dual (and dueling) trades as physician and poet. But the traversing of disciplinary boundaries between medicine and poetry that Hessel describes must encounter, in the larger context of *Keats's Negative Capability*, Britton's insistence on the poet's mediation of immediate bodily responses to the sensory surround. Because of his keen receptivity—to his own historical exigencies, in Hessel's historical parallel to Britton's epistemic figuration—the poet can refuse the single-minded encounter with the world that any strict disciplinarity requires. Similarly, what transmutes in Arsevi Seyran's essay into Elizabeth Bishop's poetic 'method of accretion', or what becomes, for Thomas Gardner, Jorie Graham's ability to keep 'the conceptual intellect momentarily at bay' registers a mediating subject at work. One might go so far as to say that every essay in *Keats's Negative Capability* posits the Keatsian subject, be it Keats himself or not, *as* a mode of mediation.

I offer this way of thinking as one reader's response, but also with a view toward marking a deeper consistency of concern in *Keats's Negative Capability* than its surface multiplicities at first suggest. One could engage in a similar exercise with each of the essays in the collection, for each of them radiates its own trajectories through all the others. In this sense there may be 'no final word', as Walter Reed avers in the collection's final phrase, but the very resistance to that finality begets a different kind of coherence from which new strains of conversation about negative capability, Keats, and Romanticism can emerge. *Keats's Negative Capability*, that is, resists in both its structure and style our moment's instantiation of the progressions Emily Rohrbach's essay so gracefully limns, offering instead an intervention that embraces, to echo Wordsworth's most Keatsian moment, 'obstinate questionings / Of sense and outward things, / Fallings from us, vanishings; / Blank misgivings of a

Creature / Moving about in worlds not realiz'd'.[1] Scholarship could do more of this kind of work, and—as *Keats's Negative Capability* shows—Romanticist scholarship could do more to take the lead in propelling it. The lack of certainty of which I spoke at the outset is thus neither virtue nor vice, but a necessary condition of the book's inquiry; and the refusal to smooth over the dissonances the volume comprises, prompting more questions, is its most Keatsian feature. Allow me to conclude, then, with just a few interrogations that these essays bring to mind. In what ways might the clinical dimensions of negative capability help us rethink seemingly unrelated inquiries—say, disability studies? Certainly 'negative capability' in such a context might realign our expectations about human capacities, or perhaps even invoke its rhetorical upside-down: affirmative incapability? How might the insistence on mediation that the phrase 'negative capability' evinces, and the letter (or transcription of a letter) that contains it emphasizes, answer the current critical affinity for speculative realism and its conspicuously post-Kantian compulsions? What would it mean to read Keats now *without recourse* to the concepts that his negative capability letter, or any of his letters, provides? How would we perceive his poetics differently than we do? How would we teach them differently? How would we rethink Romanticism altogether?

These are incipient speculations, but such are the atoms of knowledge, I think, that *Keats's Negative Capability* seeks to set in motion. No doubt each person who has encountered the book—and that includes you, who are reading it now—will spin an airy citadel or two of their own. Still, if future readers are—will inevitably be—distant in time and place from the book's original publication, *Keats's Negative Capability* will, as it makes its way into the future, prompt them to think again and anew and unceasingly on what negative capability was, is, and can become.

[1] William Wordsworth, 'Ode', in *Poems in Two Volumes, and Other Poems 1800–1807*, ed. Jared Curtis (Ithaca, NY: Cornell University Press, 1983), p. 275, lines 144–8.

Bibliography

Abrams, M. H., ed. *The Norton Anthology of English Literature*. New York: Norton, 1962.

Aitken, Robert. 'Remembering Blyth Sensei'. In *Original Dwelling Place: Zen Buddhist Essays*, pp. 23–6. Upland, CA: Counterpoint, 1996.

Allen, Donald M., ed. *The New American Poetry, 1945–1960*. New York: Grove, 1960.

Almond, Philip C. *The British Discovery of Buddhism*. Cambridge: Cambridge University Press, 1988.

American Library Association. 'Top 100 Banned/Challenged Books: 2000–2009'. http://www.ala.org/bbooks/top-100-bannedchallenged-books-2000-2009.

Archambeau, Robert. *Laureates and Heretics: Six Careers in American Poetry*. Notre Dame, IN: University of Notre Dame Press, 2010.

Ashbery, John. 'From Such Commotion'. In *Wakefulness*, pp. 14–15. New York: Farrar, Straus and Giroux, 1999.

——. 'Houses at Night: Erica Wright Interviews John Ashbery'. *Guernica* (8 February 2008). https://www.guernicamag.com/interviews/houses_at_night_1/.

Bakhtin, Mikhail. 'Toward a Methodology for the Human Sciences'. In *Speech Genres and Other Late Essays*, edited by Caryl Emerson and Michael Holquist, translated by Vern W. McGee, pp. 159–72. Austin: University of Texas Press, 1986.

Bakhtin, Mikhail and V. N. Voloshinov. 'Constructing a Sociological Poetics'. In *The Bakhtin Reader*, edited by Pam Morris, pp. 160–74. London: Arnold, 1994.

Barker-Benfield, G. J. *The Culture of Sensibility: Sex and Society in Eighteenth-Century Britain*. Chicago, IL: University of Chicago Press, 1992.

Barnard, John. 'Keats's Letters: "Remembrancing and enchaining"'. In *The Cambridge Companion to Keats*, edited by Susan J. Wolfson, pp. 120–34. Cambridge: Cambridge University Press, 2001.

Barrett Browning, Elizabeth. *Aurora Leigh*. Edited by Kerry McSweeney. Oxford: Oxford University Press, 2008.

——. *The Barretts at Hope End; the Early Diary of Elizabeth Barrett Browning*. Edited by Elizabeth Berridge. London: John Murray, 1974.

Batchelor, Stephen. *Verses from the Center: A Buddhist Vision of the Sublime*. New York: Riverhead Books, 2000.

Bate, Jonathan. *The Song of the Earth*. Cambridge, MA: Harvard University Press, 2002.

Bate, Walter Jackson. 'The Crisis in English Studies'. *Harvard Magazine* (September–October 1982): pp. 46–53.

——. 'The Endurance of Keats'. In *The Persistence of Poetry: Bicentennial Essays On Keats*, edited by Robert M. Ryan and Ronald A. Sharp, pp. 54–6. Amherst: University of Massachusetts Press, 1998.

——. *John Keats*. Cambridge, MA: Harvard University Press, 1963.

——. *Negative Capability: The Intuitive Approach in Keats*. Cambridge, MA: Harvard University Press, 1939. Reprint, New York: Contra Mundum Press, 2012.

Bates, Brian. *Wordsworth's Poetic Collections, Supplementary Writing and Parodic Reception*. London: Routledge/Pickering & Chatto, 2012.

Beaudry, Harry. *The English Theatre and John Keats*. Salzburg: University of Salzburg Press, 1973.

Beebe, Barton. 'Search and Persuasion in Trademark Law'. *Michigan Law Review*, 103: 8 (August 2005): pp. 2022–72.

Bell-Villada, Gene H. *Borges and His Fiction: A Guide to His Mind and Art*. Chapel Hill, University of North Carolina Press, 1981.

Bennett, Andrew. *Ignorance: Literature and Agnoiology*. Manchester: Manchester University Press, 2009.

——. *Keats, Narrative and Audience: The Posthumous Life of Writing*. Cambridge: Cambridge University Press, 1994.

Benton, Richard P. 'Keats and Zen'. *Philosophy East and West*, 16: 1/2 (January–April 1966): pp. 33–47.

Bernes, Jasper. 'New Criticism'. In *American Poets and Poetry*, edited by Jeffrey Gray and Mary Balkun, pp. 435–40. Westport, CT: Greenwood, 2015.

Bernstein, Charles. *Content's Dream: Essays 1975–1984*. Evanston, IL: Northwestern University Press, 2001.

Betts, William. 'Negative Capability'. *Psychoanalysis Downunder* 7B (2007). http://www.psychoanalysisdownunder.com.au/issues/8/papers/106.

Bewell, Alan. *Romanticism and Colonial Disease*. Baltimore, MD: Johns Hopkins University Press, 1999.

Bion, Wilfred R. *Attention and Interpretation*. London: Karnac Books, 1984.

——. 'Notes on Memory and Desire'. *The Psychoanalytic Forum*, 2: 3 (1967): pp. 271–3.

——. 'Notes on Memory and Desire: Author's Response'. *The Psychoanalytic Forum*, 2: 3 (1967): pp. 279–80.

Bishop, Elizabeth. Papers. St. Louis, MI: Washington University Libraries.
——. *Poems*. New York: Farrar, Straus and Giroux, 2011.
Blomfield, O. H. D. 'The Essentials of Psychoanalysis'. *Australian and New Zealand Journal of Psychiatry*, 27: 1 (1993): pp. 86–100.
Bloom, Harold. *The Anxiety of Influence: A Theory of Poetry*. New York: Oxford University Press, 1973.
——, ed. *John Keats*. Bloom's Modern Critical Views. New York: Chelsea House, 1985.
Blyth, Reginald Horace. *Haiku*. 4 vols. Tokyo: Hokuseido Press, 1949–52.
——. *Haiku, Vol. 1*. Tokyo: Hokuseido Press, 1949.
——. *A Survey of English Literature from the Beginnings to Modern Times*. Tokyo: Hokuseido Press, 1957.
——. *Zen in English Literature and Oriental Classics*. Tokyo: Hokuseido Press, 1942.
——. *Zen and Zen Classics*. Vol. 7. Tokyo: Hokuseido Press, 1962.
Bollobás, Enikő. *Charles Olson*. New York: Twayne Publishers, 1992.
Bolter, Jay David and Richard Grusin. *Remediation: Understanding New Media*. Cambridge, MA: MIT Press, 2000.
Bonnycastle, John. *An Introduction to Astronomy*. London, 1811.
Borges, Jorge Luis. 'Everything and Nothing'. In *Collected Fictions*, translated by Andrew Hurley, pp. 319–20. New York: Penguin, 1998.
——. 'Julio Cortázar, *Stories*'. In *Selected Non-Fictions*, edited by Eliot Weinberger, pp. 514–15. New York: Penguin, 1999.
Borossa, Julia, Catalina Bronstein, and Claire Pajaczkowska, eds. *The New Klein-Lacan Dialogues*. London: Karnac Books, 2015.
Bradley, A. C. *Oxford Lectures on Poetry*. London: Macmillan and Company, 1911.
Brake, Laurel and Marysa Demoor, eds. *The Dictionary of Nineteenth Century Journalism in Great Britain and Ireland*. London: Academia Press and the British Library, 2009.
Brooke-Smith, James. 'Remediating Romanticism'. *Literature Compass*, 10: 4 (2013): pp. 343–52.
Brooks, Cleanth. *The Well-Wrought Urn: Studies in the Structure of Poetry*. New York: Harvest, 1956.
Brothers, Dometa Wiegand. *The Romantic Imagination and Astronomy*. New York: Palgrave Macmillan, 2015.
Brown, John. *The Elements of Medicine; or, a Translation of the Elementa Medicinae Brunonis with Large Notes, Illustrations, and Comments by the Author of the Original Work*. Translated by John Brown. 2 vols. London: Johnson, 1788.
Browning Letters, Baylor University Libraries Digital Collections, Baylor University.
Burke, Edmund. *A Philosophical Enquiry into the Origins of the Sublime and the Beautiful*. Edited by David Womersley. London: Penguin, 1998.
Burt, Stephen. *Close Calls With Nonsense: Reading New Poetry*. Saint Paul, MN: Graywolf, 2009.

Burwick, Frederick. 'Negative Capability'. In *Romanticism Keywords*, pp. 193–5. Chichester: Wiley Blackwell, 2015.

Byron, George Gordon, Lord. *Don Juan*. Edited by T. G. Steffan, E. Steffan, and W. W. Pratt. London: Penguin, 1973.

———. *Selected Letters and Journals*. Edited by Leslie A. Marchand. Cambridge, MA: Harvard University Press, 1982.

Caldwell, Janis McLarren. *Literature and Medicine in Nineteenth-Century Britain: from Mary Shelley to George Eliot*. Cambridge: Cambridge University Press, 2004.

Calé, Louisa and Adriana Craciun. 'The Disorder of Things'. *Eighteenth-Century Studies*, 45: 1 (2011): pp. 1–13.

Chandler, James. *England in 1819: The Politics of Literary Culture and the Case of Romantic Historicism*. Chicago, IL: University of Chicago Press, 1998.

Coleridge, Samuel Taylor. *Biographia Literaria*. Edited by James Engell and W. Jackson Bate. Vol. 7 of *The Complete Works of Samuel Taylor Coleridge*. Princeton, NJ: Princeton University Press, 1985.

———. *Lectures 1808–1819: On Literature*. Edited by R. A. Foakes. 2 vols. London: Routledge and Kegan Paul, 1987.

Coleridge, Samuel Taylor and William Wordsworth. *Lyrical Ballads: 1798 and 1800*. Edited by Michael Gamer and Dahlia Porter. Peterborough: Broadview Press, 2008.

Collins, Billy. 'Keats: or How I Got My Negative Capability Back'. In *Aimless Love: New and Selected Poems*, pp. 217–18. New York: Random House, 2013.

Corcoran, Brendan. 'Keats's Death: Towards a Posthumous Poetics'. *Studies in Romanticism*, 48: 2 (2009): pp. 321–48.

Cordeiro, Will. 'All That Glitters'. *Jacket*, 38 (2009). http://jacketmagazine.com/38/r-wheeler-rb-cordeiro.shtml.

Cortázar, Julio. *Blow-Up and Other Stories*. Translated by Paul Blackburn. New York: Pantheon, 1967.

———. *Imagen de John Keats*. Biblioteca Cortázar. Madrid: Alfaguara, 1996.

Cox, Jeffrey N. '"Illegitimate" Pantomime in the "Legitimate" Theatre: Context as Text'. *Studies in Romanticism*, 54 (Summer 2015): pp. 159–86.

———. '*Lamia*, *Isabella*, and *The Eve of St. Agnes*, Eros and Romance'. In *The Cambridge Companion to Keats*, edited by Susan J. Wolfson, pp. 53–68. Cambridge: Cambridge University Press, 2001.

Cox, Jeffrey N. and Michael Gamer, eds. *The Broadview Anthology of Romantic Drama*. Orchard Park, NY: Broadview Press, 2003.

Csengei, Ildiko. *Sympathy, Sensibility and the Literature of Feeling in the Eighteenth Century*. New York: Palgrave Macmillan, 2012.

Culler, Jonathan. *The Pursuit of Signs: Semiotics, Literature, Deconstruction*. Ithaca, NY: Cornell University Press, 1981.

de Almeida, Hermione. *Romantic Medicine and John Keats*. Oxford: Oxford University Press, 1991.

de J. Jackson, J. R., ed. *Samuel Taylor Coleridge: The Critical Heritage*. 2 vols. London: Routledge, 1995.

de Man, Paul. 'Introduction'. In *John Keats: Selected Poetry*, edited by John Hollander, pp. ix–xxxvi. New York: New American Library, 1966.

———. 'Introduction to the Poetry of John Keats'. In *Critical Writings 1953–1978*, edited by Lindsay Waters, pp. 179–97. Minneapolis: University of Minnesota Press, 1989.

———. 'The Rhetoric of Temporality'. In *Blindness and Insight*, pp. 187–228. Minneapolis: University of Minnesota Press, 1983.

Deutsch, Helen. *Loving Dr. Johnson*. Chicago, IL: University of Chicago Press, 2005.

Dewey, John. *Art as Experience*. New York: Minton, Balch & Company, 1934. Reprint, New York: Penguin, 2005.

DiPiero, W. S. *Memory and Enthusiasm: Essays, 1975–1985*. Princeton, NJ: Princeton University Press, 1989.

Dower, John W. *Embracing Defeat: Japan in the Wake of World War II*. London: Allen Lane, 1999.

Duncan, Robert. *Fictive Certainties*. New York: New Directions, 1985.

Duncan, Robert and Denise Levertov. *The Letters of Robert Duncan and Denise Levertov*. Edited by Robert J. Bertholf and Albert Gelpi. Stanford, CA: Stanford University Press, 2004.

Eickhoff, Friedrich-Wilhelm. 'On Nachträglichkeit: The Modernity of an Old Concept'. *The International Journal of Psychoanalysis*, 87 (2006): pp. 1453–69.

Ellmann, Maud. 'New Introduction'. In *An Experiment in Leisure*, by Marion Milner, pp. xiii–xlii. New York: Routledge, 2011.

Ellmann, Richard and Charles Feidelson, Jr., eds. *The Modern Tradition: Backgrounds of Modern Literature*. New York: Oxford University Press, 1965.

Engell, James. '*Biographia Literaria*'. In *The Cambridge Companion to Coleridge*, edited by Lucy Newlyn, pp. 59–74. Cambridge: Cambridge University Press, 2002.

Etchegoyen, Laura. 'Panel Report: The Analyst's Response to the Effects of the Transference: On Lacan and Bion'. *The International Journal of Psychoanalysis*, 91 (2010): pp. 399–401.

Faflak, Joel. *Romantic Psychoanalysis: The Burden of the Mystery*. Albany, NY: SUNY Press, 2008.

Faimberg, Haidée. 'Whom Was Bion Addressing? "Negative Capability" and "Listening to Listening"'. In *W. R. Bion: Between Past and Future*, edited by Parthenope Bion Talamo, Franco Borgogno, and Silvio A. Merciai, pp. 79–90. London: Karnac Books, 2000.

Faure, Bernard. *Chan Insights and Oversights: An Epistemological Critique of the Chan Tradition*. Princeton, NJ: Princeton University Press, 1993.

Fields, Rick. *How the Swans Came to the Lake: A Narrative History of Buddhism in America*. Boulder, CO: Shambhala, 1981.

Finney, Claude Lee. *The Evolution of Keats's Poetry*. Cambridge, MA: Harvard University Press, 1936.

Fitzgerald, F. Scott. *The Crack-Up*. New York: Penguin, 1965.

Freud, Sigmund. *The Standard Edition of the Complete Psychological Works of Sigmund Freud*. Translated by James Strachey. 24 vols. London: Hogarth Press, 1964.

Fry, Paul H. 'History, Existence, and "To Autumn"'. *Studies in Romanticism*, 25: 2 (Summer 1986): pp. 211–19.

Galea, Sandro. 'Uncertainty and the Zika Virus: Why Scientists Need to Think Like Poets'. *Cognoscenti* (blog). WBUR, 8 September 2016. Accessed 5 July 2018. http://www.wbur.org/cognoscenti/2016/09/08/zika-sandro-galea.

Gardner, Thomas. *A Door Ajar: Contemporary Writers and Emily Dickinson*. New York: Oxford University Press, 2006.

Gigante, Denise. *The Keats Brothers: The Life of John and George*. Cambridge, MA: Harvard University Press, 2011.

——. *Life: Organic Form and Romanticism*. New Haven, CT: Yale University Press, 2009.

Gilmartin, Kevin. *William Hazlitt: Political Essayist*. Oxford: Oxford University Press, 2015.

Gittings, Robert. 'Introduction', in *Letters of John Keats*, edited by Robert Gittings. Oxford: Oxford University Press, 1970.

Goellnicht, Donald C. *The Poet-Physician: Keats and Medical Science*. Pittsburgh, PA: University of Pittsburgh Press, 1984.

Golding, Alan. *From Outlaw to Classic: Canons in American Poetry*. Madison: University of Wisconsin Press, 1995.

González, Avelino. 'Response to Bion's "Notes on Memory and Desire"'. *The Psychoanalytic Forum*, 2: 3 (1967): pp. 275–7.

Graham, Jorie. *The End of Beauty*. New York: Ecco, 1987.

——. *Erosion*. Princeton, NJ: Princeton University Press, 1983.

——. *The Errancy*. Hopewell, NJ: Ecco Press, 1991.

——. *Never*. New York: HarperCollins, 2002.

——. *Overlord*. New York: HarperCollins, 2005.

——. *PLACE*. New York: HarperCollins, 2012.

——. *Region of Unlikeness*. New York: HarperCollins, 1991.

——. *Sea Change*. New York: HarperCollins, 2008.

——. *Swarm*. New York: Ecco Press, 2000.

Green, André. 'The Primordial Mind and the Work of the Negative'. In *W. R. Bion: Between Past and Future*, edited by Franco Borgogno, Silvio A. Merciai, and Parthenope Bion Talamo, pp. 108–28. London: Karnac Books, 2000.

Greg, W. W. 'The Rationale of Copy-Text'. *Studies in Bibliography*, 3 (1950/1951): pp. 19–36.

Grose, Francis, ed. *The Dictionary of the Vulgar Tongue*. London: 1811.

Gschwandtner, Christina. 'Marion and Negative Certainty'. *Philosophy Today*, 56: 3 (2012): pp. 363–70.

Guillory, John. 'Genesis of the Media Concept'. *Critical Inquiry*, 36 (Winter 2010): pp. 321–62.

Gunn, Thom. *Passages of Joy*. London: Faber, 1982.

Hammer, Langdon. 'Art and AIDS; or, How Will Culture Cure You?' *Raritan*, 14 (Winter 1995): pp. 103–18.

Hamrit, Jacqueline. 'Nachträglichkeit'. *PsyArt: An Online Journal for the Psychological Study of the Arts* (2008). http://psyartjournal.com/article/show/hamrit-nachtrglichkeit.

Harlequin's Vision; Or, The Feast of the Statue. John Larpent Collection. Huntington Library.

Harris, Martha and Esther Bick. *The Tavistock Model: Papers on Child Development and Psychoanalytic Training*. Edited by Meg Harris Williams. London: Karnac Books, 2011.

Hart, Kevin, ed. *Counter-Experiences: Reading Jean-Luc Marion*. Notre Dame, IN: University of Notre Dame Press, 2007.

Hartman, Geoffrey. *The Fate of Reading and Other Essays*. Chicago, IL: University of Chicago Press, 1975.

Hazlitt, William. *The Collected Works of William Hazlitt*. Edited by A. R. Waller and Arnold Glover. 12 vols. London: J. M. Dent, 1904.

——. *The Complete Works of William Hazlitt*. Edited by P. P. Howe. 21 vols. London: J. M. Dent, 1930.

——. *The Spirit of the Age: Or, Contemporary Portraits*. Grasmere, Cumbria: The Wordsworth Trust, 2004.

Hejinian, Lyn. *The Language of Inquiry*. Berkeley: University of California Press, 2000.

——. *My Life*. Los Angeles: Green Integer, 2002.

——. *My Life and My Life in the Nineties*. Middletown, CT: Wesleyan University Press, 2013.

Hessel, Kurtis. 'The Romantic-Era Lecture: Dividing and Reuniting the Arts and Sciences'. *Configurations*, 24: 4 (2016): pp. 501–32.

Hoagland, Tony. 'Fear of Narrative and the Skittery Poem of Our Moment'. In *Poet's Work, Poet's Play*, edited by Daniel Tobin and Pimone Triplett, pp. 161–73. Ann Arbor, MI: University of Michigan Press, 2007.

Hobbes, Thomas. *Leviathan*. Oxford: Clarendon Press, 1909.

Holquist, Michael. 'Answering as Authoring: Mikhail Bakhtin's Trans-Linguistics'. *Critical Inquiry*, 10: 2 (December 1983): pp. 307–19.

Holt, Terrence E. 'Narrative Medicine and Negative Capability'. *Literature and Medicine*, 23: 2 (Fall 2004): pp. 318–33.

Homans, Margaret. 'Keats Reading Women, Women Reading Keats'. *Studies in Romanticism*, 29 (1990): pp. 341–70.

Hong, Cathy Park. 'Memories and Thoughts on Adrienne Rich'. *Harriet: A Poetry Blog* (blog). *Poetry Foundation*, June 2016. https://www.poetryfoundation.org/harriet/2016/06/memories-and-thoughts-on-adrienne-rich/.

Hunt, Leigh. *Imagination and Fancy; or Selections from the English Poets*. London: Smith, Elder and Co., 1845.

Jack, Ian Robert James. *Keats and the Mirror of Art*. Oxford: Clarendon Press, 1968.

Jackson, Virginia. 'Thinking Dickinson Thinking Poetry'. In *A Companion to Emily Dickinson*, edited by Martha Nell Smith and Mary Loeffelholz, pp. 205–21. Malden, MA: Blackwell, 2008.

Jacobus, Mary. *The Poetics of Psychoanalysis: In the Wake of Klein*. Oxford: Oxford University Press, 2005.

James, Ian. *The New French Philosophy*. Cambridge: Polity, 2012.

Jarrell, Randall. 'The Obscurity of the Poet'. In *American Poetic Theory*, edited by Carl Perkins, pp. 307–16. New York: Rinehart, 1972.

Jenkins, Alice. *Space and the 'March of the Mind'*. Oxford: Oxford University Press, 2007.

Johnson, Barbara. 'Apostrophe, Animation, and Abortion'. *Diacritics*, 16: 1 (Spring 1986): pp. 28–47.

Jones, Steven E. *Satire and Romanticism*. New York: St. Martin's Press, 2000.

Kahan, Jeffrey. *The Cult of Kean*. Aldershot: Ashgate, 2006.

Kandl, John. 'Plebian Gusto, Negative Capability, and the Low Company of "Mr. Kean": Keats's Dramatic Review for *The Champion*'. *Nineteenth-Century Prose*, 28: 2 (Fall 2001): pp. 130–41.

Kant, Immanuel. 'An Answer to the Question: "What Is Enlightenment?"'. In *Kant's Political Writings*, edited by Hans Reiss, translated by H. B. Nisbet, pp. 54–60. Cambridge: Cambridge University Press, 1970.

——. *Critique of Judgement*. Edited by Nicholas Walker. Translated by James Meredith. Oxford: Oxford University Press, 2007.

——. *Observations on the Feeling of the Beautiful and Sublime and Other Writings*. Edited by Patrick Frierson and Paul Guyer. Cambridge: Cambridge University Press, 2011.

Kaufman, Robert. 'Negatively Capable Dialectics: Keats, Vendler, Adorno, and the Theory of the Avant-Garde'. *Critical Inquiry*, 27: 2 (Winter 2001): pp. 354–84.

Keats, John. *Anatomical and Physiological Note Book. Printed from the Holograph in the Keats Museum, Hampstead*. Edited by Maurice Buxton Forman. New York: Haskell House Publishers Ltd, 1970.

——. Collection (MS Keats 1–6). Houghton Library, Harvard University.

——. *The Complete Works of John Keats*. Edited by Harry Buxton Forman. 5 vols. Glasgow: Gowars & Gray, 1901.

——. *The Letters of John Keats 1814–1821*. Edited by Hyder Edward Rollins. 2 vols. Cambridge, MA: Harvard University Press, 1958.

——. *The Poems of John Keats*. Edited by Jack Stillinger. Cambridge, MA: Belknap Press, 1978.

Keen, Paul. *The Crisis of Literature in the 1790s: Print Culture and the Public Sphere*. Cambridge: Cambridge University Press, 1999.

Kelley, Theresa. *Reinventing Allegory*. Cambridge: Cambridge University Press, 1997.

Khalip, Jacques. *Anonymous Life: Romanticism and Dispossession*. Stanford, CA: Stanford University Press, 2009.

Kinnaird, John. *William Hazlitt: Critic of Power*. New York: Columbia University Press, 1978.

Klancher, Jon. *Transfiguring the Arts and Sciences*. Cambridge: Cambridge University Press, 2013.

Knapp, Eloise Hay. *T. S. Eliot's Negative Way*. Cambridge, MA: Harvard University Press, 1982.

Krupnick, Marl. 'Obituary: Walter Jackson Bate'. *The Guardian*, 1 August 1999.

Kunitz, Stanley. 'The New Books'. *Harper's Magazine*, 221 (August 1960): p. 100.

Kyoko, Imamura. 'The Integration of Western and Eastern Spirituality in Blyth's *Zen in English Literature and Oriental Classics*'. In *The Force of Vision: Proceedings of the XIIIth Congress of the International Comparative Literature Association*, pp. 151–8. Tokyo: University of Tokyo Press, 1995.

Lacan, Jacques. *Écrits: The First Complete Edition in English*. Translated by Bruce Fink. New York: Norton, 2006.

——. *The Seminar of Jacques Lacan, Book II: The Ego in Freud's Theory and in the Technique of Psychoanalysis, 1954–1955*. Edited by Jacques-Alain Miller. Translated by Sylvana Tomaselli. New York: Norton, 1988.

Landon, Letitia Elizabeth. *Letters by Letitia Elizabeth Landon*. Edited by F. J. Sypher. Ann Arbor, MI: Scholars' Facsimiles & Reprints, 2001.

——. 'Lines on Seeing a Portrait of Keats'. *Examiner*, 12 September 1824. *British Library Newspapers*. tinyurl.galegroup.com/tinyurl/49fBC8.

Laplanche, Jean and J. B. Pontalis. 'Deferred Action'. In *The Language of Psycho-Analysis*, translated by Donald Nicholson-Smith, pp. 111–14. New York: Norton, 1973.

Lau, Beth. 'Authorial Disguise and Intertextuality: Scott's *The Lay of the Last Minstrel*, Coleridge, and Keats'. *Studies in Scottish Literature*, 40: 1 (2014): pp. 116–33.

——. 'Jane Austen and John Keats: Negative Capability, Romance and Reality'. *Keats-Shelley Journal*, 55 (2006): pp. 81–110.

——. *Keats's Reading of the Romantic Poets*. Ann Arbor: University of Michigan Press, 1991.

——. 'Protest, "Nativism", and Impersonation in the Works of Chatterton and Keats'. *Studies in Romanticism*, 42: 4 (2003): pp. 519–39.

Lecourt, Sebastian. 'Idylls of the Buddh': Buddhist Modernism and Victorian Poetics in Colonial Ceylon'. *Publications of the Modern Language Association of America*, 131: 3 (May 2016): pp. 668–85.

Levinson, Marjorie. *Keats's Life of Allegory, the Origins of a Style*. London: Basil Blackwell, 1988.

Levy, Jonathan. 'Reflections on Teaching Playwrighting in the Schools'. *The Journal of Aesthetic Education*, 26: 3 (Autumn 1992): pp. 103–6.

Lewis, Dearing. 'A John Keats Letter Rediscovered'. *Romantic Circles* (November 1998). http://www.rc.umd.edu/editions/keats/.

Li, Ou. *Keats and Negative Capability*. London: Bloomsbury, 2009.

Lilley, Deborah. 'Theories of Certain Uncertainty: Climate Change and Negative Capability'. *symploke*, 21: 1–2 (2013): pp. 97–108.

Lindon, John. 'Response to Bion's "Notes on Memory and Desire"'. *The Psychoanalytic Forum*, 2: 3 (1967): p. 274.

Lipking, Lawrence. *The Life of the Poet: Beginning and Ending Poetic Careers*. Chicago, IL: University of Chicago Press, 1981.

The Literary Gazette; and Journal of Belles Lettres, Arts, Sciences, For the Year 1818. London, 1818.

'The Locked Room.' *True Detective*. HBO. 26 January 2014. Television.

Longenbach, James. 'The Unfinishable Robert Lowell'. *Boston Review* (June 2003). http://bostonreview.net/poetry/james-longenbach-unfinishable-robert-lowell.

Lowell, Robert. *Robert Lowell: Interviews and Memoirs*. Edited by Jeffrey Meyers. Ann Arbor: University of Michigan Press, 1988.

Luke, David. 'Keats's Letters: Fragments of an Aesthetic of Fragments'. *GENRE*, 2 (Summer 1978): pp. 209–26.

Lussier, Mark. 'Colonial Counterflow: From Orientalism to Buddhism'. In *Interrogating Colonialism: Contextual Approaches and Pedagogical Practices*, edited by Diane Long Hoeveler and Jeffrey Cass, pp. 90–106. Columbus: Ohio State University Press, 2006.

——. *Romantic Dharma: The Emergence of Buddhism in Nineteenth-Century Europe*. Basingstoke: Palgrave Macmillan, 2011.

——. 'Self-Annihilation/Inner Revolution: Blake's "Milton", Buddhism, and Ecocriticism'. *Religion & Literature*, 40: 1 (Spring 2008): pp. 39–57.

McClane, Maureen. 'In Retrospect'. *Critical Mass* (blog). *National Book Critics Circle*, 11 September 2009. http://bookcritics.org/blog/archive/in_retrospect_maureen_n._mclane_on_john_ashberys_self_portrait_in_a_convex_/.

McGann, Jerome. 'Keats and the Historical Method in Literary Criticism'. *Modern Language Notes*, 94: 5 (1979): pp. 988–1032.

——. *A New Republic of Letters: Memory and Scholarship in the Age of Digital Reproduction*. Cambridge, MA: Harvard University Press, 2014.

——. *The Textual Condition*. Princeton, NJ: Princeton University Press, 1991.

McGann, Jerome and Daniel Riess. Introduction to *Letitia Elizabeth Landon: Selected Writings*. Edited by Jerome McGann and Daniel Riess. Peterborough: Broadview Press, 1997.

McHale, Brian. 'How (Not) to Read Postmodernist Long Poems: The Case of Ashbery's "The Skaters"'. *Poetics Today*, 21: 3 (Autumn 2000): pp. 561–90.

Mack, Maynard. *Collected in Himself: Essay Critical, Biographical, and Bibliographical on Pope and Some of His Contemporaries*. Newark: University of Delaware Press, 1982.

Mackey, Louis. *An Ancient Quarrel Continued: The Troubled Marriage of Philosophy and Literature*. Lanham, MD: University Press of America, 2002.

Macksey, Richard. 'Keats and the Poetics of Extremity'. *Modern Language Notes*, 99: 4 (1984): pp. 845–84.

McLane, Maureen N. *Balladeering, Minstrelsy, and the Making of British Romantic Poetry*. Cambridge: Cambridge University Press, 2008.

McMahan, David L. *The Making of Buddhist Modernism*. New York: Oxford University Press, 2008.

Manning, Susan. *Poetics of Character: Transatlantic Encounters, 1700–1900*. Cambridge: Cambridge University Press, 2013.

Marion, Jean-Luc. *Negative Certainties*. Translated by Stephen E. Lewis. Chicago, IL: University of Chicago Press, 2015.

Markovits, Daniel. *A Modern Legal Ethics: Adversary Advocacy in a Democratic Age*. Princeton, NJ: Princeton University Press, 2008.

Masson, David. 'The Life and Poetry of John Keats'. *Macmillan's Magazine*, November 1860, pp. 1–16.

Mathes, Carmen Faye. '"Let us not therefore go hurrying about": Towards an Aesthetics of Passivity in Keats's Poetics'. *European Romantic Review*, 25: 3 (2014): pp. 309–18.

Mayer, David. *Harlequin in his Element, 1806–1836*. Cambridge, MA: Harvard University Press, 1969.

Mellor, Anne K. *Romanticism and Gender*. New York: Routledge, 1993.

Meltzer, Donald. 'The Compartments of the Internal Mother'. In *Psychoanalysis and Art: Kleinian Perspectives*, edited by Sandra Gosso, pp. 223–8. London: Karnac Books, 2004.

——. 'New Considerations on the Concept of the Aesthetic Conflict'. In *Psychoanalysis and Art: Kleinian Perspectives*, edited by Sandra Gosso, pp. 211–18. London: Karnac Books, 2004.

Meltzer, Donald and Meg Harris Williams. 'Aesthetic Conflict: Its Place in the Developmental Process'. In *Psychoanalysis and Art: Kleinian Perspectives*, edited by Sandra Gosso, pp. 178–200. London: Karnac Books, 2004.

Merleau-Ponty, Maurice. *Maurice Merleau-Ponty: Basic Writings*. Edited by Thomas Baldwin. London: Routledge, 2004.

Middleton, Peter. *Physics Envy: American Poetry and Science in the Cold War and After*. Chicago, IL: University of Chicago Press, 2015.

Mill, John Stuart. 'The Spirit of the Age'. In *The Spirit of the Age: Victorian Essays*, edited by Gertrude Himmelfarb, pp. 50–79. New Haven, CT: Yale University Press, 2007.

Milner, Marion. *An Experiment in Leisure*. 1939. New York: Routledge, 2011.

Milnes, Richard Monckton. *Life, Letters, and Literary Remains of John Keats*. 2 vols. London: Edward Moxon, 1848.

Monteiro, George, ed. *Conversations with Elizabeth Bishop*. Jackson: University Press of Mississippi, 1996.

Moody, Jane. *Illegitimate Theatre, 1770–1840*. Cambridge: Cambridge University Press, 2000.

Mulrooney, Jonathan. 'Keats's Avatar'. *European Romantic Review*, 22: 3 (2011): pp. 313–21.

——. 'Keats in the Company of Kean'. *Studies in Romanticism*, 42: 2 (2003): pp. 227–50.

Murry, John Middleton. *Keats and Shakespeare: a Study of Keats's Poetic Life from 1816 to 1820*. Oxford: Oxford University Press, 1925.

Najarian, James. *Victorian Keats: Manliness, Sexuality, and Desire.* New York: Palgrave Macmillan, 2002.

Natarajan, Uttara. *Hazlitt and the Reach of Sense: Criticism, Morals, and the Metaphysics of Power*. Oxford: Clarendon Press, 1998.

'Negative Capability—Developing Empathy In Business'. YouTube video. Posted by 'Get Altitude'. 11 November 2007. Accessed 5 July 2018. https://www.youtube.com/watch?v=jFZaGK3GjvI.

Neuss, Meylinda. *Distance, Theatre, and the Public Voice, 1750–1850*. New York: Palgrave Macmillan, 2012.

Newlyn, Lucy. *Paradise Lost and the Romantic Reader*. Oxford: Clarendon Press, 1993.

Nicholls, Peter. 'Phenomenal Poetics: Reading Lyn Hejinian'. In *The Mechanics of the Mirage: Postwar American Poetry*, edited by Michel Delville and Christine Pagnouelle, pp. 241–52. Liège: Liège Language and Literature, 2000.

O'Brien, John. *Harlequin Britain: Pantomime and Entertainment, 1690–1760*. Baltimore, MD: Johns Hopkins University Press, 2004.

Okada, Akiko. *Keats and English Romanticism in Japan*. Bern: Peter Lang, 2006.

Olson, Charles. *The Collected Poems of Charles Olson*. Edited by George F. Butterick. Berkeley: University of California Press, 1997.

——. *Collected Prose*. Edited by Donald Allen and Benjamin Friedlander. Berkeley: University of California Press, 1997.

——. *Human Universe and Other Essays*. New York: Grove, 1967.

——. *Muthologos: The Collected Lectures and Interviews*. Edited by George F. Butterick. 2 vols. Berkeley, CA: Four Seasons, 1978.

——. 'Projective Verse'. In *Twentieth-Century American Poetics: Poets on the Art of Poetry*, edited by Dana Gioia, David Mason, and Meg Schoerke, pp. 174–81. New York: McGraw Hill, 2004.

——. *The Special View of History*. Berkeley, CA: Oyez, 1970.

Opie, I. and P. Opie. *The Oxford Dictionary of Nursery Rhymes*. Oxford: Oxford University Press, 1951.

O'Rourke, James. *Keats's Odes and Contemporary Criticism*. Gainesville: University Press of Florida, 1998.

Pachori, Satya S. 'John Keats and Zen Buddhism: An Eastern Perspective'. *South Asian Review*, 20: 17 (December 1996): pp. 12–20.

Paniker, K. Ayyappa. 'Negative Capability and "Emptiness": Keats and Nagarjuna'. *New Comparison*, 23 (1997): pp. 97–103.

Park, Roy. *Hazlitt and the Spirit of the Age: Abstraction and Critical Theory*. Oxford: Clarendon Press, 1971.

Paul, Sherman. *Olson's Push: Origin, Black Mountain, and Recent American Poetry*. Baton Rouge: Louisiana State University Press, 1978.

Perloff, Marjorie. 'Language Poetry and the Lyric Subject: Ron Silliman's Albany, Susan Howe's Buffalo'. *Critical Inquiry*, 25: 3 (Spring 1998): pp. 405–34.

Phillips, Adam. *Promises, Promises: Essays on Psychoanalysis and Literature*. New York: Basic Books, 2002.

Pickard, Zachariah. 'Natural History and Epiphany: Elizabeth Bishop's Darwin Letter'. *Twentieth-Century Literature*, 50: 3 (Fall 2004): pp. 268–82.

Pilkington, Ed. 'Children's writer Philip Pullman ranked second on US banned books list'. *The Guardian*, 30 September 2009. Accessed 14 September 2018. https://www.theguardian.com/books/2009/sep/30/american-library-association-banned-books.

Pinnington, Adrian S. 'R. H. Blyth, 1898–1964'. In *Britain & Japan: Biographical Portraits*, edited by Ian Nish, vol. 1, pp. 252–67. Folkestone: Japan Library, 1994.

Pinsky, Robert. 'The Idiom of a Self: Elizabeth Bishop and William Wordsworth'. *American Poetry Review*, 9: 1 (January/February 1980): pp. 6–8.

Pladek, Brittany. '"Soothing Thoughts": Romantic Palliative Care and the Poetics of Relief'. *European Romantic Review*, 23: 3 (2012): pp. 403–13.

Plumly, Stanley. *Argument & Song: Sources & Silences in Poetry*. New York: Other Press, 2003.

——. *Posthumous Keats: A Personal Biography*. New York: Norton, 2008.

Pollack-Pelzner, Daniel. 'Revisionary Company: Keats, Homer, and Dante in the Chapman Sonnet', *Keats-Shelley Journal*, 56 (2007): pp. 39–49.

Pope, Alexander. *Essay on Criticism*. Edited by Alfred S. West. Cambridge: Cambridge University Press, 2014.

The Princeton Encyclopedia of Poetry and Poetics. 4th ed. Princeton, NJ: Princeton University Press, 2012.

Pullman, Philip. *His Dark Materials Trilogy: The Golden Compass, The Subtle Knife, and The Amber Spyglass*. New York: Random House, 2003.

Ramazani, Jahan. *The Poetry of Mourning: The Modern Elegy from Hardy to Heaney*. Chicago, IL: University of Chicago Press, 1994.

Rancière, Jacques. *Dissensus: On Politics and Aesthetics*. Edited and translated by Steven Corcoran. New York: Continuum, 2010.

Ransom, John Crowe. *The World's Body*. Baton Rouge: Louisiana State University Press, 1968.

Ratzabi, Hila. 'Nothing Mystical About It: An Interview with Jorie Graham'. Jorie Graham (website). Accessed 11 June 2018. http://www.joriegraham.com/interview_ratzabi_2006.

Reed, Walter L. *Romantic Literature in Light of Bakhtin*. New York: Bloomsbury, 2014.

Rich, Adrienne. *Adrienne Rich's Poetry*. Edited by Barbara Charlesworth Gelpi and Albert Gelpi. New York: Norton, 1975.

——. 'In Memoriam DK'. In *Later Poems: Selected and New, 1971–2012*, pp. 190–1. New York: Norton, 2013.

Richardson, Alan. *British Romanticism and the Science of the Mind*. Cambridge: Cambridge University Press, 2001.

Ricks, Christopher. 'Keats's Afterlife'. *The New York Review of Books* (11 June 2009): pp. 59–61.

——. *Keats and Embarrassment*. Oxford: Oxford University Press, 1974.

——. 'Keats's sources, Keats's allusions'. In *The Cambridge Companion to Keats*, edited by Susan J. Wolfson, pp. 152–69. Cambridge: Cambridge University Press, 2001.

Rifkin, Libbie. *Career Moves: Olson, Creeley, Zukofsky, Berrigan and the American Avant-Garde*. Madison: University of Wisconsin Press, 2000.

Roe, Nicholas. *John Keats: A New Life*. New Haven, CT: Yale University Press, 2012.

——. *John Keats and the Culture of Dissent*. Oxford: Clarendon Press, 1997.

——. 'Mr. Keats'. *Essays in Criticism*, 65: 3 (July 2015): pp. 274–88.

Rohrbach, Emily. *Modernity's Mist: British Romanticism and the Poetics of Anticipation*. New York: Fordham University Press, 2016.

Rollins, Hyder Edward, ed. *The Keats Circle: Letters and Papers and More Letters and Poems*. 2 vols. Cambridge, MA: Harvard University Press, 1969.

Ross, Catherine. '"Twin Labourers and Heirs of the Same Hopes": The Professional Rivalry of Humphry Davy and William Wordsworth'. In *Romantic Science*, edited by Noah Heringman, pp. 23–52. Albany: SUNY Press, 2003.

Roudinesco, Elisabeth. *Jacques Lacan: Outline of a Life, History of a System of Thought*. Translated by Barbara Bray. New York: Columbia University Press, 1997.

Rousseau, George S. *Nervous Acts: Essays on Literature, Culture and Sensibility*. New York: Palgrave Macmillan, 2004.

Rudy, John G. *Romanticism and Zen Buddhism*. Lewiston: Edwin Mellen Press, 2004.

Ruefle, Mary. 'On Fear: Our positive capability'. *Poetry*, 200: 3 (June 2012): pp. 277–90.

Ruppenthal, Stephen H. 'Keats and Zen Enlightenment'. *Studia Mystica*, 1: 2 (1978): pp. 67–74.

Rzepka, Charles J. '"Cortez—or Balboa, or Somebody like That": Form, Fact, and Forgetting in Keats's "Chapman's Homer" Sonnet', *Keats-Shelley Journal*, 51 (2002): pp. 35–75.

——. 'Elizabeth Bishop and the Wordsworth of *Lyrical Ballads*: Sentimentalism, Straw Men, and Misprision'. *Romantic Circles Praxis Series* (November 1999). https://www.rc.umd.edu/praxis/lyrical/rzepka/bishop.html.

Sandbank, Shimon. 'Keats Altered by the Present'. *Comparative Literature*, 35: 1 (1983): pp. 43–54.

Schiller, Friedrich. *On the Aesthetic Education of Man*. New York: Dover, 2004.

Schleifer, Ronald. *Intangible Materialism: The Body, Scientific Knowledge, and the Power of Language*. Minneapolis: University of Minnesota Press, 2009.

Schulkins, Rachel. *Keats, Modesty, and Masturbation*. Farnham: Ashgate, 2014.

Scott, Grant F. 'Introduction: Tabloid Keats'. *European Romantic Review*, 6: 1 (1995): pp. i–xii.

——. *The Sculpted Word: Keats, Ekphrasis, and the Visual Arts*. Hanover, NH: University Press of New England, 1994.

Sedgwick, Eve Kosofsky. *Touching Feeling: Affect, Pedagogy, Performativity*. Durham, NC, and London: Duke University Press, 2003.

Shapiro, David. *John Ashbery: An Introduction to the Poetry*. New York: Columbia University Press, 1979.

Sharf, Robert. 'The Zen of Japanese Nationalism'. In *Curators of the Buddha: The Study of Buddhism Under Colonialism*, edited by Donald S. Lopez, Jr., pp. 107–60. Chicago, IL: University of Chicago Press, 1995.

Shaw, Lytle. *Fieldworks: From Place to Site in Postwar Poetics*. Tuscaloosa: University of Alabama Press, 2013.

Shelley, Mary Wollstonecraft. *The Letters of Mary Wollstonecraft Shelley*. Edited by Betty T. Bennett. 3 vols. Baltimore, MD: Johns Hopkins University Press, 1988.

Shelley, Percy Bysshe. *The Letters of Percy Bysshe Shelley*. Edited by Frederick L. Jones. 2 vols. Oxford: Oxford University Press, 1964.

——. *Shelley and His Circle, 1773–1822*. Edited by Donald H. Reiman. Cambridge, MA: Harvard University Press, 1973.

Shukman, Ann. 'M. M. Bakhtin: Notes on his Philosophy of Man'. In *Poetry, Prose, and Public Opinion: Essays Presented in Memory of Dr. N. E. Andreyev*, edited by William Harrison and Avril Pyman, pp. 241–50. Letchworth: Avebury Publishing, 1984.

Silliman, Ron. 'An Interview with Ron Silliman'. *Double Room*, 6 (Fall 2005/2006). www.webdelsol.com/Double_Room/issue_six/Ron_Silliman.htm.

——. Letter to Susan Howe, 7 December 1985. Susan Howe Papers, Mandeville Special Collections Library, University of California, San Diego.

Simic, Charles. *The Life of Images: Selected Prose*. New York: HarperCollins, 2015.

——. 'Negative Capability and Its Children'. In *Claims for Poetry*, edited by Donald Hall, pp. 399–406. Ann Arbor: University of Michigan Press, 2000.

Simmons, Dan. 'Shapeshifters and Skinwalkers: The Writer's Curse of Negative Capability'. *Journal of the Fantastic in the Arts*, 8: 4 (1997): pp. 398–418.

Siskin, Clifford. *The Work of Writing*. Baltimore, MD: Johns Hopkins University Press, 1998.

Slote, Bernice. *Keats and the Dramatic Principle*. Lincoln: University of Nebraska Press, 1958.

Spanos, William V. 'Charles Olson and Negative Capability: A Phenomenological Interpretation'. *Contemporary Literature*, 21 (Winter 1980): pp. 38–80.

Speed, John Gilmer, ed. *The Letters and Poems of John Keats, in Three Volumes*. New York: Dodd, Mead & Company, 1883.

Sperry, Stuart M. *Keats the Poet*. Princeton, NJ: Princeton University Press, 1973.

'Spontaneous Intelligence: Interview with Allen Ginsberg'. *Tricycle Magazine* (Fall 1995). https://tricycle.org/magazine/spontaneous-intelligence.

Stevenson, Anne. *Elizabeth Bishop*. New York: Twayne Publishers, 1966.

——. *Five Looks at Elizabeth Bishop*. Tarset: Bloodaxe Books, 2006.

Stewart, Garrett. 'Keats and Language'. In *The Cambridge Companion to Keats*, edited by Susan Wolfson, pp. 135–51. Cambridge: Cambridge University Press, 2001.

Stillinger, Jack. 'The Hoodwinking of Madeline: Scepticism in the "Eve of St. Agnes"'. *Studies in Philology*, 58: 3 (July 1961): pp. 533–55.

——. 'Introduction: Imagination and Reality in the Odes of Keats'. In *Twentieth Century Interpretations of Keats's Odes*, edited by Jack Stillinger. Englewood Cliffs, NJ: Prentice Hall, 1968.

——. 'Keats and Coleridge'. In *Coleridge, Keats, and the Imagination: Romanticism and Adam's Dream*, edited by J. Robert Barth and John Mahoney. Columbia: University of Missouri Press, 1990.

——. 'Multiple Readers, Multiple Texts, Multiple Keats'. In *The Persistence of Poetry: Bicentennial Essays on Keats*, edited by Robert M. Ryan and Ronald A. Sharp, pp. 10–35. Amherst: University of Massachusetts Press, 1998.

——. *Romantic Complexity: Keats, Coleridge, and Wordsworth*. Urbana: University of Illinois Press, 2006.

Sutherland, James. *A Preface to Eighteenth Century Poetry*. Oxford: Oxford University Press, 1970.

Suzuki, Daisetz Teitaro. *Buddhism and Its Influence on Japanese Culture*. Kyoto: Eastern Buddhist Society, 1938.

Suzuki, Yoshikazu. '"A candle that must melt away": Early Keats Scholarship in Japan'. In *English Romanticism in East Asia*, edited by Suh-Reen Han. *Romantic Circles Praxis* (December 2016). http://www.rc.umd.edu/praxis/eastasia/praxis.2016.eastasia.suzuki.html.

Symington, Joan. 'O'. *Psychoanalysis Downunder*, 7B (2007). http://www.psychoanalysisdownunder.com.au/issues/8/papers/108.

Talamo, Parthenope Bion. 'Laying Low and Saying (Almost) Nothing'. In *W. R. Bion: Between Past and Future*, edited by Franco Borgogno, Silvio A. Merciai, and Parthenope Bion Talamo, pp. 20–6. London: Karnac Books, 2000.

Terada, Rei. 'Looking at the Stars Forever'. *Studies in Romanticism*, 50: 2 (Summer 2011): pp. 275–310.

Teskey, Gordon. *Allegory and Violence*. Ithaca, NY: Cornell University Press, 1996.

The Theatrical Inquisitor, and Monthly Mirror. London, 1813, 1818.

Theune, Michael. 'Contradictory Keats: on Stanley Plumly's *Posthumous Keats: A Personal Biography*'. *Pleiades*, 29: 1 (2009): pp. 122–8.

——. '~~Negative Capability~~: T wang dillo dee'. *Jacket*, 40 (2010). Accessed 7 July 2018. http://jacketmagazine.com/40/theune-keats.shtml.

Thomson, Heidi. 'Keats's Letters: "A Wilful and Dramatic Exercise of Our Minds Towards Each Other"'. *Keats-Shelley Review*, 25: 2 (2011): pp. 160–74.

Thoreau, Henry David. *Walden*. New York: Library of America, 1991.

Todd, Sharon. 'Experiencing Change, Encountering The Unknown: An Education in "Negative Capability" in Light of Buddhism and Levinas'. *Journal of Philosophy of Education*, 49: 2 (2015): pp. 240–54.

Trilling, Lionel. *The Moral Obligation to be Intelligent: Selected Essays*. Edited by Leon Wieseltier. Evanston, IL: Northwestern University Press, 2009.

——. 'The Poet as Hero: Keats in his Letters'. In *The Opposing Self: Nine Essays in Criticism*. New York: Viking Press, 1955.

——. *Selected Letters of John Keats*. New York: Farrar, Straus and Young, 1951.

Turley, Richard Marggraf. *Keats's Boyish Imagination*. New York: Routledge, 2004.

Unger, Roberto. *False Necessity: Anti-Necessitarian Social Theory in the Service of Radical Democracy*. London: Verso, 2004.

The Urinals. *Negative Capability … Check It Out!* Warning Label Records, 1997.

Valenza, Robin. *Literature, Language, and the Rise of the Intellectual Disciplines in Britain, 1680–1820*. Cambridge: Cambridge University Press, 2009.

Vendler, Helen. 'The Experiential Beginnings of Keats's Odes'. *Studies in Romanticism*, 12: 3 (Summer 1973): pp. 591–606.

——. *The Odes of John Keats*. Cambridge, MA: Harvard University Press, 1983.

Vila, Anne. *Enlightenment and Pathology: Sensibility in the Literature and Medicine of Eighteenth-Century France*. Baltimore, MD: Johns Hopkins University Press, 1997.

Von Hallberg, Robert. 'Yvor Winters'. In *American Writers: A Collection of Literary Biographies, Supplement Two, Part Two*, edited by A. Walton Litz, pp. 785–816. New York: Scribner's, 1981.

von Haller, Albrecht. *Dissertation on the Sensible and Irritable Parts of Animals*. Translated by M. Tissot. London: Nourse, 1755.

von Pfahl, Linda. 'The Ethics of Negative Capability'. *Nineteenth-Century Contexts*, 33: 5 (2011): pp. 451–66.

Voyce, Stephen. 'Alternative Degrees: "Works in OPEN" at Black Mountain College'. In *After the Program Era: The Past, Present and Future of Creative Writing in the University*, edited by Loren Glass, pp. 85–104. Iowa City: University of Iowa Press, 2016.

Wang, Orrin N. C. 'Romanticism and Theory: the 1970s'. *Romantic Circles BookList* (blog). 30 August 2016. https://www.rc.umd.edu/reviews-blog/romanticism-and-theory-1970s-orrin-nc-wang.

Ward, Aileen. *John Keats: The Making of a Poet*. New York: Viking, 1963.

Wear, Delese. 'Toward Negative Capability: Literature in the Medical Curriculum'. *Curriculum Inquiry*, 34: 2 (Summer 2004): pp. 169–84.

Webb, Richard E. and Michael A. Sells. 'Lacan and Bion: Psychoanalysis and the Mystical Language of "Unsaying"'. *Theory & Psychology*, 5: 2 (May 1995): pp. 195–215.

Webb, Timothy. '"Cutting Figures": Rhetorical Strategies in Keats's Letters'. In *Keats: Bicentenary Readings*, edited by Michael O'Neill, pp. 144–69. Edinburgh: Edinburgh University Press, 1997.

Wellberry, David. Foreword to *Discourse Networks 1800/1900*, by Friedrich Kittler, pp. vii–xxxiii. Translated by Michael Metteer and Chris Cullens. Stanford, CA: Stanford University Press, 1990.

Wendel, W. Bradley. 'Methodology and Perspective in the Theory of Lawyers' Ethics: a Response to Professors Woolley and Markovits'. *The University of Toronto Law Journal*, 60: 4 (Fall 2010): pp. 1011–19.

Whytt, Robert. *Physiological Essays*. Edinburgh: Balfour, 1766.

Wilde, Oscar. 'Keats's Sonnet on Blue'. *The Hobby Horse* (July 1886): pp. 83–6.

Williams, Meg Harris. *The Aesthetic Development: The Poetic Spirit of Psychoanalysis: Essays on Bion, Meltzer, Keats*. London: Karnac Books, 2010.

———. 'Keats: Soul-Making'. In *Psychoanalysis and Art: Kleinian Perspectives*, edited by Sandra Gosso, pp. 253–68. London: Karnac Books, 2004.

Wimsatt, W. K. *Hateful Contraries: Studies in Literature and Criticism*. Lexington: University of Kentucky Press, 2014.

———. *The Verbal Icon: Studies in the Meaning of Poetry*. With two essays written with Monroe C. Beardsley. Lexington: University of Kentucky Press, 1954.

Winters, Yvor. *In Defense of Reason*. Denver, CO: Swallow, 1947.

Wolfson, Susan J. *Borderlines: The Shiftings of Gender in British Romanticism*. Stanford, CA: Stanford University Press, 2006.

———, ed. *The Cambridge Companion to Keats*. Cambridge: Cambridge University Press, 2001.

———. 'Keats Enters History'. In *Keats and History*, edited by Nicholas Roe, pp. 17–45. Cambridge, Cambridge University Press, 1995.

———. 'Keats the Letter-Writer: Epistolary Poetics'. *Romanticism Past and Present*, 6: 2 (1982): pp. 43–61.

———. *The Questioning Presence: Wordsworth, Keats, and the Interrogative Mode in Romantic Poetry*. Ithaca, NY: Cornell University Press, 1986.

———. *Reading John Keats*. Cambridge: Cambridge University Press, 2015.

———. 'Stanley Plumly, Posthumous Keats'. Review of *Posthumous Keats*, by Stanley Plumly. *Romantic Circles* (11 December 2009). https://www.rc.umd.edu/reviews-blog/stanley-plumly-posthumous-keats.

Wollstonecraft, Mary. *Wollstonecraft: A Vindication of the Rights of Men and a Vindication of the Rights of Woman*. Edited by Sylvana Tomaselli. Cambridge: Cambridge University Press, 1995.

Wordsworth, William. 'Ode'. In *Poems in Two Volumes, and Other Poems 1800–1807*, edited by Jared Curtis, pp. 269–77. Ithaca, NY: Cornell University Press, 1983.

Worrall, David. *The Politics of Romantic Theatricality: The Road to the Stage*. London: Palgrave Macmillan, 2007.

Wunderlich, Mark. 'The Glorious Thing: Jorie Graham and Mark Wunderlich in Conversation'. Academy of American Poets (website). Accessed 9 June 2018. https://www.poets.org/poetsorg/text/glorious-thing-jorie-graham-and-mark-wunderlich-conversation.

Z [John Gibson Lockhart]. 'Review of *Endymion*'. In *Keats's Poetry and Prose*, edited by Jeffrey N. Cox, pp. 272–76. New York: Norton, 2009.

Žižek, Slavoj. *Iraq: The Borrowed Kettle*. London: Verso, 2005.

Index

Printed and bound by CPI Group (UK) Ltd, Croydon, CR0 4YY
08/03/2026
14838624-0001